The Social
Construction
of Man, the State,
and War

**DATE DUE**

# The Social Construction of Man, the State, and War

*Identity, Conflict, and Violence in Former Yugoslavia*

## Franke Wilmer

ROUTLEDGE
New York and London

Published in 2002 by
Routledge
29 West 35th Street
New York, NY 10001

Published in Great Britain by
Routledge
11 New Fetter Lane
London EC4P 4EE

Routledge is an imprint of Taylor & Francis Group.

Printed on acid-free, 250-year-life paper.
Manufactured in the United States of America.
Design and typography: Jack Donner
10 9 8 7 6 5 4 3 2 1

Library of Congress Cataloging-in-Publication Data

Wilmer, Franke.
    The social construction of man, the state, and war : indentity, conflict, and violence
in former Yugoslavia / by Franke Wilmer.
        p. cm.
    Includes bibliographical references and index.
    ISBN 0–415–92962–8 — ISBN 0–415–92963–6 (pbk.)
    1. Yugoslavia—Politics and government. 2. Yugoslavia—Ethnic relations.
    3. Ethnicity—Yugoslavia. 4. Yugoslav War, 1991–1995—Causes. I. Title.
DR1282 .W55 2002
949.703—dc21

                                                                          2001048817

*To all those who struggle for nonviolent
solutions to the problem of human conflict,
for the preservation of human dignity, and in the
knowledge that in our humanity we are bound together,
particularly those whose paths I crossed in the part
of the world we now think of as the former Yugoslavia*

# CONTENTS

# PREFACE

In a 1993 interview in New York, the founding editor of the Belgrade independent news magazine *Vreme*, Milos Vasić, explained the war this way:

> All it took was a few years of fierce, reckless, chauvinist, intolerant, expansionist, war-mongering propaganda to create enough hate to start the fighting among people who had lived together peacefully for forty-five years. I acknowledge that noses were broken in barrooms over the years. But nobody was *killed*. You must imagine a United States with every little TV station everywhere taking exactly the same editorial line—a line dictated by David Duke. You too would have war in five years.[1]

I am not sure that this book will have much to add to Mr. Vasić's poignant insight. The first lesson I learned in Yugoslavia was that democracy is like water: if you have enough of it, you don't give it much thought, but if you are deprived of it, you think about it all the time. Most of the people I met in the former Yugoslavia thought about democracy a lot. But they did not think about their deprivation in terms of an authoritarian dictator imposing his will on the majority. Their deprivation was much more like de Toqueville's "tyranny of the majority." At the urging of an opportunistic leadership, the majority of people had been mobilized to behave in an undemocratic and *intolerant* way. Perhaps they were more inclined to do so because their experience of political freedom was limited in contrast to that of most Westerners. But I kept wondering: Under what circumstances could a majority (or even a plurality) of Americans (or any other people in Western, democratic societies) be mobilized to behave in the same way? Dissent in the former Yugoslavia—Croatia and Serbia specifically—was censored not only by the government, but by the majority of the people. I remembered feeling something similar not only as an antiwar activist during the Vietnam and Gulf wars, but also as an opponent of racial discrimination during the height of civil rights activism in the 1960s. Nothing can so denude the veil of democracy laid over our collective prejudices than to criticize one's own government on issues relating to its policies toward *Others,* whether internal or external. That some "Others" are internal betrays any notion that the state is not structured in ways that privilege dominant identities.

Socialized to believe that there were more differences than similarities between the United States and Yugoslavia, between American and Yugoslav society, between Americans and Yugoslavs, my first trip to the region (Belgrade) in the summer of 1995 reversed that perception—or at least led me to believe that, whatever differences there were, our similarities have much more to teach us, particularly from the perspective of how ordinary people mediate the tension between the fact of their differences from one another and the fact of their common citizenship. Nearly every contemporary state contains a multicultural population. Many states are also societies: many are not. What holds them together varies, but one thing is becoming increasingly clear: neither coercive authoritarianism nor democracy is sufficient in itself to secure multicultural societies against the disintegrative and emotional forces aroused by difference. Democracies, as we currently understand them, are probably less likely to fall apart (Northern Ireland notwithstanding), but a lot of injuries and injustices can be perpetrated without a society falling apart entirely. I think we can do better.

Arriving in Belgrade toward what we now know was the end of the war, my first "on-the ground" impressions of former Yugoslavia not only flew in the face of my idea of Yugoslavia and Yugoslavs, but also made it impossible for me to think about war as I had before. We use the term "war" to connote commonalities across the specific cases of political violence we (in the western world) readily place in that linguistic category—World Wars I and II, the Korean, Six-Day, Vietnam, Gulf, and Yugoslav wars. We may have recently added the category of "ethnic conflict" to the range of possible configurations of "war," but we think about these wars involving "nonstate actors" in much the same terms we associate with interstate wars. Some historians have already opted to uphold a state-centric view of world politics by naming the violence in ex-Yugoslavia "the Yugoslav wars of secession."

Prevailing conceptions of war emphasize strategic thinking, even if they differ over who the thinkers are—states, statesmen, ethnic groups, leaders of ethnic groups, rebels, freedom fighters, terrorists, and so on. Until the World War II, the brutality of organized (or at least orchestrated) political violence received little attention. Perhaps is was presumed to be a "normal" feature of war; perhaps we believed that among Europeans and their cousins in settler states, the brutality of war was coming under the civilizing influence of Progress. The latter was, after all, evidenced by the meetings and concluding documents of the Hague Conferences and other efforts to articulate the laws and rules of warfare, the creation of the League of Nations, various arms control and disarmament initiatives, and the Kellogg-Briand Pact which attempted to outlaw aggressive war. World War I was to be the war that ended wars.

Not only was the brutality of war overlooked, normalized, or finally the object of social engineering, but there were instances where the use of force in an overtly brutal and inhumane manner to accomplish political objectives was completely excluded from both public and academic discussions about war: more than half of the total Armenian population in Turkey killed by the Ottoman rulers; tens of millions killed under Stalin in the aftermath of the Bolshevik Revolution, including the deaths by starvation of millions of Ukrainians; millions of Tibetans and Chinese killed in postrevolutionary China; the 1937 "Rape of Nanking"; and, the subject of my own earlier research, the killing (often as a direct product of government policies) with the intent to destroy the groups as groups (to paraphrase the genocide convention) of tens of millions of indigenous peoples in the settler states of Canada, the United States, Australia, and New Zealand. By the end of the nineteenth century, the United States government was caught in its own web of denial when it realized that the failure to designate its policy of violence toward indigenous peoples as a "war" meant that the United States government soldiers who killed some 300 indigenous people at Wounded Knee in 1890 could be found guilty of murder. Colonialism itself was a brutally violent regime, though the "wars" we most often associate with it are either those among or against colonial powers.

Two things began to disturb me deeply about contemporary studies of war. First, that the category itself is embedded within linguistic practices that structure our thinking about the politics–violence nexus in ways that bolster and tacitly legitimate the state as an institution of world order and the agency of the state as a perpetrator of violence within its own boundaries, unaccountable in any ethical sense, even to the extreme of genocide. I say this even in light of the Holocaust because I believe that, for the most part, policymakers and political leaders did not see themselves in a position to object to Hitler's genocidal policies during most of the war, certainly not during his rise to power and skullduggery in central and eastern Europe and finally his annexation of Austria, which was enthusiastically welcomed by the overwhelming majority of annexees.

Contemporary portrayals of the Holocaust sometimes seem most concerned with reassuring us that we can identify, or at least locate, political evil—safely tucked away in the German past, leaving only contemporary Germans to struggle with the issue of responsibility for historical injury. But most Nazi invasions were, after all, abetted by willing collaborators. The question of why such obvious evil remained unnamed and unopposed for so long during the rise and spread of Nazism is rarely addressed. Part of the answer, I think, lies in the way scholars and statesmen (and following their cue, ordinary people) think about the state, particularly its relationship to identity and its latitude in using violence against internal Others (Jews in Germany, indigenous peoples in settler states, Blacks and other people of color in the United States, South Africa, and elsewhere). Within the discourse known as "international law" such internal atrocities and injuries are, or at least were, protected by a doctrine of "domestic jurisdiction."

The emergence of human rights as an international discourse in the aftermath of the Holocaust holds some hope for the development of norms (in Onuf's terminology, "rules")[2] that will alter social practices associated with state sovereignty, war, and the use of violence. Once we acknowledge that war is a form of violence with a potential for evil, and that war is a social practice associated with states, we must also acknowledge that states, as we currently construct them, therefore contain the potential for evil. The violence of Nazism is too often bifurcated. We talk about World War II in a strategic sense, and we talk about the Holocaust in a genocidal sense, but we rarely talk about how they co-constituted one another. As Elie Wiesel expressed in his speech honoring the opening of the Holocaust Museum in Washington, D.C. while the violence and atrocities in Bosnia raged on, the failure of the Western allies to act decisively in Bosnia made a mockery of our promise to the victims of the Holocaust: "Never Again." I need to understand that failure. It will not do for International Relations (IR) scholars and practitioners to keep using the terms "war" and "the state" without becoming conscious of the social forces that construct, and thus shape and reshape, the institutions and practices represented by these terms.

The second thing that bothers me about contemporary studies of war is the extent to which the emotional side of war has been neglected by mainstream IR scholarship and relegated to the special interest of those studying political psychology. The myth that politics, and therefore war, is rational has come under fire from a variety of camps, from the "post-" perspectives (behavioral/ structural/positivist/modern) to feminism and the adaptation of psychoanalytic theory to political analysis. I have chosen a feminist variation of the latter in order to better understand the role of emotions in creating violence, in spite of objections that one cannot extrapolate anything about collective behavior on the basis of theories about the internal psychic life of individuals. By using both psychoanalytic and constructivist theoretical perspectives, I have tried to find an intersection between our psychic and social lives. I do not see the internal cognitive and external social world as distinct, but rather as dynamic and mutually constituted. The challenge has been to find a way of understanding this relationship while locating the experiences and perceptions of actual thinking and feeling people in it. Without the willing participation of individuals, war is not possible, and their willing participation is enlisted as a result of appeals aimed at arousing them emotionally, whether as patriotism, prejudice, or pathology. I have tried to use insights from psychoanalytic theory to explain inhumanity, cruelty, and violence in so far as it follows from the politicization of Otherness.

I stopped being a complete outsider from the moment I arrived in Belgrade (actually I arrived, alone, several miles away, where the train stopped because of a railroad workers' strike, dumping its passengers to fend for themselves in arranging transportation to their final destinations). But neither am I an insider. This book aims in many ways to muddle such crisp delineations, and my own position in relation to the project is no exception. I was not, nor am I now, an "expert" on Yugoslavia, the Balkans, or southeastern Europe. This had an advantage in that I had only a very general understanding of prewar Yugoslavia, and what understanding I did have was porous. It also had disadvantages, among them that I had to read several more shelves of books as background to the contemporary conflict, in addition to the plethora of accounts that flooded bookstores during the war. I had no knowledge of Serbo-Croatian languages and no resources to invest in learning them, but I learned as best I could onsite and on tape in between trips, but did not conduct interviews in local languages. Though I had interpreters, many interviews were done in English.

Inside/outside questions had been very much at the center of my previous work. I had also been an outsider in relation to the subject of my earlier research: indigenous peoples. But what I attempted to do in that study of indigenous political activism was look at things (political) from an indigenous point of view. If I have any expertise, by which I mean a body of knowledge as a result of focusing on the same research questions over the past decade and a half, it is a growing understanding of relationships of Otherness and the political appropriation of Otherness to rationalize violence. This reflects my belief in the existence of a human capacity for empathy as well as in its importance to achieving the justice goals of politics, even though it currently has no widely acknowledged place in our political lives. To be concerned with the human capacity for evil and harm-doing is also, necessarily, to be concerned with the human capacity for empathy. If our inhumanity contains our capacity for harming others, for evacuating our own pain by inflicting it on others, then our humanity contains our capacity for caring, for making an effort to find a way to share others' burden of suffering, and for compassion—not as feeling *what* the other feels but for feeling *with* the other. If inflicting pain involves denying our connection to the Other while paradoxically regarding the Other, at least unconsciously, as an unwanted aspect of ourselves, then empathy and compassion involve acknowledging our common humanity without violating the integrity of the Other's agency. We need to acknowledge and understand ways in which we bleed into one another, and how distinctions between inside and outside create the paradox of our interdependent individual and collective existence.

# ACKNOWLEDGMENTS

As the tragedy of events in former Yugoslavia unfolded, the actions of two people from distant parts of the world led me to embark on the research that has, at last, come to fruition in this book. My good friend, colleague, and companion activist-scholar Jerry Calvert was relentless in bringing before me his outrage at both the violence in Yugoslavia and at the failure of Europe and the U.S. to fashion an effective intervention. Many hours of conversation and many cups of coffee later, I realized that my research agenda had been reshaped. At about the same time, in another part of the world, another political activist (also a professor of political economy, former leader of the People's Peasant Party and now Minister of Agriculture in Serbia), Dragan Veselinov, had the opportunity to travel to the U.S., and somehow, to include Bozeman, Montana on his itinerary. Through the Bozeman Center for International Visitors, he found his way into my classroom. His warm and reassuring invitation to visit Belgrade in the spring of 1995, his recommendation for a research assistant and interpreter, and his generosity with his time, wisdom, and passion for the political and economic well-being of his society, combined to make this work possible, maybe inevitable.

There are so many people to thank throughout the former republics and elsewhere, from the young railroad worker who gave me a lift to Belgrade when I was stranded at the Pancevo rail and bus station by a workers' strike on my first trip, to my newest friends from Skopje, Lidija and Vlatko, who puzzled with me over the uncertain future of their own troubled, multicultural country. In Belgrade, I thank Marija especially, but also her husband Vladimir, who put most imporatant life decisions on hold while they worked to defeat intolerance and political violence, and, along with thousands of others, finally, to give birth to a new democracy in Serbia. And thank you both for sharing with me the most elegant homemade ice cream sundae I've ever had! I thank everyone who took the time to talk with me, trust me, and forgive me the ignorance with which I first arrived in the region (and brought back on return trips!). Michael Szporluk taught me that, while many unfamiliar things remind us of things we already know, everything is also exactly what it is. He was an inspiration in every way, from Belgrade to Sarajevo. Thank you for your equanimity, humanity, and friendship, Michael. Milan, Judy, Milorad, Davor, Zoran, Dubravka, and Eugen, in your hands lies the future of a reconciled Croatia, and I thank you for opening your hearts (and your home, Milan and Judy!) to me. To Saso, whose patience extended far beyond untold hours of talking politics—Balkan and un-Balkan—with me, I know you will continue to make the world you live in a more just and caring place. And his father I must thank (as do my hosts in Sarajevo) for the home-brewed Pear William and the warm conversations it accompanied.

To all the antiwar activists, soldiers, displaced individuals and families, students, teachers, counselors, public servants—so many extraordinary people who longed for the return of an ordinary life—struggling to come to terms with unimaginable trauma, and who shared freely their diverse views of the events and experiences that caused it, I must both apologize and tell a story. I apologize because I feel the need to make use of what you have given me in a manner that honors the magnitude of your gift, and at the same time I feel wholly inadequate to do so. You have paid dearly for the lessons I hope this book will enable others to learn from your experiences. If I could put you all in a room to have a single conversation, what a cacophony that would be! But that *is* democracy, isn't it? The story I need to tell you is one my husband and life partner tells about a rabbi who is counseling a discordant couple. (My apologies to Talmudic scholars; I take full responsibility for the story's editing.) The rabbi listened to the husband who listed all of his wife's faults and transgressions, and recounted all of the ways she treated him badly and unlovingly, and when he finished the rabbi nodded, and said "I understand. You are right. You are absolutely right." Then the rabbi asked the wife to tell her version of things. And as her husband had, the wife explained all the ways in which her husband was unkind, unfair, and unloving, along with her litany of his faults and transgressions in the marriage. When she finished, the rabbi said "I understand completely. You are right. You are absolutely right." Well, at that the bewildered couple looked at one another, and then glared at the rabbi, and looking quite perturbed, they told the rabbi that it simply wasn't possible for them *both* to be right! So the rabbi thought about it for a moment, and then said to them "You know, I understand what you are saying. And you are right. You are *absolutely* right!" To all those I talked with and listened to, I do remember in great detail the many conversations I had with all of you, and to this day I not only feel like, but understand completely the paradoxical wisdom of the rabbi. I hope you do as well.

Stateside I have almost as many people to thank for contributions to this project. First and foremost, I must thank my life partner, Ronald, my first reader and without whose early support I would not have continued. I know he thinks that political scientists have special insights into such things, but if what I have to say cannot be both interesting and meaningful to him, I don't want to say it to anyone else. And thank you for teaching me that to love one person well is the accomplishment of a lifetime. Eric Nelson, my editor prodigy at Routledge, was the first stranger to read what I thought I had to say about this project (long before I knew what I actually would say). That he believed in its value for an academic audience gave me the confidence to say what I had to say, and then some. He is no stranger now, and has touched my thinking about many things in more ways than he knows. I thank Ben McCanna for his professionalism and understanding as a production editor, and an anonymous copy editor for a few more writing lessons. I thank Bojana for both a most careful and 'insider' reading, and for her help in making all the diacritical and grammatical corrections in words and names used from languages of former Yugoslavia. For readings and valuable comments during various incarnations of parts and/or the whole of this work, I thank Jerry Calvert again, along with Ken Lockridge, Henry Gonshak, Ray Pratt, Ronnie Lipschutz, and Colleen Mack-Canty. François Debrix and Ted Gurr were thorough, critical, forthright, generous, and constructive reviewers, and I hope they regard this as a much improved text.

Finally, for material and professional support, I must once more thank Jerry Calvert, who was Department Head when this work began; former College of Letters and Sciences Dean Jack Drumheller and current Dean Jim McMillan, as well as the various committees at Montana State University under whose watch I received support for travel and research; and Mladen Grbin and Carole Hodge and all the folks at the Southeastern Europe Research Unit at the University of Glasgow who put together a very important conference on the Island of Korcula in the late summer of 1998.

# CHAPTER I

# International Relations Theory and the Problem of Violence

Inside the nave, empty and grand, where a dark powder of dried blood marked one's footprints, a single, representative corpse was left on the floor before the altar. He appeared to be crawling toward the confession booth. His feet had been chopped off, and his hands had been chopped off. This was a favorite torture for Tutsis during the genocide; the idea was to cut the tall people "down to size," and crowds would gather to taunt, laugh, and cheer as the victim writhed to death. The bones emerged from the dead man's cuffs like twigs, and he still had a square tuft of hair peeling from his skull, and a perfectly formed, weather-shrunken and weather-greened ear.[1]

We invited the Gentile and Christian Indians to come and eat *pinole* and dried meat. . . . Then when they were on our shore we surrounded them . . . and took them all prisoners. . . . We separated 100 Christians from the prisoners and at each half mile or so these were forced on their knees in prayer, and were made to understand they were going to die. . . . Each one received four arrows, two in front and two in each shoulder. Those who were not killed by this process were killed with lances. . . . We reached the camp where we were going to stop with the 100 Gentile prisoners. . . . The Lieutenant told me to decide what was best to do. I answered him that this would be to shoot the prisoners, first Christianizing them. . . . He began at one end of the line and I at the other. We baptized all the Indians and then shot them through the shoulder. I doubled the charge for the 30 that remained and they all fell.[2]

I beheld a scene of atrocity and horror unparalleled not only in our own Country, but even in history, for it was done by men, self acting, and without necessity, color of law, or authority—the murder of little innocent babes and women, from breast to maturity, barbarously and I can't say brutally—for it is worse. . . . I beheld a spectacle of horror, of unexampled description—babes, with brains oozing out of their skulls, cut and hacked with axes, and squaws exhibiting the most frightful wounds in death which imagination can paint.[3]

On December 7, 1995, two African American residents of Fayetteville, North Carolina, were brutally and senselessly murdered by three soldiers who apparently identified themselves as neo-Nazi skin heads. Police said the soldiers were looking for black people to harass and shot the victims as they were walking down the street.[4]

According to witnesses, Tadić beat prisoners to death, raped at least one woman, forced people to crawl like pigs and drink mud from puddles, ordered others to drink motor oil from a sump pit and in the most infamous allegation, ordered one prisoner to castrate another with his teeth. In a crowning touch of sadistic creativity, Tadić, who reportedly favored military clothing and a black mask during these outrageous acts, was accused of having blasted a fire extinguisher into the mouth of a half-dead victim.[5]

The friends allegedly picked up 49-year-old James Byrd Jr., who was hitchhiking on a Saturday night last June. Authorities say they chained him to the truck and dragged him, still alive, through the town until his elbows peeled away on the pavement and his head rolled off the road. Prosecutors say Byrd's killing was to be the first act of a new chapter of the Confederate Knights of America, the group King joined during a two-year prison term for burglary. . . . Throughout his week-long murder trial, the 24 year-old white supremacist sat next to his lawyer in the same tired pose. . . . But King didn't actually speak until he was swiftly sentenced to die by lethal injection last week. On his way to death row, a reporter asked King if he had anything to say to his victim's family. "Yeah," he replied. "They can s—— my d——."[6]

According to the prosecution, McKinney and his friend Russell Henderson met Shepard at the Fireside Bar in Laramie on the night of Oct. 6, 1998. Witnesses testified that they saw Shepard leave the bar with Henderson and McKinney, who allegedly pretended to be gay in order to lure him out so they could rob him. Police testified that the two men then took him to a remote area east of Laramie where they robbed him, tied him to a fence and beat him with the butt of a .357 Magnum pistol. Shepard was found 18 hours later, but died while on full life support in a hospital in Fort Collins, Colo., on Oct. 12, 1998 never having regained consciousness.[7] . . . According to statements made during the interview, McKinney claimed to be out of control saying he felt like he was possessed and out of control during the beating. "It was like I could see what was going on, but someone else was doing it," he said. "I killed someone, and I don't know why."[8]

The men of Police Battalion 309's First and Third Companies drove their victims into the synagogue. . . . The Germans packed the synagogue full. . . .

After spreading gasoline around the building, the Germans set it ablaze. . . . A battalion member later described the scene that he witnessed: "I saw . . . smoke, that came out of the synagogue and heard there how the incarcerated people cried loudly for help. I was about 70 meters' distance from the synagogue." . . . Not surprisingly, some of the Jews within spared themselves the fiery death by hanging themselves or severing their arteries. At least six Jews came running out of the synagogue, their clothes and bodies aflame. The Germans shot each one down, only to watch these human torches burn themselves out. . . . . One exclaimed: "Let it burn, it's a nice little fire, it's great fun." Another exulted: "Splendid, the entire city should burn down."[9]

Snapshots of violence—all have political implications; all attest to the ubiquitous human capacity for cruelty. How we think and speak about these events matters. Do we think or speak of them as hate crimes? Discrimination, prejudice, or bigotry? Ethnic conflict? Genocide? What distinguishes these terms and acts from one another?

Language structures our thinking, our cognitive life. Naming—this is ethnic conflict but that is a hate crime, this is war but that is genocide—reveals how we think or instructs us as to how we ought to (or think we ought to) think about something, about an event, a policy, a behavior, a person. It is not the *differences* (what they are, whether they are) between men and women, or between male and female that matter, feminists tell us, it is the *social meaning associated with gendered difference* that matters, because it has social and political consequences.[10] Indeed, "ethnic" is not a category of meaning that constructs itself, any more than is "gender." We "identify" ourselves in an ethnic sense, we create and sustain the idea of a self identified with and by its membership in or association with the idea of a *group* believed to share common characteristics regarded by its members as self-evidence of sameness and solidarity, *only because we agree that the term "ethnic" has a certain meaning*. Social, political, economic, and legal power is then distributed and socially structured of the basis on the social meaning associated with gendered (and other kinds of) difference. Over the past two decades, language and meaning have become central concerns to a growing number of scholars in and around international relations. They are identified with a variety of perspectives—feminist, postmodern, postcolonial, poststructural, constructivist, and critical—maybe more. This development is sometimes referred to as the "rhetorical" or "linguistic" turn in International Relations (IR).

The past two decades have also witnessed the more frequent and widespread use of the terms "hate crime" and "ethnic conflict" in social science as well as civic discourses, both within and among modern democracies in the late twentieth century. "Hate crimes" are regarded not only as deviant and antisocial acts but, in most modern democracies, illegal. "Ethnic" attributes, by contrast, can be viewed as quaint at best and, primitive at worst, and in conjunction with "conflict," problematic but somewhat normal, for relatively unmodern or less modern (if not less civilized) people anyway. "Mention the term 'ethnic,'" say John Darby and Roger Mac Ginty in their introduction to reports from the "Coming Out of Violence" project in *The Management of Peace Processes*, "and you are likely to hear one of two responses: references to either folk songs, beads or rustic costumes, or to violence.[11]

So how should we think about the nineteenth-century American soldiers who killed their Indians prisoners, baptizing or "Christianizing" them first? Was it a case of soldiers carrying out a project they had come to know as "manifest destiny" and to regard as noble, even "normal" within the political and historical context of American state-building? How should we distinguish between ethnic conflict, discrimination, hate crimes, and genocide? From what position does one make such distinctions? A position of historical distance? Political authority? Who is the speaker of such a judgment—that Christianizing and murdering indigenous peoples in the name of state-building was acceptable social practice among nineteenth-century European settlers in the American West? And what of the common denominator among the opening vignettes—the cognitive process of dehumanizing those against whom brutalities are perpetrated? Can ethnic groups, whole nations, or states be guilty of hate crimes? U.S. law, for example, defines hate crimes as "acts in which individuals are victimized because of their race, religion, sexual orientation, or ethnicity." In hate crimes "the defendant intentionally selects a victim . . . because of the *actual or perceived* race, color, religion, national origin, ethnicity, gender, disability, or sexual orientation of any person."[12]

All of the introductory vignettes describe acts that can fit into this definition of hate crimes, though of course most of them did not occur within the political or historical scope of legal norms on which this definition is grounded. In most modern democracies, hate crimes are unacceptable, antisocial, and in most cases, criminal. But within the political discourse of policy makers as well as some (positivist) academics, the term "ethnic conflict," like "war," often appears as an agentless phenomenon of social life, the meaning of which is self-evident. But when does ethnic conflict become a hate crime, and vice versa? When do ethnic conflicts or hate crimes become genocides, and who are the agents? Where are the boundaries between ethnic conflict, war, state-building, and legally prohibited conduct such as hate crimes and genocide? How do people who commit hate crimes in the course of "ethnic conflicts," "genocides," "state-building" processes, and wars understand (and do they understand or think in terms of) the political implications of their behavior? How does how we think about these events and behaviors frame our interpretation of their significance, and how do meanings influence how our leaders respond (or fail to respond) to them?

This study of violence in the former Yugoslavia will attempt to problematize all of these concepts, categories, and distinctions by examining the
role of discursive practices, narratives of political identity, ethnicity, state
creation (and destruction), and war. In order to "solve" the problems of war
and ethnic conflict, it argues, we must deconstruct the narratives underlying
the practice of war, the imagined state, and the social processes that construct
(and deconstruct) the political identities in which both are grounded. The
central theme of this book is that the state is a socially constructed institution, that war is a social practice, that identity is the social and psychological phenomenon on which both rest, and that civilizing the state and
reducing the incidence and horrors of war necessitate taking the process of
social construction seriously. Paradoxically, it is often through the destruction and disintegration of the state that this becomes most evident.

This chapter's opening excerpts from trials, transcripts, and testimonials of
war, crimes against humanity, state-building, genocide and "ordinary apolitical" hate crimes also illustrate how easily the realities of other-directed
violence can muddle many of the assumptions and distinctions social scientists
make about identity, politics, violence, and the relationship among them.
From an academic perspective, only the anti-Semitic crimes of Battalion 309,
the Bosnian war crimes of Dušan Tadić, and the genocide mobilized by the
Hutu Power movement in Rwanda are of much interest to the student of
comparative or international politics. Anti-indigenous violence by settlers and
miners in North America is still so politicized in the United States that it is
most often viewed by non-Indians more as "an unfortunate chapter in
American history" rather than a problematic case of either ethnic violence or
crimes against humanity. Similarly, racial hate crimes or homophobic violence
are not really *political* problems until or unless they reach broader proportions
or are sanctioned tacitly or explicitly by governments. They are thus "priva-
tized" as "domestic" issues in the United States, interesting perhaps to sociologists or social psychologists studying deviance, prejudice, social control,
obedience, or moral development, but not all that significant politically.

But what are the emotional and cognitive processes at work in the perpetrator's construction of social reality? What are the similarities and differences in the cognitive processes of perpetrators of homophobic violence,
racial killings, the brutality of settlers and miners against indigenous peoples,
war crimes, crimes against humanity, and the otherwise "ordinary people"
who carry out genocide? How do political justifications of "war" and "state-
building" normalize behaviors that under the "civilizing" influence of
"domestic" law and order are considered marginal, deviant, or even pathological? Can and do political processes sometimes normalize otherwise pathological behavior?

The violence described in these vignettes took place within particular
social and political contexts, but it raises the questions with which I have

been struggling as a social scientist and humanist over the past decade. If social science is about solving problems and puzzles, then these are my puzzles: What are the moral consequences of exclusionary identities and behaviors? How do they rationalize human brutality and what do political processes, community, and identity have to do with it? *Are* there "real" differences between "public" and "private," or "political" and "personal" violence? Some feminists say no. How does political context shape or affect violent behavior and impulses, making them more or less likely? What psychological processes does committing wanton brutality against another human being entail, and what is the role of political variables in mobilizing and rationalizing such brutality? Are some cultures more and others less likely to produce such behavior? What is the connection between violent state-building, destroying, and maintaining processes?[13] Is war just another "hate crime," albeit writ large and rationalized by political rhetoric and statist logic? Where *are* the boundaries between madness and normalcy, civility and inhumanity, and how do we know on which side of those boundaries "war" and specific acts of political violence are located? In the case of interventions, for instance, is there a difference between "good" and "bad" violence, between evil violence and violence that stops or prevents evil? Why is identity so often implicated in both "evil" and "political" violence, and where is the nexus between identity, politics, and violence?

For social scientists, the problem of political violence takes the form of civil or interstate war, rebellion, terrorism, and more recently, ethnic conflict. Theorizing about political violence necessitates having a particular idea of "the state." It appears constant, fixed, bounded, and it is most often regarded as a kind of natural political community, the highest expression of nationhood or national identity. The case of "ethnic conflict" as a category of political violence is frequently a variation on the assumptions we make about interstate war. We either simply substitute the ethnic group for the state as the actor, or regard the ethnic group or groups as struggling against or for control of state institutions. Our theorizing and analysis of ethnic conflict, in other words, take place within the limits of statist logic, even when, as in the case of genocide, the state is the perpetrator. One distinction between the violence committed by Hutus, Nazis, and Bosnian war criminals on the one hand, and racial hate crimes and homophobic murder on the other, is that the former implicates the state as *perpetrator*. What matters is not only the fact that violence takes place in order to accomplish a political objective in the first three cases, but that violence is committed by individuals acting as agents of the state. But what, then, should we make of violence against Native Americans by Euro-American settlers and miners? Are these not also crimes against humanity? Are crimes against humanity shielded by the state-building enterprise, rationalized by the expansionist state-building ideology of "manifest destiny" (Wilmer 1993)?

These disturbing events also raise questions about our civility, the terms of our citizenship, how both are constructed in relation to the state, and how international discourse constitutes a social practice in which the state is constructed, maintained, and, in the case of the Yugoslav successor states, created and destroyed, in relation to certain international norms. There are many ways of talking about citizenship (Weiner 1998; Kymlicka 1995; Young 1990). It can be analyzed as a system of rights and/or of obligations, as a normative practice, and as a way of structuring political identity, for example. The focus here is on a somewhat minimal condition of citizenship—the obligation to refrain from violence in our relations with other citizens, and the circumstances under which it fails or, worse, leads us to commit brutality against one another. Two individuals who are citizens of the same polity *ought* to agree, at least tacitly, to such a norm of reciprocity. But is that enough? Clearly, McKinney did not feel such an obligation toward Matthew Shepard; nor King toward James Byrd, nor Tadić toward his victims at Prejidor, nor the California settlers and American military toward Native Americans, the North Carolina skinheads toward their black victims, Hutu Power supporters toward Tutsis, and certainly not Nazis toward Jews and others killed in the Holocaust. Reciprocity based on civic identity must take precedence over other forms of identity.

In the aforementioned cases the perpetrators and victims were *supposed* to be citizens within the same polity. But the distribution and intensity of "citizenship feelings," are variable in any particular society and across historical contexts. In each of these cases the perpetrators' acts of violence against those excluded from their own identity group were, in a strange way, simultaneously an affirmation of their loyalty to and membership in a group with whom they identified themselves—Hutus as distinct from Tutsis, white supremacists as distinct from people of color, Serbs as distinct from Croats and Muslims, heterosexual males as distinct from homosexual males, gentile Germans as distinct from Jewish Germans or German Jews, the emerging identity of "American" settlers contrasted with the "savage" and "primitive" indigenous peoples, and so on. If we suspend our horror and disgust for these "hate crimes," we can also see them as a way for the perpetrators to affirm their own identification, loyalty, and group membership. Is identity so unstable and ephemeral? We might further concede that the potential for other-directed violence, as well as in-group identification in ways that subvert obligations of citizenship, is present in most heterogeneous and complex societies, as antigay and racist violence in the United States, the xenophobic and extreme right-wing nationalism of Haider in Austria and Le Pen in France, and continued neo-Nazi violence in Germany indicate. In fact, the persistence of racial crimes (and, indeed, the possibility that such crimes are actually increasing in Britain and elsewhere in Europe) is some cause for concern.[14] But if the concept of civility has any meaning for modern democracies, then *instances of individuals acting violently* on the basis of exclusionary identities would or should be *marginal, not normal.*

What is still puzzling is how such marginal behavior becomes "normalized" or, worse, officially sanctioned by the state and unopposed by the international community of states. In the case of Nazi Germany, the rise of Hutu Power's campaign of genocide, or the ethnic cleansing in the former Yugoslavia, how could we have predicted that the bonds of citizenship would dissolve so quickly and disastrously, and could that dissolution and the subsequent descent into the most inhuman cruelty have been avoided, obstructed, or restrained? We need to know how civic sentiments are strengthened within the polity and under what circumstances those sentiments become vulnerable and/or deteriorate. One of the reasons these questions are more easily examined in the case of the former Yugoslavia is precisely because Yugoslavia *was* a state, and it *was* populated by citizens who felt a relatively high degree of civic identity. Contrary to the imagery of the Western media, Serbs, Croats, Muslims, and the more than a million individuals whose families were of mixed ethnic background in prewar Yugoslavia were not poised on the verge of "ancient hatreds" held tenuously in check for four decades only by the strong arm of Father Tito. In addition to an estimated more than one and a half million people in mixed marriages, there were many more people whose civic identity and loyalty were simply aligned with the idea of the Yugoslav state and civil society. Then, during the last nine months of 1990, the state of Yugoslavia ceased to exist, and while many of its former citizens descended into a very uncivil war, many also fled the violence, while others remained to oppose it. Five years, hundreds of thousands of deaths, and millions of internally and externally displaced persons later, five "successor" states remained where Yugoslavia once existed.[15] All were populated to a greater or lesser degree by citizens with multiple and sometimes overlapping loyalties and identities, and most contained a dominant ethnic group, with the exception of the impossibly multicultural Bosnia and Herzegovina.

## Ethnic Groups, Moral Communities, and States

Experts and nonexperts alike often begin with the unchallenged assumption that states and ethnic groups are constituted by individuals whose bonds of loyalty are grounded in some kind of shared identity, and that these "national" identities are, in turn, both organic and political. We sing national anthems, salute flags, and cheer for our home or national teams at international competitions as affirmations of the state's political significance, though these are by and large emotional acts. But for many, perhaps most of the world's peoples, the state as a naturalized expression of nationality does not really exist. Almost all of the two hundred or so states in the world are multinational. The term "nation-state" has until fairly recently been a used to mean what we now simply call "the state." Not surprisingly, the first scholars to evaluate critically the idea of the nation-state were those engaged with the issue of "ethnic conflict" and "ethnonationalism" *before* it was fashionable, such as Walker Connor,[16] or postcolonial critics such as Homi Bhabha.[17]

Even while international lawyers and most Western policy-makers no longer regard it as so, the discourse of the state and citizenship naturalized the state as an expression—perhaps the highest, and certainly the most powerful expression—of nationality. So it was for the eighteenth- and nineteenth-century European nationalists who wrestled authority from monarchs and handed it over to "the people." And while most citizens in modern Western states today probably believe that civic forms of identity and political allegiance have displaced the "bonds of blood," to paraphrase Ignatieff,[18] state-builders in states carved out of formerly colonized territories or in the aftermath of the collapse of the Soviet Union frequently appropriate the imagery of kinship rooted in a consciousness of nationalism as the rhetoric foundation for both their legitimacy and the legitimacy of the state itself. Zimbabwe's President Robert Mugabe, who enjoys widespread support among blacks in the former colonized and white-dominated country, announced in a June 2000 speech that: "The whites can be citizens in our country, or residents, but not our cousins."[19] The Associated Press wire story's headline, "Mugabe: Whites Must Recognize Nation's for Blacks," underscored Mugabe's claim as well as convoluting the ideas of nation and state.

Cynthia Weber deconstructs the idea of the sovereign state, claiming that:

> there is no "natural" sovereign state because there is no "natural" foundation of sovereignty. While the belief that sovereign authority resides in "the people" has become a less and less questioned foundation of state authority in the modern state system, this fact does not settle debates about sovereignty because just who the people are and who legitimately can speak for them is contested and constructed daily in international practice. And very often, debates about who "the people" are and where sovereign authority resides occur around episodes of intervention.[20]

For the purpose of the present analysis, I would suggest that "contestations of the territorial boundaries in which jurisdictional authority is asserted" occur not only around interventions but in connection with a variety of claims to justify the use of force, including civil wars, secessions, interventions, and even "ethnic" conflicts.

Although group identities are frequently presumed to be spatially fixed, in fact I think they are quite fluid, moveable, porous, and frequently fragmented by intersections, amalgamations, and contradictions. The construction of modern ethnic and national identities *as if they were organic or natural* and in relation to the configuration of territorial space, however, is central to the project of creating a system of international property rights, rights which trump all others, in the form of sovereign states. Evidence of this claim is apparent in two otherwise contradictory processes: (1) the fact that nonstate peoples' territorial claims are viewed as inferior to the claims of states, a fact used to mobilize "separatists" along "ethnonational" lines in order to obtain recognition of their "sovereign" control over territorial space; and (2) state-building ideologies, such as the American "manifest destiny," which discursively naturalized the settlers' claim to territory even when common ethnic origins (other than "white" or "European origin") were not necessarily present and there was *no connection* between people making such a claim and the territory they aimed to control. Similarly, as the conflict in former Yugoslavia progressed, norms pertaining to the naturalized relationship between organic ethnic identity, territorial space, and aspirations to sovereignty provoked incessant debates about history, archeology, and the origins of peoples in the former Yugoslavia.[21]

Not long ago, social scientists were predicting that modernity would displace ethnic identities with functional, class, and/or civic identities, or as Durkheim put it, that solidarity derived from a sense of sameness would be displaced by solidarity derived from and interdependence among differentiated individuals.[22] Instead, modernity has probably done more to destabilize and deconstruct the myth of naturalized identities. It may also, ironically, have provoked among "true believers" a more stubborn insistence on the existence of organic differences constructed in ethnic terms.[23] This may be one of the reasons for increased "ethnic conflict," even racism and xenophobia, in otherwise civil democracies as the artificiality of identities is exploded by modernity and some grasp desperately for the illusion of "authentic" difference as a psychic defense against the fear of fragmentation or of losing one's identity. I tend to view identities more in the way physicists view atoms: when you want to observe them, they show up, but who knows where they are in between observations?[24]

The modern state as a set of authoritative institutions relies on the creation of a specifically political identity in the form of "citizenship" (though many may imagine the origins of civic identity in the West as rooted in ancient Greek and Roman cultures and in the East in the tradition of Confucianism). Our identity as "citizen" is constituted through a system of rights and obligations tied to the territoriality of the state. We then make a distinction between and among citizens of different states. But these modern state identities were produced through social practices and processes that consolidated power and identity, as Bordieu has demonstrated.[25]

Although discourses of citizenship are not new, the degree of normative consensus about the meaning of citizenship and the institutionalization of the state as the purveyor of the social contract controlling citizenship are historically unprecedented. A minimal condition of citizenship as constituted by the state, or at least one that I propose, obligates citizens as a rule to refrain from violence in their relations. In the exceptional case of self-defense, the burden of proof is on the citizen to make the case that indeed his or her violent actions fit within the criteria of the exceptional case. A further and related obligation is to seek peaceful solutions to conflicts in relations with one another. The boundary between states, then, is demarcated in a moral sense by, among other things, the *absence* of such restraints between the citizens of different states. Citizens may even be called on to engage specifically in violent acts against citizens of another state. The state therefore functions as a kind of moral community in the same way that families, kinship groups, and ethnic groups do: as groups of inclusion/exclusion characterized by a moral obligation of reciprocity within the group and excluding those who fall outside its boundaries from such an obligation and from the protection it provides.

While the idea of naturalized loyalties and obligations may have a special emotional appeal, the family, kinship group, ethnic, religious, or cultural group normally does not require that we affirm our loyalties as states do—paying taxes and fighting wars—though it may ask us to show preferences for "insiders" and prejudice against "outsiders." Said differently, while other forms of group identity and solidarity (family, kinship group, and so on) may in the past have made certain claims on our loyalty which today are made by states (obedience to authority, willingness to sacrifice for collective security and economic welfare of the community), the state today makes claims on individuals on the basis of their identity as citizens which trump all other claims, past and present, based on all other group identities. There remains, however, a potential for conflict between these loyalties and those we are obligated to feel toward the state or toward fellow citizens, particularly where the state is not long or well established and/or where its legitimacy is weak.

One of the central problems of the modern state is that citizens who "find themselves" in a particular state do not simply abandon or suppress other forms or sources of group identity, nor do they relinquish the emotional bond between individual and group created by noncivic identities, nor does the sense or perception that groups of "sameness" constitute a kind of moral community disappear, nor the exclusionary practices that moral communities entail, just because the state has declared diverse individuals to be "citizens" in a common polity. The ability to arouse powerful emotions by invoking solidarity on the basis of group identities derived from symbolic as much as (or more than) substantive differences remains as pervasive as ever in modern societies, including states, even the older ones. Like gender, it is the symbolic association of difference with ethnicity that matters, and ethnicity remains one of the most potent symbolic categories of political difference.

While from a state-centric view the number of ethnic groups constituted as minorities may be fewer than several hundred, from the perspective of groups whose solidarity is grounded in cultural and linguistic affinity and narratives of identity and kinship, and who for much of their history controlled their own political destiny *as groups*, there are thousands of ethnic groups extant today. Yet these thousands of groups live within a state system made up of fewer than two hundred states. If control of state institutions offers the fullest expression of ethnic self-determination, then many ethnic groups will be less than fully expressed. I do not mean to suggest that this is so because of any legal association between ethnic identity and the state, but rather because of the normative structure of the state, its *social construction as a nation-state*, its foundation in discourses of nationalism as a *liberation narrative* in Europe in the context of the historical era of European state- (and empire-) building. The ethnic basis of the nation-state that emerged from national liberation narratives is alleged to have been more recently transformed into a civic state, a pluralist state in which no group is privileged on the basis of identity over other groups. Because this transformation occurred (if, where, and to the extent that it did) as a result of "the politics of blending and assimilation," William Connolly argues, what we actually have are not truly pluralist states in a multicultural sense but, at best, states with "layered centers."[26] Those layered centers consist of an identity regarded as foundational at the core surrounded by the "minority" identities which were to have been blended and assimilated into or otherwise treated on the basis of political legal equality with the core identity. But, he argues, we are still left with states in which the narratives of privileged groups remains at the center.

While the state is not necessarily the fullest expression of ethnic self-determination in any naturalized sense, ethnic majorities within states thus clearly enjoy a position of power in the sense of controlling and/or privileging their own cultural, religious, and linguistic practice as well as preserving and perpetuating narratives of history and identity consonant with the preferences of the ethnic majority. Additionally, since at some historical point they controlled the political and legal institutions of the states they "founded," they also control the processes of "blending and assimilation," including both the legal and political process involved in the creation of "minority" rights and protections, but also the construction and adaptation of historical and civic identity narratives. When we speak about the existence (or the problem) of ethnic minorities, we presume the existence of a status quo, a dominant or majority ethnicity. We talk about the "assimilation" of minorities, but *into what?* We talk about the "protection of minorities," but *protection against what?* Discourses about minorities necessarily implicate ethnic dominance.

Each episode of violence described at the opening of this chapter must also be understood as a specific act carried out by specific *agents*—agents located within the context of a political culture and a social context and at a point of convergence among historically situated variables within those cultures. They are acting out their own narratives of history and identity: manifest destiny, the final solution, ethnic cleansing, Hutu power, white supremacy, a particular interpretation of the Bible. Stories matter. People understand themselves, their identities, and the categories into which they place others within the framework of their own stories or narratives. The "state" is not only a structure but an agent of authority and authoritative identity situated within legitimating narratives that foster a belief in group identity grounded in notions of ethnocultural affinity. Could it be that much of what we call "ethnic conflict" may be attributed to ethnic minorities *resisting* the state as a social institution that structures power according to the ability of ethnic groups to assert control over and through it?

In approaching the question of the identity-politics-violence nexus, I begin by reconfiguring the boundaries between "us and them," between our humanity and theirs. Archbishop Desmond Tutu put it this way:

> My humanity is caught up in your humanity. I am a human being only because you are a human being. There is no such thing as a solitary human being. . . . And for that reason, the highest value is accorded to harmony, communal harmony, and anger and revenge and bitterness are corrosive of this harmony. And in a sense, it is the best form of self-interest to forgive you, because if I do not, my anger against you, which goes toward dehumanizing you, dehumanizes me in the process. The minute you are diminished, whether I like it or not, I am diminished. And so if I can enhance your humanity, ipso facto, my humanity is enhanced. . . . [27]

What if denying another's humanity also diminishes our own?

## Conflict, Violence, and War

Conflict is often said to be at the core of political life—not evil in itself, but normal. The management of conflict creates the need for mediation, dispute resolution, arbitration, adjudication, restitution or restorative justice, and other "justice functions" in social life. Adversarial judicial systems in larger, complex, modern societies may have originated with the mediating functions of societal elders characteristic of small, local, kinship-based nonstate groups.[28] The channeling and containment of conflict reduces the potential, role, scope, and impact of violence in organized social life. Anthropologists sometimes make a distinction between "primitive" and "modern" social systems on the basis of whether or not the regulation of violence is achieved through authoritative institutions empowered to use coercion in carrying out the enforcement of legal norms. This "monopoly of force" is said to be characteristic of "advanced" social organizations.

Although in a kinship-based society, "inside" and "outside" are delineated by genetic relationships, outsiders are not always or necessarily the target of inhuman, cruel, or violent behavior, nor are all outside groups necessarily treated the same way by any particular group. Anthropological literature is rich with diverse accounts of the many ways in which insider/outsider relationships can be structured, and often includes prescriptions for the admission, incorporation, or adoption of outsiders as a consequence of inter-marriage, war, or conquest (Ferguson and Farragher 1988; Bonta 1993; Turner and Pitt 1988). Some anthropological studies are concerned with questions about which variables explain why some kinship-based groups are more or less peaceful or more or less bellicose (Sponsel and Thomas 1994; Kelly 2000). Intergroup conflicts, in other words, can be more or less violent, rather like states. But the phenomenon of regarding members of one's own group with preference and outsiders with disdain, or of individuals possessing little or no obligation to restrain hostility toward out-group members or "others," is neither uniquely "primitive" nor "modern." Some psychologists suggest that constructing identity in these terms is inescapable.[29] So the assumption that the state has displaced kinship-based loyalties seems suspect, though it may in fact have, at best, simply layered over antecedent forms of group identity.

The manner in which a society channels conflict and the capacity for violence with other societies is also a function of its political culture, world-view, and "self-understanding." The Hopi, to use an example from indige-nous, kinship-based societies in North America, have formulated a worldview, self-understanding, and identity that are closely identified with pacifism. Swiss political culture, rooted in a norm of neutrality in interna-tional relations, might be an example of the political culture and self-under-standing of a state-based society in which group identity is linked with the maintenance of peaceful relations with other state societies (or simply main-taining an isolated neutrality with respect to conflicts between or among others). Narratives of collective self-understanding may reveal something about societal proneness toward highly conflicted and violent relations with Others. The state functions as a kind of a "in-group" writ large. Perhaps we flatter ourselves in thinking of it as much more than that.

The cognitive dynamics of the in-group as a moral community, a commu-nity of reciprocal obligation, suggest that members of an in-group, whether based on ethnic, cultural, or civic affiliation, ought to voluntarily refrain from violence as a means of resolving conflict in their relations with one another. Such "blood loyalty," says Michael Ignatieff (1993), provides the basis for refraining from harm-doing behavior among group members. When group boundaries are defined by kinship, members are perceived as repositories or extensions of individual identity. If all or almost all other members of a group ceased to exist, the individual's identity would lose meaning. Preservation of the group, including defense of the group, is in this sense self-interested. If civility is the basis for citizenship, and we define civility in terms of our capacity to refrain from violence and resolve disputes peacefully with others, are "citizens" whose loyalties are defined by kinship really citizens at all? Aren't they really motivated to refrain from violence in their mutual relations out of a self-interest in preserving the existence of the group on which the survival of individual identity depends?

The narrative of the nation-state claims that it represents a more advanced form of civility than "earlier" and more "primitive" forms of political organization based on kinship. Ethnic bonds have been transformed into civic bonds. Yet its roots, the norms underlying its legitimate authority over people and claim to territory, lie in kinship, hence *nation*-state. But what has occurred on a level of narration about citizenship and the state has clearly not occurred at the level of social, political, or emotional reality. States are not populated by citizens who share bonds of civic loyalty. Ethnic groups are both targets of state violence and perpetrators of violence against the state. And the emotional appeal of xenophobic movements is evident in even the most "advanced" modern states. Between 1995 and 1998 some fifty-four groups were in "open rebellion" with thirty-four states.[30] Many more cold wars are ongoing between indigenous peoples and states. What can international relations theory tell us about these forms of political violence and the grievances that underlie them?

When international relations scholars theorize about war as an interstate phenomenon, their postulates rest on an image of societies contained within the more or less solid boundaries of states, an image in which conflict is channeled and violence regulated "inside" those boundaries. Neither the boundaries of states nor the methods used to "regulate" violence within them are supposed to be contestable. "Nothing could be further from the truth," one might say, except that in addition to the very messy sites of contestation, there are also a great many cases of peaceful interstate relations as well a few genuinely interstate wars more or less consistent with the realists' view. But ironically, no sooner did classical realism prevail, perhaps regarded by some as a paradigm, in the aftermath of World War II in the still-young discipline of International Relations, than the actual events we study in the category "war" began to deviate in every direction away from the realists' image—to police actions, cold wars, civil wars, interventions, and ethnic conflict.

The way IR currently conceptualizes war as a subject seems to me to be of limited usefulness for either policy-making or academic study. It may be more productive to think about the problem of "political violence" and view it as manifested in a variety of forms. In Peace Studies we think about war as a form of conflict and ask how conflict can be more constructively channeled in political life. Political violence takes many forms. The "dirty wars" carried out as massive violations of human rights by governments in South

America and elsewhere are one kind of problematic political violence. Some of those dirty wars were considered civil wars, in Guatemala, for instance, or El Salvador. Was South African apartheid a war of the white-controlled government against blacks and other people of color in South Africa? When does a campaign of government repression become a dirty war, and when does a dirty war become a civil war? When the people who are repressed shoot back? And what distinguishes low-intensity conflict from a dirty war, civil war, or failed peace process? Perhaps most important, how useful are these distinctions either for understanding political violence or for making policies aimed at reducing or resolving it?

The inability to make a clear distinction between civil and international war in the case of former Yugoslavia was of more than academic interest. If it was a civil war, then under international law other states were obligated to remain neutral or, if they abandoned their neutrality, become a party to the conflict, which would, by definition, then be an international one. If it was an international war, then it could (or perhaps should) have been construed as a threat to the peace, breach of the peace, or act of aggression in the terminology of the UN Charter. As a violation of international law, then responsibility for war crimes would extend beyond the question of crimes against individuals and crimes against humanity to the issue of the crime of starting a war through an act of aggression. But this was never really sorted out definitively by major powers and further complicated efforts to forge a common political will and policy aimed at ending the violence.

International lawyers speak about the regulation of violence as the regulation of the use of force. But how we construct the boundary between categories of violence has real and serious consequences for policy-making. In the case of both the appeasement of Hitler fifty years earlier, and as Yugoslav republics initiated secession and war became imminent, the major powers were unable to respond decisively and effectively, and failed to make a clear judgment and undertake decisive action sooner—years sooner—in part because policy-makers could not resolve the contradictions created by thinking exclusively in terms of domestic jurisdiction (inside) versus the interests and will of the international community (outside) in condemning the rise of German fascism or toxic Serbian and Croatian nationalism. Forming an alliance to oppose German fascism or "ethnic cleansing" in the former Yugoslavia is also not simply a matter of recognizing interdependent interests among major powers, though there may be some.[31] It is a matter of political leaders choosing to use force as an intervention against the actions of a group, groups, or a state engaged in activities deemed normatively unacceptable by those in the alliance. If international law regulates the use of violence by states, then the lesson of World War II is that it cannot rule out taking action against a state misusing force within its own territory against the people whose citizenship and well-being lie in the hands of the state.

Inside/ outside boundaries, like categories, identities, and jurisdictions, are more porous than impenetrable, more fluid than fixed, and socially, rather than naturally, constructed. This calls for radical rethinking about both the structure and agency of our international social and political life.

### The Current Crisis in IR Theory

The end of the Cold War and the failure of IR theorists, scholars, and practitioners to foresee it brought to center stage an epistemological and ontological debate about practically everything that has ever been said and done in the name of IR. Everything about IR became contestable: international relations became "world politics"; states and state systems became political communities; political discourse became speech acts; war became conflict or violence; theory became epistemology; and boundaries—inside/outside— whether cognitive, geographic, or disciplinary, were decloaked as "binary categories of socially constructed space."

The ensuing theoretical and methodological debates have dragged political science, Western philosophy, and social theory into the fray and have provoked fresh interest in the old but unsettled argument about the limitations inherent in grafting the methodology and epistemology of the physical sciences onto the conduct of social inquiry. While biologist Edward O. Wilson argues that all social and physical sciences can be assimilated within a bioscience paradigm, physicist Amit Goswami claims a convergence between quantum physics and social constructivism (Wilson 1998; Goswami 1993). These are indeed exciting times to be thinking about international relations.

Some say we are experiencing a crisis in IR theory (Neumann and Waever 1997). At the same time, however, we seem to have more theories than we know what to do with. We have IR theory, classical political theory, political philosophy, modern political theory, social theory, formal theory, empirical or positive theory, feminist theory (IR and political), normative theory, postcolonial theory (and other "posts"), and constructivist theory, to name a few. Political scientists regularly draw on the theoretical work of sociologists, psychologists, economists, linguists, literary critics, and even a mathematical biologist.[32] There are currently either three or four "great debates" taking place among the "polyphony of IR voices" (Neumann and Waever 1997).

The one that most interests me here is the recent debate about structuralist approaches (including both realists and neoliberal institutionalists, because they share the view that structures matter most) as distinct from reflectivist or constructivist approaches. Prior to the poststructural/postmodern/social constructivist critiques of IR, the state, power, and political interests were presumed to be stable and to have shared meanings to all relevant global political actors. Research questions focused on institutional and structural relationships given the state, power, and interests. Poststructuralism and social constructivism share credit for redirecting our inquiry to questions of *how* the state is constituted in the first place; and perhaps most importantly, how does how we *think* about power "make it so," that is, how are states, interests, and power *socially constructed*? These do not exhaust the questions raised by ongoing epistemological debates, but they are at the core. Questions about the role of norms, normative consensus, identity, boundaries, the construction of the self, civil society, uncivil behavior, the role of culture and historicity, and others follow from the contestation of these foundational concepts—the state, power, and interests (see Ruggie 1998, Kratochwil 1989; Lapid and Kratochwil 1997; Katzenstein 1996; Neumann and Waever 1997).

My own encounter with current theoretical debates resulted from posing this question: "What sense can an academic analyst make of the global political mobilization of indigenous peoples making claims to international rights vis-à-vis their relationship to states and the state system in the late twentieth century?" (Wilmer 1993). This inquiry led me to interrogate both the role of identity in the social construction of the state, and the rhetoric of indigenous peoples' Otherness as a mechanism for mobilizing otherwise diverse European settlers to carry out the project of "modern state-building." State-building in the Americas, particularly in North America as in New Zealand/Aotearoa and Australia, meant the destruction of and dominance over the region's indigenous inhabitants. It is the question of state-building—and state destruction—as a process, and the structure of relations among diverse groups whose histories and identities are in part derived from a violent past in relation to it, that I wanted to address in a study of the violence in former Yugoslavia.

Theories ought to frame our thinking about a problem in terms of its causes, consequences, or significance. But in approaching the question of indigenous peoples" antistate grievances and activism, I did not find much in IR theory, nor indeed, in ethnic mobilization or social movement theory in sociology, that enabled me to think either systematically or critically about how identity is implicated in structuring power pursuant to state-building projects. I did find that by employing rhetorical analysis and by reading "history as text," I could understand, if not explain, indigenous peoples' activism as a response to the dominant Western normative order's construction of them as "backward and primitive others." The ideology of Enlightenment, Progress, Manifest Destiny, or the White Man's Burden all served to rationalize politically sanctioned violence against them for some five centuries. I came to see the logic of "modernization" as a kind of ideology emanating from the globalization of European social processes in settler states and later reproduced throughout the "developing" world. Indigenous activism is a form of resistance to modernizing ideology and its consequences, past and present. I also became interested in how the moral construction of indigenous "Otherness" played a central role in formation of new "modern" identities on which the processes of settler state-building rested, as well as the mobilization of "world order" imagined by the "international community." The struggle between indigenous peoples and states was a normative struggle with material consequences, and it was a rhetorical struggle—the rhetoric used to rationalize the perpetration of violence against indigenous peoples, and the rhetoric they used to combat it. Words and stories matter, I concluded. Words matter both because symbolic power matters, and because words contain meanings. They are a window into our individual and collective cognitive life.

This experience framed my own incursion into contemporary theoretical debates which I have come to see as begging a larger question about the epistemology of social inquiry and the usefulness or at least the limits of adapting the epistemology of physical science to the tasks of social science. When we think about these "great IR debates"—idealism versus realism, behavioralism versus traditionalism, neorealism versus neo–institutional liberalism, and structuralism versus constructivism—it seems to me that there are two recurring themes of contestation: the impact of agency and human cognition on social reality, and how that, in turn, affects the conduct of social inquiry. The central question underlying all of these debates seems to be: Is agency a result of cognition, and does agency, in turn shape social reality? If human cognition does influence the course of IR, then we must rectify what Wendt calls the agent-structure problem (1987). Idealists at the beginning of the twentieth century focused on the agency of structures and how they, in turn, shaped human behavior. (In fact, to assume that human nature is either inherently good—or progressive—or bad is to deny agency by predetermining that overall direction of human choice.) But this thinking was framed within the historical context characterized by the reification of "Progress," human intellect applied to scientific method and a consequent steady improvement in the material quality of life. Following a century of what many Europeans perceived as peace among, at least, *major* Western European actors in the aftermath of several centuries of war, it was probably inevitable that late nineteenth- and early twentieth-century European thinkers should reify science and translate "scientific thinking" into social engineering. But the reification of science and social engineering also manifested itself in a more diabolical form—Nazi eugenics and the Holocaust. Ironically, realist thinking was nearly as one-dimensional as idealist thinking. Like liberalism, realism also appropriated a scientific worldview, in time replacing idealism as the bearer of scientism.

The question underlying these theoretical debates is whether or not the study of *social* problems can be approached by grafting onto our disciplines the epistemology and methodologies used in the physical sciences to construct useful knowledge about the *material* world. I believe the issue that has long been lurking in, if not driving, these debates is that, as science has been under-stood for most of this century, human agency is believed to make no real difference in the structure and functioning of the physical world. But the question "Can useful knowledge about the social world be acquired by using the theoretical orientations and methodologies of physical science?" is a crit-ical one. Although the "behavioralism versus traditionalism" debate does not really fall within the scope of "theoretical debates," it is still an episte-mological debate. The larger issue is whether or within what limits we can adapt scientific theorizing and methodology—ways of thinking—to the enter-prise of acquiring useful knowledge about the social world.

My own answer is, yes, but there are limits to relying on *only* the methods and modes of thinking about physical science, and constructivist thinking has made significant inroads in opening up the question of what *other* modes of theorizing, research, and analysis can produce useful knowledge of the social world. Constructivists demand that we attend to human agency and cognition and, at least in my own work, not the "behavior" of the U.S. government toward indigenous peoples, nor the reproduction of that behavior wherever modernization projects encounter and seek domination over "primitiveness," nor the perspective of indigenous peoples, nor their persistent activism, nor the responses to it would be comprehensible without employing a constructivist perspective and methodology.

The present study of the violence in the former Yugoslavia is really a case study which examines theoretical intersections. The first is between theory and practice. When the number of states is taken into account, the number of interstate wars has dramatically declined in the aftermath of the World War II (Holsti 1991, 1996). Furthermore, since then there has been no major power war in the way we have traditionally thought of war. Inasmuch as our thinking about war was overwhelmingly framed on the basis of assumptions implied from interstate wars between major powers, it seems clear that we cannot understand the armed conflicts and collectively organized political violence of the postwar period without radically rethinking our assumptions. Drawing on Buzan's arguments about legitimacy and strong/weak states, Holsti outlines a move in this direction (1996). In this book, my aim is more theoretically modest: to examine the perceptions of those caught up in the violence in the former Yugoslavia—as leaders, soldiers, perpetrators, intel-lectual elites, antiwar activists, victims, and displaced persons—from the perspective of whether our theories about war are consistent with their expe-riences. It is not so much a "testing" of theory through empirically rigorous examination, but an attempt to engage theory and practice in a dialogue with one another: What does theory tell us about people's lived experience and what do their experiences tell us about theory?

The second intersection examined is that of the relationship between cognitive and structural variables. If, for instance, economic and political instability alone were sufficient to cause the kind of violence that occurred in the former Yugoslavia, there would be many more places in which violence or war like that was occurring. Alternatively, if one looks at psychological or social psychological variables and political culture alone, we will also not be able to answer: Why here and not there? Goldhagen (1997), for instance, makes the most persuasive argument that there was a long and well-entrenched history of anti-Semitism in *Europe* for centuries preceding the German Holocaust; but this leaves me with the question: So why Germany and not France? Why 1939 and not 1929 or 1969? So I think we need to look not at whether structural *or* cognitive variables cause conflict and violence, but how they interact and converge, and which are antecedent, precipitating, and enabling variables.

The third intersection under consideration is the relationship among levels of analysis. It may be useful to think about theorizing at different levels of analysis, but to take seriously the idea of an intersection or interaction between cognitive and structural variables also means to look at how variables at different levels of analysis interact as well as to evaluate the usefulness of prevailing formulations of "levels of analysis." Waltz (1959) dismisses the psychological level when explaining war because, he says, psychological variables can lead us to war or peace. But psychological theorizing has progressed significantly since Waltz's visitation. Perhaps we can ask: Under what conditions war, and under what conditions peace? And if our shared, external social world is not a reproduction and exteriorization of the way in which the individual psychic self is formed, then where else does it come from? Where do states come from, if not from the human imagination? Once again, this begs the "agent-structure" or ontological problem. As Waever has pointed out,[33] social scientists use the term "ontology" to describe the set of assumptions a theorist makes, the starting point, what there "is" in the social world to be explained. Does the social world consist of structures (anarchy, balance of power, alliances, markets, states, and so on), or agents (people who act, or institutions as intervening agents), or both, and what is the relationship between the two? We have to know more about human cognition in order to make sense of the social world as well as the complex intersection between agency and structure.

## What We Can Learn from the Former Yugoslavia

Holsti argues that the trends and patterns of armed conflict since 1945 are so radically different that they "cannot be explained by the standard theoretical devices of international politics." He urges us to look at the links between civil society and state institutions, into the area of "state creation and state morphology," and ask: "Why did people take up arms? What ideas, conditions, and aspirations drive them to the point of rebellion and war?"[34]

Holsti argues that wars of secession, national liberation, and national unification are concerned with issues of statehood and "the nature of community within states." But how should we classify the genocide in Rwanda or the violence in the former Yugoslavia? It seems to me that these cases also raise the most basic questions of community, of humanity, and civility, or "the nature of community within the state." But were they wars of secession? National liberation? National unification? Was an international aggression committed? What sort of state is it for which men like Tadić, or Battalion 309, or the settlers in California would so brutally torture and kill? What would Hobbes say of this Leviathan?

When it comes to the war in the former Yugoslavia, two kinds of questions seem to plague us all, expert or academic or not. The first kind has to do with "why." Why *here* (in Europe)? Why *now* (in the last decade of the twentieth century)? These questions may be answered with good political analysis, but if we pursue Holsti's questions we are likely to learn much more about the "nature of community within the state," as well as about the nature of the regional and international political community in which states are situated, and thus obtain useful knowledge applicable to a broader set of cases.

The second set of questions has to do with "why *this way*?" Why was this conflict acted out with such brutality? Why ethnic cleansing? How were people mobilized to carry out this violence? This is what we might call Goldhagen's question: How are ordinary people transformed into monsters (1997)?[35] How is it that individual people are persuaded to abandon civility in favor of brutality? Why were elites *able* so readily to mobilize them to undertake acts of inhumanity on the basis of appeals to *identity*? Why did some people resist the polarization of hate-mongering and war making rhetoric and remain staunchly opposed to the war? As Goldhagen has persuasively argued, the Holocaust was about ordinary people socialized in anti-Semitic European and German political culture carrying out acts of inhumanity willingly, even pleasurably. But I am not sure we are very much closer to understanding *why*—why in Germany and *not* France, why in Rwanda and *not* South Africa, why in Croatia and Bosnia and not (yet) Macedonia, and so on.

To understand how and why identity can be manipulated and how and why threats to identity can evoke the most virulent and violent defenses of "the self" necessitates an examination of the links between individual psychological constructions of identity and the mediating forces of culture, leadership, and history.[36] Structural explanations alone will not satisfy the need to answer the most disturbing questions raised by the wars in the former Yugoslavia. It seems to me that we need to understand not only the dynamics of identity and dehumanization (in levels of analysis terminology—"man, the individual"), but how layers of political context—local, regional, and international—frame, enable, intersect, and constitute social processes that contribute to the construction of institutions and ideologies that are the structural and cognitive arenas in which identity formation and dehumanization take place. In searching for answers to "why" and "why here" we will almost certainly learn something about why similar things can and do happen elsewhere,[37] even if figuring out how to anticipate and prevent them is a little too ambitious.

Freud said, in effect, that the psychopathic mind is really just an exaggeration of the rest of us, that studying the psychopathic mind can provide the richest and perhaps the clearest insight into the human mind because everything present in the human mind is amplified in the psychopathic mind. This is not to say that people in the former Yugoslavia were psychopathic—as Alford put it, we all participate in psychopathic qualities "by virtue of being human."[38] The starkness of the case of the former Yugoslavia may offer insights into the construction and deconstruction of civility, civic identity, and the state. The war in the former Yugoslavia and the breakdown of the polity that preceded it raise some of the most central issues of organized modern political life in multicultural societies: On what basis does an individual's sense of obligation and belonging to the polity rest and how is that bond created, sustained, and broken? What, in other words, made Yugoslavs "feel" Yugoslav, or more importantly, what made some Yugoslavs feel *more* Yugoslav and others less? Under what conditions and how can those feelings be altered? What was the relationship between Yugoslav as a political identity and other politically relevant identities—Croat, Bosnian, Muslim, Serb, Albanian, Slovenian, Macedonian, Orthodox, Catholic, and so on? Why, for some Yugoslavs, did the feeling of being Yugoslav override feelings of hostility generated by historical grievances and prejudices associated with other identities?

*    *    *

I have raised many more questions than one interpretive case study can begin to answer, but I do not think either that these are entirely original questions or that I am the only one puzzling about them these days. It is my hope that readers traveling this path of inquiry with me will come away with the kind of additional insight that will illuminate their own work on or interest in related issues. It will help to think of the social construction of the state at the core of the argument, with trajectories moving in two directions. One moves toward the individual, the citizen, and the psychological and social psychological processes involved in the formation of our inner lives as they bear on the self as citizen or as political entity. To paraphrase Benedict Anderson's assertion regarding political communities, the state must exist in the minds of its citizens, or most of them anyway. But the narratives on which our imagined states rest are neither static nor do they occur in social isolation. The other direction of the analysis looks "outward" toward the political environment, the social practices that constitute the "state system" in which the state, as a set of authoritative institutions, is created, maintained, challenged, and transformed. The state itself is understood a socially constructed set of institutions, the product of narrative and social practices constituted as international law, foreign policies, and the academic study of international relations. Both the creation and destruction of Yugoslavia as well as the creation of its successor states occurred first in the minds of men and women. In that sense, I take Anderson's widely popular characterization of our political communities as "imagined" very seriously. Whether there were 100,000 or 250,000 people killed, whether 3,500 or 35,000 women were raped, whether 1 million or 3 million people were displaced, every individual harmed was located within a network of caring relationships, as people generally are. For the millions of people whose lives were destroyed or who were deeply injured by the cruel deaths of loved ones, by their own experience as victims or perpetrators of brutality and torture, by the plundering and razing of their homes and whole towns and cities, and by the normalization of hate unleashed by the pathology of violence, the destruction of their imagined community was all too real.

# CHAPTER 2

# What Happened in Yugoslavia?

All these people in small places, they know who did what. . . .

——S.B., Belgrade, 1995

There is a crucial difference between believing, as I have heard said so many times, that "horrible things were done on all sides," and believing that this means that "*equally* horrible things were done on all sides *equally*." There is also a huge difference between asserting that "all sides are guilty" and that "all sides are equally guilty." The judicial processes employed to address the injuries against and criminal acts committed by individuals in a peacetime setting are complex enough in themselves. The problem of determining responsibility for war crimes committed against individuals as well as collectivities (which bears on the issue of genocide), by individuals acting in private as well as official capacities, and with respect to acts contributing to the outbreak of war (aggression) as well as the conduct of individuals and leaders once war broke out, is even more so. In addition to institutional processes, the restoration and reconstruction of civil society in the long aftermath of social violence and conflict entail social processes in which shared and conflicting histories continue to play out as prejudices, fears, and grievances, complicating, and sometimes obstructing efforts to achieve restorative justice and reconciliation. The power of those histories and the interplay of prejudices, fears, and grievances they contain also varies over time. A century and a half after the Civil War and the end of slavery in the United States, Americans have not yet achieved full social reconciliation. The path of social and restorative justice is a long, contentious, and often elusive one, even in relatively developed, stable, and older democracies.

Some readers may wonder as they read my historical account—a summary in which I choose some events, trends, sources, and versions and leave out others—where I stand on the issue of responsibility for the most recent conflict. So let me state my position at the outset: all sides bear *some* responsibility for resorting to violence and for subsequently violating the rules of warfare once violence broke out, but I reject the principle of equivalency, as indicated in the opening sentence of this chapter. *Responsibility must be distributed—not necessarily evenly—among political and military leaders as well as paramilitaries and middlemen, and to a lesser degree among those who followed them on all sides.* Perhaps only those who resisted war are completely free of responsibility. But I also believe that the Hague is the appropriate venue for sorting this out, though it is not without criticism. Additionally, certain individuals bear responsibility for particular acts of violence constituting war crimes, and others, as political leaders, for creating an environment provocative of war crimes. One of the deficiencies of the Hague process is its failure to address the question of aggression.

The prospect for sustainable peace, democracy, and reconciliation within and among the societies that now constitute the Yugoslav successor states will depend in large part on whether and how the institutional, social, and historical processes involved in distributing responsibility and confronting the challenge of social reconciliation are undertaken by the people of the successor states. While the Hague is the proper place to sort out legal responsibilities and consequences, the path of personal and political reconciliation among the peoples of former Yugoslavia is not yet clear. They are not alone in their need for societal reconciliation. Europeans remain engaged in post-Holocaust reconciliation, Americans have many more issues of race relations yet to deal with, some settler states are beginning to address their treatment of indigenous peoples, South Africans are coming out of the dark age of apartheid, and central and east Europeans must find a way to live with former communists as their neighbors and fellow citizens in democracies. Priscilla Hayner identifies truth commissions as attempting to come to terms with the "unspeakable truths" of "state terror and atrocity."[1]

The question of what happened in Yugoslavia (and who is responsible) ought not to be put only to the peoples and leaders of the former Yugoslavia. In my opinion anyway, some responsibility both for the events leading up to the failure to achieve a peaceful dissolution of the state, culminating in the outbreak of violence, *and* for failure to intervene decisively in opposition to activities constituting crimes against humanity must also be laid at the feet of non-Yugoslav actors.[2] What happened in Yugoslavia happened within the historical context of the last decade of the twentieth century—a century in which:

- The first world war, the "war to end all wars," occurred just after European powers believed they had "civilized" war by codifying the laws of warfare at the Hague;
- The leaders of Western democracies failed to form an alliance able to intervene decisively against Hitler during the early and critical early years of his aggression;
- Western leaders failed to intervene in the Holocaust against European Jews[3];

- Following the defeat of Hitler and full disclosure of the extent and nature of the Holocaust, the same Western allies announced "never again";
- The development of a world order and international law capable of securing such an oath was obstructed by a forty-year Cold War; and
- The Cold War itself provided the pretext for superpower interventions that rendered suspect the motives of any intervention in which major or super-powers played a role.

What happened in Yugoslavia happened at an extraordinarily ambiguous moment in the history of international relations, with the most disastrous consequences for the peoples of the former Yugoslavia. Images enable us to interpret and respond to events. The war in Yugoslavia occurred at a histor-ical moment when the dominant collective image containing an under-standing of interests, states, and war was imploding as rapidly as the conflict was escalating. The twentieth century opened with two Hague conferences in 1899 and 1907, where delegates from Western states gathered to codify the rules of warfare, including, among other things, protection for prisoners of war, wounded soldiers, and civilians. Soldiers were to wear uniforms, indi-cating their status as legitimate targets and perpetrators of warfare. World War I was the last "civilized" war in Europe. Civilian deaths accounted for 5 percent of all war-related deaths, although when those caused indirectly by the war are included, the proportion of civilian deaths climbs to 20 percent. Combat fatalities, therefore, constituted between 80 and 95 percent of all deaths in the "Great War" of 1914 to 1918. Even after the "war to end all wars," representatives of the world's democracies continued their efforts to outlaw aggressive interstate war by proposing the Kellogg-Briand Pact of 1928. During the six years of World War II, which started just two decades after World War I ended, two thirds of the sixty million who died were civil-ians. The line distinguishing civilians from soldiers continues to disappear. In Cambodia, Bosnia, and Rwanda civilians became, unabashedly, the primary targets of violence and terror. The war in Croatia and Bosnia between 1991 and 1995 was almost as far as one could get from the image of war as a contest of armed force between armies of soldiers fighting in defense of their states. ("Almost," because the genocide occurring almost simultaneously in Rwanda was worse, but then most descriptions have had the good sense not to call that a war.) Like Stanley Kubrick's Space Odyssey or Dorothy's return from Oz, it was as if all of the most significant events that shaped and challenged our understanding of international relations during the twentieth century collapsed into the time–space continuum of a place, a space, an idea, an identity, an entity called "Yugoslavia."

The destruction of Yugoslavia was incomprehensible—to many inside as well as outside its boundaries—in large part because of a kind of massive cognitive dissonance. In the late twentieth century, which we had come to call the "postwar" and then "post–Cold War" era, *European* states simply do *not* descend into a state of total warfare. *European* people in the late twentieth century do *not* commit atrocities against one another. *European* people do *not* forcibly "cleanse" ethnically diverse towns and villages. *European* political and military leaders do *not* provoke or promote any practice resembling *genocide*.[4] Atrocities, crimes against humanity, massive human rights abuses do not happen in *Europe*, and if they did, *Europeans would hold the perpetrators accountable*. Such disbelief, even denial was captured by Mark Almond's title *Europe's Backyard War*.[5] Many people in and out of Yugoslavia struggled in a kind of stunned daze for critical months and even years, asking themselves not just how this could happen, but "How could this happen *here*." And as the international community — what Almond calls "that prolix world of organisations [*sic*] hidden behind initials and acronyms" — puzzled over how to understand what was happening, the people in the towns and villages of the "cleansed" and occupied parts of Croatia, and nearly every square inch of Bosnia and Herzegovina were left at the mercy of psychopathic acts normalized as "war."

## Categories, Stories, and Allegories

This is not a book about "what happened in Yugoslavia" in the sense of making a claim of authority for presenting a single truth about the events surrounding the conflict in former Yugoslavia. It is my best understanding up to this point of what I think happened, after four trips, many interviews and conversations with "those it happened to," and a strained attempt to keep up with all of the printed material available on the subject — documents, reports, news sources, and the literally hundreds of books by journalists and academics. I remain open to new information and fresh perspectives. I have kept in mind Michael Shapiro's comments that: "All intelligible oral or textual articulations involve a temporary fix on a meaning at the expense of other possible structures of intelligibility . . . intelligibilities do not simply reveal the truth but rather establish one possibility among many" (1996: xvii).

I have also been concerned with what it all means for IR theory, particularly how we think about war, the people who cause it and carry it out, and those for whom it has the most serious and tragic consequences. I have tried to understand from talking to such people what I could not understand by reading about them. While hoping that readers will find some of the insights valuable, I remain simultaneously and acutely aware that any insights contained here are obtained at the expense of diminishing, or to use Shapiro's terminology, "impoverishing" other versions or "possible structures of intelligibility" about the events surrounding the 1991 to 1995 (and beyond) violence in the former Yugoslavia.

Where, for instance, should an account of "what happened" begin? This was in many ways a conflict about identity, but not because, as images of "ethnic conflict" might suggest, most of the people involved and affected had grievances related to their identities which they believed could be solved only by resorting to violence. Rather, it was a conflict about identity because political leaders made a conscious (and some might say irresponsible) choice to rally support by appealing to grievances which had long been a subject of political discourse, *and which were constructed in terms of identity within both political and historical narratives.* Yes, it was a war between Croats, Serbs, and Muslims (in the press often called Bosnian Muslims, since there were Muslims in Yugoslavia not living in Bosnia), but we must begin by understanding that these categories of identity were constructed in ways which had very specific and narrow meanings as the rhetorical hostility and material violence escalated. Of course the categories had social, cultural, and historical meaning, and a certain amount of public discourse before the war centered on their meaning, particularly around what came to be known as "the national question."[6] Before the war in 1990, these identities were broader, more fluid and negotiable, and, of course, less contentious. Some grievances were constructed in relation to identities. There were stereotypes, prejudices, and intermarriages. And there were other categories as well—Albanian, Shqiptar,[7] Slovenian, and Yugoslav, though as we shall see, it became harder and harder to be a Yugoslav in Yugoslavia.

The average Westerner watching events unfold became aware of the variations and hybridizations of identities in the former Yugoslavia, such as Bosnian Serb, Bosnian Muslim, and Bosnian Croat, though many are probably less aware of the existence of Serbs in Croatia. As the political climate of hostility worsened, categories of identity were reduced to stereotypes and prejudices. Perhaps worst of all, people more and more lost the ability to define for themselves what it meant to be Serb, Croat, or Muslim. One respondent, a physician from Belgrade, rather indignantly put it this way:

> My identity is a private issue. It should not be the subject of public attention. It is a matter, perhaps, of sharing certain celebrations with my family, a matter of my family history and how it is shared across generations within my family. But it is not the business of politicians what my ethnic identity is.[8]

Writer Dubravka Ugrešić (1998), whose book *The Culture of Lies* (1996 in the English translation) won the Charles Veillon European Essay Prize, claims: "My Croatian passport does not make me a Croatian writer." She refuses "to be a writer of 'my nation,' especially of a nation which destroys books,"[9] and defiantly asserts that:

I am no one. And everyone. In Croatia I shall be a Serb, in Serbia a Croat, in Bulgaria a Turk, in Turkey a Greek, in Greece a Macedonian, in Macedonia a Bulgarian. . . . Being an ethnic "bastard" or "schizophrenic" is my natural choice, I even consider it a sign of mental and moral health. (1998: 270)

So the first problem in telling any version of "what happened in Yugoslavia" is to acknowledge that ethnic categories are at least problematic—no more so in former Yugoslavia than elsewhere, just more *obviously* so. They are *naturalized* through political discourses, but not necessarily *natural*. The social construction of identity and its political consequences will be more thoroughly considered in the next chapter. For now I wish only to caution the reader against reducing and simplifying the actors represented by the terms used to refer to them.

How we talk about the actors and agents of the war is not the only interpretive problem. How should we choose a historical starting point for understanding the most recent Yugoslav conflict and violence? During the NATO intervention in Serbia, I was struck by how many Americans suddenly demonstrated an expertise on Balkan history by citing the Battle of Kosovo in 1389 as the historical basis for the 1999 war. Most of them probably had no idea regarding any other relevant historical events occurring in their own history narratives of that period. Yet they readily explained that "Kosovo is to Serbs like our Alamo is to us!" Or they offered the explanation that Kosovo had been "in" Serbia for over six hundred years and now the Kosovar Albanians wanted to secede. They seemed confused when I pointed out that European states, as we now know them, did not even exist until 250 years after the Battle of Kosovo, so how, I asked, could a claim to state territory be made prior to the creation of states?

But history is narrative, and narratives—stories—matter very much in constructing and sustaining images of a "legitimate" state. The state is presumed to be a naturalized expression of nationhood. As Homi Bhabha has very eloquently argued, it is through narrative practice that individual and collective ethnic and national identities are constituted (Bhabha 1990). Stories—or histories if you prefer—are what give us the sense that our imagined communities have a material and organic basis (Anderson 1991). Stories contain the emotions of past experiences, including trauma, and collective memories that can be conjured up by warmongering political wizards in the present. To understand how states are created and destroyed, we must understand the construction and deconstruction of the narratives that underlie them.

How narratives are mobilized to construct and deconstruct the identities and systems of meaning on which the legitimacy of state institutions rests will be the subject of much of the rest of the book. For now it is important to understand that any account of "what happened" will necessitate using terms that designate ethnic identity and refer to individuals—Serb, Croat, Muslim or Bosnian Muslim, Slovene—and terms that refer to nationality or place—Serbian, Croatian, Bosnian, Slovenian, and so on. This is not an easy distinction to maintain, as rhetorical practice regarding the construction of ethnicity, nationality, and place is in many ways the problem I am studying and is, in fact, muddled. I have tried to be consistent with the use of "Bosnian Muslim" as the ethnic labels referring to Muslims of Bosnia, though in some sources they are also called "Bosnians." I try to maintain the convention of reserving the Serbian and Croatian label to signify a relationship to place— Croatian military are the military forces from Croatia, whereas Croats para- military are individuals who identify themselves as ethnic Croats and they may or may not all be from Croatia. The Bosnian president, similarly would be the president of Bosnia, who might or might not be Bosnian Muslim or Muslim, though at present the convolution of ethnic identity and represen- tation of place in Bosnia remains problematic. We should remember that the ethnic categories are both contestable and contextual. "Ethnic groups" are neither spatially solid nor temporally fixed, though we often talk about them as if they were both.

## Pre-Yugoslavia History

Yugoslavia was a state created as the twentieth century opened and destroyed as the twentieth century closed. The history of the South Slav peoples, however, is often told—by Slavic historians, non-Slavic historians of Slavic history, and more recently by political leaders and ordinary people in the former Yugoslavia—from a much earlier medieval beginning, nearly a millen- nium before the creation of the Yugoslav state. There are several very good, comprehensive, book-length accounts of South Slav history available, and most of the recent books on various aspects of the 1991 to 1995 conflict itself also contain chapters providing historical background to the most recent conflict.[10] The movement for a unified South Slav state makes a good starting point for understanding how the process of modern state-making was played out specifically among the South Slav peoples, though it will be discussed in much greater detail in Chapter 5. First, however, we need to put the origins of the "idea of Yugoslavia" into the historical context of broader European processes of state-making and imperialism, particularly in light of attempts to ground contemporary nationalist ideologies on claims that the Serbian medieval state was conquered by the Ottoman Empire, or that the presently independent state of Croatia is the fulfillment of a "thousand-year-old dream." It should be noted that in both cases these narratives predate what most academic historians consider to be the birth of the European state system: the 1648 Peace of Westphalia. If the propaganda that flourished during and leading up to the violence is to be believed, Croats and Serbs were "dreaming" of their own states some six centuries before states existed anywhere else in Europe. Before turning to the nineteenth century movement for the unification of South Slav peoples, we should briefly discuss the experience of Croats, Serbs, and Bosnian Muslims during the medieval period, for as Lampe points out, the violent one-thousand-year history prior to the movement that culminated in the creation of the first Yugoslav state left the societies there in economic and political disarray:

> By 1800 the territories that later became Yugoslavia had suffered even more warfare and forced migration, foreign intervention, and internal division than had their Mediterranean or Central European neighbors. These lands had no chance of sharing in the economic upswing that spread through most of Northwestern Europe during the eighteenth century. Political disarray had deepened economic backwardness during the millennium between the dawn of medieval centuries and the end of the early modern period. (1996: 9)

The "Balkans," an area Hannah Arendt designated uncontroversially as including Yugoslavia, Bulgaria, Greece, and Romania, was submerged by imperial conquest and delineated by imperial cleavages in ways that would separate Croats and Serbs "even before their arrival in the region" (Udovički and Ridgeway 1997). Although the east-to-west fault line would shift as first the Roman and Byzantine empires were on the two sides, and later the Austro-Hungarian and Ottoman empires, some part of mountainous Bosnia seemed always to be the point where these rivalries erupted. Bosnia emerged with the most pluralistic population, with ethnic groups distributed across the region in checkerboard fashion. As a result, there is no contiguous relationship between ethnicity and territorial settlement in Bosnia today. The term "balkanization," which has come to mean fragmentation along ethnic lines, has more recently taken on a specifically derogatory meaning. The "Balkans," says Maria Todorova, is a "geographic appellation" that has been "transformed into one of the most powerful pejorative designations in history, international relations, political science, and, nowadays, general intellectual discourse. . . ." (Todorova 1997: 7).

Whether one is "in" the Balkans or not, then, can have a stigmatizing consequence for one's political identity, and many people living in Croatia and Slovenia today are truly offended by the prospect of being thought of (or misunderstood) as being "in" the Balkans. As one respondent recounted to me her own version of Croatian history, she began with: "Croatia is one of the oldest and most advanced nations in Europe which was forced to live with some of the most backward people in Europe in the artificial state of Yugoslavia."[11] Again, the critical voice of Dubravka Ugrešić tells us that after

Croatian secession and as the war began in the early 1990s in Croatia: "'Yugoslavia' (a country in which Croatian citizens had lived for some fifty years!) became a prohibited word, and the terms *Yugoslav, Yugonostalgic* or *Yugo-zombie* are synonymous with national traitor" (1998: 78).

In any case, prior to the breakup of the Yugoslav state, Yugoslavia, as well as all of the peoples who now live in its successor states, was widely regarded as being *in* the Balkans. Samuel Huntington's "Clash of Civilizations" (1993) describes the historical experiences of the Balkans perhaps better than, and certainly as well as, anywhere else in civilizational history. As a consequence, this region is also one of the most pluralistic areas of the world, religiously and linguistically.

Medieval Serbia—consisting of what we would think of today as south Serbia, centered near Pristina, along with Montenegro—developed and expanded as an independent kingdom, albeit, like other medieval states and kingdoms with unstable borders, reaching by some accounts the height of its development just before the invasion and defeat by the Ottoman in 1389 (Udovički 1997: 18). Byzantine authority was weaker in this area than further to the north and east, where the Croatian medieval kingdom lay. The Serbian Nemanja *zupan*, or clan, is credited with establishing the first independent kingdom in 1180, and in 1196 Stefan Nemanja was crowned king and the authorities in Constantinople declared his kingdom independent. Twenty-three years later the Serbian Orthodox Church was established by another Nemanja, later canonized as St. Sava. The defeat of the Serbs two centuries later marked the beginning of the five-century long Ottoman occupation.

Sometime between 910 and 925, the Roman pope recognized Tomislav as the first Croatian ruler of an area encompassing not only present-day Croatia, but portions of northern and western Bosnia and a larger area of the Dalmatian coast than is currently part of Croatia. In the next century, however, this "triune kingdom" fell to the Hungarians but retained a significant amount of local control under Hungarian and then Austro-Hungarian Hapsburg rule for the next eight centuries (see maps 1 and 2). The cultural and political landscape of the Dalmatian coast and Istrian peninsula was not included in the Hapsburg provinces, but was shaped instead by the intermittent assertion of Venetian influence through the eighteenth century. By the eighteenth century, Trieste and Rijeka were both free ports. Dubrovnik remained independent as a city-state until the nineteenth century.

Of the many forces converging to produce the linguistic, religious, and narrative mosaics of the Balkans, the creation of what came to be known as the Hapsburg military frontier, or *Krajina*, is perhaps the most unique and, during the violence in the 1990s, the most fractious (see map 3). *Krajina*—including areas of eastern and Western Slavonia and down the Dalmatian coast centered around Knin—is the area, in what is now Croatia and in the former republic of Croatia within Yugoslavia, where some 600,000 Serbs

**Map 1**

lived. Serb migration to this area begin in the sixteenth century as a result of two forces: peasant refugees (many forming armed bands of soldiers) fleeing from the brutal Ottoman rule, and recruitment of Serbs by the Austro-Hungarian empire to occupy a military border on the frontier of the Haps-burg Empire. In exchange for military service, families of border guards were given small land grants, freedom from serfdom, exemption from feudal dues, and religious freedom. Although there were some Croat soldiers in this force, the Croat nobility outside the region was generally resentful of the presence of such large, duty-free Serb peasant families (Lampe 1996: 30). It is worth noting, however, that historians characterize the relationship between Serbs and Croats of the same class and in the areas of mixed and neighboring communities as overwhelmingly peaceful and amicable.

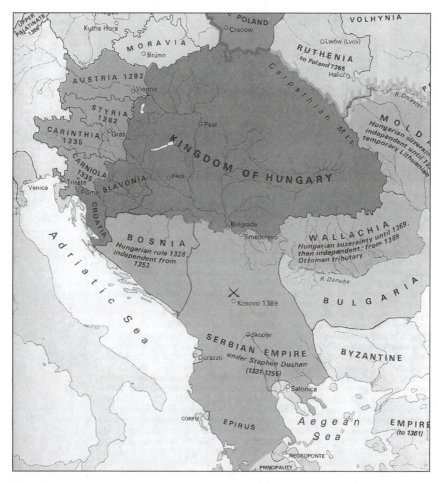

Map 2

Not surprisingly, then, the movement to create a unified "south Slav" state was advocated as a strategy for expelling and preventing future encroachments by imperial authority. It is a paradox of history that it was the centuries of domination and competition between and among religious and secular empires that both deepened the pluralism of Slavic peoples and provided them with a common interest in unification. The momentum for unification was focused by Croat scholars in the 1830s calling themselves "Illyrians" (after one of the first tribes to inhabit the Balkans),[12] who focused on the creation of a common language out of the many literary and vernacular dialects in use at the time (Prpa-Jovanovic 1997: 43). The movement settled on a dialect spoken by southwestern and eastern Croats as well as many Serbs, particularly in the *Krajina*.[13]

**Map 3**

The unification movement waxed and waned throughout the nineteenth century, as imperial, class, and to a lesser degree, ethnic fault lines began shifting. The elite-led Illyrian movement also set in motion a discourse among Croat intellectual and political elites about the shape and content of not only a "Yugoslav" but a Croat identity.[14] While Croat intellectuals engaged in this kind of nation-building, Serbian political, military, and revolutionary forces were striking at the increasingly vulnerable Ottoman Empire, until they achieved the autonomy necessary to begin state-building after the expulsion of the empire from northern Serbia in the 1830s.[15] The roots of both contemporary nationalisms, Croatian and Serbian, can be traced to this period.[16] The Austro-Hungarian empire, weakening from its own internal divisions and mounting military challenges in Europe, was being stretched beyond its capability to maintain control over its holdings and outposts. The empire had incorporated the Krajina into Croatia-Slavonia and established occupation of Bosnia-Herzegovina in the 1870s and 1880s. The independent Serbian state, emboldened by its success in throwing out the "Turks" without assistance,[17] was divided by power struggles among regional oligarchies, between those who favored a constitutional unification and those who supported a monarchy, and over the question of whether and how to incorporate, repatriate, or simply extend its boundaries to include the half million Serb peasants living in Bosnia-Herzegovina. Although Croat intellectual and religious elites were engaged in efforts to unify Croatian language and culture as a foundation on which to build support for independence, 80 percent of Croats were still illiterate and more than that were disenfranchised peasants. With such a large number of Serbs living in areas under the authority of Hapsburg rule, independent Serbia and pro-independence Croatian nation-builders found some degree of common interest in anything that would accelerate the decline and withdrawal of the Hapsburg Empire from Croatia, Slavonia, and Bosnia-Herzegovina.

Serb and Croat peasants in the area of Banija unified to expel urban tax officials from their region in 1883. In general, however, the interests of Serb and Croat peasants were less clearly aligned than their elite, literate counterparts in the urban centers of Belgrade and Zagreb. In some ways, economic class and privilege created more serious cleavages than ethnic differences. Croat nobility and later urban elites regarded the Serb soldier–free peasant families in the Krajina as a "backward and inferior race," and as "primitive Orientals" (Udovički and Ridgeway 1997: 17). To the Croat Catholics, who were strongly identified with European culture, Orthodox Serbs were "schismatics." From the perspective of many rural Croat peasants, however, their Serb neighbors enjoyed undeserved privileges—free land and tax exemption—as defenders of the Hapsburg frontier.

It was in Bosnia, however, that these divisions were most pronounced. Claims and questions regarding the ethnocultural origins of the Muslims in Bosnia abound: Were they descendants of the Bogomils? Were they Croats or Serbs who had converted to Islam or a group that solidified in the aftermath of centuries of mixed marriages between Ottoman administrators and local Slavs? During the seventeenth and eighteenth centuries, the Serb population in Bosnia increased from 10 percent to 40 percent, many, no doubt, seeking refuge in Bosnia's more remote regions from Ottoman rule. They arrived as peasants in an area largely populated by people who were Muslim, both landholders and their serfs. By the time the Ottoman and Hapsburg empires were unquestionably losing control of the region, however, the overall configuration of economic and class distribution in relation to ethnic affiliation in Bosnia was clear and became the basis in fact for Serb myths of a much resented sense of Bosnian Muslim privilege. Though comprising less than 1 percent of the population, some 90 percent of Bosnian landholders with serfs were Muslim. Nearly 60 percent of the peasants freed by Hapsburg reforms aimed at ending feudalism in Bosnia were Muslim, while 75 percent of those retained as serfs were Serb (Vulliamy 1994: 35). "Many Serbian peasants," says Jasminka Udovički, "began to view all Muslims, and not only the agas and begs, as their *dušmani* (killers of the soul)" (Udovički and Ridgeway 1997: 23).

Between the 1870s and the start of World War I, structures that had dominated the political and economic life of the area for centuries were in the final stages of decline: the two competing Hapsburg and Ottoman empires and the economic system of feudalism. The special status of the Krajina was terminated; the empires' last battle was fought by the Serb and Croat *Genzer* (military frontier guards and officers) on behalf of the Hapsburgs, on one side, and local Muslim paramilitary units on behalf of the Turkish forces on the other. Bosnia and Herzegovina was turned over to Austro-Hungarian rule (se map 3). Following their defeat, some 200,000 Muslims and Turks left Bosnia for Istanbul. The transition was marked by a series of uprisings, mostly around the Croat-majority area of Herzegovina. The annexation fueled Serbian patriotic passions by preempting plans among some nationalists for the expansion of Serbia's boundaries to include the more than 800,000 Serbs living in Bosnia. The end of feudalism was accompanied by the spread of educational programs aimed at ending illiteracy and creating an educated and skilled middle class. It also created a large number of educated young people in a short period of time, which led to the formation of student movements in the urban centers of Zagreb and Belgrade on the eve of World War I, who began rallying for an end to imperial rule in Bosnia-Herzegovina, Croatia, and Slovenia.

## The Yugoslav Civil War, 1941–1944

"Twice there was a country" is how John R. Lampe describes the creation of two Yugoslavias (1918–41 and 1945–91) in the aftermath of two world wars which, in many ways, were fought as civil wars on the territory from which the new "South Slav" state was formed. In the first case, both the world and civil wars were antiimperialist wars. Chief among the structural causes was the decline of the Hapsburg and Ottoman Empires. During the second world war, the European struggle against fascist expansionism was, as a civil war in Yugoslavia, both antifascist and anti-German with the nationalistic Croatian Ustaše party in power as collaborators with Germany. The Ustaše, founded by Herzegovinian Croat Ante Pavelič in an effort to revive the Frankist Party of the Right, formed an early alliance with the Italian Fascist Party and functioned mostly as a secessionist paramilitary organization. The first Yugoslav state was destroyed as an independent state when German occupation of Yugoslavia followed a ruthless attack on Belgrade in April 1941. When German authorities made overtures to several Croatian political parties in order to install one of them as a puppet regime in a newly "Independent State of Croatia," only the minority Ustaše party agreed. Sven Balas estimates that less than ten percent of the Croatian people actually supported Pavelič and his fascist party.[18] Following the Italian model, Ustaše supporters took a blood oath and regarded Pavelič as a heroic leader holding absolute authority over them. These and other characteristics lead some to conclude that "this was a fascist movement from the start" (Lampe 1996: 172).

Furthermore, its agenda "consisted mainly of (un-Italian) racist rhetoric blaming all of Croatia's misfortunes, including the failure to include all of Bosnia-Herzegovina within its borders, on Serbs or their partners" (Lampe 1996: 172).

Thus when the Ustaša struck a deal with the Germans, they were quite willing to recognize the annexation of central Dalmatia by their allies, the Italians, while incorporating all of Bosnia-Herzegovina, including the Eastern Slavonia region all the way to the old Hapsburg city of Zemun just across the river from Belgrade, into the Independent State of Croatia. While "enthusiastically" carrying out the Nazis final solution within the territory of an enlarged Croatia, the Ustaše's own agenda of ethnic purification extended the anti-Semitic program to include Serbs and Roma. Thousands of Serbs were "executed out of hand" under a new law allowing the death penalty to be issued by "three-man courts" against anyone guilty of speaking out against the regime (Lampe 1996: 204–205). On June 22, 1941, the Ustaše minister of education announced the official policy aimed at "cleansing" the enlarged Croatian state of its almost 2 million Serbs: one third would be deported, one third would be converted to Catholicism (and therefore would become ethnic Croatians), and one third would be executed.

In a complex ideological configuration, Serb antifascism found its outlet in the Partisan movement, though antifascism and anti-Croat sentiments were probably mixed. Serb nationalists also formed the pro-Serb, anti-Croat, and intermittently antifascist "Četniks" (Adamic 1953). The Četniks were far less united than the Ustaše, divided primarily between open collaborators who headed a puppet regime in Belgrade, and the royalist, antifascist Četniks following Draža Mihailović, in whom the allies placed their hopes for a defeat of Nazism in Yugoslavia. Some writers try to equate the collaborationists in Croatia and Serbia, but, as Lampe points out, the Četnik collaborators in Belgrade neither operated independently of their German bosses, "[n]or did they initiate the serious war crimes that stained the soil of Serbia in the late fall of 1941. Instead, according to recent scholarship, Wehrmacht instructions and a largely Austrian contingent of local German commanders bore that responsibility" (Lampe 1996: 211).

Although the Belgrade government declared an alliance with Hitler, local demonstrations belied plans for a popularly supported anti-German rebellion. Forewarned, the Germans initiated a brutal attack on Belgrade within days of the March 25 proclamation. Between April and July 1941, the German occupation forces recorded killing 23,233 people, and an order was issued that for every German soldier killed, one hundred local civilians would also be murdered (Lampe 1996: 211; Hall 1994: 106).

> At Kraljevo and Kragujevac, German and Vojvodina Volkdeutsche units, supported by Serbian State Guards, cordoned off the towns in order to execute all the adult males. When too few adults could be found in Kragujevac on October 21, schoolboys were taken as well to swell the total past 2,000. They were marched to a field outside of town, lined up in rows, and shot down the next morning. (Lampe 1996: 211)

Various writers struggle with contentions about the demonization of "Croats/Croatia" as "Ustaše" collaborators and the valorization of "Serbs/Serbia" as antifascist victims. Variations on these images were also used extensively as propaganda in arousing the virulent emotions necessary to fuel the recent conflict. Yet while each image is a stereotype used to discredit evidence which contradicts narratives of victimization and demonization, it also remains true that these stereotypes are projected from *lived* experiences. There were 168,000 Bosnian Muslims in the "Independent Croatian State." Pavelič's Ustaša regime, determined to construct an ethnically pure state, tried to persuade them that they were actually Croats of the Islamic faith. While Muslims were killed at the hands of both Četnik and Ustaše forces, in 1942 some Bosnian Muslim leaders, living at the time in the fascist puppet state, appealed to Hitler directly to guarantee their autonomy in exchange for their allegiance. Several battalions of Bosnian Muslims therefore proclaimed loyalty to Germany, but they spent most of the war "in training" before returning to Bosnia in 1944, where they committed "murder and other atrocities against Serb villagers" (Lampe 1996: 220). By far the majority of Bosnian Muslims fought with the Partisans. Muslims in Sarajevo, Tuzla, Banja Luka, and Bjieljina are also reported to have protected the 2,000 Jews who did survive World War II in Bosnia (Lampe 1996: 208).

The only ethnic group in Yugoslavia that did not participate in the Partisan movement and which in fact took up arms against the Partisans in south-Western Kosovo, were the Albanians. After decades of Serbian colonization and marginalization as a "minority" within Yugoslavia, Albanians had no loyalty to Belgrade or to Yugoslavia. When Kosovo was invaded and occupied by German and Italian forces shortly after the bombing of Belgrade in April 1941, local leaders established a working relationship with the occupying forces that ultimately allowed the Albanians a high degree of cultural autonomy in the region. Albanian leaders also wanted support from the Axis powers for their removal of Serb and Montenegrin colonists.

In the end the Partisans and the Allies won, but not before Croatian fascism had provided the ideological rationalization for killing hundreds of thousands of Serbs (and a smaller number of Jews, Roma, and various "internal enemies") in death camps as an official act of state.[19] In addition to the killings in the camps, known collectively as Jasenovac, and as part of the Ustaše "purification" program, thousands of less well documented execution-style deaths occurred elsewhere in Yugoslavia at the hands of Serb Četnik forces, Albanians, Bulgarians, and Hungarians. The Partisan victory in the Yugoslav civil war also exacted a high price on its opponents. Some Slovene and Croat collaborators were sent to detention camps. In what came to be known as the "Bleiburg Massacre," some 30,000 people were turned back by the Allies as they attempted to leave the country. Many, but not all, had been collaborators, and certainly not all were guilty of war crimes. Nevertheless, after surrendering to the Partisans, there, in the forests around Bleiburg and Kočevski Rog, they were extrajudicially executed. Justice was also hastily and questionably administered in the "show trial" of Četnik leader Mihailović, and his subsequent execution is said to have "swept perhaps 100,000 people to their deaths during 1945–46," well after the war ended (Lampe 1996: 223). These events were never acknowledged officially nor openly discussed for forty-six years. When brought to light in 1990, on the eve of Slovenian and Croatian secessions as nationalist leaders spearheaded the destruction of the Yugoslav state, it was probably too late. Revelations about the "dark side" of Yugoslav communism, founded on the narrative of Partisan valor, simply played into the hands of Yugoslavia's destroyers.

The political identity of succeeding generations of Yugoslavs, both as Yugoslavs and as Croats, Serbs, and Muslims, was profoundly shaped by these events. Both wars thus heightened the salience of (particularly Serbian and Croatian) nationalisms as a basis for identity and political mobilization within the second Yugoslavia. In spite of efforts by Tito and by the Communist Party *apparatchiks* to control the processes through which historical narratives were constructed, then as now the "people in small places ... know who did what," and their own versions of events survived as local and family histories.

### Structural Causes I: The Domestic Context

The 1943 Partisan congress, meeting in the Bosnian town of Jajce, voted to reconstruct the Yugoslav state as six republics and two autonomous provinces with three official languages—Serbo-Croatian, Slovenian, and Macedonian, though, particularly when written, the Serbian and Croatian variants were used. Ethnic identities were represented in two ways. *Narodi* signified the status of Slovenes, Croats, Serbs, Macedonians, and Montenegrins, and, after 1971, Muslims,[20] including only the Bosnian Muslims, as nationality groups who enjoyed equal constitutional status. They were known as "constitutive nations." *Narodnosti* referred to nationalities that existed in Yugoslavia as protected minorities, including Albanians, Hungarians, Turks, and Slovaks. *Narodi* were also distinguished by the fact that they had no homeland outside of Yugoslavia.[21]

The structure of political power in the second Yugoslavia — six republics and two autonomous provinces — roughly corresponded to ethnic identities and historical experience, although the discontinuities were as deeply rooted in historical experience as the continuities. For example, even after centuries of living in Eastern Slavonia, which was "in" the republic of Croatia according to boundaries constructed by Tito, many Serbs there certainly did not think of themselves as "Croatian" but rather as members of the Serbian *Narodi* who happened to live in Croatia. This became problematic when, along with other nationalistic moves, the newly recognized independent Croatian government declared "a Croatia for Croatians" in 1991. The secession of Croatia the republic from the Yugoslav state and the designation of Croatia as the state of the "Croatian" nation in which Serbs would live as a "minority," however protected they might be, was a move with intensely significant and tragic political consequences. After enjoying nearly fifty years as members of a Serbian constituent nation within Yugoslavia, Serbs in Croatia were, with the stroke of a pen, "demoted" to the status of a minority.

Kosovo is another territorial space identified with many rich, complex, and contested histories. Although evidence of Albanian presence in the area of Kosovo far predates the Turkish invasion, the medieval Serbian kingdom asserted authority in the region for several centuries prior to the Ottoman invasion. The region includes the historically significant site of the pre-Ottoman Serbian capital as well as the site of the "Serbs' last stand against the long Ottoman occupation," Kosovo Polje (see map 2). Between 1961 and 1991 the proportion of Albanians and Serbs in the region shifted dramatically from 67 percent Albanian and 24 percent Serbs to 90 percent Albanians and 10 percent Serbs (Woodward 1995). According to census figures, the 1945 Albanian population of 350,000 in Kosovo had grown to 1.7 million by 1981, an annual increase of 24 percent (Kovačević and Dajić 1994: 16). In Bosnia-Herzegovina the ratio of the Serb-Muslim population had literally been reversed between 1961 and 1991, from 43 percent Serbs and 26 percent Muslims in 1961 to 31 percent Serbs and 44 percent Muslims in 1991 (Woodward 1995: 33).[22]

Tito attempted to check Serb domination and balance the distribution of power along ethnic lines across the republics and the autonomous provinces of Vojvodina and Kosovo so that, except in Bosnia with the Bosnian

Muslims, each republic and province contained a clear ethnic majority of between 65 and 90 percent. From the perspective of some Serbs, because Serbia alone had autonomous provinces within its boundaries, this appeared as an unfair infringement on republican authority to administer affairs within the territory of the republic, a perception exploited by Milosević when he revoked the autonomy of the provinces. Serbs constituted the largest ethnic group on a statewide basis (around 40 percent), but, like the Croats in Croatia, Macedonians in Macedonia, and Montenegrins in Montenegro within Serbia (including the autonomous provinces) they represented around three fourths of the population. With the exception of relative homogeneity in Slovenia and Montenegro and the impossibly heterogeneous Bosnia-Herzegovina, this meant that in each of the four remaining republics there was both a large majority (around 70 to 80 percent) ethnic population and at least one substantial minority (of between 20 to 30 percent)—in Croatia, the Serbs, and in Serbia and Macedonia, the Albanians.

This majority–minority relationship within the republics reveals several potential cleavages at the level of the republics: a perceived or actual discrimination against minorities; a tendency for majority decision making and officeholding to coincide with ethnic distribution; and a large enough minority population to sustain a critical or discontented political voice but too small to translate political demands into policy changes. Nationwide, there were fears of Serb hegemony among the non-Serbs, and among Serbs, a suspicion that the boundaries of the republics were drawn so as to deliberately thwart their cohesiveness as a national group. The volatile constitutional history of Yugoslavia reflects numerous efforts to achieve balance among these precarious relationships at both republican and federal levels. The relationship between Kosovo Albanians and the Serb majority in Serbia was chronically at risk. At a very superficial level, the relative homogeneity of Slovenia and, at the other end, the heterogeneity of Bosnia-Herzegovina foreshadowed the least and the most conflicted secessions which began in 1991.

The discontinuities between structure and identity were furthered by worsening economic conditions, both internal to Yugoslavia and as a result of changes in Yugoslavia's international position after the fall of the Soviet Union. Internally, Slovenia's economy was the most industrially developed, prosperous, and diversified. The Croatian economy was less diversified, with sharper cleavages between the wealthier urban and coastal areas on the one hand, and the extractive and agricultural economies of the interior on the other. The Croatian coast generated substantial profits from tourism. Some of the best farmland lay in Eastern Slavonia, where a majority of the Serbs in Croatia lived.[23] Both Slovenia and Croatia were much more integrated into the European and global economies and enjoyed dramatically lower unemployment rates than the other republics. Prior to the outbreak of violence in 1990, persistent full employment in Slovenia generated labor shortages, and unemployment in Croatia remained well below 10 percent until the outbreak of the conflict in 1991. This contrasts sharply with 20 to 25 percent unemployment elsewhere in prewar Yugoslavia, with rates up to 50 percent in Kosovo (Woodward 1995). Many in the wealthier republics expressed chronic and growing resentment toward federal redistributive policies aimed at fostering development in the poorer regions (Tanner 1997). Slovenia and Croatia were associated with being more "progressive, hardworking and western," while republics and nationalities further east were negatively stereotyped as backward, lazy, and even parasitic. Like prejudices cutting across class and ethnic cleavages elsewhere, this was used to explain the higher poverty and lack of development in Bosnia and Serbia and the worst impoverishment in Kosovo.

## Structural Causes II: Interplay between Domestic and International Structures

Through a combination of superpower politics and Tito's strategic maneuvering, Yugoslavia came to play a unique role in the Cold War world order. As elsewhere in central and eastern Europe, postwar communism in Yugoslavia strongly correlated with the fact that victory over fascist forces was credited to the Partisan movement, which was probably more populist than communist (Adamic 1943). As war hero and leader of the Partisans, Tito articulated Yugoslav identity as his own version of communist ideology, which was oddly both nationalist and internationalist at the same time. It attempted both to provide a normative basis for the development of a Yugoslav civic identity while serving simultaneously as an antidote to antagonistic nationalisms. Sabrina Ramet calls it "patriotic communism" or "Yugoslav socialist patriotism" (1992: 54). Breaking off relations with Stalin in 1948, Tito positioned Yugoslavia as the first socialist "nonaligned" state. Yugoslavs were "good communists," people with whom the West could do economic and political business. Yugoslav guest workers in western Europe and western European tourism on the Croatian coast provided huge foreign currency earnings used to balance trade deficits. Yugoslavia received financial assistance from the International Monetary Fund (IMF), World Bank, and the U.S. Import-Export Bank, and in 1979 opened talks with the European Free Trade Association (Woodward 1995). Yugoslav citizens (except for the army, who were not allowed to leave the country) went shopping in Italy. The relative prosperity of Yugoslavia in contrast with other central and eastern European socialist states was probably attributable to the combination of liberal international assistance, the relative openness of the Yugoslav economy, and the fact that the normative basis for communism, at least initially, was grounded in the goodwill following from the support and success of the Partisans.

By the same token, economic decline in Yugoslavia occurred as a consequence of two parallel developments that by the time of Tito's death in 1980, had reached a critical juncture. As the Cold War warmed into a more peaceful coexistence and appeared to be manageable through a more "rational," negotiated, superpower relationship, Yugoslavia's strategic importance to the West began to diminish. Simultaneously, the entrenchment of political and economic conditions within the communist bureaucracy resisted efforts to implement critical reforms in either area. Noting the interdependence of political and economic life, political economist Marija Obradović argues that this "political and economic monopoly" sabotaged efforts at reform as early as 1958, and was initiated six years earlier (Obradović 1995).

Unlike other central and east European socialist states, the Yugoslav League of Communists recognized the need to move toward a more market-oriented economy and reduce the role of state planning as early as 1958. By the 1960s, successful reforms had led to significant increases in income in the more industrially developed republics, where industry generated both higher profits and higher wages, but had the opposite effect on areas where income was tied to extractive industries (mining and timber). Thus the gap between rich and poor grew, and with it, the political unrest to which a one-party communist state is particularly unprepared to respond effectively. These problems were compounded by the fact that economic stratification followed ethnic and republican lines—Slovenia and Croatia became wealthy, while Kosovo suffered increasingly entrenched poverty.

Whatever political and economic structural stability Yugoslavia enjoyed — during the first three decades of its existence therefore began to crumble in the late 1970s. A slumping world economy precipitated a fiscal and economic crisis in Yugoslavia, leading to international demands for austerity, the return of hundreds of thousands of guest workers, layoffs in government-owned firms, annual inflation of 50 percent and more by the mid-1980s, and a series of currency devaluations. The majority—nearly 60 percent by 1985—of unemployed Yugoslav workers were under the age of twenty-five, and a growing number of young professionals were underemployed, thus eroding the middle class on which both political and economic reform depends. Work stoppages, strikes, and protests became increasingly common and widespread, and they began to take on nationalist tones. Then, in 1980, Tito died.

Like other heavily indebted developing states during the 1980s, the Yugoslav government struggled with attempts to restructure its economy and, at the same time, with the political instability exacerbated by Tito's death. It should be noted, however, that political stability was elusive even before Tito died. Neither the recognition of Bosnian Muslims as a constituent nationality nor the 1974 constitutional reforms giving Vojvodina and Kosovo nearly the same power as republics ameliorated mounting political tensions. These reforms may have made things worse by further implicating national identities as the primary mediating force between individuals and the state. In pluralist democracies, political parties, interest groups, and social institutions combine to form the basis for civil society through which individual grievances are mediated and transmitted to political leaders and institutional actors. In a one-party communist state, only national identities were left to play that role. As the Cold War came to an end, Western strategic interest in Yugoslavia declined. Pressure on the Yugoslav government to implement economic reform and austerity was increasing, while economic aid declined.[24]

Nationalist rhetoric and demonstrations in the republics waxed and waned for at least several decades before Milosević gave his now infamous and inflammatory speech in 1989 before an audience of one million in Kosovo on the six hundredth anniversary of the Battle of Kosovo. Both Croat and Serb intellectuals, for example, had made claims to separate Croatian and Serbian languages in the 1960s; a "Croatian Spring" nationalist movement, peaking between 1967 and 1971 met with severe repression from the Tito government; a number of Muslim nationalists, including Alija Izetbegovic, were tried and sentenced in Sarajevo; and Serbian intellectual nationalism found a unified voice with the publication of the *Memorandum of the Serbian Academy of Sciences and Arts* (SANU) in 1986. Albanians protested against discrimination and repressive police tactics, while Serb demonstrators protested against growing Albanian nationalism and "separatism." Constitutional changes reduced the autonomy of Vojvodina and Kosovo in 1988, and in 1990 Milosević unilaterally revoked what little local control they had retained. By the time Ante Markević, committed to both political and economic reform, became prime minister in 1989, the disintegration of Yugoslavia was well under way. In the fall of 1989, the Slovenian parliament declared a right of "self-determination, including the right of secession."

The convergence of a variety of structural variables at this stage—failure to achieve institutional political stability under Tito's rule, inability to respond to the challenge to move from a federal to confederal system, rapid escalation of an intractable economic crisis, failure of the West to foresee the likely horrible consequences of hasty republican secessions—produced a legitimacy crisis. In the absence of other institutional mechanisms for mediating conflict in a civil society, grievances were mediated by the network of national identity–related institutions and actors. The Communist Party itself had decentralized into a league of republican-based communist parties; a relatively free and prolific media had become more local, republican, and nationalist; churches were already more or less nationality-based; even the pluralistic, cosmopolitan world of Yugo-rock began to show some signs of national disintegration (Ramet 1996). The legitimacy crisis was occurring not only among political leaders but in the minds of the Yugoslav people. As Susan Woodward has insightfully observed:

While politicians and parliaments bent on sovereignty or radical change were challenging the legitimacy of the federal government and party, all the less visible bonds that hold any society together were collapsing—the rules of mutual obligation, the checks and balances, the equilibrating mechanisms, the assumption of minimal security of one's person and status. (Woodward 1995: 116)

## The Destruction of Yugoslavia

The emperor, who was scantily dressed before, now wore no clothes at all, and politicians in the republics—most vigorously in Croatia and Serbia—exploited the opportunity to cloak their own claims to legitimacy in the sentiments of increasingly extreme, emotionally charged, and exclusive nationalism. The "rules of mutual obligation," in Woodward's terms, changed. Or, as one of my informants said despairingly when I asked her to talk about her identity in 1995, "Well, you see I am a Yugoslav. But then there is no more Yugoslavia."[25] While this sentiment was shared by many people, nationalist emotions, fomented by what was essentially hate speech broadcast by the Croatian and Serbian controlled media, increasingly polarized people into categories of sameness and otherness based on new rules of obligation *and exclusion*. Almost overnight, "Yugoslavs" and "Bosnians" became "stateless persons." Suddenly one had to be Slovene, Croat, or Serb—or, almost by default, Muslim. Of all the people I talked with between 1995 and 1998, the Muslims in Bosnia seemed most grounded—even now—in a cosmopolitan "Yugoslav" identity.

Shifting emotional boundaries of identity and moral obligation, of course, were mobilized in support of shifting political boundaries. With the most homogeneous population of between 90 and 95 percent of people identifying as Slovenes speaking their own language distinct from Serbo-Croatian, a historically stable and robust economy, greater wealth, and a high degree of contact with and integration into the western European and global economy, Slovenia's secession was relatively peaceful, if premature. The Croatian government welcomed it as the pretext for its own secession, and the Belgrade regime, acting as the Federal Republic of Yugoslavia (FRY), opposed it but saved the strength of its opposition for a showdown with President Tudjman. Ironically, the first casualty of the "war," which at the time was constructed as Belgrade-as-FRY using the force of the "Yugoslav" state to put down an illegal and militarized secession in Slovenia, was a Slovenian soldier in an FRY uniform flying an FRY helicopter with supplies into the FRY bases in Slovenia. He was shot by a Slovenian soldier fighting for the "independence" of Slovenia, to which his government claimed it was legally entitled.[26] Ten days after the war in Slovenia began, Milosević ordered the Yugoslav National Army (JNA) to withdraw.

Prior to the secessions, a series of six meetings was held among the presidents of the republics. Milosević and Tudjman also met separately. Though the meetings failed to resolve the crisis, many suspect that Milosević and Tudjman may have conspired, or at least tacitly colluded, so that each could lay a claim to a divided Bosnia. They subsequently did nothing to stop and in fact much to accelerate the momentum of local hostilities, which erupted in open conflict in Slavonia and Bosnia. This would then strengthen the position each is suspected to have supported: the partitioning and subsequent annexation of a divided Bosnia to each of their new states.[27]

Some of the facts of the conflict and violence that followed are undisputed, others are highly contestable, and many are not yet, nor may they ever be, known. Irregular forces began to mobilize everywhere, soldiers and republican governments outside of Serbia renounced allegiance to the JNA, and the Slovenian and Croatian governments authorized their own military forces. On June 25, 1991, the Slovene and Croatian governments passed acts of separation and independence, and on June 26, the Belgrade government authorized JNA interventions. On July 9, the European Parliament passed a resolution which did not support unilateral acts of secession. Special committees were formed and crisis monitoring projects created. Local violence between police and citizens, irregular forces and the JNA, and police and irregulars broke out in multiethnic areas, including the Krajina on the Western border between Croatia and Bosnia.

While Europeans attempted to facilitate arbitration and enact a cease-fire, the UN called for an arms embargo against all the republics of "Yugoslavia." A referendum among Albanians in Kosovo, calling for the creation of "a sovereign and independent state," carried the support of 99 percent of Albanians. But in December, Germany broke ranks with those withholding recognition from the republics, and extended official recognition of Slovenia and Croatia. This was followed in January 1992 by European Community (EC) member-states opening the process of recognition to Slovenia and Croatia. Austria, Belgium, and Great Britain did so immediately, and within days some fifty countries had joined them. In April the EC Ministerial Council recommended recognition by all member-states, and a day later the U.S. recognized Slovenia, Croatia, and Bosnia-Herzegovina on April 7, 1992.

What Tudjman and Milosević discussed at their several meetings in 1991 may never be known. The Croatian government made moves signaling increasingly exclusive and nationalist antagonism toward the 600,000 Serbs living in Croatia. These moves included reviving symbols used by the Ustaše, rewriting the constitution so that Croatia was the homeland of the Croatian nation instead of "the national state of the Croatian nation and the state of the Serbian nation in Croatia," and rescinding the official status of the Cyrillic alphabet (both Latin and Cyrillic alphabets had enjoyed official status in Croatia). Serbs serving in the Croatian police were removed from office and replaced with Croatians in Zagreb as well as in the Serb-majority regions (Tanner 1997: 230). The Serb response was to begin to mobilize as an autonomous entity within Croatia, and numerous reports followed of both sides manipulating the media with propaganda aimed at further fomenting local violence. Many people became convinced that their neighbors had been overnight transformed into their enemies.

The Croats claimed a right unilaterally to declare independence from Yugoslavia and constitute a state territorially delimited by the boundaries of the Croatian republic. The Serbs claimed, before the actual secession, not that secession and independence itself were out of the question, but that *unilateral* secession was. Officially, anyway, the option of negotiating a new structural relationship, including new territorial boundaries, and which might then include secession and independence, remained open. The status of Serbs in Croatia and Bosnia, they argued, would be dramatically (and unacceptably) altered. Whereas within the Yugoslav state for over forty years they had been a "constituent nation," within a Croatian (or Bosnian) state they would become an ethnic *minority*. As Tanner put it, under the new Croatian constitution: "The Serbs were relegated to the rank of a national minority, along with Hungarians, Italians and other ethnic smallfry" (1997: 230). By the same logic, in a "rump" Yugoslavia minus Slovenia and Croatia, Bosnian Croatians and Bosnian Muslims would become minorities living within a state dominated by a relatively much larger Serb majority. This would leave the Bosnian Muslims in a particularly vulnerable situation as, unlike the Croats, they would have no patron successor state in which Muslims were a majority.

What followed was the killing of a quarter of a million people, 70 percent to 75 percent of whom were civilians,[28] including many elderly, and rapes of girls and women from eight to eighty years old of the most brutal kind — the conservative Hague estimates were that by the end of 1994 (before Srebenica) approximately 35,500 women had been raped, and half of them subsequently killed in summary executions[29] — the forced displacement of more than one million refugees, and the destruction of many of their homes. Many people died of starvation, both in "camps" and in cities under siege. The level and scope of torture and brutality in Europe was unmatched since World War II. Testimony in the War Crimes Tribunal alleges that some men were forced to orally castrate fellow prisoners. Journalists broadcast and photographed some of the conditions as early as 1992. For three more years Western policy-makers and international organizations debated the political costs of intervention and settled on a "no arms to anyone" embargo which tacitly sanctioned the military advantages of the Serbs and Croats, leaving the Muslims virtually defenseless while Western strategists searched for "structural" solutions.

Until July 1995, a "dual key" required approval by both the UN and NATO in order to authorize direct multilateral intervention. That policy changed during the London Conference (Holbrooke 1998: 73–74). On August 30, 1995, the NATO initiated air strikes against key Serb positions, which emboldened an offensive by the tenuous Croat-dominated Muslim–Croat "alliance" and brought all parties to the negotiating table within two months. The strikes were not a response to the 1992 revelations of the existence of Bosnian Serb death camps at Omarska and elsewhere. They were not a response to the hundreds of thousands of civilians killed during "ethnic cleansing" operations. They were not a response to the more than 35,000 rapes reported to the Hague Tribunal. They were not a response to the three-year siege of Sarajevo, during which thousands starved while children were murdered in the streets by snipers and mortar shells pounded the city, including several direct attacks on the open-air central city market. They were not a response to the more than fifty French peacekeeping soldiers killed, nor to the taking of 350 peacekeepers as hostages on May 25. Nor were they a response to Bosnian Serb massacres in the UN-declared "safe areas" (Muslim enclaves surrounded by Bosnian Serb–held territory) Srebenica and Zepa, though they followed these pinnacles of horror by six weeks. After a "military" victory in Srebenica, Bosnian Serb General Mladic's forces carried out what has been called "the biggest single mass murder in Europe since World War II" in Srebenica (Holbrooke 1998: 69). The International Committee of the Red Cross estimates that 7,097 people were mass executed in four days while some 370 Dutch peacekeepers were made to witness the massacre (Honig and Both 1997; Holbrooke 1998: 70). Following the massacre, British Prime Minister John Major rejected a French proposal for direct intervention (Holbrooke 1998: 71).

The "final outrage" that provoked the overdue NATO response was a combination of events perceived to be an affront to American leadership: the killing of three American diplomats on Mount Igman pass on August 19, 1995 (a month after the Srebenica massacre); another mortar attack on August 28 on the Sarajevo market, killing 38 civilians and wounding 85 others; impassioned calls for action by Republican leaders Dole and Gingrich; and a decision by President Clinton to break the NATO impasse of forty months by supporting Operation Deliberate Force (Holbrooke 1998: 101). Within weeks, the siege of Sarajevo ended.

### Dayton: Peace or Another "Peace Process?"

Like Korea, Vietnam, Northern Ireland, and the Middle East, the structural solution negotiated at the cessation of violence in Bosnia in 1995 involved territorial partitions (viewed as temporary by some and permanent by others) and an ambiguous legal and political status for the inhabitants. The war in Croatia had begun in June 1991. An unconditional cease-fire signed in January 1992 left the Serbs—many originally from the area and others from

Bosnia and Serbia moving into towns "cleansed" of Croats—in control of a third of the republic's territory. The war in Bosnia-Herzegovina started in April 1992 and ended with the cease-fire in October 1995. The violence between Croats and Muslims in Bosnia ostensibly and officially ended with the formation of a Muslim–Croat alliance in March 1994. With the formation of the alliance, the war in Bosnia began to turn against the Serb forces. Croatian army operations Storm and Flash reversed the situation in occupied Croatia in the spring and summer of 1995, with some 250,000 Serbs fleeing the area as it returned to Croatian control. Weakened by defeat in Croatia and weakening in Bosnia, Serb forces moved into the UN-declared "safe areas" of Srebenica, Gorazde, and Zepa in June, in a final burst of brutality and barbarism.

President Clinton announced the cease-fire on October 5, 1995, to take effect five days later. On November 1, all three of the leaders whose rise to power marked the move toward war, and who had presided over four years of violence, met to make peace, regardless of any evidence of their connection to events that by any measure clearly constituted crimes against humanity.

The Serb negotiators knew they would have to give up territory in Bosnia. As I watched the "peace process" unfold from my home in the United States, I chillingly recalled comments made to me by an influential member of the Serbian Socialist Party in Belgrade exactly at the time we now know the Serbs to have been massacring somewhere between 7,000 and 8,000 men and boys in cold blood in Srebenica.[30] He offered a hypothetical: "This cannot go on much longer," he said, "What if the Bosnian Serbs made a move right about now to take, for example, up to seventy-percent of the territory in Bosnia, then they would go into negotiations and give up some, and still come away with something like fifty-one percent." From his perspective, this was not ethnic cleansing or the mass killing of innocent civilians. It was war, and this was a strategic move to control territory which could be used to achieve better results in negotiations that seemed both inevitable and impending. A few days later I sat in the office of an antiwar activist who during my visit received a phone call from eastern Bosnia. "Something just terrible is going on there," he said, "just absolutely unbelievable."[31]

The Muslim and Croat negotiators also knew that Bosnia would be partitioned. The gravest issues lay in the status of border areas between Croatia and Herzegovina, where Bosnian Croats had proclaimed "The Croatian Community of Herceg-Bosna" in 1992, in the "Brčko corridor" in western Slavonia, on the front line between Bosnia and Croatia, and in eastern Slavonia, the area of Croatia on the eastern border with Serbia, where, as the Dayton talks opened, the Serbs maintained control even after operations Storm and Flash. The Brčko corridor was on a narrow strip of land on the Bosnia–Croatia border in a formerly Muslim majority area. It formed a crucial link between the territory of the Republic of Serbia and two large swaths of land in eastern and northern Bosnia cleansed and controlled by Bosnian Serb forces (the so-called "Republika Srpska). Without control of the Brčko corridor, there would be no contiguity between these two areas of Bosnia under Serb control. It would be difficult to make any case either for an independent Serb "entity" within Bosnia or for any contiguous territory which could be annexed to the Republic of Serbia. Sarajevo, a city already divided by Serbian control in the suburbs and Federation control in the urban center, had nearly become an enclave within Serb-controlled Bosnia, with Bosnian Serb leadership headquarters just a few miles away in Pale. The formerly Muslim majority towns of Srebenica and Zepa had fallen under Bosnian Serb control, while Gorazde and an area of about 10 kilometers surrounding it remained nominally under the control of the federation.

Summarizing the Dayton Accord and the Erdut Agreement governing the transition of eastern Slavonia, and conditions and events that have followed them in the past six years, is almost as difficult as trying to do justice to a summarized account of the histories and events surrounding the conflict itself. Copies of the accord are available on many internet sites and Richard Holbrooke's *To End a War* (1998) provides a detailed account of the negotiations themselves. Bosnia was partitioned into a boomerang-shaped "entity" in the northern and eastern areas of Bosnia under the control of Bosnian Serbs and another "entity" in the region contiguous to Croatia and controlled by the Muslim-Croat Federation (formerly an alliance) in the western and central areas of Bosnia (see maps 4, 5, and 6). There are joint as well as distinct "entity" institutions, with provisions for their gradual integration. An international peacekeeping force was created, with provisions for local participation. There has been little progress toward integration, and many Bosnian Serbs regard their entity as a state or as in the process of becoming a state.

What is both clear and disturbing is, first, that no one could find an acceptable alternative to negotiating with exactly those leaders whose nationalistic rhetoric, preying on prejudices and vulnerabilities, were in one way or another responsible for the war and its atrocities, and second, that their efforts were rewarded with the partition of Bosnia.

Recently, some of former President Tudjman's closest advisors and members of his government were among those calling for annexing all or part of the federation entity. In late February 2001, the HDZ leader of the Bosnian Croats, Ante Jealvić, declared the federation "null and void" and threatened Croat secession from Bosnia and the (re)creation of a Bosnian Croat "entity." At a rally held by Tudjman's Party HDZ in Herzegovina, "speakers condemned the Hague-based tribunal," and when reference was made to Croatian President Stipe Mesić, who supports the tribunal, crowds chanted "kill him, kill him."[32]

Though the Hague Tribunal has not yet convicted any of the accused of

**Map 4**

genocide (they have been convicted of crimes against humanity and war crimes, and accused but not convicted of genocide), new evidence related to the events in Srebenica in July 1995 may provide the critical link to the charge of genocide against General Radislav Krstić.[33] As of June 2001, Milosević himself, in prison in Serbia, draws closer to extradition to answer charges at the Hague.[34] Ten months after winning the presidential election, opposition candidate and now-President Kostunica and his government were able to issue a decree allowing extradition of accused war criminals and cooperation with the Hague Tribunal. Though a subject of considerable domestic controversy, the Croatian government had long been cooperating with the ICTY—and complaining as well that doing so was tantamount to achieving one-sided justice. Like the partitioned status of the two Bosnian "entities," reconciliation efforts in Bosnia are tenuous, as is the first postwar, post-Tudjman government in Croatia.[35]

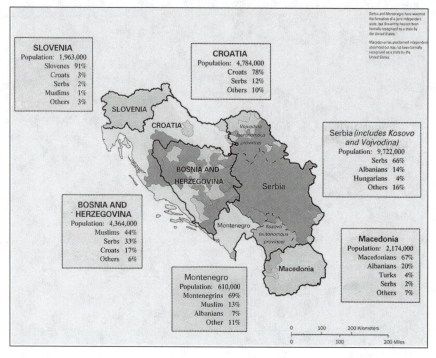

**Map 5**

There are and will continue to be many conflicting views of the success of or failure to implement the Dayton Accords in Bosnia, but the effort itself is both unique and remarkable. It is unique in that it represents a truly international effort, though NATO-led, to keep the peace in a postwar environment, even though the peacekeepers were not direct participants in the conflict. At the same time, Dayton attempts to implement structural provisions for economic and political recovery. In that it resembles the occupation and reconstruction of postwar Germany and Japan. It is a grand social experiment in which soldiers from Ukraine, Italy, German, France, Russia, Netherlands, Canada, Finland, the United States, and elsewhere are taking turns on tours of duty in war-torn Bosnia, cleaning up rubble, protecting civilians from further random violence, and puzzling over what this assignment has to do with the tasks for which they have been prepared as soldiers (Ackerman 2000; Maly 1999). The UN and various regional organizations involved in peacemaking and humanitarian service are known to the locals simply as "the internationals." Daily NATO briefings in Sarajevo are held by the Office of the High Representative (OHR), the Organization for Security and Cooperation in Europe (OSCS), the European Union (EU), the United Nations

**Map 6**

Mission in Bosnia-Herzegovina (UNMIBH), and the United Nations High Commissioner for Refugees (UNHCR). This January 11, 2000, statement to the press from the EC representative provides a glimpse of the intricate interplay among international functional organizations, regional political organizations, the international security forces authorized by the UN but under NATO command (SFOR), and local companies, public institutions, and the everyday lives of ordinary people in Bosnia:

Dobar Dan for the European Commission. I would like to invite you all to the formal opening of the bridge over the Usora River near Doboj on Monday 17th January 200 at 11:30. The bridge will be formally opened jointly by Mr. Zivko Radisić, member of BiH Presidency, and Ambassador Hansjorg Kretschner, Head of the European Commission Representation Office to Bosnia and Herzegovina. This project was completely financed by the European Union to the value of 2.5 million euro and the reconstruction was completed by the local construction company, ZGP Doboj. An important part of this project was de-mining of the area, which was done by HELP. This bridge is a part of the vital North-South motorway M17, linking Bosanski Samac, Sarajevo and Capljina. Its reconstruction will improve transport links through Bosnia and Herzegovina between the coast and central Europe. And I would also like to announce the signing of the contract with SFOR for rehabilitation of central heating in Poblobodj Primary School in [unintelligible] area. This will provide central heating for over five hundred and fifty pupils in twenty-five classrooms which is mainly a refugee population. Thank you.[36]

## Peace, Peace Processes, and Civil Society

During the campaign for congressional support to establish the U.S. Institute for Peace in the 1980s, advocates argued that resources had long been going into the development of war-making technology and education, and that the time had come to put some resources into the study of peace. There were active peace studies and conflict resolution communities and programs, and to some extent academic studies of the "causes of war" have always thinly veiled the hope that understanding the causes of violence will contribute to the development of policies capable of reducing its incidence and scope. But most of these endeavors have focused on the process of negotiation, on the conditions that make negotiation more likely, and on how to de-escalate conflict interactions as they move from rhetorical hostility toward the precipice of physical violence. There has also been an emphasis on how to move parties toward compromise in order to achieve structural solutions, which is understandable in light of the assumption that the inability to resolve grievances peacefully is the underlying cause of violence.

Structural negotiations, however, often leave territories divided and the people in them possessed of uncertain political status. Examples include East and West Germany, North and South Korea, North and South Vietnam, Northern Ireland, Cyprus, and the failed partition of Palestine in 1948. Following World War II, wars have tended to conclude with indeterminate outcomes and peace "processes" that go on for many years.

Talking, or a willingness to negotiate leading to periodic efforts to move toward a more stable peace outcome, even when accompanied by low-intensity conflict, is still better than all-out war. But we need to move forward in our thinking about peace to the question of how to get beyond the nego-tiation of structural peace. Peace is more than the cessation of violence, and even more than an agreement about how to achieve compromise over mate-rial interests. How do we move from violence to the cessation of violence, to building a *sustainable* peace and the reconstruction of a civil society, or, in the case of international actors, civil relations in the aftermath of conflict? How do former parties to a conflict, parties formerly engaged in a relation-ship of violence, whose identities interlock historically and include histor-ical injury, reconcile their relationship so that both can live within a civil framework of mutual obligation?

ductory classes on IR, by the unabashed and rather unsympathetic realism reflected in many American university students' perception of war. It is as if studying history as a series of events often organized around the way war restructures perceptions of power in the macrohistorical sense leaves them with a fatalistic, if not also dispassionate, sense that wars are an inevitable feature of political life and that the "nature" of war is simply tragic. Neither the scope nor innocence of its victims, nor the severity, depths, and scope of the intentional cruelty on the part of perpetrators seem to make much difference to their fatalism. I always wonder what combination of socializing influences produces such an attitude, and whether their families see things very differently. My impression is anecdotal, yes, and perhaps what I've seen is only an American attitude, but in itself it is more than disturbing enough.

While mass emigration, mass murder, and mass graves make it difficult to give precise figures, the oft-cited number of 250,000 people dead seems plausible, if not conservative. By the end of 1994—nine to ten months before the war ended, there may have been as many as 75,000 victims of war crimes in the territory of the former Yugoslavia, with up to 15,000 individuals suspected of having committed them. There were more than 450 completely destroyed towns, in which approximately 800 mosques, 128 churches, ten Orthodox churches, and three synagogues had been demolished. Two hundred fifty-eight "detention camps" were known to have existed in Bosnia, fifteen in Serbia, and two in Montenegro. Forty-four mass grave sites had been discovered. An estimated 35,000 women had been raped, over half of whom were subsequently murdered in approximately 200 incidences of mass execution.[3] As many as 4.5 million people out of 24 million prewar inhabitants of Yugoslavia, had fled their homes to "move to areas where their ethos was dominant, or emigrate to other countries, even other continents."[4]

To treat war as an agentless social phenomenon tends to obscure the human suffering, the thousands of compound tragedies that make up the experience of mass violence. For those attentive to the events in the former Yugoslavia, the massacre of seven thousand men and boys in Srebenica in the summer of 1995, and the deprivations of a detention camp known as Omarksa, discovered and reported in the Western media in the spring of 1992, are well known.[5] Less well known, but still widely reported and the subject of the award-winning film *Calling the Ghosts,* were the experiences of the individuals, many of whom who became Omarska's prisoners, who were living in the Prejidor district of Bosnia in the spring of 1992 when the "cleansing" began. Of the 112,500 people reported by the 1991 census living in the district's seventy or so ethnically mixed villages, Muslims made up 44 percent of the population, Serbs 42 percent, Croats 6 percent, and the remaining 8 percent were other ethnicities, including those who identified themselves as Yugoslav. Alexandra Stiglmayer, author and editor of *Mass Rape: The War against Women in Bosnia-Herzegovina,*[6] who worked as a freelance journalist in the region during the war, reports that:

Fifty thousand Muslims and 15,000 other non-Serbs were driven off or murdered, twenty-five mosques and eleven Muslim sanctuaries were blown up, more than 10,000 houses and apartments were searched, looted, and destroyed. . . . Thus there were approximately 65,000 non-Serbs. Of these 65,000 people (according to reliable calculations of the Prejidor Homeland Club in Zagreb) 20,000 were murdered, 30,000 were driven away, and approximately 3,000 were still living in Prejidor. (Stiglmayer 1993:86)

Excerpts from the Hague Tribunal proceedings against Ivica Rajic in 1996 take us a step closer to the lived traumas and tragedies of individual people.[7] The tribunal in this excerpt is questioning the prosecutor about the testimony of several protected witnesses regarding a massacre alleged to have taken place on October 23, 1992, in the towns of Vares and Stupni Do, in north-eastern Bosnia:[8]

Q: I think there was some discussion amongst these HVO soldiers,[9] which indeed the witness told you about, as to whether or not to shoot them or burn them alive; is that correct?
A: That is true.
Q: Can you tell the court in the words of the witness what happened next?
A: Witness B distinctly remembered that when she was being taken to what she called the "summer house" she saw soldiers throwing two dead bodies. There were three men who had been killed and one woman, and she saw two dead bodies being thrown into a burning house which was at that instance house No. 3 here. That house had meanwhile been put on fire, and in this house she saw two dead bodies being thrown, she went inside and all of them were locked up in the summer house. She eventually saw lots of smoke through the glass panes of the window of the summer house. There was lots of smoke, and after a while she saw that the glass of the windows was shattering and she also saw flames outside. She concluded that the summer house that they were confined into was on fire.

And later, Witness B, describes how these "soldiers" held a knife to her son's throat:

Q: How old was the boy, did she say to you?
A: Yes, his age was 7 years of age at that time.
Q: Thank you. I think the witness then said something to you about Sido's house; do you recall what she said?
A: The witness said that after murdering three men, the soldiers turned to this line of women and children and they said that we should kill them now and they should stand properly in a line, and when they were saying this, Sido said: "Don't do this to us; what have we done? I have

gotten a house here and I will give you my house," and Witness B recalled that when she said this, her house was not burning at that time, but one of the soldiers ordered her house being burnt and her house was burnt with the help of something that was put on the rifle and fired and her house was burnt. . . .[10]

Q: I think again this witness confirmed that the soldiers discussed amongst themselves whether or not these people should be shot or, in fact, burnt alive; is that correct?

A: That is true.

Q: I think that this witness also confirmed too, did she not, that the remaining group of women and children were taken into the summer house which was duly locked by the HVO; is that correct?

A: That is true.

And so witnesses entered testimony into the record of the tribunal regarding their experience and perception of events occurring in the small northeastern Bosnian town of Stupni Do, a town off all main roads between areas of confrontation, admitted to have no military significance. A Swedish peacekeeper who was in the area in 1992 provides the court with a chilling account of the scene in Stupni Do by the time his battalion arrived there early the next morning:

Q: Tell us something about the houses? Were they burnt or shot at or exploded?

A: They were exploded. It was just ruin.

Q: Was there any building in the city left unhurt?

A: No.

Q: Did you see any living person or living animal there?

A: No.

Q: No living animal either?

A: No.

Q: Did you see many dead animals?

A: Yes, there were dead animals on the, let us say, fields, on the road, among the houses. Everything was killed.

Q: Killed, shot?

A: Shot, burnt, sliced up throats, whatever you want to call it.

Hundreds of hours of testimony and evidence have been presented to the court since it began hearing cases in 1996. The historical account summarized in the previous chapter relies on conventional sources about events surrounding the war. I do not deny that there is significant explanatory power in such an analysis; by all structural indications, Yugoslavia was perhaps a war waiting to happen. Yet similarly unstable political and economic conditions, similarly conflictual configurations of intercommunal relations, and similar tensions arising from competing and intersecting claims on civic and ethnic identities occur in other parts of the world. And in those many other countries, societies, or states, where structurally unstable conditions and intercommunal tensions do occur, they do not always result in such brutal violence. Structural explanations may tell us why *leaders* and *institutional actors* did what they did, but they do not tell us why the soldiers discussed whether to shoot or burn civilians alive, why they then lined up women and children, herded them into a house, and set the house on fire. It may be "rational" for political elites to calculate interests and to think strategically about the value of unleashing forces that motivate ordinary people to commit horrible acts, but is it rational for ordinary people to respond? Do we need to know something of the structure of the inner, psychic, emotional, and social life of human beings in order to account for and ultimately lessen the likelihood of this kind of behavior? Structural accounts do not tell us why ordinary people did what they did, yet certainly without ordinary people, there would be no wars.

## Is There Something "Terrible" in All of Us?

Like the vignettes at the opening of Chapter 1, the above excerpts raise two questions that I see as central to the issue of uncivil behavior and exclusionary violence. First, is there something terrible in all of us, or is there something terrible in just *some* of us? And second, what does identity have to do with it? If only some of us are capable of brutality—Dušan Tadić, Idi Amin, Adolf Eichmann, Pol Pot, Matthew McKinney—or if some categories of us are more likely to engage in exclusionary violence—members of the Ku Klux Klan, Germans, Hutus, English settlers—then we must ask why in *this* person or *these* people, and not others? And how do we make the leap from exceptional instances of brutality to the political rationalization and normalization of violence? If the capacity for inhumanity is contained within all of us, however, then why is that capacity acted on by *this* person or *these* people in *this* instance and not others in other instances? Are some individuals, some cultures, or some conditions of group life more prone to exclusionary and inhumane behavior than others, and if so, why?

These issues ultimately point to the perennial political and philosophical question regarding "the nature of the self": Is the self by nature "good" or is it "evil," does it tend toward progress, creativity, and enlightenment, or toward violence, destruction, and cruelty? It seems, as Waltz argues in *Man, the State and War* (1959), that we can find ample evidence to support as well as contradict either claim. But do political culture, practice, and institutions constitute variables intervening between the capacity for cruelty or caring and our actual behavior? Can they make either caring or cruelty more or less likely?

Both because Freud redirected the debate by recasting the "human nature" question in terms of "the psychic structure of the self," and because modern philosophers have problematized any ontology that proceeds from assumptions that "naturalize" human character, we can restate a more contemporary version of the question by asking: How is an understanding of the self formed, and under what conditions is it more likely to result in behavior that can be characterized as "taking pleasure in hurting others without remorse," or, more simply put, evil?[11] In this light we might ask whether the vignettes in Chapter 1 and the war crimes trial excerpts here also raise the question of whether "war" itself is evil. Certainly evil things are done in the context of war and by individuals behaving within the cognitive framework of war. When psychologist Sam Keen interviewed David Rice, who confessed to killing an unarmed family of four in Seattle because he believed they were "communists," Rice explained that "he was a soldier" and "this is a war."[12] For Rice, the distinction between wars officially sanctioned by states and his own private, psychotic war was imperceptible. But what is the distinction? Is this really just a matter of scale and, in Foucauldian terms, socially agreed upon boundaries between politics and madness, or can war be "civilized," as international law attempts to do? Even when wars are fought primarily by "trained soldiers," the psychological objective of military training is aimed at *enabling* ordinary people to kill, not necessarily *enabling them to kill while maintaining an integrated psyche capable of feeling remorse*. As a consequence, one can argue that war as a political practice certainly makes "hurting for pleasure without remorse" more likely.

The issue of harm-doing versus civility is much more complex than an oppositional positioning—good versus evil—suggests, as I will argue here and elsewhere. Civility, it seems, should not simply be a matter of *refraining* from "hurting for pleasure without remorse," though we may regard this as constituting a minimal condition for civility in human relations. But ethical choices are seldom so stark. We have the possibility of (1) "hurting for a noble cause," though without remorse; (2) hurting for a noble cause with remorse (as some Nazi defendants claimed); and (3) hurting some in order to prevent or end the suffering of a larger number of others (were Hiroshima and Nagasaki evil acts?). There are probably more choices. The concept of civility used here, or rather the capacity for civility as the antidote to the capacity for harm-doing without remorse, begins with a shared agreement to regard others as one's moral equals; an obligation to regard others as entitled to the same benefits and ethical obligations one expects for oneself. In the case of regulating violence, for example, one agrees to refrain from the use of force to inflict harm or to coerce others and to submit one's grievances with other moral equals to an institutional process for remediation. One agrees not to "take the law into one's own hands" when rights are violated. In the exceptional case of self-defense, the burden of proof lies with the individual to show that the act of force constituted an allowable exception.

What do these accounts of violent, inhumane acts carried out through individual or collective, institutionalized, human agency tell us about civility? Is there something terrible, a capacity to do terrible things, in *all* of us, or just some of us? All states, or just some states? Discussions of the Holocaust often begin with the assumption that such cruelty is exceptional or that it must be explained in terms of exceptional qualities attributable either to individual war criminals or collectively to the family structure, or to anti-Semitic political culture. Alice Miller (1983), for instance, focuses on the authoritarian family and patriarchal society. Goldhagen's argument rests on a historical account of European anti-Semitism. Arendt explores the intersection between anti-Semitic and totalitarian ideologies on the one hand and the psychological effects of terror and isolation on the other.

The Holocaust stands, at the same time, as an incomparably horrific crime against humanity and as an invocation to those social scientists and humanists concerned with the issue of citizenship constituted as a moral obligation. It is because of the Holocaust that we study genocide, inhumanity, and evil. Yet for all the ways in which it is unique, we must inevitably make comparisons if we are to address the questions "why" and "how." Perhaps the Holocaust is also like Freud's psychopath, an exaggeration of other genocides, or of other cases of politically sanctioned inhumanity, however different from the Holocaust they may seem.

In asking, "is there something terrible, a capacity to behave inhumanely toward others, in all of us?" I am struck by how pervasive, rather than exceptional, politically sanctioned brutality, rationalized by exclusionary ideologies, has been. For example:

- The private and public violence toward indigenous peoples sanctioned or carried out directly by various European empires, settlers and settler-controlled states throughout the nineteenth and early twentieth centuries, throughout the Americas, Australia, New Zealand, South Africa, and elsewhere;
- The brutality of British colonization, first directed toward the Scots and Celts;
- The "religious hatred" of the St. Bartholomew's Day Massacre;
- The Ottomans' genocide against the Armenians in 1915;
- Communist counterrevolutionary purges under Stalin and Mao;
- Tens of thousands of people disappeared, tortured, and arbitrarily or summarily executed in Argentina, Chile, Guatemala, and elsewhere under Latin American dictatorships;
- Pol Pot's anti-intellectual, anti-middle-class genocide;
- African genocides in Uganda, Rwanda, and Burundi.

Politically sanctioned violence rationalized by exclusionary ideologies is clearly ubiquitous, however scarcely it appears in academic discourses. It is very often presented as a problem of "others," an indication of their backwardness and "our" civilization. Historical accounts of war are mostly silent on the brutality of political violence, emphasizing instead their "strategic" significance. Historical narratives of "religious warfare" normalize a full century of killing arising out of conflicts between old and new forms of religious identity in western Europe. That killing, often in mass murders, was instigated by political leaders struggling over the question of their (the political leaders') own legitimacy in competition with the authority of the Catholic Church, but was carried out quite often by *ordinary* people who killed on the basis of "hatred." Their significance, we are told, is that, brought to an end by the Peace of Westphalia, these wars resolved the issue of church and state.

It is European cultural mythology that produced the "modern" identity. But "modernity" relies on our ability to make and maintain a distinction between nonmodern and modern, a distinction dependent on constructing non-Western cultures as "primitive," "backward," and ultimately "barbarian." According to the logic of modernity, non-Western or "oriental" cultures are more inclined to engage in brutality, however unselfconscious or innocent their primitiveness is. The mythology of modernity can be traced to the interplay between Christian discourses articulating a totalizing and hegemonic moral system and the social processes which produced the Westphalian state in Europe. Brutality became "barbarism," which provided a crucial dividing line between "civilized" Europe and "uncivilized" non-Western, non-European Others. The maintenance of European identity *requires* the construction of the Holocaust as exceptional. The 1991 to 1995 "wars of Yugoslav sucession" similarly unsettled European identity, though variations on the "ancient hatreds" hypothesis, reinforced by the longstanding construction of eastern and central Europe as backward and primitive, were deployed in defense of European civilization.

Trying to understand the Holocaust by studying German political culture or German family structure, then, presumes it to be a *German* problem. Yet if we take seriously Goldhagen's argument regarding the pervasiveness of anti-Semitism in *European* history and cultures, then we must ask: Why did the Holocaust occur in Germany, and *not* in France, Holland, and so on? My answer is that, well, it *did* happen in France, and Holland, and Austria, and elsewhere in Europe. It simply did not *begin* nor was it conceptualized elsewhere but rather in Germany. Europeans are just beginning to come to terms with the ethical issue of collaboration. If genocide is defined as: "the widespread killing of members of a national, ethnic, racial or religious group, or causing mental or bodily harm, or deliberately inflicting on the group conditions of life calculated to bring about its physical destruction carried out with the intent of destroying, in whole or in part, the group as such"[13] then how else is one to think about the widespread deliberate killing of some 15 to 40 million indigenous people *because they were indigenous people*, the majority killed within the first three quarters of the nineteenth century? Does the destruction of indigenous peoples' economic base—such as the U.S. government–sponsored killing millions of Western buffalo in the late 1800s—count as "deliberately inflicting on the group conditions of life calculated to bring about its physical destruction carried out with the intent of destroying, in whole or in part, the group as such"? Rewriting the history of settlers, empires, and indigenous peoples as "manifest destiny" enables Americans to view historical facts from the vantage point of a cognitive distance. Similarly, violence in the former Yugoslavia was often dismissed in the Western media by portraying it as a problem of "ancient hatreds," and even after the term has fallen into disuse and has been renounced as an unfair simplification, many ordinary Westerners are still wont to explain the continued violence in Kosovo (where Serbs are called "Serbs" and Albanians are called "ethnic Albanians," presumably to distinguish them from "citizen Albanians" in the state of Albania) in these terms.

Cognitive distancing serves as a way of reassuring ourselves that "we" will not or are unlikely to be a party to the horrible things done not only to, but by, Others. Similarly, the term "ethnic conflict" naturalizes the notion of "ethnic" as a basis for collective behavior, including violent behavior, while excluding from consideration other problems such as the "troubles" in Northern Ireland or "race relations" in the United States and elsewhere in the Americas. The term "ethnic conflict" has increasingly appeared as a central problem of international relations—particularly since the end of the Cold War—a problem, not coincidentally, that happens almost exclusively in non-Western "places." Uncritical use of such terms enables the construction of discourses claiming that brutality and inhumanity are exceptional and uncommon, at least among "civilized" Western societies. Perhaps we have been asking the wrong question. Instead of "why does it happen here, and not there," maybe we should be looking at instances in which harm-doing and brutality rationalized by an exclusionary ideology have occurred *wherever they are to be found*, and then ask "why?"[14]

## The Structure of the Self

My theoretical inquiry begins by conceptualizing the problem of exclusionary violence as the capacity for doing harm without remorse or where remorse is overcome by (political) rationalization,[15] and by thinking of civility as grounded on the ability to engage in reciprocal moral obligations. Civility involves the capacity of individuals to empathize or "identify with" others, to "see something of themselves" in others, or at least to value others equally and submit to a social rule that requires, minimally, that all individuals regard one another as equals (legally constituted as "equality before the law"). Conversely, where no such identification and/or rule exists, there may be no prohibitions against rationalizing harm-doing in exclusionary terms, in terms of inequality derived from difference, and, at the extreme, without remorse. Thus we can begin to approach the problem of whether there is something terrible in all of us and how it operates in relation to identity by interrogating psychoanalytic theories regarding the structure of the self and its identity in relation to others.

For roughly the past decade, a growing number of social scientists—political scientists and theorists in particular—have become increasingly interested in the question of identity. Identity is implicated as a corollary to the problem of ethnic conflict (Carment and James 1997), as a mechanism for disturbing the presumption of an agentless social structure (Wendt 1987; Shapiro and Alker 1996), through inquiry into gendered epistemologies and to reveal the way gender is encoded into social structures (Enloe 1990; Peterson 1992), as the central problematic of poststructuralist IR theory (Lapid and Kratochwil 1997), and as the platform from which postcolonial critiques of Western cultural imperialism are launched (Said 1979; Sardar 1998; Nandy 1995). Interrogating the limits of self/other perspectives, Neumann and others have also challenged the interchangeability of the concepts of "self" and "identity"(1997).

While I will not here enter into this labyrinthine theoretical discussion of identity and selves, I would like to extract from it several features salient to the question of how violent behavior is provoked through the political mobilization of identity. First, identity is neither stable nor fixed but rather fluid and contextual. Second, identity is multifaceted, perhaps even consisting of layered, intersecting identities. Third, identity is referential. It exists only in reference to something other than itself, an order, an Other, or multiple orders and Others, orders *of* others. Finally, the referent in relation to which identity is perceived is linguistically collectivized and, therefore, categorical. That linguistic order, in turn, contains the rules through which we constitute identity.

For the purpose of my argument, the self is both the basis for and the sum of identity narratives. But it is more. It is a position from which we experience ourselves as agents in a given time in a particular space. It is our ability to reflect self-consciously on our agency—our ability to act on or in relation to orders and others. As Joane Nagel has said, identity is how we answer the question "Who am I?"[16] The difference between self and identity may be expressed in this way: we know when "I" has acted without being affirmed of the self's existence by others, but we only know what it *means* to be "I" as a consequence of the interpolation between orders, Others, and the self as the cause or agent of an action with consequence. The self is a locus of subjectivity and agency. At the same moment, the self is an individuated space onto which identities—meanings—can be grafted, and can exist as only *bounded* because of its encounter with Others and orders of Others.

Unable initially to make a distinction between her own experience of and agency "in the environment," the infant begins the process of acquiring a "sense of self," becoming conscious of herself as a bounded being by learning to negotiate the expression and gratification of needs within a complex system of ongoing relationships rooted in social practices, processes, expectations, and socially produced shared meanings. Perhaps one of the earliest developments impacting the formation of identity is the relationship with Others whom we come to identify in gendered terms. Associating gender with Others and, eventually, with ourselves is not an agentless process, but rather through linguistic order and the mirroring of Others, we learn gender distinctions even before their meanings are clear. This takes place during the same period in which an infant is developing a sense self, agency, and separation from her environment, and becomes apparent between six and eighteen months of age. Thus cognition of the self as a bounded and individuated entity and as a *gendered* self develops within the framework of one's relationship with others—caregivers—during this very early period of life.

In more or less patriarchal cultures, where early caregivers are exclusively or as a rule female, narratives of selfhood and difference are bound up with gendered, hierarchical orders. As Will Roscoe (1991) has noted, it is through gender identification that we first encounter difference. From a state of unity, of unboundedness, of immersion in an environment, self-consciousness emerges into a two-dimensional world of sameness and difference, and the development of identities begins. From this two-dimensional cognitive framework we develop a capacity for more complex orderings, indeed, our capacity for tolerating difference, for empathy, and for critical thinking depends on our ability to do so. But we enter the cognitive world within as two-dimensional selves, so to speak. Klein relates this to the subsequent development of categories she calls the "good" and "bad" self and the good and bad Other (Alford 1989; Klein and Riviere 1964).

The self is not only the standpoint or position from which we experience and interpret life experiences, but also an agent engaging in interpretive acts, which in turn necessitates the use of linguistic categories, which in their turn contain the meanings through which social order is constructed, maintained, and even altered. It is as an interpretive agent that identities are constituted. In this paradoxical beginning, identity is constituted by referring the bounded self to something else, something with which the self is either *identified* (as the same) or from which it is *different,* something that contains our capacity for both hatred and empathy, harm-doing and caring, critical thought and the capacity to understand ourselves and our world in more complex terms, in terms of alternatives to dichotomous constructs.

Thus, whether from Wittgenstein's philosophical or Lacan's psychoanalytic perspective, the self can be known only as it is constructed within the social world of language and the psychological world of Otherness, the meaning of which is embedded within language. In discussing the "metalinguistic material" used to construct literature, Dzevad Karahasan, the former dean of the Academy of Theatrical Arts in Sarajevo, captures the relationship between the social world and its linguistic representation:

> Literature therefore dictates, or at least determines, our behavior through the values that culture imposes with an objective feeling that things make sense in the world. It also provides an instrument for interpretation of human experience in the world, and the reasons for our dwelling in it. The choices made within an accepted value system quite immediately determine human behavior, because the selection of values and the way we relate to them are the foundation of human ethical existence. . . . Hence literature shapes human behavior and perception of the world, making selections from the value system that people use to give meaning to their existence.[17]

There is no way to know or experience the self apart from its social existence, and its social existence is contained in categories of identity. The self and the Other, so to speak, are twin-born. The self is born as we become able cognitively to distinguish between the location of the agent "I" and the world of objects on which we act. But the self is also the object of actions of which the Other is the agent. In the mirrors of our emotional life the self is shaped, and with it a perception of what sort of "world" it is in which we live. If we are the object of the Other's scorn, we will live in a threatening and hostile world; if the object of warmth and tenderness, a world of caring connection.

But I am getting a bit ahead of myself. Before considering the impact of sociocultural interventions, I need to summarize an account of the structure of the self which I find most cogent as the starting point for understanding the human capacity for "doing harm without remorse." It derives from psychoanalytic theory and the application of psychoanalytic theory to the political theory of group life and critical theory (Alford 1989, 1994),[18] enemy-making and intergroup conflict (Volkan 1985; Volkan, Julius, and Monteville 1990), and the social construction of gender (Chodorow 1978; Balbus 1982) and its consequences for political action (Di Stefano 1983, 1991).[19]

Prior to birth, we know of no Other and we know of no self. We are boundless. There is unity between the organism of the body that will contain the self and the Other on whom it depends for the fulfillment of basic needs. Our needs appear to be met effortlessly, and there is no distinction between us, our needs, and that which satisfies them. Whether at birth or soon thereafter, there comes the moment at which we lose the illusion of boundless oneness, but of course we cannot articulate the experience. In fact, this prelinguistic stage is also "precategorical" in that we can locate neither ourselves as subjects nor others as objects (nor of course the social order that mediates between the two) until we begin to realize, or emotionally sense, or in some way become aware that the satisfaction of our most basic needs comes from a source that does not emanate from our own agency, from our own will, and over which we have no control. In Lacan's terminology (and Freud's to some extent) this is experienced as a sense of *lack*, or absence, and it is from this sense of lack that we begin to develop identification, which is, again, bound up with difference: "At the psychological level the partial object conveys the lack which creates the desire for unity from which the movement toward identification springs—since identification is itself dependent upon the discovery of *difference*, itself a kind of absence."[20]

Upon realizing this difference, we should not mistake the lack of language to describe the emotions we experience from our capacity to experience the emotions aroused by an awareness of our incompleteness. Psychoanalysts refer to the anger and frustration we feel at the realization that we do not control that which fulfills our needs, the realization that the source that does contain the capacity to fulfill them is "outside" or detached from the self, as "infantile rage."

As we enter the world of communicative action, feelings of frustration, anger, and rage can be channeled into attempts to verbalize as a means of eliciting needs-fulfilling action by the Other, the source on whom we depend. And so social life begins. The more our ability to act on feelings by verbalizing effectively develops (our self-expression seems to "cause" the desired response), and the more we learn the social and linguistic rules that repeatedly prove effective in eliciting needs-fulfilling responses from others, the less we experience ourselves as powerless and engulfed by our own frustration, and the more we feel competent to act in the social world in ways that result in the fulfillment of needs and the abatement of frustration.

So far the account is fairly straightforward. From the beginning humans are dependent on Others and they enter the social world by becoming participants in language games through which their relationships with one another are structured. Learning the rules of these language games is literally a matter of survival. The psychoanalytic account of the self is a good place to begin our interrogation of those variables that produce different inclinations toward the social world and different understandings of the self in the social world in which it is located, as well as varying inclinations to act in Other-destructive and Other-caring ways. In light of the widespread occurrence of Other-destructive behavior among and across human cultures and histories, it would be useful to consider the underlying psychological dilemma of incompleteness, of dependency on others, as more or less a universally human starting point. Variations in culture, encoded in linguistic practices, may then function as intervening variables, mitigating the impulse to act out infantile rage, creating social structures in which dependency is ameliorated by complex relationships of work, play, and distribution of goods and values, and providing various ideological and religious narratives containing "expla-nations" about our destructive impulses which in turn may relieve our anxi-eties about them, or through which our anxieties can be manipulated.

## Psychoanalytic Theory, Identity, and Conflict

There are three ways that psychoanalytic accounts of the development of our emotional life can inform an inquiry into the breakdown or absence of civility characterized by harm-doing and rationalized by ideologies based on exclu-sionary identities. First psychoanalytic accounts highlight the significance assigned to the meaning of difference, particularly as it is gendered and gender-coded, and its role in structuring social relations.

Rather than making assertions as to what is "true" about the self and iden-tity, let's just think of the self as a kind of ego structure, or container, and identities as the "content" of the structure, and ask whether this is a useful way of thinking about the relationship between the two. Identities endow structure with meaning, and identities are constructed within a system of linguistic order. Following Iver Neumann's advice that while the self cannot have ontological status, to engage in any kind of political theory we must "have an 'as if' story to tell about it,"[21] this is my "as if" story of the self. More correctly, it is my story of the Western self.[22] Male, female, Serb, Croat, European, Oriental, mother, daughter, father, soldier, all are socially constructed categories containing identities. These identities are then poured into the vessel of the self, so to speak, as a consequence of the interplay between our agency, the agency of others, and the language rules and speech acts through which agents construct meanings. From Lacan and Klein we learn that between the ages of six and eighteen months, an infant struggles with two cognitive issues that give the structure of the self its initial shape — the location of agency and the source of needs satisfaction/frustration. This struggle has emotional consequences. According to Klein, early awareness of needs being met or frustrated arouses feelings of contentment or, in the case of need frustration, anger. Klein argues that an infant, not immediately able to understand the agency (not being able to disentangle self from Other) asso-ciated with these contrasting experiences and feelings, exists in an emotional world in which the Other is the object of both anger and devotion, or nega-tive and positive attachment, however you like to phrase it. The contradiction in these feelings is coupled with confusion about self/Other boundaries or the location of agency so that an infant's contentment is a blissful state of unity, while the experience of needs frustration and the associated anger provoke guilt to the extent that she is becoming aware of the Other as separate and as the same Other for whom she feels a positive attachment at other times.

Thus early cognitive constructions begin as two-dimensional systems of agency and, according to Klein, a two-dimensional emotional world — an action, an utterance, or an emotion originates either with the self or with the Other, and it is either "good" or "bad." How can the Other be both the source of one's pleasure and the source of one's pain? At first the infant resolves the contradiction by perceiving the Other as if it were two objects — one good and one bad. This splitting of the Other is reproduced in the self, so that early emotional life is characterized by the belief that we are *either* good *or* bad, and that we are essentially two selves (imagine how a child hears the statement "Be a good girl now!" or "Don't be a bad boy!"). Under the best of circumstances, in the care of a loving and narcissistically mature caregiver, the infant will come to understand that the Other is a single but complex person who possesses a dual capacity for caring and for harming (even if only emotional harm), for being *either* good or bad. By internalizing this lesson, we can resolve the dilemma of two selves, which enables us to integrate them into one self capable of contradictory emotions and agency. The infant *identifies* with or, in Lacan's terminology, *mirrors* the Other in order to become herself.

Our capacity for empathy as well as critical thought depends on constructing the self and the world in more complex terms than dichotomous or binary thinking — learning to tolerate ambiguity and contradiction and understanding ourselves and others as having the capacity both to care and to do harm. This is not a particularly contentious point, and it is easy to see that a world consisting of only two categories is a world lacking ambiguity, a world of idealizations and demonizations. Yet this is exactly the world one lives in when it is populated *only* by enemies and allies, when we feel the need to see ourselves as "good" (enlightened, modern, progressive, redeemed, reborn, Western, civilized) and others as "bad" (backward, barbarian, unenlightened, unredeemed, oriental, uncivilized). It is a world of simple questions and easy answers. It is a world of absolutes. It is a world of certainty, however misguided and short-lived it may be. It is a world in which things are either one or the other — they cannot be both. It is a world of right and wrong, good and evil, enemies and allies. It is a knowable world. And it is a world of male and female, and only male and female. A world of opposition and clarity.

Steven J. Kull notes that: "During war, things become very simple, very clear. There are no ambiguities. In times of war suicide rates go down by half, mental health is better, even physical health gets better. It is simpler. All the ambiguities evaporate and we know what we are supposed to do."[23]

Perhaps we can speak of infantile experience only metaphorically, but it is nonetheless useful as a way of talking about the development of cognitive complexity. Our understanding of the world and ourselves in it does move from simple to complex. Returning to the proposition that the bounded self (and therefore the Other) comes into existence during the same period in which we begin to develop a linguistic capacity as well as an awareness of the self as situated within at least initially dichotomous gender categories, our original encounter with identity as *either* male or female entails making a distinction between being *either the same as or different* from the Other. Since the Other is in control of the means of satisfying our needs, we attribute the agency of satisfaction to the Other. Of course, we also attribute agency to the Other when our needs are frustrated or unmet, or when, from an infantile perspective, their fulfillment is withheld.

In a society of woman-monopolized early child care, or where child care is nearly an exclusively feminine activity, especially during our infancy, infants will associate the fulfillment or frustration of needs with the other-who-is-female. From an infant male (a self-who-is-male) perspective, I think it not a stretch to make the argument that some of the anxiety associated with this relationship will be compounded by the perception of *difference*, and that in patriarchal cultures, this may account for the perpetuation of gendered hierarchy. It is also a rationalization for structural violence in the form of male privileging and female marginalization, as well as the prevalence of more directly violent male behavior toward women, such as rape. Female infants, alternatively, perceive the Other as "same," one with whom the infant *identifies*, with whom the infant shares a category. "Sameness but separateness" may be one basis for the later development of empathy, thus female infant anxieties about the Other are mitigated by the perception of sameness, of identification *with* the caregiver.

Here is one area in which cultural interventions can matter a great deal, for it is not so much the "fact" of difference as the *meaning* assigned to difference that matters. But while gender can indeed be constructed differently across varying cultural contexts (Roscoe 1991), I am here concerned with how it is constructed and socially encoded in states, in identities of citizenship, and in the Western European social order from which the idea of the state was born. Having read and studied both the poststructural critique of modernity as well as some of the diverse cultural and social orders of non-European, indigenous peoples, I find a striking contrast between European social practices and those of many (but certainly not all) nonstate indigenous societies in the form of a relatively higher incidence of more complex constructions of both gender and difference among indigenous cultures and the tendency of modernity to reduce tolerance for ambiguities, including gender ambiguities, in favor of absolutist generalizations, as David Campbell has put it (1998: 90).[24] Although not well studied, this contrast suggests that feminist and other theorists are on the right track when they propose a correlation between patriarchal social order and intolerance of ambiguity.

Cultural variations can matter very much in how or whether the anxieties of infantile dependence are moderated, particularly in relation to gender differences. Infantile dependence is diminished in general, for example, as one grows into a capacity for self-care and self-reliance and as one learns to negotiate the social world through communicative action. But these devel-

opments may play out very differently for girls and boys becoming women
and men, as well as vary across cultures. Combining Kleinian and Lacanian
accounts, the realization of dependence on the Other, accompanied by a
growing awareness of one's gender identity, can generate more anxiety for
boys than girls in the care of women, and may account for what Di Stefano
calls a "fear of engulfment" (1991). For girls, the realization of difference
entails less anxiety only because a female infant understands herself as dependent on one who is the *same*.[25] Someday, she will *become* a woman. If this
is true, then the social structure and relationships surrounding boys during
their maturation process can also make a great deal of difference. To the
extent that infants and young boys have positive contact or even caretaking
relationships with older boys and men, these experiences can ameliorate the
anxieties generated by associating dependency with difference. In Lacanian
terms, boys will look into the mirror provided by such relationships and see
themselves in the future, empowered and mature.[26] Chodorow argues
precisely this when she says that it is the increasing absence and distance of
the father under conditions of modernity that exacerbate the preexisting anxieties of boys attempting to form masculine identities while remaining in the
primary care and company of women. [27]

The second contribution psychoanalytic theory can make here is by
providing a way of discussing how we perceive the world of objects or
Others, particularly in the form of in-group/out-group relations and the widespread phenomenon of enemy-making. Whether one agrees with my arguments about the structure of the self from a psychoanalytic perspective or
not, or whether one can assert a kind of universality to the basis for human
emotional life, we are still left with the fact that group life is frequently
constructed in terms of enemies and allies, in terms of "we" who are the same
and "they" who are different. *This* phenomenon, whether in the form of
sustained adversarial relations or simply ethnocentrism is widespread and
cross-cultural. Whether we approach differences in terms of cultural regions,
or metanarratives, or civilizational streams, the articulation of group identity by contrasting one's own group with a negatively regarded other is widespread, if not universal.

We hate what we are trying *not to be*, and we love those who we think
affirm the qualities we hope to find in ourselves. Perhaps paradoxically, the
belief that the qualities we despise are located in others and *not* in ourselves
enables us to indulge in a denial of our own capacity to express precisely
those qualities. We are most evil when we believe we are not. We alternate
between *demonizing* the Other as a means of disowning what Burack calls
the "disagreeable emotions," or what Alford calls the "unwanted parts of
the self," and *idealizing* the Other in an effort to associate and identify with
and even possess those we regard as embodying qualities we wish to believe
reside within ourselves.

Are there alternative ways of structuring intergroup relations, or, at the very least, are there ways of ameliorating Other-destructive tendencies? The work of Vamik Volkan suggests that enemy-making is inevitable, that we "need" to have enemies, but are there ways of structuring identity that do not rely on negative projections?[28] While the construction of identities based on enemies and allies, good selves and bad others, binary and hierarchical contrasts between "them" and "us," inside/outside, or self/Other relations does seem pervasive, some writers and theorists have struggled with the limits of such analyses. Rhoda Howard-Hassmann, for instance, believes self/Other discourses work against recognition of universal human rights and argues that the insertion of "identity politics" into international relations excludes of the possibility for empathetic relations.[29] Ziauddin Sardar argues that postmodernism "is simply a new wave of domination riding the crest of colonialism and modernity."[30] Iver Neumann struggles with the consequences for theorizing without a subject at all, agreeing with Bauman (1996) that we can neither theorize subjects possessed of fixed and stable identities, nor by destroying all subjectivity in order to avoid fixation.[31] The fact remains that people still very often behave in ways suggested by psychoanalytic theories of self/Other projection in their personal relationships, in the construction of group identities and intergroup relations, in ways that affect public life and political discourse, and in ways that can be mobilized by public leaders. Yet democratic and civic discourse rests on our ability to be self-critical, to see ourselves in a critical light, to acknowledge that *we can do bad things*; and it requires that we develop a capacity to view ourselves from the perspective of others. So there is a direct relationship, I think, between achieving and maintaining psychic integration and emotional maturity on the one hand, and carrying out the cognitive tasks required to keep democracy and civility functional, if not improving, on the other.

Finally, by employing psychoanalytic theory to help us understand the breakdown of the psyche and specific incidences where hatred toward the Other is acted out, we must think in terms of cognitive *positions* rather than stages. Our psychic, emotional, and cognitive lives become more complex, but cognitive simplicity is not displaced by cognitive complexity. Maturity consists of the growing recognition of and coming to terms with the agency of others, and our interdependence on others, our own capacity for both caring and doing harm, and an ability to understand the consequences of our actions (agency) and take responsibility for them. This is achieved by integrating the psyche, creating our own boundaries, respecting the boundaries (and therefore the agency) of others, and being able to empathize with others. Maturity occurs within a network of relationships, familial and social, and within a sociocultural and historical context. Thus the paranoid-schizoid perspective of immature narcissism constitutes both a developmental position experienced in childhood *and* a psychic position to which we may revert at any later time in response to conditions of vulnerability, such as severe stress or trauma.[32]

In the cognitively simple world of the paranoid, immature narcissist, where others are either "same" or "different," different, demonized others are regarded as lacking humanity, as subhuman or inhuman. The ability to acknowledge the humanity of others is thus a benchmark of moral maturity. Most, if not all societies distinguish between the moral competence of children and adults to understand the consequences of behavior and accept responsibility for causing harm to others. The ability to acknowledge Others' humanity entails regarding the Other as distinct and separate, even different from oneself, *while at the same time seeing the sameness of the Other*. Joseph Campbell, discussing the phenomenon of self-sacrifice in Schopenhauer's essay, "The Basis for Morality," argues that in those instances where we respond spontaneously to another's pain or suffering—acts of heroism by ordinary people—the boundaries between self and Other also seem to dissolve, with positive, and caring consequences:

> [W]e forget what is the first law of nature—self-preservation—and that is dissolved, and the impulse is not to preserve yourself but to lose yourself. What is it that makes this possible, not only possible but actual? ... [Schopenhauer] says that this comes from the transcendent realization that you are that [O]ther are the same life, you are the same consciousness. . . .[33]

Self-sacrifice may represent a higher level of moral development, but in structuring our own relationship with other members of our society, it is minimally the ability to acknowledge simultaneously *a connection and a separation—including separation by difference*—on which our ability to respect a basic rule of moral reciprocity and our civility rest.

## Identity, Historicity, and Socialization

The foregoing account portrays a self whose structure can be characterized as moving from a precategorical, preboundaried, and unconscious state of unity with its environment toward a more complex, even fractured and multidimensional existence in which self-consciousness becomes possible, and perhaps we can even say, necessary. In Aaron T. Beck's terminology, as we mature, we develop the ability to intervene in both our cognitive and emotional processes.[34] We do not change how we feel, but we can *choose* how we interpret the significance of our feelings, what stories we tell ourselves about our feelings, and we can choose how to act in relation to our feelings. The self does not "spring forth," mushroomlike, as a fully formed entity. Rather, its contours emerge within a preexisting social world populated by other previously formed selves whose thoughts are structured within the context of linguistic practice. It is within this world of social meaning that self-consciousness develops, in a linguistic world of categories, identities, communicative rules, and actions.[35]

A social constructivist approach takes issue with assertions of both gender and ethnic difference that rely on notions of objectivity, where difference is conceived as organic and essential. It is not the "fact" of difference but the *meaning* assigned to difference that matters. This does not mean that differences are not "real," but that it is the significance they have to social action and analysis in the way in which they are constructed within social processes that counts. The ways in which two people are different[36]—language, religion, cultural affinity, how each identifies herself within a historical narrative—are not as important as *how those differences structure their social relations.*

Unlike our bodies, our social life is not contained within a bounded and unified space. If identity is the way we answer the question "Who am I?" then we may answer the question differently depending on who is asking, when it is being asked, for what purpose the question has been asked, our own purposes in responding to the question, and so on. The answer changes in relation to temporal, emotional, and social context. And if we answer the question by referring to categories, then we are answering by referring the questioner to "signifiers," signs or symbols intended to convey a body of information believed to be mutually understood by the questioner and respondent. Those categories—identities—are constructed through social processes.

But answering the question "Who am I?" does more than convey mutually understood meaning from the respondent to the questioner. It *structures the relationship between the two.* Many, perhaps even most cultures—or rather the languages and symbolic systems of meaning through which cultures are created, maintained, and transformed—contain concepts of unity, difference, opposition, contradiction, and multiplicity, though the meanings vary. When I argue (in my "story of the self") that cognitive and emotional development proceeds from a position of undifferentiated unity with the environment toward the split dimension of an emergent self/Other and then toward a self/Other capable of experiencing and acting on a range of emotions delineated initially by apparently contradictory feelings, I believe that we should be less concerned with whether it is "true" in a fixed an absolute way than with whether it is useful as a basis for cross-cultural comparisons. I have tried not make assumptions about *how* difference, contradiction, opposition, unity, and multiplicity are understood, but rather propose that human cognitive development, and the structure of the self it produces, follows a path from unity to duplicity, to multiplicity, from simple to complex, and that the significance of that experience is interpolated by cultural practices, including language.

Thus when we encounter a culture in which the firmness of individual psychic boundaries seems weak, nonexistent, highly variable, negotiable, and so on, in contrast with the highly bounded individualism of Western cultures, it may not be because the self does not emerge in relation to an Other, but because cultures interpolate the experience of separation and Otherness in different ways.[37] Early child care may be more or less woman-monopolized, or child care may be more or less collectivized, or families may be larger or extended, forming a kind of community in themselves. Specific cultural practices pertaining to the relationship between infant girls and older girls and women, and infant boys and older boys and men, may vary in ways that produce "selves" more or less prone to polarization and projection, to victimization and blaming, on the one hand, or more or less prone to a more complex cognitive structure with a greater sense of agency, responsibility, and tolerance of ambiguity, on the other. One can imagine many other variations on these themes.

Alford, for example, after studying the way Americans/Westerners experience evil, noted that a concept of evil seemed to be absent in Asian cultures. So he interviewed hundreds of Koreans representing many diverse identities (religious, professional, age, gender). What he found was that, although the concept of evil was not present, a fear similar to the fear experienced by Western informants as "evil" in another study was present, though it took the form of a fear of "globalization." Another example pointing to the interpolation of culture in constructing the mutually shared meaning of concepts such as contradiction and opposition comes from Native American cultures, not only in comparing across Native cultures but, broadly speaking, in comparing Native with European cultures. Many Native cultures include religious or metaphysical systems of thought in which the concepts of contradiction and paradox play a central role. Among the Athabaskan it takes the form of Raven, for the Pikuni (Blackfeet) it is Napi, among many Plains, Midwest, and Southwest indigenous cultures it is Trickster or Coyote, and among the Ojibway it is "the inimical figure of Nanbozo who brings positive outcomes from contrary behavior."[38]

At present, there is a tendency for Western writers to assume that the way in which Western thinkers construct opposition and difference is universal, or, according to some postmodern critics, to decloak the socially constructed quality of opposition and binary thinking and then decry all oppositional thinking. In doing so they fail to see among the alternatives that thinking about difference differently itself constitutes an alternative. Egalitarian instead of hierarchical difference, complementarity instead of opposition, mutually constituted and interdependent difference instead of separation. Differences or oppositions can also represent unity. Why can we not accept that opposition is but one dimension of our cognitive life, multiplicity another, and unity another? There is a critical distinction between saying, on the one hand, that "opposition" exists because it is our first stop in the process of developing a bounded self, because opposition is a way of structuring *some* meanings, and quite another to say that the sign "opposition" represents a basic, inescapable, natural, or essential order of objective reality, or that all reality can be understood in oppositional terms. The *meaning* of opposition is epistemologically variable. For example, instead of defining opposition in terms of exclusivity and hierarchical relationships, we might see opposition as mutual constitutive, each element in the opposition necessary to sustain the other, a meaning suggested by the *Tao Te Ching*.

> When people see some things as beautiful,
>     other things become ugly.
> When people see some things as good,
>     other things become bad.
> Being and non-being create each other.
> Difficult and easy support each other.
> High and low depend on each other.
> Before and after follow each other.[39]

The identity of the self, therefore, develops a particular system of meaning. A child learning to speak frequently refers to herself in the third person, eventually locating the named thing other people refer to as "myself." To "learn" that one is a "girl" is also to learn, in Western cultures, what one is *not*—a boy—and so it is with identities constructed in oppositional (and still hierarchical) terms. Identity also develops within the framework of group life, created, contained, and maintained through narrative systems. Two such systems are relevant to this study: identity narratives, and historical narratives. They are not mutually exclusive. "Identity" narratives are often "ethnic,"[40] but religious identity often structures political identities in the same way, as in the case of Northern Ireland, the former Yugoslavia, and the Middle East, and the two are not always entirely distinct (some versions of an Irish Catholic narrative claim also to constitute the "true" or "indigenous" Irish ethnic identity in contrast to the Protestant "settlers," while the Irish Protestant narrative is "British but not English" and so on).

Narratives of collective identify are often "located," at least partly, in historical narratives, although the historical narrative is more inclusive and makes reference to a particular selection and interpretation of events. The historical narrative is then constituted as the "fact" of history, *but told from the perspective of a particular (imagined) collective self.* While collective identity and historical narratives are not mutually exclusive, the distinction is useful because historical narratives tend to be more top-down ("official or authoritative"), whereas narratives of collective identity tend to be more bottom-up (folk knowledge and societal prejudices). Historical narratives, while often perpetuated in private venues such as family, community, and circles of intimate association, have become, as a consequence of publicizing education, an instrument of political agency. Narratives of collective identity, while referencing "official" versions of history, not only fall more into the sphere of informal and private discourse, but often contain folklore, prejudices, and anecdotal accounts. Historical narratives, in contrast, are routinely appropriated to legitimate political acts. This does not mean that the rhetoric of identity collective narratives does not find its way into political discourse—indeed it does—but here we are treading on the territory of nationalism, patriotism, ethnocentrism, and enemy-making. Finally, of course, political leaders frequently convolute the two, particularly in an effort to arouse emotional response.

### Ethnic Conflict Revisited: Inside Looking Out

Until the end of the Cold War, the study of ethnic conflict in political science remained primarily within the domain of comparative politics, with a few exceptions.[41] Since then, the relationship between ethnic conflict and international relations has attracted attention from a growing number of scholars.[42] Three views of the political significance of ethnicity emerge from these studies: a view of ethnicity as primordial, organic, essential, or natural; an instrumental view of ethnicity as a mechanism used by groups for underscoring the legitimacy of political claims to self-determination and/or nationhood; and what is sometimes called a "constructed" view of ethnicity appropriated by elites as a bit of both—the primordial basis for political claims.[43] The more sociohistorical approach taken by Anthony Smith and Benedict Anderson emphasizes the narrative basis for both ethnicity and nationhood.[44] Though opening a space for considering how these narratives operate in the lives of ordinary people caught in extraordinary conflicts, theirs is a more cultural and historical project, one that has been enormously influential in interrogating the link between narratives, identity, and the politics of the modern state.

The perspective I have outlined here conceives of the self as a work in progress, moving from a more or less unconscious sense of unity with its environment, a self that is relatively undifferentiated from the world in which it is born, to become a more bounded being, possessing a separate consciousness of agency of increasing complexity. The self develops a capacity for multiple, variegated, and complex configurations of identity, selfhood, and Otherness, of agency and structures, of ambiguities and contradictions, *including* separation, difference, unity, opposition, and pluralities. The way in which these dimensions of the self and self/Other social relations are structured, understood, and interpreted varies within different cultural and historical contexts. Self/Other boundaries, for example, may be more or less rigid, more or less porous. Opposition does not necessarily generate hierarchy, though in patriarchies it does. Cultures can encourage the development of individual selves that are more or less tolerant of ambiguity and contradiction, maybe even more or less complex or capable of encountering complexity with more or less anxiety.

In the next chapter I will begin taking up the relationship between historical narratives, identity narratives, the construction of the state, and intergroup conflict. Here I have been concerned mainly with laying the theoretical groundwork for arguments pertaining to the social processes involved in the construction and destruction of political identities, the state, intergroup conflict, and the relationship between these processes and a psychosocial account of the self as a citizen of the polity. While such an argument calls into question theories of ethnic conflict that rely on a primordial, organic, or naturalized account of ethnic identity and its consequences for group life, we are still left with two theoretical propositions. First, people often think of their political interests *as if* ethnicity mattered, and second, political leaders employing images of primordial solidarity make rhetorical claims to political entitlement grounded in the presumption of a relationship between imagined primordial identity and political authority.

# CHAPTER 4

# Identity and (Ethnic) Conflict in the Former Yugoslavia: In Their Own Words

I really don't know what identity is, but certainly it is a powerful source of grievance, or explanation for grievance. Everybody believes that he was wronged in the former Yugoslavia. . . .

—V.D., Belgrade, 1995

The belief that problems of identity and political violence at the end of the twentieth century occur primarily in non-Western, non-European settings may serve more to reassure to Westerners that they are insulated from such threats than to usefully or accurately circumscribe a category of political violence. As a term reserved for twentieth-century political violence in mostly non-Western settings, ethnic conflict also conspicuously excludes the experience of Western societies historically, so that we might imagine that "ethnic violence" is somehow different from the history of violence associated with Western state-making.[1]

Like most citizens of modern nation-states, people living in Yugoslavia identified themselves in terms of multiple, intersecting, and sometimes overlapping identities, particularly those to which we attribute political significance—ethnic, religious, ideological, and national. Yugoslavs could be Slovenian, Croatian, Serbian, Montenegrin, Macedonian, Hungarian, Albanian, Wallach or Vlach, Turk, Slovak, German, Romanian, Bulgarian, Italian, Ruthenian,[2] Russian, and, at the same time Yugoslav. Just as one could be French, Anglo, or Native *and* Canadian; black, white (Swedish, Italian, Irish, English, German), Hispanic, Native, Asian *and* American; Protestant or Catholic *and* Irish; Huguenot or Catholic *and* French, and so on. The problem is that many compound identities have been constituted as categories serving to rationalize marginalization, discrimination, outright violence against certain groups at the hands of another. These conflicts have not been rectified satisfactorily or peacefully. Many remain problematic.

## Problematizing "Ethnic Conflict"

A recent educational film entitled *Ethnic Identity, Regional Conflict, and Peacekeeping Initiatives*, made in 1999 by Palm Plus Productions, identified eighteen ongoing so-called "ethnic wars": one in Europe, it said, and one in Latin America, six in Asia, and ten in Africa (without being more specific). But are such uses of the term "ethnic conflict" (and its corollary, "ethnic war") just a variation on terms like "ancient hatreds" or "age-old antagonisms" that once dominated reports in the Western media on violence in former Yugoslavia? Does the notion of "ethnic conflict" really just bolster the image and identity of "Western" societies as "progressive" vis-à-vis the non-Western Others who are still mired in "tribalism"?[3] In the words of a well-educated respondent from Belgrade:

> *S.S., Belgrade, 1995*
> I'll give you an example of an arrogance. Very often people talk about European identity, but by that they *really* mean western European, of course, pretending that half of Europe—eastern and central Europe— doesn't exist or doesn't count. Then of course if you are the modest European, you will explain that European identity is based on humanism, democracy, human rights, a market economy, and so on, but what about Nazism? Nazism originated in Europe! *Western* Europe! It wasn't in the Balkans that six million Jews were killed but rather in the midst of Western Europe.

We seem too eager to use the term "ethnic conflict" uncritically, as if its meaning were self-evident, as if the category "ethnic" were organic, and most often, as if it were primarily a non-Western problem. But should the public violence committed and the private violence sanctioned against Native Americans in the nineteenth century count as "ethnic conflict"? To many nonindigenous peoples, it was "state-making," albeit within the ideological construct of Manifest Destiny. For many indigenous peoples, it was a genocide. U.S. government policies intentionally mobilized the European settler population to carry out a variety of actions including publically sanctioned violence, aimed at destroying the ability of indigenous peoples to continue living their way of life, dispossessing them of their economic base, and forcing their cultural assimilation The objective of American state-building was deliberately to reduce the number of indigenous people—some argued to the point of nonexistence—and take control of their resources. These objectives were accomplished for the most part by force. The project was mythologized in American historical narratives as the American Manifest Destiny, and it rationalized the intentional starvation, forced relocation, and "ethnic cleansing" of enough Native people in the territory west of the Mississippi to reduce the extant Native peoples from between ten and twenty million in 1789 to fewer than a quarter of a million a century later, to occupants of small, economically marginal enclaves known as "reservations."

Similarly, should we talk about the violence of South African apartheid as a case of "ethnic conflict"? What about the inner-city riots prompted by long-standing racial discrimination and sparked by the civil rights movement in the United States? Why do we include conflict involving "Slavic" Catholics (Croats), Orthodox (Serbs), and Muslims (Bosniaks or Bosnian Muslims) in the category of "ethnic conflict," while excluding conflicts in Northern Ireland and the Middle East in which parties are distinguished primarily by religious identities?

I am not arguing that high intensity intergroup violence characterized by the rhetoric of ethnic tension has not occurred most recently more frequently in non-European settings. Nor am I arguing that there are not important differences among the cases cited above. But let me open a space to consider two things precluded by a presumption that the violence of American Manifest Destiny, South African apartheid, the "troubles" in Northern Ireland, and war in the Middle East are categorically distinct from the "ethnic conflict" in Yugoslavia, Rwanda, Ethiopia/Eritrea, and elsewhere in non-Western settings. First, the similarities may be as important as the differences, and second, such distinctions do not adequately problematize the relationship between identity and political violence, including state-building violence. The fact that Western policy-makers and journalists eventually abandoned the language of "ancient hatreds" does not tell us why it was such an appealing explanation to begin with, nor does the use of the term "ethnic conflict" in reference to what happened in Yugoslavia enable us to interrogate its causes free of the assumption that such problems are more likely to occur in "undemocratic," politically "underdeveloped," and generally "non-Western"—in other words, backward—societies.

Returning to the configuration of multiple, intersecting, and overlapping identities that exists today to some extent in all states, how is it that "Yugoslav" as a unifying and civic identity failed in the face of challenges hurled at it through inflammatory nationalist rhetoric? Should we think of "Yugoslavia" as an "artificial" state and "Yugoslav," therefore, as an "artificial" identity and one therefore ultimately doomed to failure at some point?

One problem with the idea of "artificial" states is that it implies that "natural" states or "natural" national identities also exist, in fact are the norm against which we perceive the "artificiality" of other states. But was Yugoslavia *more* artificial than, for example, the United States? Canada? Britain? Why and how did "American" identity and the "American" state survive and Yugoslavia fail? One might argue that "democracy" makes the difference. But democracy is not a solid and absolute condition. Rather, it is a set of conditions—among them, free and competitive elections; the presence of pluralistic associations; free and open expression of ideas; majority, plurality, or coalition rule *coupled with* the right of minority expression and participation; free and open borders; and more. Yugoslavia was certainly more democratic than certain other communist states and, I think it is fair to say, less democratic than its Western European neighbors. But we cannot simply say it was an undemocratic society and, for that reason, a failed state that descended rapidly into the most personal, brutal, and deviant forms of mass violence.

Neither does the democracy explanation work when applied to the presumed "success" of Western societies in averting conflict and violence. Less than one hundred years into its own experiment with democracy, a less democratic America *was* embroiled in civil war, and the existence, structure, and future of an American state was, at that time, uncertain. Democracy in Great Britain, a state where the "ethnic" identities of the Scots, Welsh, and Irish were supposed to coexist peacefully even though they were incorporated into "Great Britain" by force or at least without consent, has not succeeded in resolving the identity conflict between Irish Catholics, many of whom do not consider themselves British, and the Irish Protestants, many of whom consider their British identity—as citizens—to take political precedence over their "ethnic Irishness." Do indigenous peoples in Canada consider themselves Canadian citizens, or citizens of their indigenous communities, or both?[4] A significant number of Iroquois (Haudenosaunee) for instance, maintain that they cannot be citizens of both the Canadian state and the Haudenosaunee (or Iroquois Confederacy), and so in World War II, refusing to be drafted by the American state, the Haudenosaunee traditional government independently declared war on the Axis powers.[5] Though unlikely to produce the kind of violence associated with the breakdown of Yugoslavia, identity conflicts between French and Anglo Canadians have forestalled constitutional revision for over a decade. Democracies are more likely to channel identity conflicts peacefully, but they are not immune to such conflicts.

Perhaps the problem of "ethnic conflict" can more usefully be conceived as conflict mobilized around *identity discourses*. Antagonistic responses by those marginalized on the basis of identity often culminate in violent behavior rationalized through politically constructed narratives of oppression/liberation. This does not mean that narratives of oppression/liberation are not based on lived experiences, though historical and cultural symbolisms are also often appropriated in support of political projects. Neither does it mean that narratives of oppression/liberation *ipso facto* constitute legitimate grievances and claims. But in order to develop a picture of how the relationship between identity and political violence is constructed in cognitive and emotional terms, we need to suspend evaluations of "truth" claims made in connection with identity and conflict and focus instead on how identity and historical narratives figure into peoples' stories about the conflict and their experience of it. For the remainder of this chapter I will examine testimonial evidence regarding the way people in (and escaping from) the conflict environment understood the issue of identity in relation to the breakdown of civility and descent into violence. Much of the evidence comes from interviews done between 1995 and 1998,[6] but I have supplemented it with rather lengthy passages from several testimonial sources covering earlier stages of the conflict. These include two of former Yugoslavia's most outspoken critics, Dubravka Ugrešić and Slavenka Drakulić, both originally from Croatia, though whether they are "Croatian" only each of them could say,[7] and excerpts published by Central European University from essays by young émigrés. These firsthand, witness accounts offer unique insights into questions such as: How was "Yugoslav" identity constituted and how did it interface with various "ethnic" identities? How did people in Yugoslavia encounter "Otherness"? And what was the role of historical narratives in constructing Yugoslav and other identities?

## Well You See I Am Yugoslav, But There Is No Yugoslavia[8]

"Twice there was a country," says Lampe, and so twice there were Yugoslavs. Some referred to the "first" Yugoslavia as the "old Yugoslavia."[9] For others, the (his)story of Yugoslavia was more or less continuous, if not seamless, and cohesive. Like most histories, the earlier chapter was simply reinterpreted, in the case of Yugoslavia, with the hindsight of Tito's particular version of Marxist historical inevitability. Structurally speaking, if the first Yugoslavia was created to secure the independence of various South Slav peoples from the competing imperial Goliaths during a historical moment of imperial weakness, then the second Yugoslavia represented both a continuation of the first and an extension of that security against a future of competing postimperial superpower states. Anti-imperialism has historically been a powerful force for unity in both the nineteenth and twentieth centuries among the peoples western Europeans called "South Slavs," taking the form of nationalism in the nineteenth century, and culminating in the Austrian archduke's assassination. But since the fascist enemies during World War II ascended under the banner and rhetoric of nationalism, anti-imperialism in Yugoslavia and elsewhere in central and eastern Europe was tied to the antifascist partisan movement, which was subsequently transformed from a force of resistance to an ideological basis for the new Yugoslavia. In the words of one young émigré:

> We knew that this state was no recent creation, that it dated from 1918. But, at the same time, we were convinced that our state's real history did not begin until the Second World War, that everything before then was just a necessary prelude to the real thing. I use the word "necessary" delib-

erately, to evoke the official Yugoslav line of the late sixties and seventies, which linked the Marxist ideology of the inevitable transition of capitalism to socialism to the Titoist proclamation of "socialism with a human face." This version of socialism centered on the worker and on dismantling the power of the state.[10]

Yugoslav identity in the aftermath of World War II was thus grounded in two centuries of anti-imperialism, the heroism of the partisans, and an emerging socialist ideological program. As the tentacles of Cold War competition extended their global reach, however, and Europe became increasingly polarized around the East–West axis, Tito articulated a Yugoslav identity distinct from the alleged excesses and extremes of both Soviet-style communism and Western capitalism. Having worked for Comintern in Moscow before the war, Tito knew Soviet communism from the inside out. In contrast with Soviet communism, Tito's postwar communist model was based on popular support (though as much or more as an antifascist than a communist movement) and intellectual openness.[11] "Titoism," was constructed as a counterdiscourse to both Western capitalism and Stalinist communism. Rejecting Stalin's idea of an international communism with Moscow at the center, Tito officially split with his former ally in 1948. Thus the Otherness out of which postwar Yugoslav identity was carved was complex. Onto the normative foundation of anticapitalist Marxist populism, a distinctly Yugoslav identity was grafted. It was embodied in the anti-Stalinist, partisan hero Tito and articulated through a variety of constitutional and policy moves that increasingly emphasized the "socialist" rather than communist basis for Yugoslav society, "self-management" in the economy, and the coexistence, however uneasy, of national ethnic and socialistic civic identities as the former, like the state, would presumably wither away. Thus, in contrast to Soviet communism, Yugoslavia embodied "socialism with a human face," with schoolchildren daily reciting the slogan "Brotherhood and Unity" while their parents traveled from Belgrade to Zagreb on the highway bearing the slogan's name. Dubravka Ugrešić reflects on reminiscences of her "Yugoslav" childhood:

> When I went to school I learned that Yugoslavia was a country which consisted of six republics and two autonomous regions, six national communities and several national minorities.... I learned that Yugoslavia had three large religious communities—Catholic, Orthodox and Muslim— and a lot of smaller ones. I learned that Yugoslavia was a small, beautiful country in the hilly Balkans. I learned that I must preserve brotherhood and unity like the apple of my eye. This was some kind of slogan, whose true meaning I did not really understand. I was probably confused by the poetic image *apple of my eye....*
> In my first documents, where I had to fill in "nationality," I wrote

"Yugoslav." I grew up within an ideological framework historians and political scientists call "Titoism."[12]

The history lessons Ugrešić learned—and more—also appear simply but eloquently stated in an essay written by this young émigré:

The second Yugoslavia, which encompassed six republics, several nations and nationalities of difference religions and cultural and political persuasions, violently disintegrated in mid-1991.... The entire region of the former Yugoslavia and all its peoples who now live in their own separate little states have been set back in every respect. The reputation of this once universally acknowledged country has been torn to shreds....

The year 1991, when the entire Eastern socialist bloc collapsed, brought Yugoslavia the possibility of deciding its future and fate in a new, democratic way. For the first time people were able to take part in genuine democratic elections, with real choices. The problem, in my opinion, was the absence of an interim period, a psychological pause....

1991 was a humiliating year for everyone who upheld, in mind and deed, the idea of a democratic, open society....[13]

There were two groups for whom identification with "Yugoslav" as a category of national identity was also primarily a practical matter: Bosnian Muslims, who prior to 1971 were not represented in the census as a category of ethnic nationality,[14] and the people in, or the children of, ethnically mixed marriages—somewhere around 1.5 million, though I often heard "nobody knows, really." But this does not tell us what Yugoslav *meant* to the 1.5 million people who identified themselves this way in the 1980 census, nor does it say anything about those who were not from mixed marriages and identified themselves as Yugoslav, either officially or unofficially. It does not tell us whether "Yugoslav" had different meanings to different people. For some it was inclusive and pluralistic by definition, a way of locating oneself within a cosmopolitan political landscape, providing such an identity in ways that "ethnic" identities could not, as the words of another young student reveal: "I am a Yugoslav from Belgrade. And let's get something straight: I am not the product of a mixed marriage, that's not why I feel Yugoslav. I am a Yugoslav by conviction."[15]

The following interview passages reveal how complex Yugoslav identity could be—how contestable and contradictory, particularly as people attempted to rectify the relationship between Yugoslav identity and the "ethnic" identities of their "nationality."

*R.N., Belgrade, 1995*
I think there was a deeper kind of identity that referred both to the Yugoslav position in the world, the non-alignment, a sort of a special status in

the Eastern European world as well, the importance that we attached to this country, the fact that we could cross the borders very easily in comparison to the other Eastern European countries, there was a general identity on that level . . . and as soon as this structure was dismantled, other levels of identity became dominant.

*S.S., Belgrade, 1995*
Now we have in all ex-Yugoslavia some people who are Yugoslavs—1.5 million said they were Yugoslavs, not a big amount. Maybe five percent of all inhabitants. But they were the people who had a background from various nations and also some who chose to be identified as Yugoslav for a political reasons. For example, the people who were involved in the Partisan movement. They wanted to be citizens in a Yugoslav state with all the people of all the nationalities. To be honest, there is also something political in my wish to be a Yugoslav, something in my political background . . . but now other people do not think like me.

*A.J., Jajce, 1997*
I was a Yugoslav before the war and nothing else. We were all Yugoslavs in my family. For me it meant that if I went somewhere and said that I was Yugoslavian, I didn't want to be asked about my religion, about politics, I just wanted people to see me as a guy from the Balkans who wants to have fun and is always ready to make a joke about something.

*D.S., Belgrade 1995*
I always say when asked "What is your identity?" that I am a Yugoslav. Why? I explain that because I was born in the Yugoslav state, and also the fact that both of my parents and grandparents are Serbs, although my father is from Bosnia. But I also mean that without Yugoslavia Bosnia would be part of another country, so that was my reason for saying I am Yugoslav. It included all my family who were Serbs. Yugoslavia holds the best possibility for all Serbs living in one state. Now I say "ex-Yugoslavia."

*S.R., Sarajevo, 1997*
Yugoslavia was a place where people who were different could live together as neighbors. People who lived in that place were Yugoslavs. I was a Yugoslav. I still feel myself to be Yugoslav, which does not conflict with my being Muslim. You can't just make the feeling go away. We kept believing in that spirit, even during the worst of the bombing here.

*S.B., Belgrade, 1995*
Maybe I am a special case because since childhood I have been living all over the world. Maybe by talking about Yugoslav identity I could talk about social values, certain social values that we had been socialized to

believe in. There are certain things common to a whole generation. I was
born in 1948. So I was in the postwar generation. The people I know
and I can compare my identity to are liberal, because Yugoslavia was a
liberal idea.

### D.C., Zadar, 1997

This was a private thing. . . . No, I was a Yugoslav. For me national identity didn't mean anything. The way I was raised, I didn't feel that I was a
Croat because I was surrounded by Albanians, Serbs, Croats, and we were
all Yugoslavs. My father was a Yugoslav, so I was a member of the
Communist Party. Afterward I found out it was the biggest lie they sold
me in my whole life.

   Three years ago I was living the life I wanted. And then my country
was torn apart by political and national conflict. My father is a Croat, my
mother a Serb. I was supposed to be a Croat. We lived in Belgrade, the
capital of Serbia. When war broke out, anyone who had any links to
Croatia, or was a Croat, was threatened, physically, and mentally
mistreated. Many lost their jobs, like my father, although he had been very
successful in his work. I dared not mention my national origin at school.
But then questionnaires were introduced into all schools, asking students
about their place of birth, their nationality, where their parents were from,
and so on. Under "Nationality" I wanted to say: "Yugoslav," but it was
not allowed. (Young university student in exile, from *Children of Atlantis:
Voices from the Former Yugoslavia.*)[16]

The following passages indicate how differently two individuals from
"Croatia" felt about the issue of Croat versus Yugoslav identity. Some difference can be attributed to their generations; the first was in his early thirties
at the time of the interview, and Drakulić, author of the second, was about
ten years older. But they were *contemporaries* at the time of the breakup of
Yugoslavia:

### M.B., Zagreb, 1997

Being Yugoslav never had much meaning for me. It was a Serb identity. It
was their reward for being on the winning side in the two world wars. They
were the ones who wanted a communist government. They were mostly
the ones who worked for the government, and the capitol of Yugoslavia
was in Belgrade. Maybe it should have been in Sarajevo, but it was in
Belgrade, and the perception was that Yugoslavia was dominated by Serbs.

Says Drakulić:

I have to admit that for me, as for many of my friends born after World
War II, being Croat has no special meaning. Not only was I educated to

believe that the whole territory of ex-Yugoslavia was my homeland, but because we could freely travel abroad (while people of the Eastern bloc countries couldn't), I almost believed that borders, as well as nationalities, existed only in people's heads. Moreover, the youth culture of 1968 brought us even closer to the world through rock music, demonstrations, books, and the English language. We had so much in common with the West that in fact we mentally belonged there.[17]

Even while some non-Serbs — Croats are most willing to make this observation — maintained the perception that Yugoslavia was "dominated by Serbs," from the perspective of at least some Serbs, Yugoslavia itself was the fulfillment of an (imagined, perhaps) historic wish to "unite all Serbs in one state," although they did not all live in one republic.

### D.S., Belgrade, 1995

I think about my national identity very seldom, maybe because I am living in Serbia where Serbs are the majority, but maybe the other thing is that Serbs who are living in Bosnia or Croatia, where the question of national identity is a daily question, must think about it more often. But as for me personally, I see myself as a Serb, and as Orthodox, but I feel this is my private life. In official life before 1991 I never spoke or thought about my national identity, only if someone directly asked me, then I would say "Serb" or "Orthodox." But it should not be important in public life. Unfortunately in the past five years it became very important, you know.

In Croatia some developed a feeling of resentment toward Serb hegemony, which was in part expressed during the nationalist revival of the Croatian Spring in 1971. Discontent among Croatians was aggravated by other developments following Tito's death, including a commercial banking scandal with ties to Belgrade and the perception that Belgrade was responsible for the policy of redistributing wealth from Croatia and Slovenia to the most "backward" areas of Yugoslavia, Kosovo, and Montenegro.

In addition to the linkage between grievances and identity, patterns regarding the meaning of and relationship among various identities were clear among people I interviewed between 1995 and 1998. Bosnian Muslims, for example, were as a rule more inclined to identify themselves as Yugoslav, particularly in a civic and multicultural sense. This was no doubt in part attributable to the fact that prior to the 1971 census, "Muslim" (used by Bosnian Muslims) was not listed as a nationality, and the majority had been accustomed to dentifying themselves in the "Yugoslav, ethnically undeclared" category until then. The positive identification of Bosnian Muslims with the idea of being civic Yugoslavs to some extent follows from the fact that Muslim nationalism had only recently become politicized. "Yugoslav" may have been a "safe" place to be Muslim in Yugoslavia, and in Europe. Although many Muslims were partisans, the fact that some Muslim leaders during World War II did ally with and participate in the Croatian puppet regime left Bosnian Muslims as a group vulnerable to the charge of collaboration. Identifying themselves as "Yugoslavs" was therefore a way of insulating themselves against these charges, of proving their loyalty to the partisan vision of Yugoslavia, affirming a positive relationship with Yugoslav state-building and its partisan roots. And while some Bosnian Muslims were religious before the onset of nationalized violence and antagonistic nationalisms, there was a strong feeling that "Bosnian Muslim" constituted an identity with as much cultural as religious significance. Bosnian Muslims were perceived to be the *least* nationalistic of the peoples who formed the second Yugoslav state.[18]

But I met people everywhere, not only Bosnian Muslims, who even in 1995 and afterward still positively identified themselves with Yugoslavia in a civic and multicultural sense. There were "Yugoslavs" in Croatia, though when I was there in 1997 and 1998 it seemed more difficult to be Yugoslav in Croatia than, for instance, to be "Yugo-nostalgic" in either Slovenia or Bosnia. The situation in Serbia is slightly different, because some still claim that Serbia and Montenegro together constitute "Yugoslavia," albeit a "rump state" Other Serbs see this as nonsense. The loss of a civic and multicultural Yugoslav identity is also deeply deplored by some in Serbia:

*M.O., Belgrade, 1995*
I belong to that way of thinking, of being a Yugoslav and living my whole life in Yugoslavia. That was my life and this Serbian nationalism is something I just can't believe now. For me Yugoslavia and my Yugoslav identity was reality, that was my life, and now it doesn't exist at all. The way they put it forward now, and what they understand being Yugoslav here in Serbia is not what I identify with.

*S.B., Belgrade, 1995*
I don't have a national ethnic group identity. I was brought up as Yugoslav. I am well traveled and I have only a Yugoslav identity. I can't help it. I can't relate to any ethnic identity. I have maybe a regional identity, maybe from my childhood—my grandmother was from Dalmatia. I am from Belgrade. I had only a Yugoslav identity and you see there is nothing left to compare it to; there is no Yugoslavia. I immediately rejected the situation here when it started, this new nationalism, and I was very much against the idea of an ethnic identity. I just don't feel affinity with any national identity. I could not identify with Serbian national interests. I don't see what that is.

Or again, in the words of Slavenka Drakulić:

> It was usually on 29 November, Republic Day, or some other national holiday. . . . Dressed in blue caps decorated with red stars and with red kerchiefs around our necks, we dutifully waved paper Communist Party flags, chanting "Long live Comrade Tito! Tito! The party!"—while black limousines drove by. There was another slogan we used to shout on such occasions, glancing at our teacher, who would give us a sign to start. "Bro-ther-hood! U-ni-ty!" We yelled with all our might, as if we were casting a spell . . . we were told to shout the slogan and clap our hands but never to question what those words meant. And when I did it was too late. Brothers started to kill one another, and unity fell apart, as if Yugoslavia were only part of a communist fairy tale . . . the communist state never allowed devel-opment of a civil society; it oppressed ethnic, national and religious beliefs, permitting only class identification; and in the end, communist leaders manipulated these beliefs, playing one nationality against another to keep themselves in power for as long as they could. Even if the price was war.[19]

"Yugoslavs," said the man in Belgrade, "are dinosaurs. Disappeared."[20]

## National and Ethnic Identities

It is sometimes said that Tito constructed republican boundaries so that the largest ethnic group—the Serbs—would be territorially and jurisdictionally split between Bosnia, Croatia, and Serbia, preventing them from dominating Yugoslav politics. Milošević and other Serb nationalists mobilized the Serbian masses on the basis of the alleged grievance that the move of granting autonomous status to Vojvodina and Kosovo was deliberately aimed at reducing Serb capacity for effective self-determination within Serbia proper. The Slovenes, Croats, Montenegrins, and Macedonians, Serb nationalists complained, all constituted majorities within their republics and their self-determination was not impaired by the presence of any "autonomous" regions.

There were other ways in which Tito is said to have created "ethnic balance of power"—interlocking checks and balances, a plural presidency, and multiethnic federalism. Although we will never know what Tito was thinking or—perhaps more importantly from the standpoint of the mythology surrounding his leadership—his motives, it seems unlikely that any sort of arrangement other than some attempt to find accommodation between ethnonational and federal-national interests would have been viable in 1945, whether undertaken by Tito or anyone else. This is underscored by the way Hitler's attempt to create a fascist empire played out among competing nationalisms in the complex Yugoslav civil war. Perhaps, like a good communist ideologue, Tito really did expect ethnic cleavages, like those of economic class, to "wither away." Americans at the time were, after all, expecting their own "melting pot" to create an American stew. In any event, institutionalizing the link between ethnic identities and political participation in Yugoslavia created a contradiction that was never resolved.

As in other communist states, institutional relationships were overshadowed by party politics. In Yugoslavia, the federal-republican party structure further thwarted efforts to achieve a level of party unity on which any Yugoslav-wide civic culture could be grounded. These tensions climaxed, between 1967–1972 during the "Croatian Crisis,"[21] so-named because of the leading role played by Croatian liberal-nationalists. Though its leaders were defeated and purged, the question of republican decentralization as a response to fears of Serb hegemony and assimilation was never resolved. Solidarity within the Yugoslav state depended on the creation of a Yugoslav civic identity, but the structure of multiethnic federalism only punished people for declaring "Yugoslav" as their indentity by diminishing their capacity for political participation. This seemed quite clear to a Belgrade man:

*M.P., Belgrade, 1995*
In the ex-Yugoslavia one could not politically identify as an individual, you know, because all political representations went through the nationalities. So I had to be Serb in order to have my identity on a federal level because we did not have one normal citizens' chamber. So I could not be represented as an individual or a citizen member of civil society because it was necessary to have representation through a national group at the federal level. In Yugoslavia at the end of the eighties we had to be Serbs, Croats, Muslims, which is why "Muslim" became a nationality in 1974 due to constitutional amendments. But privately it didn't seem to matter.

And so as "in the new state of Croatia, no one is allowed not to be a Croat,"[22] in former Yugoslavia, ex-Yugoslaiva, the Yugoslav successor states, in fact it also became impossible to remain a Yugoslav, even if one wanted to, as the following story illustrates:

I was born in 1974 in Zenica, Bosnia-Hercegovina. My father is a Serb and my mother is a Muslim. Tradition and my family name dictate that I should be of Serbian nationality, but I have always felt Yugoslav. I spent the first six years of my life in Zenica, then we moved to Karlovac, Croatia, where I finished high school. . . . But then the war broke out in Croatia. . . . My entire family was persecuted. Eventually we were forced to leave and go to Belgrade, where my father's sister lived. But our troubles did not end there: my mother was Muslim, and I had a Croatian accent. Nobody wanted to talk to me. I was bullied because of my dialect. We realized that we could not stay there either. Again we had to flee. And, even worse, to separate. . . . My father had to find a job, to support us. He went to Krajina to work for the Serb army. (S.Z., London; Lešić, 1995, p. 75)

As one of the 1.5 million people from mixed marriage families who identified themselves as "Yugoslav," this young person's family flees from one new "state" to another, telling us finally that his or her father, unable to settle and secure his family in the climate of war and nationalism, must *become* a "Serb" in order to find employment—as a "Bosnian Serb" soldier in the Krajina. This is not at all consistent with "ethnic conflict" explanations of the war. It was in no way "natural" for him to be a "Serb"; in fact he tried *not* to reduce his identity to nationalistic terms. Likewise, there was nothing "natural" about his participation in "ethnic conflict" with those Croats or Muslims who, just months before, had been his fellow Yugoslavs.

Drakulić laments her own struggle against nationalism:

In the end, none of that helped me. Along with millions of other Croats, I was pinned to the wall of nationhood—not only by outside pressures from Serbia and the Federal Army, but by national homogenization within Croatia itself. That is what the war is doing to us, reducing us to one dimension: the Nation. The trouble with this nationhood, however, is that whereas before, I was defined by my education, my job, my ideas, my character—and yes, my nationality, too—now I feel stripped of all that. I am nobody because I am not a person any more. I am one of 4.5 million Croats.[23]

While in Zagreb, like Belgrade, streets and squares were being renamed to reflect the symbolism of various historical nationalist movements, in Bosnia-Herzegovina efforts to create large swaths of ethnically homogeneous territory contiguous to the new Croatian and Serbian states included forced relocation, or "ethnic cleansing," forced assimilation, and cultural destruction. By the end of 1994, it was estimated that some 450 villages and towns had been completely destroyed, including 800 mosques, 128 Catholic churches, ten Orthodox churches, and three synagogues.[24] In a sealed indictment issued in 1995, General Tihomir Blaskić was charged with violations of international humanitarian law against Bosnian Muslims while commanding the armed forces of the Croatian Defense Council (known as the "HVO") in the Lasva Valley area of Bosnia-Herzegovina, where Bosnian Croats had declared independence for the "Croatian Republic of Herceg-Bosna." Although the area contained an ethnically mixed Croat and Muslim population and many Hague witnesses described good interethnic relations before the war, the Croatian-controlled government of the so-called Republic initiated a policy requiring the use of Croatian language throughout the schools and in other public venues. During General Blaskić's trial, the prosecution read from an HVO policy statement: "There is no Bosnian language, and it is an insult to the Croatians when anyone tries to make the Croatian language into some kind of Bosnian language."[25]

Official acts aimed at evoking ethnonationalist sentiments contrasted sharply with the resistance I heard so often expressed by many of the "ordinary" people in all of the former republics. In the words of one man from Belgrade: "My identity is a private matter. It is the business of me and my family, what holidays we celebrate, for example, but it is not and should not be the business of politicians. It should not be a matter of public, political concern."[26]

People in the Yugoslav successor states think now much more about the question of identity, about the difference between civic and ethnic identity, and about the possibility and significance of a distinction between the two. When asked to discuss their own identity and to comment on the general problem of identity in relation to the conflict, people were very reflective, as the following passages indicate.

### D.C., Korcula, 1998

When I am outside of Croatia I am more Croatian, but when I am here it doesn't matter, I am a local guy, I am from Dalmatia. I love my coast, my sea, Dalmatia, Zadar is my place where I was born. When I go to Zagreb, I like the people there, but there is a difference. When you travel outside of Croatia you show people that Croats are not some barbaric tribe, that we have a civilized way of thinking . . . if I meet someone from Great Britain or France, he respects me because I am from a civil society which is Croatia. But if we have to spend too much time every day of our lives proving that we are Croats among ourselves, we are going to lose the point of national identity and we are going to look very stupid.

### D.J., Belgrade, 1995

Now we have a crisis of identity. It is not easy for ordinary people to say what is their identity. Yugoslav, for example. What is that? . . . I have friends who were born in Croatia. What is Serbian national identity? Is it an ethnic community? But it is not possible to keep together all Serbs. Okay at the beginning of the war people accepted this idea of national identity as the reason for the war. But how shall we make Serbia into an organization based on national identity? Serbia is a multinational state, even without the other republics—Croatia, Slovenia, Bosnia-Herzegovina—it is still a multinational state. We have Albanians in Kosovo, Muslims in Sandzak, Hungarians and Croats and others in Vojvodina. We cannot ethnically cleanse even Serbia!

*R.N., Belgrade, 1995*
I would think that all along the Yugoslav category was rather a minority in itself, the figures were always very small. People identified themselves as Yugoslavs, and that is one of the most unprotected minorities now. I would think that with the disappearance of the state, whatever was the prevailing image of Yugoslavia has become so negative that very few people will identify with it, or at least it is perceived as so negative or as a completely futile project, so units of national identity became dominant.

*S.R., Sarajevo, 1997*
Economic development usually brings people in one country into contact with one another so they realize their interdependence, and from this develops a sense of civic identity. A small percentage may think like me, but for the majority their identity was much more tied to their nationality at the local or regional level, like Muslims. So they identified on the basis of their own local differences.

*R.S., Belgrade, 1995*
We had trouble in ex-Yugoslavia because every nation had a different factor on which they based national identification—Serbs and Montenegrins, Serbs and Croats and so on. Now we are supposed to base our identity on religious differences. I must also say that before all of this conflict, people did not make so much of their religion, it was more like a cultural practice than strongly held religious beliefs. We didn't have that many people who went to church. Something like 97 percent of Muslims did not practice religion. I even heard this morning of Muslims who came from Bosnia to talk to Milošević who even had a drink with him. But when the war started they suddenly profess faith in the company of others. Because of the war they need to profess religion now, so they won't be criticized by their own people.

In the following interview, the respondent tries to explain that there have always been multiple identities among the people in the territory of Serbia, but that state-building heightens nationalist mythologies. The respondent has also obviously been influenced by the metaphor of a multicultural "melting pot"—ironically calling it a "boiling pot"—and the idea of a civic identity distinct from ethnic identity, but is not entirely clear about the relationship between civic and ethnic identity.

*R.N., Belgrade, 1995*
With the state, for example in Serbia under Turkish rule, there were many different people. Many Serbian people now try to say that there were always only Serbs here, but there were the Vlachs, Albanians, Muslims and

so on. It was always a boiling pot. But national identity became important when we began to try to build an independent state. There were people who thought they were Serbs because they were born in Serbia, even if they were Jewish. A lot of people changed their names to Slavicize them. A lot of people had cultural or religious celebrations in their homes. A lot of Jews wanted to become Serbs and practice Serbian traditions.

The following respondent is quoted at greater length because here we see how confusing it can be to think in a logical way about the relationship between identity and political community when the relationship between the two becomes contestable:

*D.S., Belgrade, 1995*
We have two possible bases for national identification—religion and territory, though people are now trying to make language a basis for their differences. But religion is not enough by itself for one's national identity. For example, Montenegrins and Serbs are both Orthodox, but we have differences with some people in Montenegro who say they are not Serbs, they say they are Montenegrins and they base that on a claim of territory and some historical idea of a Montenegrin state. Maybe thirty percent of Montenegrins at this time think like this, and they say they want independence. Maybe this is similar to the relationship between Austrians and Germans, the relationship between Montenegrins and Serbs. Or maybe like Swiss Germans who say they are not Germans, and what makes the difference between them is territory and to some extent, language, and local identity.

[The respondent is somewhat confused when he then tries to apply this logic to the national identity of Serbs in Croatia.] In Yugoslavia we have a mixture of various principles on which national identity can be based. Language is not enough by itself. Culture, well that is not enough because our cultures are similar. We have a mixture, and different people base their national identity on different things. Religion, for example. The Serbs in Croatia know they are still Serbs because they are Orthodox. This is odd because many Croats say that religion is the main trait for their national identity, Croats are Catholics, Serbs are Orthodox. But the Serbs in Croatia are supposed to believe that they can be citizens of Croatia when they call it a Catholic state? Some say that the state is constituted through history. But for Muslims we have only one characteristic and that is religion. When the Muslims became a nation thirty years ago, the main fact was that they had a distinct religion, but also there are Albanians who are Muslim, but they were not included in the Bosnian Muslim. Still the fact of difference was supposedly based on religion.

In a letter to her daughter, Drakulić speaks to the frustration of living in the climate of intolerant nationalism and the loss of individual agency:

> The tragedy and the paradox of this situation now is that you will have to decide, to take his or my side, to become Croat or Serb, or to take on and suffer his and my "guilt" of marrying the "wrong" nationality. In the war there is no middle position. All of a sudden, you as Croat or Serb become responsible for what all other Croats or Serbs are doing. You are reduced to a single nationality—almost sentenced to it, since nationality in the war brings a danger of getting killed just because of it.[27]

## Encountering the Other

Contrary to the media portrayal of people in former Yugoslavia as uniquely programmed to act on primordial impulses that prevented them from seeing the world in any terms other than the pathology of enemies and allies, I found them extraordinarily cognizant of and reflective about the problem of "Otherness," much more so than in my own country, and no doubt this is an awareness heightened by the fragmentation of their own country. Many people in former Yugoslavia have been deeply injured by violence motivated by hatred and intolerance of others. Still it seemed striking that so many people I encountered had such an intricate, sophisticated, and self-conscious understanding of both the more immediate problem of scapegoating and marginalizing internal enemies (which they recognized in the media and regime rhetoric as "hate speech") as well as the broader necessity of cultivating pluralism in the development of civic culture.

But there were paradoxes and exceptions. Many Croatians were quick to regard their republican boundaries as Croatian "national" space, so that when it became evident that the violence there was partly engineered by the Belgrade regime, they understood it simply as "aggression against Croatia by Serbia." The sense of violation among many ordinary Croats[28] tended to override their sensitivity for the situation of Croatian Serbs and the possibility that the policies of the new "Croatia for Croatians" government had any part in provoking fear among the Serb minority.

Among Albanians, many of whom are Muslim, Albanian identity generally remained more significant, while their identification with Yugoslavia and being Yugoslav was much weaker. Again, there were exceptions, more so before the breakup of the Yugoslav state and the disintegration the Communist Party. But no doubt the long-standing pattern of discrimination and social prejudice against Albanians left many feeling more alienated by than identified with the idea of a Yugoslav civic state. "We are all Albanians," writes Slavenka Drakulić in an article for *The Nation*, on June 7, 1999. But, she claimed, this lesson had not yet been learned throughout

Yugoslavia, and even before ethnic fragmentation it had not been learned by those Croats, Serbs, Slovenians, and Macedonians related by shared Slavic language, to whom Albanians were always the "Other within." In order to rationalize discrimination as well as to commit violence against Albanians, she explains,

> There was no need to construct their "Otherness" — as, for example, with Jews in prewar Germany or recently with Serbs in Croatia. The Albanians were never integrated into the country's social, political and cultural life. They existed separately from us, barely visible people on the margins of our society, with their strange language that nobody understood, their tribal organization, blood feuds, different habits and dress. They were always underdogs. What was their place in the Yugoslav literature. In movies and popular culture? What famous Yugoslavs were Albanians? Because of that estrangement, not many voices were raised in protest during the past ten years, when Albanians in Kosovo lived practically under apartheid (*The Nation*, June 7, 1999)

Drakulić takes all Yugoslavs to task for marginalizing Albanians and thus failing to integrate them into Yugoslav society as equals, a policy continued by the Serbs in their "rump state."[29] Even among Serbs engaged in the antiwar effort there seemed generally to be a significant level of denial about the reality and seriousness of anti-Albanian prejudice in Serbian society. I was reminded of how long it took for a small but critical mass of white Americans to become self-conscious of their own prejudices toward African Americans (some may argue that it remains a small but critical mass), a consciousness which I have seen emerge in my own lifetime.

These anti-Albanian prejudices were apparent even to a nonexpert outsider, and though they were clearly not shared by everyone, they were conspicuously exploited by political leaders and their loyal media. But there were (and remain) those critical of such prejudices. The Helsinki Watch Group and the Humanitarian Law Center in Belgrade have both publicized anti-Albanian and anti-Muslim police brutality, discrimination, harassment, media censorship, and human rights abuses in the Sanjak area of Serbia as well as in Kosovo. The Humanitarian Law Center has been critical of police conduct in Kosovo during popular demonstrations. During the NATO intervention, at a time when 64 percent of Serbs did not believe reports about atrocities against Albanians in Kosovo, Nataša Kandić, of the Humanitarian Law Center, traveled to western Kosovo to investigate reports of atrocities for herself.[30]

One international lawyer and human rights and antiwar activist from Belgrade spoke at length about the problem of prejudices, dehumanization, and enemy-making in Serb-Albanian relations:

*V.D., Belgrade, 1995*

The most important thing is to dehumanize the enemy. So, for instance, you have strained relations with many of the Albanians, they call themselves Šiptar, but before the war many Albanians were not hated because to Serbs and to Yugoslavs they were "useful little beings" who were busy taking menial jobs. For some reason the communist Albanian nomenklatura decided that they should call themselves Albanians. Now the Serbian nationalists who hate them call them "Šiptar" in a derogatory sense—and you immediately know that this is the kind of thing that dehumanizes. The Serb nationalists are deliberately provocative by spelling "Muslim" with a small "m," and I saw a publication by a Yugoslav embassy abroad which in English also spelled Muslims with a small "m." This is a way of reducing the other person so that it is easier to kill them.

At the same time this plays into the Serb complex of superiority and inferiority. The stereotype is that the Albanians, being poorer and more primitive, have more children. So this is a point for rallying hate. The "white pestilence" they call it. The "white plague." They are going to take us over by overpopulating. This is perceived as the danger. Actually I think the birth rate among urban Albanians is the same as for other urban people. But the most difficult thing here in Serbia is to be accused of being an "Albanian lover." Whenever you say something in favor of Albanians as human beings . . . you are a traitor.

Like people in most complex modern societies, there was a vast difference in the understanding of pluralism and civic culture among the better educated urban population and at the rural village level. I heard many times in Belgrade that "the Serbs outside of Serbia are different," or that there was a clear distinction between urban and rural Serbs even in Serbia. In Croatia, or Zagreb at least, I was told that the Croats in Herzegovina were "different," that, for example, they lived in very small towns where "everyone was related" and that they would "do anything in defense of their families first, that they were parochial; some even referred to them by using the U.S. term "rednecks." The difference, however, cannot be simply understood as "cosmopolitan tolerance" in the urban setting versus "provincial prejudices" of small towns, for life in many multiethnic villages, particularly in Bosnia, was frequently characterized by a high degree of community cohesiveness, good-neighborliness, and a self-consciously shared interest in harmonious intercommunal relations,[31] while, conversely, there was ample evidence of prejudices among urban dwellers. The peaceful qualities of village life before the war are echoed throughout the testimony of the witnesses speaking to the Hague tribunal.[32] People in the villages often heard of the violence occurring elsewhere, even in nearby towns and villages, and among themselves would say that they were still sure it would not happen to them or that they could prevent it.

One American-born woman, whose parents had emigrated from the former Yugoslavia in the 1960s, returned to Croatia toward the end of the war; she worked for an international development agency after having spent time working on the archeological investigation of mass graves in Bosnia. Briefing me on the "Croatian perspective" as she understood it, she described how there was a very strong feeling among many Croats that they had been misunderstood by outsiders, by the "international community," and that "Serb propaganda" had been very "effective." I did indeed encounter those who expressed this perspective, and soon learned that it was a kind of defense against accusations regarding war crimes alleged to have occurred during the conduct of operations Storm and Lightning, when the Croatian army recaptured the Krajina and most of Eastern Slavonia. People assumed that I had heard this "propaganda" and so invariably brought up the operations in order to make sure I understood what "really" happened. A common explanation was that one had to make a distinction between violence committed as aggression and violence in response to aggression. Any war crimes committed in retaliation were different from those committed as aggression. Especially in Herzegovina, I was told, any excesses committed by Croats were "after their villages were destroyed by Serbs."[33]

For many in Croatia, this was a war between two sovereign national states, and the Serbs were the aggressors. There was real and widespread suffering, and emotions ran high on the subject of nationalism, in whose name the suffering had been endured and inflicted. What had been ethnonational prejudices in Yugoslavia became, as the civic state disintegrated, the basis for the new nationalisms. Croatians, many respondents said, do not consider themselves "Balkan" and some even found it insulting to be included in that category. In this view, not shared by everyone but in many ways consistent with the "official" line of the ruling HDZ party, Croats had been "Europeanized" as a result of living under the Hapsburg empire for so many centuries, especially when contrasted with the Serbs, who had lived under the more oppressive, backward (and of course oriental), and "barbarian" rule of the Ottomans. One learned from one's oppressor, apparently.

Croats, I was often told, associate the idea of Yugoslavia with backwardness. The Croats equated Yugoslavia with Serb dominance, and indeed, a propaganda film I watched while in Zagreb in 1998 went so far as to claim that the reason Serbs "liked" communism so much was that they were lazy, and that they had learned to be lazy and to be taken care of by a strong cental power as a consequence of having lived under the Ottomans for so long. The film implied that long association with the backwardness of the Ottomans as oppressed people under the Ottoman Empire "explained" Serb affinity with communism. One respondent explained that for Croats, being in the Ustaše was "like being in the Nazi army," that is, it was not a crime in itself, and most Germans were in the Nazi army during World War II without being stigmatized afterward as war criminals. Many people I talked with explained that there was the perception, at least, that under Tito's rule, Croats had been collectively punished for the crimes of the Ustaše leadership and were disproportionately arrested and imprisoned. Finally, Croat respondents in Zagreb explained that Croats from Herzegovina were "different," they were crude, conservative, and more "Balkan" (apparently for some a synonym for "backward"). Parochialism thus struggled against a more civic Yugoslavism, though as things fell apart the former gave way to nationalist ideologies, and Yugoslavism was marginalized as a form of resistance.

One of Drakulić's most poignant essays in *Balkan Express* tells the story of an actress simply referred to as "M," apparently a Croatian Yugoslav living part-time in Belgrade. In her "Letter to the Citizens of Zagreb," published in the Belgrade independent newspaper *Borba* just before leaving for a self-imposed exile, she writes of her resistance to the growing nationalism, the climate of intolerance, and her desperate and failed attempt, in an increasingly polarized and hostile climate, to find a way in that climate of sustaining her own "human" identity above all else:

> I am sorry, my system of values is different. For me there have always existed and always will exist, only human beings, individual people, and those human beings (God, how few of them there are) will always be excepted from generalizations of any kind, regardless of events, however catastrophic. I, unfortunately, shall never be able to "hate the Serbs," nor even understand what that really means. I shall always, perhaps until the moment the kind of threats on the phone are finally carried out, hold my hand out to an anonymous person on the "other side," a person who is as desperate and lost as I am, who is as sad, bewildered and frightened. . . . I reject, I will not accept such a crippling of myself and my own life. I played those last performances in Belgrade for those anguished people who were not "Serbs" but human beings like me, human beings who recoil before this horrible Grand Guignol farce of bloodshed and murder.

"M" felt herself to be a citizen of both Croatia and Serbia, a Yugoslav citizen. But according to others, her experience was not shared by a majority of Yugoslavs. A number of people attributed the failure to develop a widely shared civic Yugoslav identity not only to the lack of interaction and integration between urban and rural sectors of the society but also to the lack of integration across republican boundaries, as the following interview passages illustrate:

*S.T., Belgrade, 1995*
In other states modernization and development brought people possibilities to move to various places and spend a few years in one part of the new country, and then a few years in another part of the country. But in Yugo-

slavia we did not have that possibility. This made it more difficult to develop a sense of citizenship in spite of our regional differences. Our development was very poor and only the army officers are trained in all the different towns and provinces in the first Yugoslavia, and in the second also the bureaucracy. But ordinary people, for example, and even students, tended not to travel to other universities. If they went to Belgrade University they usually didn't have the possibility to change to another university. This would have been essential for the development of the idea of one Yugoslavia.

*D.C., Korcula, 1997*
The main problems were that we hadn't the possibility to get to know the situation and problems of people in other parts of our country.

*R.S. Belgrade, 1995*
Another problem for ex-Yugoslavia was that some people had the chance to get to know different people better than others. Serbs, for instance, tended to remain more isolated, especially outside of Belgrade. Eighty percent of Serbs spent their whole lives in Serbia because they didn't have the possibility to go to the seaside. Or there were a lot of Slovenians who did not have possibility to study in Belgrade. They might visit one or two days and that's all. So it did not make us feel like one country.

*D.T. Belgrade, 1995*
We have a lot of examples in history. In France, for instance, they thought that the railway would connect France and make people feel like one country and be able to travel more around that one country. But in our country we haven't a connected railway and people do not travel in three hours' drive to Ljubljana and drink coffee with your friends and so you do think you live in the same land with them. Yugoslavia is small but we didn't have a lot of possibilities to move. This affects not only political development, but also economic development.

The comments seemed directed toward a general perception that there was *not enough* integration, that people may have traveled temporarily, but they did not relocate across republican boundaries. Of course people did travel from one republic to the other for vacations, and even some students from one republic would attend university in another. Another respondent believed that people knew of and accepted their regional differences as normal.

*S.S., Belgrade, 1995*
The people did not have a lot of opportunity to move throughout Yugoslavia and this is not unusual, for example the people in the north of Germany are very different from the people in the South of Germany, even more different than Serbs and Croats, for example.

In other settings, we would call this a problem of "regionalism," and in itself it is not a cause of civil unrest and uncivil violence. Swiss society, for instance, is extremely regionalist, but with a stable economy and high standard of living, a historical narrative based on a certain positive idea of the raison d'être for creating a Swiss state over six centuries, and various mechanisms (such as mandatory service in the army for some seventeen years, where "soldiers" from all ethnic groups serve side by side) that promote and sustain a civic Swiss identity.

In the following interview, the idea that ethnic identity is most fully expressed through unity in one state appears as a central feature of both Serb and Croat identity. We also see how people struggle with the problem of minority status within the state and that majority status is implicitly empowering.

*S.S., Belgrade, 1995*
Something in the Croatian identity makes them simply unable to define themselves positively, so they define themselves negatively vis-à-vis Serbs. This is the trouble of all the nations is which one is smaller than the other. Their identity develops around the contrast between them and the larger group. Then by the 1980s and 1990s some nationalities would not define themselves without defining themselves in an anti-Serbian way.

When Yugoslavia was created in 1918 I think different nationalities entered Yugo with different understandings, at least potentially. Croats never lost their historical craving for a national independent state. Serbs on the other hand thought that they did resolve their nationalities problem by creating Yugoslavia because Serbs in Bosnia and Croatia were embraced. Slovenes at that time were just recognized more or less but they didn't have national ambitions.

A Croatian man in his late twenties, the son of a Yugoslav army officer, tried to explain how "Serbs" can live "in" Croatia and whether they should be thought of as Serbs or Croats. He struggled with some confusion about ethnic versus civic identity, particularly when it comes to the question of Croatian Serbs. For him, the idea seemed to be a bit of a contradiction:

*D.C., Zadar, 1998*
When I was twenty-two years old [in 1988] I started thinking about what I am, and I thought: "Well, my mother and father were born in Croatia, and we live in Croatia." And I thought to myself: "What do you want Croatia to become? A recognized country." So who I am is determined by the fact that I grew up here, and I live here, and everything that I have is here, so a Serb, I am Croatian. But are there really any Serbs in Croatia? How can someone whose great-great grandfather came here in the

fifteenth century and after all these generations which were born in Croatia, and which were buried in Croatia, how can they declare themselves as Serbs?

He went on to explain how one can be *ethnically "different"* from a majority population but adopt the civic identity of the dominant population. This was the solution, as he saw it, evidenced by his acquaintance with a Vietnamese man who had become an Australian citizen. He thought of civic identity to some extent in ethnic terms, as he understood the Vietnamese man to be assimilated into an Australian civic identity while able to enjoy free cultural expression in his private life. He had even "layered on" an Australian identity. In his thinking, "Australian" is constituted as "white" and "Vietnamese" is "different," in the same way that "Croatian" is "ethnically Croatian" and in Croatia "Serbs" are "different":

> Like in the U.S. or Australia where I lived for a year I met this Vietnamese guy and when he was in his home he was Vietnamese and he spoke Vietnamese language, listened to Vietnamese music, everything there was Vietnamese, but when he was outside he didn't look white of course, but in all the other actions, he was drinking lager beer, cheering for cricket games, singing Matilda in school and so on, so he was Australian but he treasured his national identity as Vietnamese too.[34]

As we talked, it seemed that the problem for him was that the idea of "Yugoslavia" had clearly constituted a civic identity, but one concretized by its *inclusion* of multiple and historically conflicted ethnic and national identities. The death of Yugoslavia meant the death of that inclusive, civic identity and the emergence or "liberation" of "Croatian" identity as some kind of organic and naturalized identity. But there were "Serbs" living in Croatian space, and had been for centuries, so now Croatia needed a Croatian *civic* identity that would also be inclusive, at least inclusive of those Serbs who had lived there for centuries. Coupled with the perception of Serb aggression as the cause of the conflict and the mobilization of Croatian nationalism as an ethnic project, "Croatian" as a *civic* identity seemed to be a contradiction. He knew that somehow this whole issue is related to the question of prejudice, but he was not entirely clear how. He explained that although he was a "Croat" *without* prejudices, he understood that other Croats, now nationalists, were and always had been prejudiced toward Serbs living in Croatia and/or Yugoslavia:

> ... but also you had guys whose father and mother always said inside closed doors, you know, we are Croats, we are Catholics and we cannot have a Serb in our house ... and I was having a party and I had a Muslim

guy, an Albanian guy, Macedonian, a guy from Serbia, a guy from Slovenia, from Montenegro . . . so I never saw these differences, I am not saying that they weren't there, I am just saying that for me they weren't there, I didn't care. I could be a Muslim, but I am not a religious person, so why should it matter if I say I am Bosnian, or Serbian for that matter, or Slovenian. . . . The Serbs from Krajina spoke very nice Croatian language, but when the war started they learned Serbian language so that they could divide themselves by differences. And the [Croat and Serb] people in Slavonia speak a Serbian language because they were very close to the border [between Croatia and Serbia]. But then in Knin it became very fashionable to declare yourself as a Serb, they started speaking Serbian. (D.C., Korcula, 1998)

There is ample evidence that people understood that their common humanity, if not their civic relationships, transcended ethnic identity. It is terribly difficult to obtain accurate reporting on racial or ethnic prejudices, whether in former Yugoslavia or in the United States. It is also difficult to determine the extent to which education and class played a role in mitigating prejudices, since many of the most intolerant political elites were highly educated, well traveled, professional, and middle class. And of course it was the aim of socialist ideology to reduce class differences.

In spite of these prejudices and the contradictions and tensions between national and civic identities, many people did develop a sense of Yugoslav identity, and understood it to be both pluralistic and inclusive, cultural as well as civic. "Yugoslavia without Croats is not Yugoslavia," said one Serbian man to me, and another said: "I was Croat when Serbs bombed Dubrovnik, I was Muslim when Croats bombed the old bridge in Mostar. It is all part of my culture, it's part of who I am."[35]

"We are the war," says Drakulić, "we carry in us the possibility of the mortal illness that is slowly reducing us to what we never thought possible and I am afraid there is no one else to blame. We all make it possible, we allow it to happen. Our defence is weak, as is our consciousness of it. There are no us and them, there are no grand categories, abstract numbers, black and white truths, simple facts. There is only us—and, yes, we are responsible for each other."

## In War, Everything Turns Black and White

As Steven J. Kull says, "During war, things become very simple, very clear."[36] Indeed, it *is* more difficult to live with ambiguities, to wonder about something and think to ourselves, or to be asked something by someone else and say simply "I don't know." The classical imagery of war is one of interstate conflict, where states are well-bounded communities of solidarity in which (male) citizens agree to come to the defense of the community if threatened. The "ethnic conflict" model of war substitutes "ethnic group" for the state to the extent that the ethnic group is viewed as a community of solidarity, with clearly demarcated boundaries and evenly distributed and equally intense loyalties among members of the community. "Ethnic conflict" thus appears to the realist as being as "natural" as interstate war.

But what exactly is it that is threatened either in our classical state conflict or ethnic conflict models? Both, it seems, are metaphors for family and kinship. Either one's family is injured or threatened, or *those we regard as equals on the basis of something shared, something that makes us "similar"* are threatened. In Yugoslavia, family and identity group commingled in the minds of many people. In light of the number of deaths, rapes, and displaced people,[37] a conservative estimate that nearly 20 percent of the prewar population directly suffered injuries and loss does not seem improbable. The greatest proportion were from Bosnia-Herzegovina. But if we add to these numbers those who committed atrocities, at least *some* of whom suffered psychological trauma as a consequence, the number of injured persons will rise much higher.[38] In interviews with psychologists I learned of former snipers who committed suicide after the war and young men—many of them still teenagers—who suffered what they were calling "Vietnam syndrome," psychic disorientation resulting from the inability to make the adjustment from war to postwar life, with symptoms of posttraumatic stress disorder including a predilection for violence. Collective centers regularly received reports of domestic and family violence, particularly among families "hosting" refugees from Bosnia.[39] War is by definition traumatic and therefore highly emotional. Even people in Zagreb, for instance, who were less likely to be personally and directly attacked, suffered the psychological trauma of vulnerability as they listened to the bombs hitting targets just thirty miles from the city:[40]

> Standing there, I feel I am approaching an edge, an abyss, a turmoil of feelings which I cannot identify, but know it is dangerous, and I know I must stay away from it, because then it would be too late for reason, for doubts, even for fear. While I stand there, everything clicks into place with perfect clarity: they attacked us, we responded. Here, war is a simple matter. There are no politics any more. No dilemmas. Nothing but the naked struggle for life. I know that if I had to stay here, this would soon be my reality, too.[41]

The essays of student émigrés captured that same frustration, and even despair as they struggled to resist the polarization that follows from political violence:

> To disagree with the prevailing political credit and the government was dangerous. As time passed, I became aware of things that had not been important to me before. My mother is Muslim, my father Croatian, but he was born in Belgrade and brought up as a Yugoslav. The time came

when I had to decide what to be: Muslim? Serb? Croat? Or simply disappear.[42]

...in 1991, when hatred between the Serbs and the Croats started to grow in Croatia, I began to feel pressure in my immediate environment to take sides, something I did not want to and could not do. I could not identify with the increasingly aggressive nationalism of the Croats, or with the militant aggressive aspirations of the Serbs. Above all, I resented the unjustifiable idea of killing as a way to resolve social and political problems, not to mention the problems of "national destiny." Whatever one's beliefs and national identity, everyone has the right to life.[43]

There is a very small window in which it is even possible to talk about war as "rational," and in that window stand elites, not the masses of ordinary people who become its perpetrators and victims, whose experiences of loss, terror, anger, frustration, regret, and despair, are undeniably emotional.

### The Erdemović Case[44]

The model of "ethic conflict" presumes that intergroup violence is some kind of "natural" response carried out by individuals because they are identified with a particular ethnic group. It presumes a hostile and Other-destructive impulse driven by organic qualities that follow from one's ethnic identity, that violence is psychologically rationalized by difference, and even that such violence comes easily, especially when "ancient hatreds" or long-standing "ethnic rivalries" between groups are present. So I went to ex-Yugoslavia to talk to "ethnic" people as individuals, to find out how *they* understood their ethnic and civic identities and how they understood the conflict that had consumed them for nearly a decade and which had destroyed the lives of so many.

One of the most intriguing cases with respect to the relationship between ethnic conflict and ethnic identity is that of Drazen Erdemović, who was charged with crimes against humanity and violations of the laws of warfare in connection with the massacres taking place in and around the UN "safe area" of Srebenica in the summer of 1995. Between July 6 and 16, 23,000 Bosnian Muslim women and children were expelled from the town of Srebenica in eastern Bosnia, approximately 10 kilometers from the Serbian border. Approximately 7,000 men and boys of Srebenica were taken by the Bosnian Serb army and summarily executed. At his trial, Erdemović pleaded guilty to the charges.

The case of Mr. Erdemović is intriguing because it was people like Erdemović who enacted the violence of "ethnic conflict" in former Yugoslavia. His would be classified as violence by "Bosnian Serbs" against Bosnian Muslims. Yet Erdemović was not a Bosnian Serb, though his wife was. Nor was he aroused to action because of any identification or emotional attachment to the cause of the Bosnian Serbs. In fact, he had tried to escape the violence but could not afford to take his family with him into exile. Thus it was that Erdemović, a Bosnian Croat from Tuzla, initially convicted on one count of a crime against humanity, appealed his case and pleaded guilty to violations of the laws of war but not guilty to crimes against humanity. His cooperation would help the tribunal build its case against the military and political leadership of the Bosnian Serbs, including, at the top of the list, Bosnian Serb "president" Radovan Karadzić and his general, Ratko Mladić. Erdemović confessed to "participation under duress," in the first of two massacres he witnessed on July 16, 1995. A pivotal reason given by the judges for accepting his plea to the lesser charge and reducing his sentence was his demonstration of remorse. In the following excerpts from the trial transcripts of the International Criminal Tribunal for Former Yugoslavia (ICTY), Jean-Rene Ruez, Investigative Team Leader for allegations respecting crimes committed at Srebenica in 1995, discusses his interviews with Mr. Erdemović in response to questioning from the prosecution, represented by Mr. McCloskey:

MR. MCCLOSKEY: On the third point, can you give the judges some of the background into the incident that leads you to believe that there was duress present when he committed these crimes and this duress should be used as mitigation?

MR. RUEZ: I have a personal belief that indeed he was under duress at that time, but the reason for that would need to re-explain a certain number of facts, which have probably for some of them not been raised in front of a court until now. He knew about the behavior of some of the members of the unit he was part of, the unit was split into two locations, one was in Bijeljina and one was in Vlasenica. The rumor he was aware of was that members of the unit in Vlasenica had committed numerous crimes since the beginning of the war. It was public knowledge inside the unit. He also witnessed where under the order of a commander, people were killed only because the order was given. He was himself in a very difficult situation at that time because of his ethnic background he was not fully trusted by his comrades. Also he already had some strong arguments with his commanders, because he did not fulfil the assignments he was given. The reason why he did not fulfil them was that for especially one of them, there was a big risk of civilian casualties and he did not fulfil the assignment, which led that he was from his rank, so he was stripped already at that moment in a very weak position in front of his superiors and also in front of his comrades.

Mr. McCloskey then asks him to describe the circumstances surrounding the events, how Mr. Erdemović came to be in the area that day with his squad, and where they went:

A. The factual circumstances of the situation we know them also only through his testimony, was that on the morning of 16th July, he was designated to go with a few men to Zvornik, he did not know about the assignment at that moment. The fact is that the team leader of the group was a member of Vlasenica platoon which is not normally his own chain of command. The reason is that the man who was designated team leader had a close relationship with the commander of the unit and was part of these people who committed allegedly and according to the rumour bad actions since a couple of years. When he arrived in Zvornik, a lieutenant colonel came out of a building which is currently the Zvornik brigade headquarters. He was accompanied by two military policemen and led the team of the 10th diversion unit to the Branjevo farm where the civilians arrived and the assignment was given to execute all of them. He knew that when he was at the farm and all these buses were arriving, understood very quickly that all this was part of a quite huge operation and it would be out of the question for him to rage against it. Most certainly he would get in very deep trouble if he had done so, so he made a few attempts, but very quickly found out that it was absolutely unuseful [sic] and even received the command that if he was sorry for these people, he could line up with them. At that point, he made the choice to participate in this, not to be killed either on the spot, either very shortly afterwards and also had in mind the will to protect his wife and his kid, who were both in Bijeljina at that time.

In his confession, when asked why he dared to refuse to participate in the second (which resulted in the killing of 10,500 people), he explained:

... they already had spent five hours on this killing field, killing all the people who were arriving on the spot, and having fulfilled this part of the assignment, they felt secure enough to oppose the order of the lieutenant colonel, since they had the feeling that they had already done far enough that day, so they had a feeling that this man could not take action against them at that moment, and also the fact that other comrades of him immediately stepped behind him, saying "no, we are not willing to do that." He felt that the lieutenant colonel could not take the risk at that moment to have a kind of rebellion among this execution squad, which was also in— the confrontation was unuseful [sic], since this officer also had at his disposal a few members of soldiers coming from Bratunac who were obviously volunteered for the task....

In the summation, his counsel argued for contextualizing Erdemović's participation as a young man who, but for the misfortune of circumstances which made his emigration from Yugoslavia difficult to impossible, would rather have joined other students who left the country for Austria, Germany, or the United States. He was in their age group, though married and a father, rather than a single student in the university.

> ... the accused, as a member of the 10th sabotage detachment of the army of Republika Srpska, participated in the shooting of approximately 1200 unarmed Muslim civilians at the Branjevo farm near the village of Pilica. ... At the time of the commission of the crime, the accused Erdemović was only 23 years old. He is a Croat and a Catholic. He comes from a working class family, in which the children were brought up in the spirit of religious and ethnic tolerance, and as Yugoslavs. This he adopted in his own life without reservation, and he acted accordingly. The different religions and ethnic groups in his environment were his true wealth, and as crowning proof of this all, he married a woman from another ethnic and religious group, with whom he has a three-year-old child. His family lives in the Tuzla area, which is where they lived before the war and during the war, and they have fallen on hard times. Therefore his family will suffer hardship due to his serving a prison sentence. He did everything he could to avoid these winds of war and to leave the country and go abroad with his family. However, unfortunately, he did not succeed. So the confluence of many circumstances in the territory of the former Yugoslav, and I think that the Trial Chamber is aware of this, and the unavailability of other choice took him to all three warring sides. This was his modus vivendi and not only his, this was a fate shared by all. He never belonged to any nationalist party. He resisted as much as he could all propaganda advocating intolerance, just as he was taught at school, by the community and family. He has no criminal record, and he does not even have any misdemeanor charges against him. All this makes it clear that the accused Erdemović poses no danger for his environment and that his character is reformable. This is also borne out by the expert commission findings.

While the circumstances of the student emigrés enabled them to escape military mobilization and the horrors of the war, Erdemović's circumstances trapped him. And so it was that a Croat from Tusla found himself accused of committing war crimes with Bosnian Serbs in the killing of 1,200 Muslim men in Srebenica in this "ethnic conflict" in the Balkans.

## Conclusion

Considerable controversy surrounds the relationship between the citizens of Dachau, where the first official Nazi concentration camp was so designated by Heinrich Himmler on March 21, 1933, and the 300,000 prisoners of that camp who suffered and died there from 1933 until its liberation twelve years

later in late April 1945.[45] The first prisoners, indeed, were political opponents of the Nazi regime: communists, social democrats, members of trade
unions, and some of the opposition political parties, conservative and liberal
alike. Soon, Jewish political prisoners were taken there, along with homo-
sexuals, Romani, and a variety of Hitler's religious opponents. Although prisoners came to Dachau from more than thirty countries, the largest national
group was the Poles. Upon liberation, the American soldiers, politicians, and
the public were outraged by the realization that by normalizing the existence
of a concentration camp in their midst, the citizens of Dachau had silently
assented to the camp's mission, though we may never resolve whether they
did so out of fear, helplessness, or depraved indifference.

I raise the question of Dachau now because it symbolizes the issue of
responsibility for witnessing genocide. The people of Dachau, the film *Shoah*
suggests, lived, worked, and walked daily by the barbed wire surrounding
the camp. Perhaps the citizens of Dachau did have a moral duty to protest
and reveal its atrocities to the world, but was American and European indifference to the events taking place in Bosnia (as well as Dachau) any different?
Modernity and its technology in a sense makes us all witnesses to the injuries
of others. Visiting the U.S. Holocaust Memorial Museum after having made
three trips to ex-Yugoslavia, I had to wonder if "never again" really meant
"never again would leaders of the transatlantic alliance stand by while a
Western European leader implemented a plan to annihilate more than six
million European Jews, but that smaller scale atrocities in eastern or central
Europe (or Africa, Southeast Asia, and elsewhere) would be tolerated." It
did not seem to mean that "never again" would the Western allies witness
atrocities in their own backyard (much less in Rwanda, further afield) and
fail to intervene. Citing the questions raised by Dachau as symbol and reality,
Drakulić put it this way:

> For by closing our eyes, by continuing our shopping, by working our land,
> by pretending that nothing is happening, by thinking it is not our problem,
> we are betraying those "others"—and I don't know if there is a way out
> of it. What we fail to realize is that by such divisions we deceive ourselves
> too, exposing ourselves to the same possibility of becoming the "others"
> in a different situation.[46]

CHAPTER 5

# The Social Construction of the State: State-Building and State-Destroying as Social Action

Without crimes of ethnic cleansing it is impossible to create new states based on national identity, new Serbian state, new Albanian state, new Croatian state, and so on.

—M.Z., Belgrade, 1995

It was July 1997 when the three of us—my friend Michael, an American I first met in Belgrade when he was working as a translator for the antiwar campaign, Elma, a high school student from Sarajevo who was working as a translator for the "internationals" who now occupied her city, and I—climbed into a cab headed for an interview with the director of the nongovernmental organization (NGO) "Žena-Ženema" or "Women to Women." We asked the driver to take us to Hamdija Čemerlica 25, but the exchange between Michael, Elma, and the cab driver soon heated up until the cab driver was positively irate, furrowing his brow and shaking his hands in dismissive gestures toward us, toward the streets, toward an invisible provocateur. I gave Michael a "what's wrong?" look, to which he replied in a subtle, quiet voice, "Oh, it's nothing really, but he's angry because the names of the streets have been changed and he wasn't sure where 'Hamdija Čemerlica' is, but when I tried to explain to him where I thought it was he got angry and said "I don't need foreigners telling me how to get around my own city!"

Oddly, there had been much less street-name-changing in Sarajevo than in the Croatian and Serbian capitals of Zagreb and Belgrade. After all, Sarajevo still had a Marsala Tito Boulevard. I first encountered the street-renaming phenomenon in Belgrade, but for me the larger problem at the time was reading Cyrillic-only street signs. For residents of ex-Yugoslavia, I can imagine how frustrating it must have been when the places where, for fifty years, they had lived, and shopped, and met friends for coffee, suddenly ceased to exist, and in their stead were boulevards and squares named after mostly long-forgotten nineteenth-century nationalists and cultural heroes. (Though in some cases there were interminable debates about whether particular heroes were really Serb, Croat, or Muslim.)

In light of the recent history of fascistic nationalism in Croatia in World War II, however, in the areas of Croatia where Serb majorities lived, the renaming of streets in their hometowns in honor of Croatian nationalists, even long-past historical ones, was perceived as especially foreboding, particularly in conjunction with other policies that seemed overtly or covertly aimed at marginalizing and intimidating the Serb population in Croatia. Even before seceding from Yugoslavia, the Croatian republican government amended its constitution unilaterally to alter the status of Croatian Serbs from "constituent nation" to "national minority." According to Ejub Štitkovac, at a party rally over a year before Croatia seceded from Yugoslavia, Franjo Tudjman declared that: "The NDH [Independent State of Croatia, as the collaborationist regime was known] was not simply a quisling creation and a fascist crime; it was also an expression of the historical aspirations of the Croatian people."[1] To some Serbs, this was tantamount to Holocaust denial. Thus renaming streets and squares throughout Croatia after individuals known for their support of and association with the pro-Nazi Ustaše regime further fueled their fears. Tudjman's "reconciliation" program rested on the premise that the Ustaše and the Croatian army regulars were the unmourned victims of World War II.

The new Croatian "national" flag restored the flag used by the Ustaše, though the new regime claimed it was a symbol of historical continuity with long-standing Croatian aspirations for statehood—the "Thousand Year Old Dream," as it came to be known. The distinguishing feature of the flag was the *sahovnica*, a white-and-red checkerboard insignia, which also began to appear on Croatian national military uniforms. The flag was raised not only on public but also private buildings, shops, cafes, and homes.[2] Serbs serving in the police were fired and replaced with Croats. Mass firings of Croatian Serbs in the public and private sectors followed.[3] These developments, of course, gave tacit permission to the more extreme Croatian nationalists to express openly and even act on anti-Serb prejudices, while Milosević's government in Belgrade exploited these tensions for its own propagandistic purposes. Serb paramilitaries began to infiltrate mixed or primarily Serbian communities in Croatia. New states were in the making. These developments are described by one of the young émigrés writing to the Open Society Institute:

A culture that had been "stifled for centuries" was revived in a matter of weeks. Serbia was not alone in its renaissance—people all over Yugoslavia became much more aware of their origins, customs, and religion. . . .

What initially seemed to be a cultural appreciation and patriotism developed into a complete misunderstanding and depreciation of other cultures and then into various separatist movements. (J.P., Corvallis, Oregon; Lešć 1995: 111–112)

Drakulić describes her experience crossing the new "border" between Slovenia and Croatia for the first time:

> There we were, citizens of one country falling apart and two countries-to-be, in front of a border that is not yet a proper border, with passports that are not any good any more. . . .
>
> Until then, the Slovenian state, the Croatian state, borders, divisions, were somehow unreal. Now, these people with guns in Slovene police uniforms stand between me and Slovenia, a part of the country that used to be mine, too.[4]

## Where Do States Comes From?

Americans particularly, but Westerners in general, tend to take the state's existence for granted, albeit within the context of their own romanticized historical narratives and foundational myths about the events and social processes through which it "came into existence." We speak uncritically, casually, and often patriotically, about the "birth" of "our nation." But, as I often tell my students, the United States is not really "orange," Canada is not really "yellow," and Mexico is not really "green." Maps matter. Maps are instruments of political socialization. We internalize an image of the geopolitical reality in which we locate our own experiences, and our identities are bound up with place and place *meaning*. The political entities we call "states" only exist as a set of governing institutions because they are recognized as such by both internal and external agents. Unless those acting authoritatively as agents of the state are willing and able to rely on repressive tactics to maintain power, the existence of the state relies on agreement among most of those living inside its boundaries as well as recognition by agents of other states. In both cases—inside and outside—recognition of some agents is more important than others. *Some* antigovernment activity can be tolerated as long as it remains *marginal*. But it would be quite another story if business, political, and media elites began to defect from their recognition of a state's existence. This is more or less what happened in Yugoslavia. But like most people in Europe and the Americas, whether they live under more or less democratic governments, most of the people in ex-Yugoslavia never expected that their state would cease to exist.

The destruction of Yugoslavia and the apparent ease with which so many of its citizens abandoned their "Yugoslav" civic identity in favor of antagonistic ethnonational identities brings us face to face with the question of state creation: How *do* states, and the identities on which the link between citizen and state rests, come into existence?

Recent criticisms of the organic model of the nation and nation-state, whether from sociological and historical perspectives on group identity and national myths,[5] postmodern and poststructural political analyses,[6] or by inquiring directly into the relationship between narrative and nation,[7] call into question both the basis for social solidarity and the assumption of a normative foundation for the "modern" state. Taken together, critics raise a set of questions crucial to our understanding of both the state and the state system: How do/did states come into existence, and are there important differences in the processes of state creation? What is the basis for solidarity in the state where the citizenry constitute a group? What is the role of identity and what is the role of normative beliefs? Once we denaturalize and demythologize the state, it becomes clear that the state is a set of institutions created through human agency, it is a product of *social processes:* human agents engaged in social relations, the production of meaning, and social acts including speech acts. This is what I mean by the "social construction" of the state; what are the social processes that produce, sustain, and transform the role, functions, and normative basis for the state?

In Chapter 3 I argued that psychoanalytic accounts of the self situated its development within social processes, but what about the state? The state is in a sense an association of selves whose authoritative and allocative acts are structured by institutionalized as well as normative rules about, as Lasswell would say, who gets what, when, where, how, and why. *Where else could the state have come from if not from the minds of men?*[8] And in this case, I do mean men. As Peterson has argued, the modern state has its origins in the political order of the Greeks, an order founded on essentialized sex difference, a privileging of masculine over feminine roles and spheres of action, and a dichotomy between private and public spheres of social life.[9] It is from the public life of the Greeks that Western discourses about the polity as a civic space proceed.

As Michael Ignatieff argues,[10] the narrative of the modern state is often stated in terms of a transition from ethnic to civic identity, but this presumes a preexisting relationship between ethnicity and the state as well as the neutrality of ethnicity with respect to the allocation of values within the state-as-political-community, both of which are highly contestable. Indeed, there is a relationship between ethnicity and the state, but it is much more of a Gramscian relationship of hegemonic ethnic identity, because it is frequently the basis for relations structured by dominance and subjection or more and less privileged (or underprivileged) forms of citizenship. It is precisely because ethnicity is *not* a neutral factor that the justice with which values and goods are allocated by those institutions we collectively call "the state" is so often impaired.

## Ethnic Groups, Nations, and States

While I normally disapprove of using dictionary definitions to build academic arguments, it seems useful here because they reflect language practices that represent widely shared meanings within a particular historical setting.

Connolly deconstructs the political mythology of "nation" in his essay "The Liberal Image of the State" by critiquing dictionary definitions of "nation." Here he finds that "nation" means "a birth, origin," also a "breed, stock, kind, species, race, tribe," and "race of people" and: The *OED* seconds this, saying that in early European uses race or stock was primary to the idea of nation, while in later usage a people formed through common history takes on more salience.[11]

Although this kind of naturalization of ethnicity as "stock" may seem archaic to more sophisticated thinkers, it was taken seriously enough by the government of Australia in its official treatment of Aboriginal Australians well into the 1960s and 1970s. Aboriginal Australians had difficulties obtaining passports because the Australian government claimed that their Australian nativity could not be verified since their births had often been recorded in "stock books."[12] Australia was not alone. The history of policy toward indigenous peoples in European settler states, as well as the whole of European "colonial science" generally, was rife with the rhetoric of "race" and human "stock" within a schema that cast Europeans as a kind of genetic "crown of creation." In this context, it does not seem such a huge leap to Nazi ideology. In discussing the Western philosophical roots of the modern state, Ernst Cassirir, writing in the mid-1940s, says of the nineteenth century French diplomat and social philosopher Joseph Arthur, Comte de Gobineau, a contemporary of Toqueville whose writings became the basis for twentieth century anti-Semitism:

> One of his firmest convictions was that the white race is the only one that had the will and power to build up a cultural life. This principle became the cornerstone of his theory of the radical diversity of human races. The black and yellow races have no life, no will, no energy of their own. They are nothing but dead stuff in the hands of their masters—the inert mass that has to be moved by the higher races.[13]

European Americans went so far as to claim that Native Americans who had any European blood were by virtue of that blood morally competent to manage title to property responsibly, while their "full-blooded" relatives would have to wait twenty-five years to establish "competency."[14]

Like the *Oxford English Dictionary*, Webster's *International Dictionary*, which probably reflects a more American usage but with an effort to take into account international uses of English, also offers a series of definitions for "nation" that seem grounded in an organic notion of relationship:

1. Kindred; race; lineage.
2. A people connected by supposed ties of blood generally manifested by community of language, religion, and custom, and by a sense of common interest and interrelation; see *people*.

3. Popularly, any group of people having like institutions and customs and a sense of social homogeneity and mutual interest. Most nations are formed of an agglomeration of tribes or peoples either of common ethnic stock or different stocks fused by a long intercourse. A single language or closely related dialects, a common religion, a common tradition or history, and common sense of right and wrong, and a more or less compact territory are typically characteristic, but one or more of the elements may be lacking and yet leave a group that from its community of interest and desire to lead a common life is called a nation.
4. Loosely, the body of inhabitants of a country united under a single independent government; a state.

These definitions begin with the simplest and perhaps most commonly associated attributes related to the idea of *organic relatedness*—"kinship, race, lineage"—and culminate with the more modern equation of nation with "state."[15] But the intermediate elaborations emphasize the perceptual—the "supposed ties of blood"—and social dimensions of "nation," perhaps reflecting a more American orientation. The importance of shared history and language are acknowledged in "tradition," "related dialects," and in combination through "long intercourse," pointing to importance of shared meanings, a single, agreed-upon history, and by implication, a tacitly shared worldview. Finally, a normative dimension is indicated both as a social contract in the form of "mutual interest" and "community of interest," and perhaps most important, as a "common sense of right and wrong." The last definition reflects the most recent association of "nation" with the *institutional structure of the state* and its exercise of authority over the people and resources within a territorial space, something ordinarily thought of simply as "country." Surely we do not expect that "countries" can simply cease to exist.

Ideas of "national" and "ethnic" identity do indeed evoke images of kinship, organic relationship, familial loyalties, or, as Donald Horowitz calls it, "a family resemblance."[16] But if the basis of national and ethnic identity is *not* natural, if it does *not* represent common ancestry, then what is it? If the set of markers to which we often make reference as evidence of ethnonational identity—shared history, culture, language, or religion—are not naturally occurring phenomena, how should we think of them? National identities, including ethnic identities, are narrative practices. Some theorists even think of them as metaphoric, though metaphor is itself a narrative practice.[17] They are constituted through "bottom-up" processes: people tell stories of family and regional history; people practice culture and often alter it in the process or, more recently, they "consume" popular culture and by doing so shape its content to some degree; language, of course, contains and transmits culture and structures cognitive development; and both formal and informal religious groups can be influenced to some extent by their practitioners, depending on how hierarchical and flexible the group structure is. But they are also constituted as "top-down" processes, or elite-induced and -manipulated practices, whether in democratic or undemocratic environments.

Let's look at the case of the United States. In order to overcome the ethnic bias of European origins and move toward a more civic-based political culture, the articulation of historical narratives must remain open and contestable. However disturbing and destabilizing "multicultural" discourses are, they have become a persistent as much as contentious feature of civic life in the United States. The production of political culture in the United States is limited only through complex political and legal struggles that engage multiple institutions and actors (the public funding of the arts authorized by Congress, Supreme Court decisions pertaining to the limits of free speech, agents of cultural practice, and direct action by citizens, for instance). Religion remains, for the time being at least, separated from state authority, with multiple institutional and individual actors lined up on both sides of the issue and no lack of religious activists who, arguing that "America has lost its moral foundation" (an argument often made in conjunction with an indictment of multiculturalism), would like to abolish that separation.

The United States, therefore, *aspires* to a civic based identity, though ethnic and religious pluralism seems gripped by perpetual struggles over multiple histories, languages, cultural and religious practices, and right-wing "identity" and "values" groups ever waiting in the wings (and sometimes taking to the streets) to undermine that aspiration. Although the United States was "founded" on the rhetoric of equality, full citizenship was quite exclusive. Because equality originally extended only to a small ruling class of male property owners, it would be difficult to view that ruling class in terms of any kind of pluralism, particularly ethnic pluralism. To the contrary, the norm among early American/European colonists was the *subjugation* of east Europeans, Asians, Africans, and indigenous peoples. At best, then, what we have in the United States is an ongoing process of *transition* from an *implicitly* ethnic (and/or cultural) basis of political identity to *the ideal* of a civic identity and culture. That transition has been marked by demands—often through direct action and "extraordinary" political action, and sometimes violent—for expanding the basis of inclusion, eradicating traces of second-class citizenship, and emancipating various categories of people subjugated or marginalized on the basis of ethnicity, gender, and/or religious and national identities. American state-building entailed a kind of exclusionary nationalism based on a distinction between "European/Christian/white Americans" and "indigenous/primitive Others of color."[18] Even in the absence of any "ancient hatreds," Euro-Americans managed to kill literally millions of Africans and Native Americans in the course of building their democracy.

Many Western European states are similarly engaged in making a transition from ethnic to civic identities while simultaneously struggling with the process of forging a new "European" civic identity (Weiner 1998). The devolution of authority in Great Britain in response to demands for cultural pluralization, the question of citizenship for Turks and other non-Germans, the persistence of xenophobic political movements and parties in France and, most recently, Austria, all attest to a variety of "ethnic versus civic" identity struggles and adjustments. Meanwhile, the collapse of communism as the ideological basis for states-as-societies has raised a slightly different version of "the identity question" in central and eastern Europe.

These developments, along with violence mobilized around ethnic identities in formerly colonized non-Western states, have given renewed significance to one of the central questions of social theory: *What is the basis for group solidarity within the state?* For no matter how powerfully we imagine that the state is a naturally occurring or "emerging" unit of social order, the creation of real states has been an enormously violent process. The people who live in or "find themselves" living in modern states must confront the consequences of that violence. It is not only the winners who survive to write narratives of political identity, not only the state-makers and their descendants, but a variety of groups, each with its own historical narrative, many who were victimized or exploited by state makers. There are between four and five thousand ethnic groups and fewer than two hundred states. Virtually every state is multiethnic, though some less so than others. Yet every state has an official language and a foundational narrative, however tenuous and unstable it might be. State-making conquers the "Others" within imagined boundaries; assimilates, often brutally, those marginalized as "minorities"; unifies and imposes official languages on speakers of dialects and "non-native" languages;[19] and excludes particular ethnic groups from citizenship and/or restricts their immigration and emigration. Sometimes states even target specific ethnic/identity groups for forcible relocation. State-making has been violent, both directly and structurally.

## Theories of the State

In contrast to realist and neorealist international relations theory, which "takes the sovereign state as a given,"[20] feminist theory, comparative politics, and political theory and philosophy have, in different ways and at different historical moments in the practice of political inquiry, addressed the question of the origins of the state.[21] We have the liberal state, socialist state, welfare state, multiethnic state, totalitarian and authoritarian state, we have states "emerging" from the convergence of historical and social forces, and we have the state-as-polity and the Marxist state withering away. Theorizing the state comes (as it did in the 1960s, as the subject of "political development"), goes (as it did in the 1980s, when theorizing turned to the "states system") and returns (with a rise in poststructuralist, postmodern, and feminist theorizing in the 1990s).

It seems to me that discussions and theories of the state suggest, broadly speaking, five different though not mutually exclusive ways of thinking about the state. One involves an anthropological or sociological relationship between society and state. "Society" precedes the state, so that the state is understood as representing a certain level of societal and organizational complexity, hence it is often thought of as an "evolutionary" model. Gellner summarizes this view:

> Mankind has passed through three fundamental stages in its history: the preagrarian, the agrarian, and the industrial. Hunting and gathering bands were and are too small to allow the kind of political divisions of labor which constitute the state; and so, for them, the question of the state, of a stable specialized order-enforcing institution, does not really arise.[22]

Here, a "prestate" unit of social order, a "society," with perhaps self-evident boundaries, presumably evident also through a shared language as well as shared social norms, reaches a kind of critical evolutionary point of choice: to state-build or not to state-build.[23] Although used primarily by sociologists and some political historians and scientists, an evolutionary model of human society suggests that its roots are in anthropological thinking, even though anthropologists now often acknowledge that their discipline has revealed at least as much about the Western anthropological gaze as about that upon which it gazes.

A second way of thinking about the state also holds that the process of state-building is a function of social complexity, but elaborates and emphasizes the role of *institutions*. Increasing complexity moves social forces in a centralizing direction, producing corporate interests, which in turn create patterns of "behavior," norms, rules, procedures, and decision-making bodies. If this sounds like the basis of regime theory in International Relations, I think it is—an extrapolation from thinking about the state as a particular outcome of political development driven by increasing complexity which both broadens and deepens relationships of social and economic interdependence. According to this view, the state as a set of institutions is a particular response to an evolutionary problem. In a variation on this theme, these institutions can be viewed as the outcome of collaboration and recognition of mutual interests among *elites*, rather than social processes involving collective action in the sense of mobilization by the masses. Again, though employed explicitly or implicitly by nonsociologists, because of its focus on elites and social structures, I tend to think of the state from a sociological perspective.

A third, more overtly political way of thinking about the state views it as the expression of national self-determination. Again, though it draws on and interfaces with anthropological and sociological thinking, the association of statehood with the ability to exercise the fullest capacity for self-determination has the most direct and serious political consequences, particularly as nineteenth-century nationalism gave way to twentieth-century self-determination, notwithstanding the very conflicted and paradoxical relationship between the possible *right of peoples* to self-determination and the *right of states* to sovereignty. The state as an expression of self-determination presumes that the state has an ethnic basis, though a variation on this theme suggests, like the first view, that it is really *societies* that precede states, but that ethnic solidarity is the basis for prestate societies. The idea of *nation* is important here because it does not represent a kind of prestate merging of society with ethnicity. There are currently huge controversies over the international definition of "a people" precisely because that particular unit may, under international law, possess the right of self-determination, though the exercise of that right does not at this point include engaging in any act that violates the sovereignty of an existing state.

Of course the obvious problem here is the discontinuity between the number of ethnic groups and the number of states. It must be possible to exercise the right of self-determination through some means other than by taking, as a group, control of state institutions. The fact (Durkheim would say "social") that there are Chinese people who live in a Chinese state, Japanese people in a Japanese state, Swedes in Sweden, French people in a French state, and so on appeals to our unconscious or at least uncritical assumption that a natural relationship exists between ethnicity and state: ethnic groups, like families, are the basis for societies, and as societies "progressed" they developed into states. This obscures the fact that there are some 55 million people of marginalized ethnic groups in China, and assimilated indigenous Ainu in Japan along with second- and third-generation Koreans denied Japanese citizenship; indigenous Saami have been marginalized in Sweden; and the Frenchness of the French people was achieved (and is still maintained) through a kind of linguistic imperialism,[24] not to mention a very contestable border in the Basque country to the south.

A fourth view of the state has been suggested recently by feminists and various other critical theorists. I alluded to the feminist critique of the state earlier, but it is worth restating here. The state is a "reproduction" of the dominance and subjection socially institutionalized in gender hierarchy, with roots in the Greek *polis*,[25] a defensive response to the "fear of [female] engulfment,"[26] a product of the psychic trauma associated with the realization by the maturing male that control over one's needs is in the hands of one who is "different," and a demonstration of manhood.[27] As in previous cases, there is some overlap between feminist and other views, particularly those emphasizing elite domination, though feminists point out both that hierarchies of dominance may have their roots in gendered hierarchy and that elite structures are, in Western societies anyway and especially under conditions of modernity, dominated by men. Thus in hierarchies of race or class, for example, gender relations within a particular "race" or class will still reflect masculine privileging, both as male dominance and as the privileging of behaviors associated with the socially constructed category of masculinity. Men rule. There is something of each of us in the things we create. The creation of states is a process that both reflects and reproduces gender hierarchy. Therefore the states created by men embody and are understood in terms of "masculine" characteristics and the masculine experience of cognition.

The last perspective on the state follows from discourses on political philosophy within the historical narrative of "Western civilization." It appears sometimes as the image of the modern state as the institutional embodiment of classical liberal ideals, but it could just as well be a Marxist, communitarian, or associationalist state.[28] Here state-building is a humanistic and liberatory project. I include in this category the Marxist variation, for although subverted by the argument that ordinary people could not navigate their own liberation and required an intermediate dictatorship, the modern welfare state in its various shades of social democracy, can, I think, be traced to Marxist influences. The important thing about this perspective is that state-building is understood as a normative project involving the mobilization of *civil society* on the basis of common values and civic, rather than organic, relationship.

Underlying all four perspectives on the foundation of the modern state is an assumption that each attempts to address the basis for legitimacy or, in some cases, social cohesion to the extent that it provides and sustains legitimacy. The first three locate cohesiveness in the realm of organic identity (in the ethnic, rather than Durkheimian, sense), a self-conscious cultural affinity among members of the group, and a shared or at least agreed upon historical narrative, often commingled with the group identity narrative. The fourth — feminist and critical theories of the state — identifies hierarchy, elitism, and patriarchal structures and ideologies not only as the basis for cohesiveness within a race/class/gender-stratified society, but as pitfalls in the progressive development of political institutions legitimized by consent and on the basis of social equity within the framework of the ideal of a liberal polity.[29]

Finally, we have the state as liberator, whether in the form of the liberal state created by the populist revolutions against oppressive, despotic, and arbitrary monarchies of the seventeenth through nineteenth centuries in Western Europe, or in the form of the socialist revolutions in central and eastern Europe, Cuba, and China. In both cases, Marxist and liberal, the *struggle* for liberation provides the normative basis on which postrevolutionary legitimacy rests, and that struggle is mythologized within ideological narratives.

States are, as Giddens and others note, structures of social organization. It is possible as well as useful, I believe, to generalize about social structures to some extent, though we must keep in mind at least two analytical dimensions of distinction: time and complexity. The organization of social life and the structures through which social life is organized vary across time, so they must be historically contextualized, and, if I might add a kind of evolutionary dimension, they will vary in their degree of social complexity. Complexity is indicated by the scope of the organization, that is, the number of individuals whose social life is governed by the organization's norms and rules, and by the breadth and depth of social interaction, that is, the distance between interactive agents as well as the complexity of their interactions. Thus if we compare the Roman and British empires, the latter would constitute a more complex structure than the former.

The state as a structure of social organization carries out functions that have been carried out by a variety of other social organizations over time, such as the fiefdom, tribe, clan, village, kinship group, and so on. Today, however, as a result of the convergence of a variety of social forces as well as the agency of European political actors, the state is the preeminent structure carrying out or, in Giddens' terminology, "containing" the resources necessary to carry out two kinds of political activities: allocative and authoritative.[30] Any other form of social organization must reckon either with the existence and preeminence of the state, or with agents attempting to construct states in spaces where other forms of organization—tribes, clans, mafias, warlords, and so on—structure social life. Allocative activities involve the distribution of economic opportunities and resources such as jobs, regulating wages, provision of social and welfare services, property rights, access to technology (applied collective/community knowledge, including health care), and so on. Authoritative functions entail regulating social action, mobilizing resources for coercion, and enforcement of allocative rules. In a sense, this combines Laswell's concept of politics as "who gets what, when, where and how," with Easton's idea of politics as the allocation of values.[31] Or almost, for politics is not only about *who gets what* but *who does not get what*. It is, in other words, about allocating *and excluding*, and it is about *mobilizing coercive resources in order to enforce exclusion*. But what is missing, though Easton's emphasis on values nearly gets it, is what Onuf has outlined in his constructivist theory—the *normative* rule on which the basis of allocation, exclusion, and coercion rests. And while we would like to believe that the normative rule on which allocation, inclusion/ exclusion, and coercion in modern societies rests is some kind of social contract or citizenship, is it more often, in the end, based on a *perception of sameness*, whether articulated in terms of narratives of organic sameness or narratives of shared historical experience.[32] It is, therefore, identity that secures the social cohesiveness necessary to create and maintain the boundaries of inclusion and exclusion among those who identify themselves as "members" of the social group or "citizens" of the state.

## Legitimacy and Social Cohesion

If the state is not "natural" polity or community, then what is the basis for its social cohesiveness, when and where it does exist, and how can cohesiveness be cultivated and, when contested, maintained? As Cohen, Brown, and Organski have shown,[33] most states "came into existence" as a result of violence or by incorporating diverse social groups into a single administrative unit within which a dominant group's identity achieved hegemony. I will limit my remarks, therefore, to the general case of states created through various forms of struggle and conflict, including varying degrees of direct or structural violence. Once such a state "comes into existence," it faces the task of obtaining and maintaining some kind of popular support, even if it is not what Westerners would call a "democratic state." It is, I believe, more a matter of *degree* than *kind* when it comes to the relationship between relying on coercive force (or the threat of it) and relying on consent as the basis for regime legitimacy, for not only direct force counts, but the coercive force of economic survival, and consent is often support given by individuals (even an elite sector of the population, such as religious leaders in South and Central America before Liberation Theology upset the system) in exchange for or in expectation of receiving some kind of personal privilege or benefit, even if only in the form of association with the ruling class or regime.

In explaining civil strife and war or attempting to anticipate states at risk of civil war, we should begin by asking questions about the basis for legitimacy and social cohesion and how cohesion and legitimacy are positioned historically relative to a conflict or potential for conflict. Thus, for example, legitimacy in the United States was weakened during the 1950s and 1960s as social cohesion was stressed as a result of demands for greater inclusion and for ending discrimination and second-class citizenship for blacks and women. The Vietnam War also weakened both social cohesion and legitimacy. While normally the balance between coercion and consent in the United States weighs more heavily on the side of consent, in response to civil unrest arising in connection with both civil rights and antiwar protests, the federal government more than once employed force against those who challenged its legitimacy. The backlash of this period continues to some extent today, as social conservatives continue to chastise various liberation and antiwar movements of the earlier period and claim the need for a "return" to "family values" in order to rebuild the fabric of American society.

Legitimacy in communist countries rested on a combination of coercion and consent, with emphasis on overt and covert coercion. But this does not mean that communist regimes did not also attempt to mobilize consent and, as a consequence, create cohesion. In Poland social cohesiveness was mobilized around both religion and eventually workers' organizations, creating a parallel social structure that undermined the ability of the communist regime to rule with any support other than a minority willing to support the Communist party. In Romania, direct coercion played a larger role than state-sponsored socialization and indoctrination, probably more so than Poland and with less pretense toward consent. In communist states in general, legitimacy would have to rely on intellectuals because social cohesion was based on ideology—the sameness of beliefs—rather than on the sameness of so-called naturalized identities. This was also consistent with Marxist doctrine. Prejudices of ethnicity, class, and gender were supposed to wither away under an enlightened Marxist society, and religion was to become completely irrelevant. What varied among communist countries was the degree to which a particular regime relied on coercion (usually a mixture of direct coercion and state-sponsored socialization) and the degree to which the perception of sameness followed from narrative and ideological abstractions as opposed to organic or concrete naturalized or religious identities.

This emphasis on state-building as an intellectual project, even if it necessitated an interim dictatorship of the "unenlightened masses," profoundly shaped social life in communist societies. Regimes attempted to recruit intellectuals and artists, to censor their cultural production, and, of course, to censor if not fabricate historical narratives consistent with Marxist ideology. Dissidents thus also came to play a critical role in undermining the legitimacy of communist regimes, and Yugoslavia was no different. The historical narrative on which communist Yugoslavia was founded construed "South Slavs" as the relevant kindred identity and a shared struggle against imperialism (Austro-Hungarian and Ottoman) as the basis for creating a liberatory state. Marxist anti-imperialism supplanted earlier forms of anti-imperialism such as Serb, Croat, or Illyrian nationalism. The effort to discredit nationalism, which sometimes took the form of outright government repression, never entirely succeeded, however, and eventually nationalism became an important expression of both demands for reform and outright anticommunist dissidence.

Within this framework, many elements of the breakdown of Yugoslavia and the ability of certain leaders to incite violence becomes much more comprehensible. Alija Izetbegović's publication of *The Islamic Declaration*, often cited by Serb nationalists to arouse fears of Islamic nationalism in Europe, was more an attempt to articulate Bosnian Muslim dissent from the contradiction of a communist system that claimed to transcend ethnonational identities while at the same time providing unique opportunities for participation on the basis of Serbian, Croatian, Slovenia, Montenegrin, and Macedonian nationalities. The last, failed president of Yugoslavia, Dobrica Ćosić, was a nationalist, a dissident, and a writer. His novel *Vreme srmti*, which tells the story of Serbian "betrayal" and "herosim" during World War I, is said to be one of the two most influential novels in fomenting a climate of toxic nationalism in the 1980s.[34] The 1987 Memorandum of the Serbian

Academy of Sciences, often credited with providing the rationale for Serbian hegemonic aspirations and even with starting the war, was influential precisely because it was an intellectual product. Franjo Tudjman was an historian, Radovan Karadžić a psychiatrist, his successor, Biljana Plavšić a biologist, and so on. The role of intellectuals varied across the various communist states, and I do not mean to oversimplify with generalizations, but in contrast to Western democracies, the party and its ideology functioned as the basis for legitimacy much more than did the constitutions.

Compared to other communist states, the Yugoslav regime relied more on socialization and less on direct coercion, which also meant that Yugoslav intellectuals played a relatively large role in creating and sustaining the legitimacy of the state. Ugrešić notes that Yugoslav intellectuals did not have to play the role of dissidents to the extent that their counterparts did in other communist states.[35] Additionally, as a war hero and symbol of pan-Yugoslavism, Tito embodied a naturalized, organic identity, so that when he died, intellectuals began to defect from communism and toward nationalism as the normative basis for solidarity. On a purely rational, intellectual level, the transformation of communist leaders into nationalists (with the exception of Izetbegović, the secessionist and nationalist leaders of Slovenia, Croatia, Serbia and Macedonia were all former party leaders) and how, when they transformed themselves, the people followed, makes no sense without understanding the legitimating role of intellectuals and the intellectual role of communist leadership. This also explains why Vaclav Havel, a dissident intellectual, was able to lead the Czechs and Slovaks toward a peaceful dissolution, and why the Polish Solidarity movement provided a network for the maintenance of organic identity and later, transition to market democracy.

Both socialist and democratic liberal states attempted to engineer a transition from organic, ethnic conceptions of sameness as the basis for solidarity and cohesiveness to a normative, civic, or ideological basis for reciprocity, sameness, and commensurability among citizens subject to state authority. Communist states may have failed, but that does not mean that liberal states have yet succeeded. Only recently the liberal, democratic, western European state of Austria witnessed the rise to power of a xenophobic nationalist party and leader, to the surprise and outrage of the people and leaders of other EU states. In the process of such a transition, much weight falls on the shoulders of historical narratives, articulating and even mythologizing shared experiences. But why do we assume that democracy is not impaired by the fact that "history is written by the victors"? Why do we seem to be in denial about the distortions of history and their capacity to hinder the democratization of our societies? Why do we assume that the political appropriation of history is unlikely or relatively harmless in our liberal democratic states? I knew from previous research that the construction of indigenous peoples as the backward Other was not as much a thing of the past as more high-minded

Western liberals might like to believe. And indigenous people (and other people of color) know that "the victor's history" is neither harmless nor apolitical. Why do marginalized people demand the inclusion of their perspectives, and why do social conservatives so fear this? I have come to believe that an unstable, as contrasted with a "fixed," history, a history inclusive of multiple and conflicting claims, is probably a very good sign in a democracy aspiring to the liberal ideals of social justice.

## Balkan Ghosts, Narrative Practices, and Politics

The first breakup of Yugoslavia and subsequent descent into brutal, personal violence rationalized mostly on the basis of imagined ethnic differences occurred during World War II. One-tenth of the population—1,700,000 people—was killed in combat, mass murders, or concentration camps.[36] If we wish to evaluate the broader societal tramatization, then we must also take into account those who killed them, either as members of the collaborationist regime or as fighters for the Serbian nationalist Četniks. If we add together the number of people who were either victims or perpetrators, the number of those directly affected is probably doubled, and multipled again by the number of family members affected. Put differently, something like three million families were directly involved in or tragically affected by the atrocities of a war fueled by both internal and external forces of hatred, even if there was no "natural" basis for it. As the economic and political situation became increasingly unstable after Tito's death, politicians willing to exploit these "open wounds" had little trouble arousing those repressed but not forgotten fears. Drakulić writes poignantly of the interlocking logics of unreconciled grievances, fear, and nationalism:

[N]ow the time has come to count the dead again, to punish and to rehabilitate. This is called "redressing the injustice of the former regime." In the spring of 1990, the monument to the nineteenth-century Croat hero Duke Jelašić, removed by the communist government after World War II and relegated to what was known in the official lingo of the day as the "junkyard of the past," has been returned its original place; Republic Square has been renamed after him. The name of the Square of the Victims of Fascism, where once stood the notorious Ustaše prison, has also been changed. The names of virtually all major streets and squares in the cities throughout Croatia have been changed—even the names of the cities themselves. The symbols, the monuments, the names are being obliterated. . . . Thus altered and corrected, the past is in fact erased, annihilated. People live without the past, both collective and individual. This has been the prescribed way of life for the past forty-five years, when it was assumed that history began in 1941 with the war and the revolution. [37]

Mirko Tepavac, former foreign minister in ex-Yugoslavia, finds it miraculous that Tito and his partisan followers, meeting at Jajce in the aftermath of war, managed to establish any basis for peaceful coexistence at all, however coercive, in the aftermath of the war. "[W]ithin two years," he writes, "one could travel safely from one end of Yugoslavia to another, irrespective of nationality, religious beliefs, or language."[38] Pro-Axis war criminals were tried and punished, as well a few political opponents, expressions of nationalism essentially became criminalized, and the slogan of "brotherhood and unity" silenced any open discussion of the horrors of the war. "Terror by remembering is a parallel process to terror by forgetting," writes Dubravka Ugrešić, and "Both processes have the function of building a new state, a new truth."[39]

As I formally interviewed and informally chatted with people in the Yugoslav successor states, I was repeatedly struck by their mistrust of history and historians.

*M.P. Belgrade 1995*

I think it is often the case of history, not only here, being used for political purposes. But it is very clear now, and I agree, it is very difficult because everything has been colored by these very intense emotional issues which were never addressed after World War II. It is very difficult to distinguish between facts and inventions, and we need to learn how to do that. We keep falling into stereotypes of being insufficiently nationally conscious, or of being a traitor, and so history is a battlefield. A lot of my foreign colleagues say "you have to get over the past, you have to look toward the future." But when we try to explain what happened here, that it has some relationship with what happened before—they think this is sort of irrelevant. But this is an extremely complex land geopolitically, and it is not only our choice, but our fate that history has not yet become fully the past here.

*R.N., Belgrade, 1995*

I don't know if anyone can explain why this is, but so many dimensions of European civilization meet here in such a way that once you touch it, it is just so disruptive and it has been so many times, perhaps like Huntington says.[40] The roots of the religious conflict, relations of central Europe civilization, the division lines between the East and the West, these are things that have been with us, the manipulation by the external powers of the conflict sides, these are all old stories, so obviously the past is a very key dimension in understanding why all this has happened.

And how can you know where you are going until you know where you are coming from? It is overwhelming, that history, once you begin to take it into account, then all other stereotypes and explanations don't hold. So if your intention is not to understand, then you have to ignore history.

When Others take the historical dimension into account then it is always something like "those Balkans people are always fighting" and "ancient hatreds" and so on. But there is something like a posttrauma from these events, and it is passed on from one generation to the next and will continue to do so unless we begin to openly address it.

The question of history, of who gets to decide what constitutes an official or correct version, is not an easy one. How do we not only remember the Holocaust, but remember it *correctly*? And what is the purpose or motivation for remembering? One would think it is in part to draw ethical lessons from the tragedy, the "never again" lesson. But even as Elie Wiesel gave a speech in Washington, D.C., at the dedication of the U.S. Holocaust Memorial Museum in 1992, he reminded his audience of its failure to intervene in Bosnia. All of the people I talked with in ex-Yugoslavia seemed to spend a lot of time thinking about history and the role of history in relation to politics and conflict. Of course, I asked them about the role played by history (see Note on Methodology), but their answers were lengthy and reflective, as if they had been waiting for someone to ask.

*M.B., Zagreb, 1997*
We were not told the whole truth about World War II, about Bleiburg, and about how most Croats did not support the quisling state. But we were punished as a people for it. I learned later that the symbols used by the Independent State of Croatia were really historical symbols of Croat nationalism long before they were adopted by the Ustaše. So when I display those symbols now, like the flag in my car, it is a *historical* symbol, not a fascist symbol. You know that's how I can tell when I pass other Croats in their cars. They have either the Croatian flag or a rosary, or both, hanging from their rearview mirror.

*M.P., Zagreb, 1997*
In school of course I learned a lot about World War II, but like everyone else, much more from an ideological and political perspective, not a real historical perspective. We definitely got a one-sided picture, the picture of the winners, of Partisans, which became the official communist point of view. So communists wrote history from their ideological and political perspective, for their political purposes, and in that case Ustaše, Četniks, and others were demonized, stigmatized, and we never had the possibility to experience or to be exposed to the real dimension of that historical tragedy. It was much more a part of the ideological framework of the communist period than a real historical education.

Of course, historical narratives are not only politicized, interpretive acts. They are also the telling of lived experiences. Said one respondent:

*S.S., Belgrade, 1995*

To speak about how nations or nationalities developed here in Yugo-slavia, there is the issue of actually suppressing histories and mythologies. We simply forgot our history as a result of communist education since 1945, which provided us with an internationalist version of history, so to speak. I would add to that the illusion, the official Yugoslav line which the West bought into, that the nationality problem was resolved in Yugo-slavia, when in fact it was not resolved. We forgot that it was only rela-tively recently that there was a fratricidal war here in Yugoslavia, plus another factor—the genocide. The role of genocide in World War II is still very influential among people today, and it is exactly on the territory of Croatia and Bosnia where it occurred that now you have the most intense fighting because, as you know, Bosnia was mainly part of the Ustaše state. Serbs I think suppressed this but never forgot about it. Unlike in Germany, there was not an open discussion about World War II in Yugoslavia since 1945.

The implications of basing state legitimacy on national identity conceived in organic terms were perfectly clear to one very influential philosopher and antiwar activist. He was very angry when I spoke with him; among other, more obvious reasons, he was angry because so many of his graduate students had left the country. This made the prospect for a democratic future even grimmer.

*M.Z., Belgrade, 1995*

Okay, on my own identity. I am by origin Serb, you know. But I am educated as Yugoslav. In high schools, elementary schools, in the whole of my life I was Yugoslav. And I think that a Yugoslav identity exists. Yugo-slav people also exist biologically, in mixed marriages, you know, that would be a biological example of Yugoslav identity, but that is not really the problem. To speak of *biological* Yugoslavs is to take a racist view of identity. The problem is that we were educated as in my generation (I am now 65) not only in Serbian literature, but in Croatian literature, in Slovenian literature, in Macedonian literature. That was our Yugoslav liter-ature. Now people are fighting over whether this or that writer was a Croat or a Serb or a Bosniak. We Yugoslavs don't, for example, have our own philosophy. You know I am philosopher, but I am not interested what nationality, for instance, is Emanuel Kant or Hegel. I was simply educated in philosophy, which is the heritage of humankind. And in that sense I can tell you what my corporeal identity is, but the problem of national iden-tity is the problem of cultural identity, it's not some kind of racism or Nazism which stresses biological identity.

I just came from a symposium in Novi Sad and I had a great dispute with my old friends who were philosophers because now they think that

Muslims are "biologically" Serbs. That may be true, but they overlook the fact that the problem of national identity is the problem of *cultural* identity. It is a problem of the historical destiny of some people which existed in Bosnia, and Bosnia was not Serbia during any time of its existence, so those people never lived in Serbia even though they were Serbs. I think that there exists, for example, Bosniak national identity now which was denied at the beginning of this war. Now I think they must have their own identity, but it will depend on the results of this war. Serbs from Pale, these nationalistic Serbs, they leave them only one choice. The Bosniaks had to become nationalistic whether they wanted to or not. But to "cleanse" Bosnia, they are saying "If you are Serb, okay you will stay in our country, if you are not Serbs, if you deny that you are Serbs, then please leave our country. We want to have an ethnically cleansed country." This is insane. This is a move backward, a racist move backward.

*D.V., Belgrade, 1995*

How did national identity change during the last decade and last several years? Before and during the war? I think that identities have not been changed in the sense that people who are Croats suddenly changed their identity. Most probably thought of themselves as both Croat *and* Yugoslav, both Serb *and* Yugoslav, and it was not a problem for them. Political elites tried to make identity an issue. During the existence of last Yugoslavia, the identity of Yugoslav existed. Period. Probably as the institutions that embodied the Yugoslav state disintegrated, people became frightened, perhaps they could not identify Yugoslavia with something that could solve their problems. There is so little difference between the cultural heritage among Croatian, Serbian, people, especially, they have common language, even common history. The only thing they don't have in common is religion. According to Max Weber, the difference in religion is the main source of the difference among nations in this part of ex-Yugoslavia. But I think that we are now faced with the problem of the identity of Muslims in our country. If your question is how national identity has been changed I must say that the first problem is the appearance of a new question—do we have to neglect the existence of Muslims as special national identity or to affirm it? This was central to the "nationality question" which arose in the sixties and seventies and was never resolved.

I think we must affirm it, must recognize that there exists a type of new national identity which wants to be recognized here. And the main problem is not when we recognize it, but if we neglect those demands for the identity of nations within existing states. Every nation in ex-Yugoslavia wants to have their own state, and this is completely impossible. The right of self-determination was the main ideological model of Serbian nationalists. They say all nations in ex-Yugoslavia had this right of self-determination—Slovenians, Croatians—not only for Serbs, and Serbs must have their own country, a new country in which all Serbs live in a new Greater Serbia. This is completely impossible. Imagine that all Russians want to be in one state!

*R.N., Belgrade, 1995*
All the nations now aspiring to become states have, in developing their national dreams or aims, recruited various historical myths, so the reconstruction and reinterpretation of history is being done all over the place. You have literally hundreds of books on behalf of each nationality now attempting to prove that either they are the oldest nation in this region, or that they dissociate themselves from the others, that the others come from somewhere else, that their origins are different than they were, that they belong more to Europe and not Balkans, the so-called Europe-Byzantine question. The roots of our existence here are really being reinterpreted, and there are all sorts of preposterous theories coming out. I think it is hard sticking to this kind of mythological legitimation of the national dreams and trying to prove that what they are doing now is actually carrying a continuation of something thousands and thousands of years old. In that sense the machinery of inventing an reconstructing the past is very present, and there are serious problems from the past, and memories and tensions, and mutual ill memories, but also this whole political industry of producing false history.

I think it is often the case of, not only here, [history] being used for political purposes. But it is very clear now, and I agree, it is very difficult because everything has been colored by these very intense emotional issues and it is very difficult to distinguish between facts and inventions and it needs to be, falling into stereotypes of being insufficiently nationally conscious or a traitor, and so history is a battlefield. This is one aspect, and another aspect is that I think (a lot of my foreign colleagues say "you have to get over the past, you have to look toward the future, we are not interested in" — when we try to explain what happened here, that it has some relationship with what happened before — they think this is sort of boring) but this is a very, very complex land, and it is not only our choice, but to some extent, our destiny.

*B.J., Belgrade, 1995*
Serbs living in one state, it was Yugoslavia, and now they want all Serbs living in one state, but why destroy Yugoslavia? Yugoslavia was where all Serbs lived in one state!

And one of the student émigrés recalls:

I remember that I had never known my grandfather—he had been hanged by the Ustaše. I remember being told that my family had not been allowed to take him off the gallows for four days because the Ustaše were setting an example for the rest of the village. And I resented the Croats for that.

But at the same time I knew that there was nothing intrinsically evil about the Croats, and nothing inherently altruistic about the Serbs. The Croats' reasons for hating the Serbs seemed reasonable, too. Furthermore, some of my best friends were Croats. I could not resolve the dilemma between love for my own culture and respect for cultures that differed from mine.... (J.P., Corvallis, Oregon)

In the case of Yugoslavia, the interpretation and reinterpretation of historical "truths" are often regarded as a major factor contributing to the creation of a hostile climate that made war carried out as personal violence almost inevitable. "The terror of remembering," says Ugrešić,

is, of course, also a war strategy of setting up frontiers, establishing differences: we are different from them (Serbs), our history, faith, customs and language are different from theirs. In the war variant this complex (which profoundly penetrates the Croatian collective consciousness) is used like this: we are different from them (Serbs) because we are better, which is proved by our history; we always built, they only destroyed; we are a European, Catholic culture, they are only Orthodox, illiterate barbarians. And so on and so forth.[41]

On the six hundredth anniversary of the Battle of Kosovo, Milosević evoked the "terror of remembering" in his now infamous 1989 speech in which he grounded Serb nationalism in historical victimization, a move would enable him to contort Serbian aggression in Bosnia and provocation in Croatia into noble and liberatory acts:

Today, it is difficult to say what is the historical truth about the Battle of Kosovo and what is legend. Today this is no longer important. Oppressed by pain and filled with hope, the people used to remember and to forget as, after all, people in the world do, and it was ashamed of treachery and glorified heroism. Therefore it is difficult to say today whether the Battle of Kosovo was a defeat or a victory for the Serbian people, whether thanks to it we fell into slavery or we survived this slavery....

The lack of unity and betrayal in Kosovo will continue to follow the Serbian people like an evil fate through the whole of its history. Even in the last war [World War II], this lack of unity and betrayal led the Serbian people into agony, the consequences of which in the historical and moral sense exceeded fascist aggression....

The concessions that many Serbian leaders made at the expense of their people could not be accepted historically and ethnically by any nation in the world, especially because the Serbs have never in the whole of their history conquered and exploited others. Their national and historical being has been liberational through the whole of history and through two world wars, as it is today. . . . Let the memory of Kosovo heroism live forever! Long live Serbia! Long live Yugoslavia! Long live peace and brotherhood among peoples! (From Milosević's speech on the six hundredth anniversary of the Battle of Kosovo, Gazimestan, June 28, 1989)

The Battle of Kosovo came up in virtually every interview in Serbia because it was widely believed to have become a symbol around which the most intolerant and even racist form of Serbian nationalism was aroused among ordinary people. So powerful is its symbolism that I found Americans quoting Serb propaganda during the NATO intervention in Kosovo in 1999. They told me again and again how "Kosovo is to Serbs like the Alamo is to Americans," one of the official lines coming out of Belgrade at the time.[42]

*S.T., Belgrade, 1995*
If you asked people on the street what year was the Battle of Kosovo, many people wouldn't know, but the idea of having been conquered by the Turkish empire is what is important in their version of history. The Kosovo played a role in Serb identity for two reasons: (1) to liberate all the Serbs, specifically, and (2) identifying Serbs as liberators vis-à-vis imperial conquest. In the nineteenth century nationalism was important in all of Europe, that was the time of nationalism, not in today's sense, but the nineteenth century was the century of nationalism in a romantic sense. Then between the two wars and after the Second War it was not so important to Serbs, but now they have made it important again. . . . It is a revival of Kosovo and revival of nationalism.

*D.T., Belgrade, 1995*
In the minds of ordinary people, the Battle of Kosovo is a powerful symbol of oppression as told in our history under the Ottomans. The central feature of the story was liberation from the Muslims [Turks] because Kosovo battle was the symbol of this liberation from the Turks. They [the nationalists] repeated this theme all through the nineteenth century very much to create support for [Serbian] uprisings and then finally the Balkan wars. And now they do the same, because after the uprising in Kosovo and the conflict between Albanians and Serbs some intellectuals from the nineteenth century have also been revived as cultural heroes. Serbian national identity has been created by defining itself as a struggle against Muslim— meaning Turkish—domination.

*S.T., Belgrade 1995*

I have thought about this Kosovo battle. I am not sure that it played some role in the development of national identity because Kosovo was important for identification of Serbs in the nineteenth century but that is not the only fact because we have the same thing in Bulgaria and Macedonia. But it played a greater role in the creation of Serb national identity in the nineteenth century than now because the main goal then was the independence of Serbia, the main interest of Serbs was to liberate Kosovo field and that was important for national identification and for national unity. The main slogan for the Balkan Wars was to liberate Kosovo.

As Milosević's ranting in Kosovo elevated his influence among the growing number of elite nationalists, some more and some less extreme, Franjo Tudjman the historian had just published his controversial book entitled *Bespuča* (Wilderness), just a year before he was elected as president of Croatia. His revisionist history of Ustaše atrocities gave a figure of 60,000 Serbs and others killed at the compound of camps known as Jasenovac, in contrast with the claim under the postwar communist regime that between 750,000 and 1 million people died there. Many Croats hailed Tudjman for "finally revealing the truth" about the war, relieving them of the collective guilt Tito had manipulated in order to subdue them and any national political or cultural aspirations. His claim not only set off a furious debate in what was still an undivided Yugoslavia (structurally, at least), but provided chilling evidence of how historical narratives as "truths" had structured both identities and interpersonal and intergroup relations in postwar period. The book provoked a campaign to disinter mass graves in order to discredit Tudjman. The crusade was carried out on the ground and in the media, with publically displayed remains and televised funerals. In the process, the heretofore unacknowledged fact of the Bleiburg Massacre of unarmed Croatian refugees also received substantial publicity, and this, in turn, coupled with the implication of collective Croatian guilt for the brutalities of the quisling regime, provoked a significant anti-Yugoslav, anti-Serb backlash in Croatia. Tudjman's book was considered by some as tantamount to hate speech. Croatian and Serbian nationalist narratives became mirror images of victimization and paranoia:

*D.C., Korcula, 1997*

Of course the Serbs have a fear of so-called Croatian nationalism by the stories given to them by their people who lived through the Second World War. It was not intended to scare them, or to provoke them with talk about what Croats had done to them in the Second World War. In the socialist education system when you talk about history you get the partisan version of history, when you talk about the Croatian situation in the Second World War, you got a very bad picture about the Ustaše and the Croatian nationalists and what they did. Of course the numbers are very interesting, they always played with the numbers. The official line was always to talk about communism as the savior against the Ustaše enemy. But I actually I think that more than that it was just to keep Croats under control. Tito was seen to manipulate the collective guilt of Croats for crimes of Ustaše, and that was also seen [by Croats] as a way of keeping Croats under control. On the other hand, from the Serb perspective, Tito was seen as splitting up Serbs into three different republics and then making autonomous regions in Serbia was a way of controlling Serbs. So each had a paranoia about the other and about the communist system or Tito as the oppressor.

*V.D., Belgrade, 1995*
The time of Communist totalitarianism as an era in the history of the idea of Yugoslavia, as a Yugoslav state, it was comparatively a very long period in the history, almost fifty years, which is longer than the eleven years of democracy in Serbia before. So you can disregard all the propaganda about this tradition and that tradition, because what they learned under communism lasted longer than any of these other periods when the Serbian state was supposed to have existed as a democracy aspiring to self-determination. And now textbooks have been rewritten, and most of the Stalinists have become nationalists. You have kids here who were twleve or thirteen when Milosević came to power and now they are seventeen or eighteen. They grew up with one version of things and now they find another. The totalitarian mind has adapated perfectly well to the politics of Milosević and other, sometimes even more extreme nationalists. I don't believe personally that Milosević is really a nationalist. He is an opportunist.

*J.B., Zagreb, 1997*
The Serbs always identify with their own victimization. They tried to manipulate the Croats through a sense of collective guilt for what happened in World War II. Under Tito, with mostly Serbs in the bureaucracy, Croats were disproportionately arrested and imprisoned for crimes against the state. Serb nationalism was expressed as Yugoslav patriotism, since really Yugoslavia was a state where most of the government jobs were taken by Serbs. Croats, on the other hand, were industrious, and preferred not to work in government jobs, but to be educated and more professional. We were punished for expressing any Croat nationalism.

*K.V., Belgrade, 1995*
Some people are concerned that there will be three Serbian states, and they are concerned about whether they will need a passport to go from, for example Serbian Krajina to Republika Srpska, to Yugoslavia. You know if this was a situation of normal European states it would become quite

normal for people to travel without passports as they move from one state to another. It doesn't really matter so much what state you are from. And I say there have been many examples, you know, where people of one nation are not allowed to unite into one state for strategic reasons. Austria is not a part of Germany. But this obsession . . . these creatures of myth, the nation, they have a powerful influence on the imagination and, consequently, on our ideas of reality.

*D.S., Belgrade, 1995*

So okay, there are principles, you know. One is the principle of group identity, a second is the identification with or within the territories or republics, and finally the identity of the man as an individual. You know these are the three principles. And the misalignment of these three was always a problem of Yugoslavia. It began to subside in the twentieth century in this so-called modern Serb state. It has its roots in the nineteenth-century independent Serbia, although it was from Belgrade to Niš, but in this part it was organized administratively in this way, and the political parties were established in the nineteenth century. So some kind of formal political culture existed within Serbia, and some kind of territorial identification. But let us discuss Serbian history. People will talk about Serbian tradition, they talk about heroism, fighting against invaders, but what about five hundred years of Turkish rule, and only occasionally some uprising. It is again very contradictory. So Serbs are some heroic, and some very subservient. People make mythologies about themselves, and about the Others, of course people make mythologies.

*S.T., Belgrade 1995*

There is not much history of Serbia as an independent state, but the mythology goes to the Middle Ages, the feudal state of Serbia. Then of course, this is where the idea that Kosovo is in Serbia comes from. But it was not until after World War I that Kosovo and Metohija became part of Serbia as a modern state. From some Serbs you get the impression that they had killed all the Turks when they talk of overthrowing their oppressors. . . . But Serbs and Croats, Muslims and Croats are essentially the same people. In some sense it is a biblical war between brothers. I mention our case simply because at times it becomes ridiculous. In the case of Yugoslavia, Serbs became, in the eyes of the others, a very big nation, but actually it is a very small nation. Serbia is one of the most megalomaniacal nations in the world. By that I mean this idea that although you are a small nation, you can claim something much larger, which was in fashion at that time. In the eyes of Slovenes or Croats when they talk about Greater Serbia you would think they were talking about the Soviet Union or U.S. or at least Canada or something like that.

S.S., Belgrade, 1995

As a matter of fact my wife is a Serb from Croatia who escaped the geno-
cide there in 1941, her family was killed. People moved back and forth, it
is in some sense one nationality, but it is not necessarily homogeneous.
There are some differences in traditions, but historically speaking,
Montenegrins are in some ways more Serb than I, who come from central
Serbia, and still they wouldn't like to be ruled always from Belgrade. If it
ever came to some unification or reunification with the Serbs in Bosnia or
Croatia, it would have to be some kind of federal state or decentralized
state because in spite of how much we try to convince ourselves that being
Serb is enough to make us all alike, there are very sharp differences, for
instance, between the rural Serbs of Bosnia and the majority of urban Serbs
in Belgrade. There has always been a difference between Serbs living in and
out of Serbia proper. But speaking about so-called Greater Serbia, it has
never been developed as a project. There were some talks historically, but,
I think that was at the time of World War I, 1914 to 1915, when there was
the possibility that if Serbia and Montenegro became victorious—as they
did, later on—they would be able to choose what sort of state to create as
a result of their World War I victory, as a result of helping to defeat the
crumbling Austro-Hungarian empire. Whether to unite only parts of the
southern Slavic areas, primarily Serb majority areas, or to opt for something larger. Today some people think that Serbs made an historical
mistake—I don't know, it depends on how you look at that, whether a
mistake or not, it certainly was a reflection of Serbian megalomania, self-
determination, Versailles, the idea that somehow the Western Allies wanted
to get the Balkan parts together, and there were several factors.

Drakulić laments the loss of cosmopolitan identity and the way in which
Yugoslav realities collapsed into Manichaean opposites in a political climate
of escalating and mutual intolerance:

Some of my foreign friends from that time cannot understand that being
Croat has become my destiny. How can I explain to them that in this war
I am defined by my nationality, and by it alone? There is another thing that
is even harder to explain—the way the awareness of my nationality, because
of my past, came to me in a negative way. I had fought against treating
nationality as a main criterion by which to judge human beings; I tried to
see the people behind the label; I kept open the possibility of dialogue with
my friends and colleagues in Serbia even after all telephone lines and roads
had been cut off and one third of Croatia has been occupied and
bombed. . . .[43]

## Conclusion

Perhaps the nation is not entirely imagined. Perhaps there was a time when the boundaries delineating communal life were marked by sharper distinctions in language, physical appearance, and cultural practice, as with many indigenous peoples today, in spite of unrelenting efforts to force their assimilation. But it has been the project of the state to incorporate and expand its control over people and resources. We may even one day come to see imperialism as an historical chapter in the logic of state expansion. In any event, as a consequence of state and imperial expansionism, virtually all states today are to some degree multiethnic, multicultural, and multinational. Their boundaries are more artificial than natural, and their roots lie in violent processes rather than consent. To many of the people living within them, the boundaries of the polity appear contestable. Perhaps we should be surprised that they are not challenged more often. That they are not is probably a result of several factors: the relative openness of some (more or less democratic) states to participation and changes that restructure power; the ability of states to persuade those within their jurisdiction that they can secure basic needs for order, access to economic resources and opportunities, collective decision-making, problem-solving, and so on; and the production of legitimating narratives constructed out of both historical interpretation and a belief that identity and political life are linked—that the inside/outside boundaries between "us" and "others" are real.

Perhaps what we in the Western world call "ethnic" identities today are the remnants of a more organic form of kinship. But modernity, with its capacity for the widespread movement of people and ideas (not to mention guns, germs, and steel), its migrations, conflicts, and logic of domination, has left in its wake many fractured, fragmented, and interpenetrated identities living within the boundaries of a relatively small number of states. We might view the century of conflicts in southeastern Europe, including former Yugoslavia, as postcolonial. "State-making" has been a violent process involving both direct and structural domination, which in turn has led to struggles among groups for and against cultural hegemony. But it is not only a matter of establishing, albeit through violent means, *whose* language will be the official language, *whose* version of history will represent the official history, and *whose* cultural practices and identity constitute the basis for a (mythologized) "national" identity on which the legitimation of the nation-as-state rests. One identity achieves dominance through state-making by *destroying* (assimilating, marginalizing) "other" cultures, languages, histories, and identities. Yet here we are, as the twenty-first century begins, living in a political world in which thousands of groups who do or might claim nationality on the basis of ethnic, cultural, or religious "sameness" live within a system of fewer than two hundred states.

Historical narratives do not constitute truth, nor can they ever consist of complete knowledge. They attempt to resolve competing truths in accord with struggles over power and interpretation in order to produce legitimating narratives (American history, French history, British history, Irish history, Russian history, and so on). In actuality they can do no more than settle such questions temporarily and in relation to the structure of power underlying complex relationships (including those of domination and subordination) among agents. Historical narratives are a kind of repository for the ongoing project of interpreting collective human experiences. From historical interpretation meanings and identities are constructed; however, neither meanings nor identities are stable and fixed. The stories themselves are less important than either the meanings we assign to them or the way meanings structure power. Only in a democratic environment can multiple histories be told, contested, and become the subject of inclusive civic discourse. But that is not enough. The liberal model of the state as we know it today remains centered on the idea of majority–minority relations, where majority is most often expressed in terms of identity, whether in ethnic, national, or cultural terms or some combination thereof. Perhaps, as both Connolly and Rosenau argue,[44] what we need are decentered identities, where no identity is privileged within a truly pluralistic normative environment.

# CHAPTER 6

# The Social Construction
# of War

History is a battlefield. It is a tragedy, but it is our fate that history has not
yet become the past here.

—R.N., Belgrade, 1995

Structural approaches to the causes-of-war question rest on an assumption
of rational agency, often represented as the basis for strategic decision-making
by political elites. This does not, however, tell us why it is rational for "ordinary people," the people whose lives and property are put at risk, whose
towns and villages become battlefields, and whose loved ones will die, to
carry out the violence of war. War may or may not be rational from the
perspective of elites. It may strengthen or erode their hold on power, if that
is what we mean by rational, or they may obtain personal economic gains
for themselves, their families, and friends, if that is what we mean by rational.
But elites do not fight wars. Violence may also be "rational" for criminals
whose exploits create a lucrative black market for stolen and contraband
goods. But for the millions who become internally and internationally
displaced persons and the hundreds of thousands of victims and families of
victims raped, tortured, and murdered, wasn't the war, in ex-Yugoslavia
anyway, at least as emotional as it was rational? How is it that ordinary
people are persuaded to *act* on the wishes of elites, rational, strategic, or
otherwise?

There is a point in the course of political violence when the experience
and climate of violence creates and sustains its own logic without regard for
either the rationality of "strategic thinking" or the primordial imperatives of
"ethnic conflict."[1] This is more likely to happen when the locus of violence
is decentered, lacking organization and a clear line of command and responsibility, as in ex-Yugoslavia or Rwanda.[2] This is partly Goldhagen's point—
that many "ordinary" Germans willingly and voluntarily engaged in acts of
inhumanity, including murder, against Jews, with little or no authoritative or
official prompting.[3] Once violence is experienced personally, however, its

emotional underpinnings are laid bare, and perhaps the only real question then is whether one will remain content, and restrained, in the role of victim, or not. In 1997 I heard the story of one young woman who finally found her way to a rape crisis program in Zagreb. She had been captured and imprisoned by Serb soldiers at the age of fourteen. During six months of captivity, she was repeatedly raped, including sexual assaults involving penetration with the barrel of a rifle. At first, she said, she had no idea why she was released after six months rather than killed, though she guessed that her captors expected that her trauma would suffice to send her family fleeing their home, never to return to the site containing the memory of such unimaginable horrors. She was not content to be a victim, however, and upon release she became a "soldier" in this "ethnic war," and, by her own admission was driven by rage to "kill as many Serbs as possible" over the next year as the war continued. At the age of sixteen, after seeking treatment in Zagreb, she emigrated to the United States.[4] So what should we say, from her perspective, or from the perspective of her perpetrators and later her victims, was the "cause" of war?

When the violence of "war" is experienced in such a personal way, neighbor against neighbor, as it often was in ex-Yugoslavia, the window in which social scientists might look for explanation when they approach causes-of-war questions is really very small. Perhaps our questions regarding the causes-of-war are implicitly directed toward elites or leaders who "are rational" in the sense that they seek to remain in power or prove themselves "right" about the reasons they have used as a pretext for calling their citizens to arms. Perhaps what is "rational" for elites is embedded within the rationality of international discourses about power, sovereignty, the state, and state system. But why elites "go to war" may be very different from why the ordinary people who are its perpetrators and victims on the ground "go to war," yet wars cannot be fought without the tacit, willing, or enthusiastic support of ordinary people.

The political rationalization of violence matters only to some people for some time during a very brief period we call the *onset* of war. Certainly it matters to political elites who articulate "reasons" for going to war, and whose speech and other political acts are aimed at mobilizing support for war both vertically among their supporters and horizontally among elites from other sectors, such as the media, churches, intelligentsia and other cultural agents. Ultimately, however, their call to violence must target "ordinary" though not necessarily politically attentive people who listen to, read, or watch media reports, or who might be influenced by church leaders, teachers, or university professors, who talk with one another about "the war" or about reports of violence taking place in a neighboring village. Swept along by the tides of war and ultimately becoming the majority of its victims, for ordinary people it becomes "impossible not to get involved," as the young exile said, as "People were fighting wars in their heads, on the ground, in the air, in their homes."[5] Once a causes-of-war discussion turns to the subject of elites and their relationship with ordinary people, we are talking about a complex network of *social* relationships, processes, and interactions which, for the most part, are overlooked by structural accounts of war.

Milosević's military mobilization initially met with widespread resistance. As many as 200,000 young men of military age openly resisted the draft in Serbia alone,[6] contrary to the image of "ancient hatreds" driving the "backward" people of eastern Europe into an "ethnic conflict" arising out of their still predominantly "tribal" identities and affinities. Among Croat conscripts there was also opposition to their being transferred to fight in Bosnia-Herzegovina.[7] Those who refused were reportedly beaten and threatened with violence against their family members. Stipe Šuvar, former president of the Communist Party of Yugoslavia, estimated that by June 1995 somewhere around 700,000 people eligible for military service had left—300,000 from Serbia, 100,000 from Croatia, and 300,000 from Bosnia—because they did not want to fight in the war.[8] It took a combination of propaganda (including, by some accounts, staged violence) and paramilitary terrorism to provoke enough fear in the general, particularly rural, population to ignite violence.[9] Once a civil society has been transformed into a war zone, however, violence provides its own logic. Said differently, once one's family has been killed—one's mother and father, wife, brother, sister, husband, infant, or young children murdered—the immediate psychic and emotional effect is devastating. Ambiguities collapse into the "simplicity" of agony. Political "interests" and military strategies give way to grief, fear, terror, and rage. War may be "rational" from the perspective of those elites whose political careers hinge on it, but the environment of war is overwhelmingly emotional and irrational.

David Campbell argues that "violence is the *ultima ratio* of politics. The basic subject of modern politics," he says, "in the sense of the foundational understanding of what politics is ultimately about, is consequently violence."[10] From the perspective of critical feminism, modern politics is about using good violence to control bad violence, or, because violence is socially constructed as both a masculine subject and a masculine characteristic, it can further be said that modern politics is about getting *good masculinity* to control *bad masculinity*. Anarchic violence—the centerpiece of realist theorizing—makes no distinction between "good" and "bad" violence and is in many ways the antithesis of civility. Civility is predicated on the assumption that politics can assert discipline over unruly, arbitrary, gratuitous, bestial, irrational, antisocial, Other-destructive violence.

How does it do so? By the formulation of rules distinguishing between "bad" or unacceptable violence, on the one hand, and "good" or necessary violence, generally *restricted* to the role of rule-enforcement, on the other.

Thus discourses about the laws of war, beginning centuries ago with the "just war" doctrine, signify a distinction between the "right" and "wrong" reasons for going to war, though more recently, leaders of states have attempted to outlaw war by distinguishing between aggression and defense, and by codifying law regulating the conduct of war, or use of force once war breaks out.[11] "Bad" violence, then, can be though of as *arbitrary* because it is conducted without regard for, or in violation of, social norms or legal rules.

So politics *is* about violence, but in being about violence it is also about the social construction of normative rules distinguishing between arbitrary violence and rule- or order-enforcing violence. It is also about how (and by whom) order is constructed, maintained, and transformed, or in Lasswell's terminology, who gets what, when, and how. The process of constructing normative rules gives rise to perennial philosophical questions of morality and ethics. Politics is also, after all, about the conduct of discourse through which ethical conceptions of justice and welfare are articulated; the recognition of our interdependent interests and fates on which a concept of collective or community life rests; our collective efforts to solve our common problems; and about a vision of the good, or at least better, society. There is no doubt, however, that violence can trump all other concerns of political life.

## War as Social Practice

My argument does not aim to refute structural accounts of "causes-of-war" but rather to examine the cognitive and emotional elements, both social and psychological, that also figure into the experience of political conflict and violence by the ordinary people without whom violence would not be possible. It claims, as do other critics of purely structural approaches, that there exists today a serious discontinuity between the prevailing way war is conceptualized, on the one hand, and the way war is actually conducted and experienced, on the other.[12] In spite of the now-substantial debate among academics about the changing nature of war, I am still struck every semester by how persistently and effectively incoming college students have been socialized to understand war both as the Clausewitzian extension of the politics of the state and, perhaps more lamentably, in the tradition of realism, as inescapable and unmitigable. War for them is a "fact of life." Feminist theorists like Di Stefano (1991) and Peterson (1996) make a persuasive argument that such "realism" is really an intellectual projection of the cognitive construction of "masculinity" to which all of us, in the West at least, are socialized to regard as the norm. I do not really have anything to add to that argument, but wish instead to examine its consequences for the way not only my students but a substantial number of policy-makers and scholars conceptualize the problem of "war."

Clausewitz viewed war as an instrument of statecraft, a means of achieving foreign policy objectives. This view undergirds the philosophical and theo-retical assumptions of realism and neorealism by assuming that, in the absence of a higher, supranational authority (which constitutes anarchy by some accounts), the sovereign state must resort to force or the threat of force in defense of its interests (presumed to be monolithic and shared uniformly by all citizens). The absence of supranational authority is taken by realists as the condition of international anarchy. They apparently cannot think of order in other terms. Often overlooked by such analyses, however, is another assumption made by Clausewitz, discussed in greater detail by both Peter Paret and Martin van Creveld.[13] "Clausewitzian wars," as we have come to call interstate wars, were fought by citizen-soldiers, even professional, merce-nary soldiers, whose voluntary participation indicated their willingness to be perpetrators as well as targets or victims of war's violence. War, like dueling, was to be "civilized" by the laws of warfare; political violence would be monopolized by the state, in Austinian and Weberian terms, and then regu-lated. It could even be deployed as a legitimate means for settling, if not resolving, disputes. "Why do you think," I always ask my students, "the British army ran around in the green forests of the Atlantic coast wearing red coats during the American Revolutionary War?" It was, of course, because wearing a uniform signaled one's willing participation in the violence of war. Civilians were not to be targeted, and prisoners of war were not to be mistreated. May the best man win.

Codified in the Geneva Convention, the rules of warfare sought to "civi-lize" the practice of war as calculated and instrumental violence carried out by the sovereign European state. Critical analyses of the history of war abound, and I will not provide another here,[14] but they do raise a serious challenge to those social scientists who would limit the study of war as a problem or puzzle to be "solved" solely by using scientific methodology without interrogating the sociolinguistic processes involved in the construc-tion of the category used to define the problem: war. Without historicizing and contextualizing the problem to be solved, causes-of-war theories and studies err by generalizing and extrapolating from European experience to everyone else, as if even the European experience of war-making can be understood in a historical vacuum, isolated from other relevant social processes occurring over the past four centuries. Whatever we think we know about "war" is really no more than what we know about *a social practice we call war* within the historical and epistemological context of European experience and interpretation.

By contrast, war as a social practice among indigenous peoples of North America, for example, was so different from the European practice in terms of its participants, decision-makers, purposes and objectives, and the rules and norms governing its conduct that there can be almost no useful gener-alization about the two. This is military historian John Keegan's argument when he says: "it is at the cultural level that Clausewitz's answer to his question, What is war? is defective."[15] Kalevi Holsti, whose academic career has long been focused on the problem of war and conflict, takes such criticism seriously by offering a culturally and historically contextualized account of the war-state relationship in an effort to shift the focus of the discipline from interstate to internal state-building (and state-destroying) wars "of the third kind."[16]

Critiques of the Clausewitzian image of war conclude that it fails today because (1) states are neither monolithic nor impenetrable and people, their goods and services, and their ideas, move easily across state boundaries; which also means that (2) issues are neither easily identified nor aggregated; (3) efforts (dominated by Western states and leaders) to regulate the use of force, both by "agreeing" that the state possesses a "monopoly of force" and by agreeing to rules of warfare, including attempts to outlaw aggressive war, have not led to a decline in political violence; and (4) participants in political violence, including actors in positions of authority in states and citizens of states acting as citizens, are often mobilized around intangibles, such as identity, beliefs, or ideology. To these I would add, along with John Keegan (1993), that Clausewitzian perspectives on war fail because they do not account for the cultural and historical contexts in which both state- and war-making occur. These critiques cast significant doubt on the utility of analyses that proceed from assumptions about states as the primary agents of war and about agents as rational actors.

An alternative to the Clausewitzian model is to conceptualize war as a social practice. Vivienne Jabri and other peace researchers argue for the examination of the "war-society interface."[17] In *Discourses on Violence*, Jabri quotes Martin Shaw, who argues that: "war must be seen as a social activity related to the whole complex of social life and organization."[18]

John Keegan's critique similarly faults the formulation of questions about what is and what causes war on the grounds that war is a social phenomenon varying across cultural spaces and historical periods. The "state interest" and "rational calculation" version of war is specific to the sociocultural context of and historical discourse among European peoples.[19] This is not to say that other societies have not been restructured "in the image of the European state" and that, as a consequence, war as a social practice emerging out of European history and culture has been adopted by these states. But just as surely as European cultural hegemony spread to global proportions, European social practice has been reshaped by the Others it has encountered as well as by more invigorated internal critics. Discourses about war are, as a consequence, becoming multidimensional, contestable, more complex, and critical. Those engaged in "peace studies," for example, have long regarded war as a function of underlying social conflict or as the product of certain socialization practices.[20]

Though David Campbell and other contributors to his edited volume on violence and politics interrogate the ontology of violence in Western political discourses, their concern is more with building a theoretical and even philosophical critique than with exploring the practical implications of acknowledging war and violence as social practice, though they do claim that taking such a critique seriously brings us to "the end of philosophy and the end of international relations" as we know it.[21] Jabri, on the other hand, takes a more constructivist approach albeit in the intellectual stream of Giddens's (1984, 1987, 1991) structuration theory." She explores both the theoretical and practical consequences of taking political violence, including war, to be a social phenomenon, with a particular eye to the necessity of intervening in and transforming the social practices that perpetuate violence and war, including the construction of political identities in exclusionary terms.[22] "The ability to wage war," she says, "requires a high degree of control and an ability to impose and reinforce disciplinary power."[23] Taking a postmodern, Foucauldian approach to the role of language in producing and reproducing relationships structured by power, Jabri argues that:

> The emergence of dominant constructions of identity within specific locations in time and space suggests a point of intersection between structures of domination, symbolic orders, and legitimation. . . .
>
> The nation, that most commonplace of identities, is the location of discursive and institutional practices which at one and the same time generate legitimation and exclusion. It is the location of a remembered past, of repetitive symbolic reification, and of total mobilization in time of conflict.[24]

By declaring war a social practice, constructivists like Jabri as well as critical poststructuralists like Campbell interrogate the discursive processes through which the violence of war is constituted and sustained. From a constructivist perspective, theorizing (speaking theoretically) about war is itself a speech act contributing to its social construction. Speaking about war, including theorizing, acknowledges certain meanings while denying others. At the very least the act of theorizing takes place within the context of scholarship, even if no one "outside" international relations discourses listens. As Onuf argues, however, theorizing can also have consequences for people acting in the context of violence who take on a variety of roles, ranging from the civilian victim whose rage and grief turns into violence, to paramilitaries, regular military commanders, and political provocateurs.[25] When discourses of "outside" observers and theorists are heard by those acting in the context of violence, and when the theorists" meanings are employed by "insiders" to interpret their own experiences, theorists becomes agents.

Shapiro and Alker (1996) argue that by examining who benefits from the inclusion of some meanings and exclusion of others reveals the way in which theorizing and speaking about war structures power. So, for example, the killing (murder) of millions of indigenous peoples in the British settler states was, for the most part, never constructed as "war" because doing so would have invoked international discourses and meanings, and would have risked acknowledging the international and therefore potentially sovereign status of indigenous nationhood. "Hate crimes" occurring today within the United States are aberrations in an otherwise civil society, while similar acts occurring within an environment of war in ex-Yugoslavia or Kosovo are normalized or at least obscured by discourses about "ethnic conflict" arising out of "ancient hatreds," prejudices which we Westerners congratulate ourselves on having overcome.

These assumptions were evident in remarks made by Major-General Lewis MacKenzie, who, on leaving his UN command in Sarajevo in 1992, said that there could be no peace in Bosnia because "the people here hate each other too much."[26] The quintessential realist, Mackenzie found the explanation for violence in the former Yugoslavia simple and straightforward. All sides were responsible for the war, and in the realist tradition of purely strategic thinking, he suggested capitulation to Serb control of Sarajevo as well as the mostly "cleansed" territory held by Serb forces in Bosnia and Croatia as the only means of ending the violence, stating that "Force has been rewarded for the last twenty centuries. "That's the reality," he said.[27]

## Where Structural Accounts Fall Short

Structural accounts generally refer either to international, systemic variables, such as the transition from a bipolar to either a hegemonic or multipolar system of major power dominance in the aftermath of the Cold War, or to domestic, internal, or national variables pertaining to the specific case of the former Yugoslavia. The second orientation is implicated by various accounts referring to the fall, breakup, disintegration, or dissolution of the Yugoslav state. On the issue of systemic change, I have no doubt that power transitions generate system instability, and in order to exploit that instability, political leaders contemplating controversial moves to challenge the international status quo (such as internationally recognized boundaries) recalculate likely international responses to their prospective adventurism. Saddam Hussein's move into Kuwait may be such a case in point. But system instability alone does not tell us *why* such moves are made in one particular setting, by the leaders of one particular state, and not another. I suggest, therefore, that we think of systemic variables as necessary, but not sufficient causes, as *antecedents* to conflicts that contest the international status quo, but not sufficient in themselves to *cause* such conflicts.

Among the internal structural antecedents to the war in ex-Yugoslavia were some underlying weaknesses in the Yugoslav political system that threatened instability even before Tito's death. There is, of course, the perennial (post)communist issue of succession. But in the case of former Yugoslavia, the "national question" that plagued both the first and second Yugoslavia, and with which it seems that everyone, including Tito, struggled throughout the entire history of the second Yugoslavia, was probably its most fatal structural flaw. It came up repeatedly in my 1995-to-1997 interviews, and Ivo Banac's 1984 work *The National Question in Yugoslavia* is still highly regarded as the most influential account of the problem by those both inside and outside the successor states.[28] But I am not so sure that "the national question" in Yugoslavia was all that different from the question of multiple identities and histories in many pluralistic, multiethnic societies, albeit, like Freud's psychopath, exaggerated or "writ large" in the case of Yugoslavia.

The "national question" was really, I believe, a series of related questions with which many multiethnic, multicultural societies struggle. For example, how to construct and maintain an inclusive but pluralistic identities without privileging one identity and marginalizing others (the Swiss Confederation Helvetica and its plural presidency often come to mind as the most or only successful case of decentering national identities within a multiethnic state). Other problems confronting multinational, multiethnic states include how to balance interests associated with multiple identity groups, particularly when distribution across groups is pluralistic (a situation found in many postcolonial African societies); how to provide for participation on the basis of group identities in addition to participation as individuals; how to conduct societywide civic discourse without privileging one "national" language over others; and how to engage in redistributive policies where historical patterns of discrimination are evident without provoking class resentments, especially when class cleavages coincide with identity differences.

But I do not find the argument that internal structural sources of conflict in Yugoslavia alone in some way *caused* the war persuasive primarily because these problems—an unresolved "national" (multiethnic power-sharing) question and a succession crisis—preceded the war by at least a decade, so we are left with the question: Why war in 1990 and not before? What happened between 1980 and 1990 that culminated in what has been called the worst and most brutal violence to occur anywhere in Europe—west, central, or east—since World War II? An explanation might even combine internal and international structural change by adding to the succession crisis the fact that in 1990 profound changes were taking place in the external, regional, or international structure as a result of the ending of the Cold War, but this still does not answer the question why such a brutal and sustained violent conflict in Croatia and Bosnia, and not Macedonia, Czechoslovakia, or elsewhere?[29] Nor does it provide sufficient explanation regarding the particularly personal and cruel nature of the violence in ex-Yugoslavia.

Structural variables have cognitive dimensions or, at least, cognitive consequences. Structural crises or changes in themselves do not contain meaning. They must be *interpreted* by political leaders, media elites, and so on. If we take into account the convergence of structural with cognitive variables and the interplay between the two, then we achieve a better understanding not only of the causes of violence but of violence in particularly personal and brutal forms, and how it became not inevitable, but *more likely* in the Yugoslav republics of Croatia and Bosnia-Herzegovina in 1990 and 1991. Psychologists I interviewed, for instance, spoke of how expressions of nationalism were suppressed and punished, how both Serb and Croat nationalism were perceived negatively in the aftermath of World War II because of their association with the Croatian Ustaše and Serbian Četnik movements, and how a positive identification with Yugoslav communism had begun to take root within some sectors of the population, in mixed marriages, among those who opted for distancing themselves from the nationalistic identities of the war, and among some Bosnian Muslims for whom "Yugoslav" was a kind of national identity. Yugoslav socialism or communism was perceived to be more liberal than its Soviet counterpart. Still, with the end of the Cold War it was not Soviet communism that collapsed as an ideology, but east/central European communism, which was grounded or centered in the Soviet Union. From the perspective of psychologists who saw the mobilization of exclusionary nationalistic identities (and the negative emotions that followed) as the primary cause of the 1991-to-1995 war, the collapse of communism precipitated the collapse of Yugoslav identity because Yugoslav identity had been constructed as a derivative of Soviet communism. A better understanding of the relationship between structural and cognitive variables will enable us to consider how and where else similar conflicts might develop, and what sort of intervention strategies can be implemented in order to preempt the escalation of violence.

## Prologue to War: Hate Speech and Media Control

Many will agree that here, as well as in the Bible, "in the beginning there was a word." A word malicious, hysterical, and criminal. . . . It is absolutely clear that the mass media in the entire territory of Yugoslavia, which has remained under state control, as property of the regime, regardless of the various privatization and ownership transformations, has fundamentally contributed to the beginning of the war and its brutalization.[30]

—from a report on hate speech,
Centre for Antiwar Action, Belgrade, 1994

Whatever structural, societal, political, or cognitive discontinuities bedeviled the citizens of the second Yugoslav state before 1980, the next decade was unquestionably one of severe and seemingly unstoppable descent into political and economic chaos. By the time Ante Marković was elected in March 1989 with a program for economic reform, which might have succeeded in stabilizing the economy had he had the chance to implement it, the reasoned voices of reformers were being drowned out by the increasingly belligerent and highly emotional tirades of the new nationalists.

While many societies undergo economic and political crises without descending into a brutal and uncivil war, societal breakdown along economic and political lines simultaneously is the equivalent of going bankrupt and getting divorced in the same week. These are psychic traumas, whether on a societal or personal level. Individuals living within the context of these traumatic experiences are inclined to emotional volatility and vulnerability. In a context where material and security needs are so threatened, individuals are more likely to abandon ambiguity in favor of the sense of control that simple explanations, such as scapegoating, seem to offer. Said differently, when psychically traumatized, we look for easy answers. All we need is someone to give them to us. The difference between societies experiencing economic and political instability without descending into violence and those that do may just be the timely emergence of leaders willing and able to engage in speech acts which exploit the emotional vulnerabilities of ordinary people whose psychic life is unsettled by societal crises. Hitler. Pol Pot. Milosević. Tudjman. Hutu Power. Whether the society is or was relatively democratized or not may make a difference in two ways: how the rules that bring individuals into power affect the ability of such leaders to come to power; and whether people in a democracy are more likely to have been socialized in ways that enable them cognitively to recognize and resist efforts to mobilize them emotionally to support or engage in exclusionary scapegoating and collective violence.

It is not rational for ordinary people to go to war; it is irrational. People do not think: "Oh, well, there is much to be gained by putting my life and property at risk, even if my children, parents, husband, wife, or neighbor are very like to be killed; but my life will be better afterward." People, even people in the Balkans, prefer peace and security to violence and fear. War both requires and provokes fear, anger, and a willingness to do harm to others that is very often rationalized on the basis of the other's inferiority, guilt, or both. The ordinary Others of our daily lives must be transformed into despicable Others. They must be transformed into *threatening enemies*. It seems abundantly clear both that the political leadership in Belgrade and in Zagreb knew this, and that to accomplish such a transformation, to provoke fear and insecurity, to induce support for a war, they would have to assert significant control over the media. In 1992 the Canadian newspaper *The Gazette* reported on a campaign of media persecution in Zagreb:

> Six reporters are facing charges of publishing "false information," "disturbing the public," and "offending the state president, Franjo Tudjman." Members of the ruling Croatian Democratic Union (HDZ) are said to want

to *take over* the country's leading independent newspaper, *Slobodna Dalmacija*, which has been consistently critical of the Zagreb leadership.[31]

Following a report critical of human rights and political freedoms in Croatia, the Croatian Helsinki Committee published a statement in July 1993 expressing concern about the effective state monopoly over printing, distribution, and sales of newspapers, suppression of independent magazines, and lack of access to all media, including television and radio broadcasting, by anyone other than the ruling party.[32] Its Serbian counterpart, the Helsinki Committee for Human Rights in Serbia, published similar reports in 1994, denouncing the government's "abuse of the Right to Information," with special reference to the official propaganda that Serbs in Bosnia, Croatia, and Kosovo were in fact victims rather than perpetrators of genocide:

> Almost all media are under control of SPS, and even those which are not, the working space for the independent media is limited to such an extent that one can speak about the regime's intention to put all the relevant media under its control. In the past years media were in function of the systematic propaganda of war and ethnic cleansing. The media have a great responsibility for justifying many war crimes and crimes against humanity by declaring that they are the necessary patriotic obligation to help compatriots endangered by a new genocide.[33]

The report further condemned the dissemination of hate speech and xenophobia by the media in service to the regime, and listed the three print and three broadcast media which, in the opinion of the committee, were the only sources of independent news and which were not used to promote war through propaganda. The Independent Media Union in Belgrade published a report entitled *Three TV Years in Serbia*, detailing the conduct of the media between 1990 and 1992.[34] In his preface, writer Filip David says of the work:

> The first year is in many ways critical and inescapable for a complete understanding of what happened on the territory of the former Yugoslavia, for an understanding of how the state-party media created stereotypes and prejudices greatly responsible for the escalation of the war and interethnic hatred. The claim that without such a television or such televisions the war would not have been possible, or at least would not have been so brutal and remorseless, is not very far from the truth.[35]

The crucial role of the media and the strategy of openly disseminating propaganda, particularly in the form of hate speech aimed at provoking or exacerbating xenophobia, was equally clear to my respondents. Said one:

*M.O., Belgrade, 1995*
They created fear in order to influence the ordinary people, so ideas of ethnic prejudice were provoked among many more people than had been the case before the war, and these people did not have any notion of human rights and civil society. Remember that at the beginning of the war there were something like 200,000 people who deserted because they did not want to fight. So it was not as if there were lots of people filled with so-called ethnic hatred just waiting for an excuse to begin killing each other. *People did not want to fight. The people did not want a war. They had to be emotionally mobilized first, and then militarily mobilized.*

A report on military deserters prepared by the Helsinki Committee for Human Rights in Serbia in 1994 summarizes the earliest attempts by Milosević to mobilize an army, and the extent of resistance to mobilization:

During the war in Croatia until 4 October 1991 reserves were formally summoned for military drills and sent instead into the battlefield. They were, in fact, sent into a battlefield in their own country, and to take up arms against their fellow citizens. Very many persons did not respond to the military summons during the war in Croatia. In Belgrade the military authorities succeeded in drafting only 17 percent of those called up, and 1/3 of them had to be taken in. In towns and villages in Serbia sometimes as many as 50 percent of recruits failed to turn up. In Knjaževać (eastern Serbia) practically all the recruits at the first junction stopped the trucks that were taking them north and refused to go into the battlefield. After several attempts to send them to the front line the military authorities gave up. Massive refusals to go to war were also recorded in Niš (southern Serbia), Valjevo (western Serbia: the reserves protested by blocking the roads for two days), Gornji Milanovac (Šumadija), Trešnjevac (Votjvodina)....[36]

According to Women in Black, an antiwar nongovernmental organization, criminal charges were filed against 3,748 and initiated against another 5,497 persons for desertion in 1992 alone.[37] An estimated 200,000 people had left the country to avoid military service. Stipe Šuvar, former Croatian member of the Yugoslav Federal Presidency (1989–90) and now a professor at Zagreb University, reported that the number of people who left the country, including those from Serbia, Croatia, and elsewhere, was by 1995 approximately 700,000.[38] Ordinary Yugoslavs—Bosnian, Serb, or Croat—did not want to fight a war. A war had to be orchestrated. People had to be mobilized, more or less willingly.

Far from seething with ancient hatreds or even intercommunal animosities, most of the people living in small, rural, as well as the larger urban, multiethnic communities got along very well.[39] Both in testimonies at the Hague and in my own interviews, people tell over and again how many families of different identities celebrated birthdays and even religious holidays with their neighbors, how they had in their own family a mixed marriage or knew someone who was from a mixed marriage (in Bosnia alone an estimated 27 percent—nearly a third—of all marriages before the war were mixed),[40] and of a variety of community practices or norms that fostered cooperative interethnic relations.[41] This is not to say that prejudice was absent or that no one was intolerant or disapproving of interethnic romances and relationships. Some people told of knowing someone or some family who was "prejudiced," or of knowing that interethnic prejudice was more common among those of the older generation, particularly those who had lived through World War II. No doubt much of what people were attempting to convey in their testimony both to me and to the tribunal was just how unexpected was the bitter and brutal nature of the violence they experienced during the war.

Still, the picture that emerges is one in which intergroup prejudices in general were not necessarily more pronounced or widespread, or even any more malignant than those found in most contemporary Western democracies. People in Western democracies are freer to discuss and debate their prejudices in public and private forums, and to wrangle over public policies aimed at remedying the historical effects, of prejudices and develop policies aimed at reducing or eliminating prejudices through more enlightened educational socialization. In former Yugoslavia, not only was such open discussion suppressed, but also the more positive expressions of cultural pride were always vulnerable to punishable prohibitions against nationalism. Here is how one respondent put it:

*B.V., Belgrade, 1995*
One hundred years ago, we had here in this region a type of patriarchal family, and this type of family socialized us to a very chauvinistic expression of national identity. This was present in all aspects of everyday life. It is expressed by the socialized habits of ordinary people in their everyday lives. Fifty years ago we adopted a communist system, and a central objective or belief of communist ideology was that the relevance of national identity should decline and even disappear. Additionally, because of the negative association of nationalism with World War II, every kind of expression of national belonging under the postwar regime was forbidden by law and punished by the authorities. Children who belonged to the Communist Party were encouraged to turn their parents over to the authorities if they expressed any type of national identity. Punishments consisted of losing a job, going to prison. Parents were denounced by their own children. So we were socialized to view nationalism as the opposite of communism.

As an expression of opposition to communism, nationalism in some ways became identified with dissidence, not only in Croatia, where cultural revival finally erupted during the Croatian Spring of 1966 to 1971, but in Serbia as well, where dissident writers and intellectuals such as Dobrica Čosić and Mihailo Marković, were ultimately implicated in the intellectual position outlined in the now infamous 1986 Memorandum of the Serbian Academy of Sciences. The first Bosnian president elected during the first multiparty elections in Bosnia-Herzegovina in 1990, Alija Izetbegović, had been jailed between 1983 and 1988 for his alleged advocacy of Muslim nationalism.[42] Thus Tito's death, combined with the collapse of European communism, destroyed the symbolic, ideological, and normative basis for Yugoslav identity. So while nationalist movements had already been apparent a decade prior to Tito's death and two decades before the end of the Cold War and the failure of communism, these watershed events also effectively eliminated all prohibitions against the full-scale political mobilization of nationalistic identities and emotions. Said another respondent:

*M.P., Zagreb, 1997*
One cannot comprehend how this war began without knowing something about the political culture in which we had lived for five decades. It was in the context of that political culture that people came under the influence of nationalist propaganda. I don't know what percent of the people may have had ethnic prejudices before. Some, but certainly not a majority. But from the beginning of the war this historical background is very important. All of us grew up in this atmosphere of tension between nationalism and communism. Many of the key figures in nationalist revivals—in Croatia the Croatian Spring leaders Mika Tripalo and Savka Dabčević-Kučar, and Franjo Tudjman, and in Serbia Mihailo Marković, Milosević, and so on, created the atmosphere in which this war started. So there was already this ideological conflict, and then they started this political propaganda, and the Serb leaders and the Croat leaders wanted simply to destroy Yugoslavia and get the best deal they could as they went their own ways.

## Ethnic Prejudices in Ex-Yugoslavia: The Emotional Side of War

Against a backdrop of pernicious, chauvinistic, and potentially exclusive nationalistic movements from the 1970s onward, there were important ways in which actual or potential ethnic prejudices and intergroup hostility did profoundly affect the violence that erupted in 1990 and 1991. Interpersonal prejudices were apparent along at least two lines—the "Otherness" of Albanians living in Yugoslavia, and interethnic prejudices in specific local settings.

As discussed in the previous chapter, Albanians were marginalized or were targets of prejudice to some degree by all other sectors of Yugoslav society, so that when Milosević moved against them first, using anti-Albanian prejudices to mobilize Serb fears, there was little protest from either among the Serbs or elsewhere in Yugoslav society. The relationship between Kosovo Albanians and other Yugoslavs generally as well as Serbs in particular was structured on the basis of their moral exclusion within Yugoslav society. Slavenka Drakulić argued this point in an article published in *The Nation* in the aftermath of the NATO intervention in Kosovo:

> They lived among us, but we chose to ignore them. If we did happen to notice them, we despised them, laughed at them, told jokes about them. . . . It was clear that they belonged to a different category from Serbs, Macedonians, Montenegrins or Slovenes. Serbs could even fight a war against Croats, but they never perceived each other in the same way they both perceive Albanians. The prejudice against Albanians can be compared to that against Jews or blacks or Gypsies in other cultures. Today every Serb will tell you that Albanians multiply like rabbits—that this is their secret weapon in the war they are waging against Serbs in Kosovo. This is not nationalism; this is more or less hidden racism.[43]

As economic and structural instabilities worsened, Milosević, not surprisingly, began by exploiting specifically Serb prejudices against Albanians in order to incite public scapegoating.[44] If the disintegration of the "Serb nation" within Yugoslavia by the political chicanery of the 1974 constitution was the issue, then Serbs could begin to remedy the structural injustices in their own backyard by restoring Serb control of Kosovo, both politically and demographically. Between 1961 and 1991 the percentage of Albanians in Kosovo had grew from 67 percent to 90 percent, while the percentage of Serbs declined from 23 percent to 10 percent.[45] Tensions in Kosovo provoked a growing separatist movement that erupted into violence in 1968 and 1981. No doubt the demographic shift occurred as a combined result of some Serbs leaving, some Albanians emigrating from Albania and even Macedonia, and the higher birthrate among rural Albanians. Vuk Drašković, President of the Serbian Renewal Movement and deputy prime minister of Yugoslavia during the 1999 NATO intervention, made the patently ludicrous claim that the declining proportion of Serbs in Kosovo was due to an Albanian genocide against them.[46] That would be the equivalent of arguing that the "white flight" from American cities in the 1950s which left majority Black populations in Washington, D.C., and elsewhere, was caused by a genocide against whites.

But I do not mean to paint too dark a picture of prewar Kosovo. In spite of anti-Albanian prejudices in general, and in spite of the fact that as a proportion of the total Yugoslav population, Albanians were roughly equal to the number of Slovenes, Muslims, and Macedonians,[47] Albanian language was not recognized as one of the national languages of Yugoslavia. The rate of criminal offenses in Kosovo overall was, on a per capita basis, comparable to other regions.[48] Julie Mertus reports that between 1981 and 1987 the crime rate in Kosovo was actually the lowest in Yugoslavia, with only five interethnic murders in the same period.[49]

A second way in which ethnic prejudices figured into war mobilization was the fact that such tolerance and prejudice were unevenly distributed across the society. Not only were urban areas in general more likely to have a more tolerant majority, but there were specific rural areas in which prejudices were more deeply entrenched within the local culture and associated historical narratives. Not only were intolerance and prejudice more common and widespread in the rural population, but in particular geographic areas interethnic hostility was both more concentrated and more dangerous. This was the case in Herzegovina, joined with Bosnia for over five centuries. The Herzegovinians, says Misha Glenny, who chronicled the war and the events leading up to it,[50] "consider themselves the greatest Croat patriots and consider the association with Bosnia an insult."[51] This perception was supported by Croats I interviewed both from the Dalmatian coast and from the cosmopolitan center of Zagreb, who variously described their brethren in the poor, mountainous region of Herzegovina in southwestern Bosnia-Herzegovina on the border with Croatia, as "different," "rednecks," "parochial," "patriotic," "Big Croats," and people whose identity was "focused on their own families and villages where everyone is related to everyone else." I could think of places in, for example, the more remote areas of West Virginia, North and South Carolina, and Montana (where I have lived), which I might describe in similar terms. Western Herzegovina was not only known as a hotbed of militant Croat nationalism today, but it was also home to many major supporters of the fascist Ustaše from World War II.

Neighboring eastern Herzegovina, bordering both Croatia and Montenegro, is also known for its militant nationalists—but Serbs, rather than Croats. Vojislav Šešelj, a paramilitary commander who served in the Serbian parliament, is from eastern Herzegovina, as are, says Glenny, many of the most radical politicians in Belgrade.[52] In Herzegovina, as in the eastern region where Bosnia borders Serbia and the northeastern area of Posavina on the Bosnian border with Croatia, lived the most ardent Serb and Croat supporters of partitioning Bosnia between their two republics. For them, Bosnia was an artificial republic filled with Muslim heretics. The more urbanized Muslims constituted a majority in the Hercegovinian capital, Mostar, also the scene of some of the worst atrocities during the Bosnian phase of the war. It should not be surprising, then, that the Bosnian war started in these areas.

As I mentioned in Chapter 5, Belgrade respondents frequently referred to the "difference" between Serbs living in and outside of Serbia as well as between urban and rural Serbs. Serbs living in Bosnia, they pointed out, lived in a political environment in which they were not a majority and were descended from people whose persecution under the Ottoman Empire was passed on to subsequent generations through family histories. Of course, the Ottomans did not distinguish between Serbs in Bosnia and Serbs in Serbia, but the Muslims in Bosnia were perceived by some Serbs as descendants of those who adopted Islamic identity and, as a result, received privileges and favorable treatment under Turkish rule. Serbs in Bosnia, in other words, were still living among descendants of their former oppressors.

Interviews in Zagreb indicated that Croat identity, for some at least, relied on the distinction between having been subjects of the imperial rule of the Catholic, Western, European Hapsburg empire on the one hand, and the Serbian experience under the imperial rule of the "backward," "barbarian," Eastern, Islamic Ottomans. This contrasted sharply, respondents suggested, with the Croats" experience under the Hapsburgs. Croats were therefore more European, more Western, hardworking, enterprising, and oriented toward the individualism and eventual liberation of Western democratic movements. They were, it implied, clearly the more civilized people as a result of their association with Western European imperialism.

In the agriculturally rich region of Slavonia, where the first Serb–Croat violence took place and which remained occupied until the Croatian offensives in the spring and summer of 1995, similar prejudices were reflected in the prejudices of *starosedioci,* or old settlers, against the newcomers, the *došljaci,* who came from the south—Bosnia and Herzegovina—after each world war. These were less ethnic than class and regional identity differences, but embedded within the structure of imperial and postimperial identities. The old settlers of different ethnic identities, which included not only Serb and Croat but Hungarian, German, and others, got along very well. But especially after the World War II, a significant population of *dosljaci* were relocated to eastern Slavonia from precisely those areas of Bosnia and Herzegovina where the most virulent Serb and Croat nationalists who had fought in the region's civil war lived. They were moved into the homes vacated by those (mostly Germans) who fled or were expelled after the war. The newcomers brought their prejudices with them.

"Before we make war," says Sam Keen, "even before we make weapons, we make an idea of the enemy."[53] If we wish to understand the war in structuralist terms, we need only decide whether the republican boundaries of Croatia were recognized or duly constituted as international boundaries, and if so, then the movement of troops or militias under a Belgrade command can be construed as a simple act of international aggression. But even the Hague Tribunal, created by the UN Security Council, is not authorized to address the question of aggression in relation to the Yugoslav war. That question aside for the moment, both the Croatian and Serbian leadership exploited what they knew to be rather specific ethnic prejudices, more prevalent, influential, and provocative among certain regional populations, as they attempted to mobilize political support on the basis of new or renewed nationalisms as both Tito and communism disappeared as the symbolic and ideological basis for civic or at least political identities. But it would be a mistake to view the ensuing violence in the simplistic terminology of "ethnic conflict," "ancient hatreds," or something inherently Balkan. Many people resisted both military and ideological mobilization on these terms. Many people, particularly young people, left Yugoslavia in order to escape the conflict. Others organized war-resistance efforts. Many felt like the young refugee who said:

> [I]n 1991, when hatred between the Serbs and the Croats started to grow in Croatia, I began to feel pressure in my immediate environment to take sides, something I did not want to and could not do. I could not identify with the increasingly aggressive nationalism of the Croats, or with the militant aggressive aspirations of the Serbs. Above all, I resented the unjustifiable idea of killing as a way to resolve social and political problems, not to mention the problems of "national destiny." Whatever one's beliefs and national identity, everyone has the right to life. (L.Z., London; Lešić, 1995, p. 77)

### Identities, Historical Narratives, and Unreconciled Grievances

In addition to interpersonal prejudices characterized by intolerance (not unique to ex-Yugoslavia), historical narratives and experiences also figured into structure of both ethnonational identities and intergroup relations in ex-Yugoslavia. Narratives of national or ethnic identity in ex-Yugoslavia were largely constructed as exclusionary. They were structured by cultural and historical narratives of Otherness, persecution, victimization, exploitation, and collective guilt, particularly Croat and Serb identities, though not necessarily only in relation to one another. Croat identity, for example, was tied to its "progressive Westernness" in contrast to the "backward, barbarian, superstitious Easternness" of both Orthodox Serbs and Bosnian Muslims. One Croat respondent went to great lengths to explain to me the different ways a Croat, Muslim, and Serb would slaughter an animal, and he clearly intended the descriptions as a metaphor for differences in the civility of each culture, contrasting the more "civilized" Croats (who killed quickly to minimize suffering, and therefore humanely) with the "barbarian" Serbs who, according to his description, actually enjoyed both inflicting pain and the act of killing. Muslims were also said to kill not of out of necessity, but as an expression of religious fanaticism. Croat respondents also often explained the alleged Serbian affinity with communist ideology, which in the aftermath of the Cold War became incorporated into narratives and metaphors of backwardness.

Here is how one respondent discussed the relationship among these identities in relation to historical narratives.

*S.S., Belgrade, 1995*
Both Croat and Serb identity are now exaggerated. Croatian identity, for example is a very strange mixture of megalomania and inferiority. You have this megalomaniacal idea of a thousand years of Croatian statehood and culture and so on. Serbs also have this idea of simply forgetting five hundred years under the Turks. Let me tell you an anecdote. Our leading writer, [Ivo] Andrić was hosting one of the leading Turkish writers of the time in Belgrade, I forget which writer it was. While they were dining, the Turk asked Andrić "Would you tell me some good jokes about Turks?" Andrić hesitated, but under pressure he agreed. "For whatever our faults," he said, "we Serbs always have a good excuse for them. We say "No wonder we are like this because the barbarous Turks ruled for five hundred years." But his Turkish counterpart said "I know this is funny, but it is not that funny, so there must be something else." So the Turkish writer thought about it, and then said, "Yeah, well we have a similar saying in Turkey, only we say "no wonder we are messed up because we ruled over Serbs for over five hundred years."

Prejudices against Bosnian Muslims were often expressed in terms of Muslims as "race-traitors" — Serbs who converted to Islam in order to obtain privileges or to exempt themselves from mistreatment under the Ottomans; or they were simply referred to as "Turks." The Muslims are the blondest of all the Slavic people," said one respondent, "because they converted to Islam in order to save their women from being raped by the Turks." This was more than a curiously twisted view of the relationship between historical interpretation and contemporary identity, because during the war in Bosnia, Serbs burning Muslim homes and killing their inhabitants would often refer to their victims as "Turks," which was understood to have a derogatory meaning, illustrated by as the following excerpt from Hague Tribunal testimony regarding the events surrounding the commission of alleged war crimes in and around the Bosnian town of Prejidor:

Q. Around this time did you begin hearing the use of offensive terms regarding Muslims used in public and in the media?
A. At that time, not in the local media, I could not hear it that often, but I could hear and read it in other media where we, the Muslims, were always called "Turks."
Q. What did that term connote when it was used in the media?
A. It is very easy to conclude if you take all the time into account, the constant syndrome that we, Muslims, have, the syndrome of Turks, they

were constantly repeating about the Kosovo battle, the Czar Dušan and the Prince Lazer [*sic*] and carrying around about symbols of Prince Lazer, and all the preparations for the 600th anniversary of the Serb battle, and the Turks are presented as the people who kill; and if we were called the "Turks," it is not very difficult to conclude what they mean.[54]

Theories regarding the origins of "authentic" identities, the role of conversions, and theories attributing psychological and biological significance to "ethnicity" commonly appeared in war propaganda. The Belgrade based Center for Antiwar Action's analysis of propaganda during the war reports the following:

In the August 1993 issue of the Serb Radical Party Bulletin "Western Serbia," Radoslav R. Unković, director of the Republican Institute for Protection of the Cultural-Historic and Natural Heritage of the Bosnian Serb Republic, tried to explain the Bosnian war and policy circumstances by using a slightly simplified variation of the ostensible psychoanalytic race theory made widely popular by the late Dr. Jovan Rašković. "We have not forgotten our cultural tradition or perhaps our genetic instinct for enlightenment even in the most difficult and darkest of times," proudly says Unković. "The Bosnian balija (a Turkish word meaning scoundrel, most often used to designate a religious convert—so we're not being offensive) is of Serb origin, oh woe is us. And he is ashamed of the ancestral sin and carries it in his subconscious, and therefore wants to exterminate our roots along with his own to obscure a shameful remembrance. The Catholics, who since not so long ago called themselves Croats and whose inherited mother tongue is the Serb language, also used to be orthodox Serbs through to the time of Mary Theresa, and therefore they want to erase from their subconscious all traces of their origin and their ancestors' moral disgrace."[55]

The claim that religious conversions concealed "authentic" ethnic identity was not limited to the construction of Muslims as "race-traitors." In 1997, as I began a slide presentation after returning from one of my trips to former Yugoslavia with a few maps regarding the ethnic distribution before the war, someone in the audience immediately raised her hand to explain to me that there weren't really any Serbs in Croatia, but rather there were Croats who had converted to Orthodoxy living in Croatia. One prominent Croatian writer, Dubravko Horvatić, explains it this way:

The Croatian Catholic population living in the areas occupied by the Turks suffered violence and big taxes that forced many to convert to Islam to protect their families and properties. Numerous Islamicized Croats achieved high office in the Turkish administration, army, and court.[56]

He goes on to explain that the Turks forcibly removed many Catholic Croats from occupied Bosnia, saying that "An estimated two million Croats emigrated or were removed from Croatian lands from the fall of Bosnia util 1723."[57] Perhaps most interesting is the explanation regarding how both Croatia and Bosnia became multiethnic, particularly regarding the presence of Orthodox Serbs, which I will quote at some length and annotate in italics:

Vlahs, Serbs, Tzinzars, Greeks, and members of other nationalities who were mainly Greek Orthodox from the interior of the Balkans colonized the areas abandoned by the Croats. *[Presumably this abandonment occurs because of the forced migration.]* Thus the Orthodox religion first appears in the area west of the Drina and Neretva Rivers at the beginning of the sixteenth century. Turkish authorities, who had always been suspicious of Catholics since the pope was outside Turkish reach, trust the Orthodox since the head of the Orthodox church was under Turkish control. Furthermore, Turkish authorities permitted Orthodox priests to collect church taxes from Catholics as well. *[This constitutes a collaboration between the Orthodox/Serbs and the brutal Ottoman conquerors from the east.]* Persecuted both by the Turks and the privileged Orthodox population, many Catholics converted to Orthodoxy; in addition, the Turks killed a large number of Catholic priests, and many Croats converted to Orthodoxy from Catholicism because of the shortage of priests.[58]

From this eighteenth-century struggle emerged a weakened Croat nation which finally obtained peace and security through a "personal union" between "civil Croatia" and the Austrians. But by the nineteenth century a struggle reemerged, this time against encroachment perpetrated by both Hungarian and Serbian imperialism, and finally, against moves by the Austrians to assert a more centralized and absolutist control over Croatia. This, in turn, gave birth to a national revival movement as well as a pan-Slavic movement, with the latter prevailing when the first unified South Slav state was created after World War I. Again Dubravko Horvatić explains that: "This new state was called the Kingdom of the Serbs, Croats and Slovenes but the Serbian military authorities not only called Croatia and Bosnia and Herzegovina 'occupied territories' and 'enemy districts' but also acted as if they were."[59]

Horvatić explains the struggle against Serb oppression from this time until the collapse of the second Yugoslavia:

In addition, national identity was denied to the Croatian people from 1918 to 1939, and not only partially as in the past but for the first time in history totally. The continuity of the Croatian state, which had lasted since the ninth century, was interrupted for the first time from 1918 to 1939; from 1920 to 1939 the Croatian Diet was abolished; the Croatian state disappeared from the map and sank into the unitarist kingdom that the Belgrade authorities unofficially called Greater Serbia, which it really was . . . parts of Croatian national territory . . . were surrendered to Italy; and Croatian national symbols such as the flag and coat-of-arms were prohibited. Serbs started settling in Croatia, and they even renamed Croatian villages . . . many had the adjective Serbian added to their names. . . . During the Independent State of Croatia *[This was the state run by Ustaše collaborators]* the old names returned, but after the war, in 1945, the imposed old-Yugoslav (actually Serbian) names were reestablished and they remain today.[60]

Croatian historical narratives also contain elements of victimization, both by reference to a long struggle for independent statehood and in connection with being made (unfairly) to bear the burden of collective guilt — often referred to as "Jasenovac Complex" — after the Ustaše camp for war atrocities committed during World War II by a minority of Croatian collaborators. According to the version of Croatian history that underlies contemporary claims, the history of the Croatian nation is one of perpetual struggle against domination and encroachment on its sovereignty and self-determination. The "Catholic Croat" nation enjoyed a special relationship with the Austro-Hungarian empire which allowed for maximum local autonomy. Depending on the account, the association is often characterized as voluntary.[61]

The Preamble to the Croatian Constitution adopted in December 1990 contains a lengthy summary of the "historical facts" of the "millennial national identity of the Croatian nation," said to have begun in the seventh century and to have culminated in:

[T]he historic turning point marked by the rejection of the communist system and changes in the international order in Europe. [T]he Croatian nation was reaffirmed, in the first democratic elections (1990) by its freely expressed will, its millennial statehood and its resolution to establish the Republic of Croatia as a sovereign state.[62]

Of course, what was more disturbing to Serbs living in the Krajina of the secessionist republic was the Constitution's declaration that "the Republic of Croatia is hereby established as the national state of the Croatian people," even though the document goes on to list the various non-Croatian "minorities" who "are guaranteed equality with citizens of Croatian nationality." It was not the declaration regarding the protection of minorities which upset some Serbs, but that by accepting that constitution the status of Serbs was immediately altered from that of a "constituent nation" to a minority. These changes occurred in conjunction with the renaming of streets and squares after pro-Hitler and other nationalist figures in Croatian history,[63] the revival of symbols associated with the quisling regime, massive firings of Serbs primarily but not exclusively in the public sector, and allegations that Serb children in Croatia were being subjected to pressure to convert to Catholicism or at least to take Catholic catechism.[64]

While Croatian discourses of anti-Serb prejudice located Croatian identity in the context of "European" history and culture as an affirmation of their higher level of civility as compared to Serbs, discourses of Serbian prejudice toward Croats turned the claim of "Croats as Europeans" into a criticism. Serb identity narratives attempted to locate Serbian identity within a discourse that elevated eastern over western European culture, critical of western European imperialism. Thus the Croats" willingness to identify themselves as European indicated, within Serbian identity discourses, a flaw in Croatian national character. The Croats were (according to this discourse) class-conscious elitists, the character flaw that made the Holocaust possible and, closer to home, led the Croats to ally with Hitler. When partisans defeated the fascists and the Communist Party was created as the peacetime political successor to the partisan movement, the capitalist–communist, West–East rhetoric of opposition was superimposed on preexisting Croat–Serb prejudices. Croats *were* more Western, according to Serb prejudices, but in a negative sense. They were greedy, selfish capitalists who would allow self-interest to prevail over the welfare of the community. After all, the West had given rise to fascism. Serbs, on the other hand, were more community-oriented, egalitarian, and concerned with social welfare. Marxism was more progressive, it was the wave of the future, and Serbian national character was already better suited because it did not have to first overcome its Western capitalist orientation.

Serb respondents I interviewed often discussed Serbian identity in terms of an inferiority complex vis-à-vis Croats, or by equating Croats with Germans, particularly as obedient conformists unable or unwilling to think for themselves. Such perceptions also insinuated that the alliance between the quisling government in Croatia and the Nazis during World War II reflected an affinity between the negative aspects of Croatian and German national characters. There was a kind of a joke in Belgrade that, though it seems silly, was very revealing about the popular construction of Serb identity. When waiting on a street corner for the pedestrian light to turn green before crossing the street, people would cross on the red light and say jokingly "nesam nemački" (I am not German) as an affirmation of Serbs as independent thinkers and Serb character as distinct from the conformist character of Germans. The fatal flaw in German character was the failure to question authority, and thus Germans were possessed of a predilection for fascism. In her study of "Bellicose Virtues in Elementary School Readers," Vesna Pešić found Germans to be the second most frequently cited enemy of the Serbian people, following closely behind "Turks."[65] To be Serb was also to be brave enough to stand up to and overthrow their oppressors, whether Ottoman (in the several Serb uprisings), or Austro-Hungarian, or German. This distinguished Serbs from the timidity of the Croats, who managed to tolerate imperial domination.

Along with the juxtaposition of historical experience, identity, and intergroup prejudices and stereotypes, the violence in ex-Yugoslavia was also fueled by unreconciled grievances arising out of the lived experiences of World War II, particularly the atrocities. Tito's Yugoslavia made no effort to reconcile the past, and thus intergenerational fears remained among those directly and indirectly affected by a relatively recent war trauma. Paul Parin, a physician who served with the partisans during World War II and a Swiss-trained psychoanalyst, argues that Yugoslavia's failure to reconcile grievances arising out of the 1941 to 1944 civil war legitimized the war of aggression. He discusses the contemporary impact of the "unresolved past" in former Yugoslavia:

> For forty-five years the mass murders of Serbs by the Ustasha guards (soon after the Ustasha state was founded in 1941, in many locations and then in the death camp of Jasenovac), the mass murders of Ustasha supporters by Serbian Chetniks, and the murders of war prisoners of the Ustasha state by the victorious Partisan army were never elucidated and put in order, either in publications or within the context of parliamentary or legal discussions. By no means have these events been repressed—that is, forgotten. They have not been extinguished in the memory of the survivors.[66]

Parin's observations are echoed in the following comments by a respondents from Belgrade and Zagreb:

*J.B., Zagreb, 1997*
There are clearly deep traumas that have remained silenced over forty years, and then with this breakdown now have again become first of all a problem, and second of all they have been manipulated in very different ways by all the parties involved, and third they've become a part of the present issues as well. So evoking fears related to the imagery and for many families, the experience of Jasenovac, is part of the political strategy now. It is a part of historical interpretation that is propagandized. It is part of the mythology of the present regime. The key unresolved events of history are still with us. There was no dialogue after the war and under Tito to resolve these questions, to bring closure so we could move on as a society. Many of these things were taboo, and there was great pressure to suppress them in the name of an artificial kind of reconciliation. It was not a *real* reconciliation, that was the problem. There was not a real process of reconciliation after the Second World War.

*R.N., Belgrade, 1995*

The whole thing has been very much put under the carpet because of this [communist] ideology of internationalization, of "brotherhood and unity" within Yugoslavia, and the idea that with communist rule that all national questions have been resolved and subsumed. Communism was antinationalist and nationalism was anticommunist. It was a way of actually not only sweeping under the carpet but really leaving very crucial traumas completely silenced and memories that played a very major part in determining the radical responses to provocations. I was listening to something on television yesterday, and Misha Glenny was talking about the case of Glina in Croatia. Glina was absolutely an example of two very bad massacres during the Second World War. When Tudjman sent the police there with the Sahovnica with the flags, for them this was just a signal that a third massacre was going to occur. But Jasenovac, the concentration camp, the numbers, the political issues, the parties during the Second World War, what was really the civil war and what was the national liberation war, who was who, it has been all muddled by propaganda and the failure to address history openly and honestly. This is particularly true for the Serbian people and how they understand themselves as the "Serbian nation" with respect to the issue of the concentration camp Jasenovac. Neither Tito nor anybody made a gesture of reconciliation regarding the way the Holocaust was enacted here in Yugoslavia like Willy Brant did in postwar Germany. The camp was just totally destroyed and then just the memorial was built there.

Now the problem has just been compounded because you have not been able to initiate a real reconciliation process so that the trauma of forty years ago has become a part of this new conflict, and how are you going to achieve any kind of reconciliation when all these traumas are not addressed, but just piled on top of one another?

During my 1995 visit to the collective (refugee) center in Šabac, Serbia, I interviewed a seventy-three-year-old Serb woman who had been displaced from her home in Eastern Slavonia in 1991. According to her, the Croatian soldiers had came to her town to attack and terrorize the Serbs. From her account it was clear that the events in 1991 reignited the trauma of her war experience in 1941. Her story is one of a continuing history; she was born before World War II, was nineteen years old when the Croatian soldiers of the Ustaše terrorized her town and killed her husband, and was in her seventies when the new Croatian nationalists came to, depending on your perspective, either put down a Serb rebellion in Slavonia, or terrorize the Serbs in Slavonia into abandoning their villages. Her own version of that history reveals the interplay between traumatic experience, the historical and identity narratives in which she found herself, and the context of neonationalist propaganda in the 1990s wars: "I was just running," she said, "and so was everyone else. The soldiers came, and I saw the Ustaše symbols on their hats and uniforms. They had already killed one thousand children and thrown their bodies into a nearby lake."[67]

Kaja, a young Serb college student, active in the antiwar effort in Belgrade, had accompanied me to the collective center. Kaja knew that the woman's perception of what happened may also have been influenced by the propaganda broadcast by the official Belgrade media into the Slavonia region, so she asked her: "How did you know that they killed one thousand children? Did you see them kill the children?"

"No," said the older woman, "I didn't see that. What I did see was the woman who was running next to me with her child in her arms. The child was about seven or eight and the Ustaše soldiers grabbed the child and they killed her by sticking a pole in her, like a roasting stick."

"Do you mean they impaled her?" asked the younger woman.

"Yes," she said, "They impaled her." She went on to tell us the story of her experience fifty years earlier:

> I was nineteen and my husband was twenty-one when the Ustaše came one day. They rounded up all the men and boys and put them in the church. The blood in that church was running up to my knees [pointing to her calf] and I will never forget it! Only one boy survived by climbing a tree. Thousands were killed that day. Later [after the war] Tito sent one of his generals to that town and he gave a speech, saying that Serb and Croatian blood alike had been spilled there. But that boy who survived was a man now, and he stood up and said "If you can show me the bones of one Croatian killed here I will slit my own throat."

This story illustrates not only how the violence in 1991 evoked emotional trauma and confusion, particularly when, as was likely in this case, propaganda and hate speech had already been deployed to frighten people in the more rural and ethnically mixed small towns and villages. It also confirms the criticism of Tito's so-called "evenhanded" policy of postwar reconciliation that I had so often heard thoughtful people in all of the republics express. That policy functioned as a kind of denial, critics said. It denied that there was any difference between the guilt and responsibility of individuals and collective guilt and responsibility. It denied any difference between having a collaborationist government, the Ustaše, in power in Croatia and a nationalist Četnik movement (who flirted with collaboration) in Serbia, and it officially denied any difference in the quality and quantity of atrocities committed by each. The massacre of (alleged) Ustaše supporters and sympathizers at Bleiburg and some hasty monkey trials in which verdicts were predetermined, followed by executions of the accused collaborationists immediately after the war only made matters worse, both because such sloppy, brutal, and indiscriminate "justice" laid the ground for a new level of grievance among Croats and because it was meant to preclude the need for any further societal reconciliation.

Perhaps the general sent by Tito to the elderly woman's town was referring to the deaths of Croat and Serb partisans who fought against and defeated the Croatian Ustaše and Serb Četniks. But in the woman's understanding of these events, the civil war in 1941 was perpetrated by Croatian collaborationists against Serbian victims. War is a condition of organized political violence between enemies, one a perpetrator, possibly an evil perpetrator, one a noble defender, and only one will win.

The view of the sort of "ordinary people" we speak of when we use that term was the rather uncomplicated view of solid and organic ethnonational identities that made the violent experiences of both perpetrators and victims comprehensible to her. I do not mean to suggest that such "ordinary people" as a rule live in a cognitively, psychologically simpler world, but that when traumatized, we are all more likely to seek the comfort of simplicity. The woman also claimed, like so many of the "ordinary people" I interviewed, that before the violence she had no problems living with her neighbors — Serb, Croat, and Muslim. But the trauma of her earlier war experience and the loss of her young husband to violence would have been more than enough cause for her to regress to a more infantile emotional interpretation of events, roles, and agency constructed in the oppositional terms of enemies and allies, a world of stark contrasts, of two dimensions, of victims and perpetrators distinguished by their ethnic identity. Perhaps the trauma, which occurred when she was only nineteen years old herself, locked her into the cognitive world of a teenager for the rest of her life. The trauma of her earlier war experience was easily provoked by a deadly combination: the instability of the political environment, the reinvention of the Croatian state by renaming public spaces after Croatian nationalists, the deployment of Ustaše symbols by the police and military, and propaganda broadcast by the state-controlled media in nearby Belgrade.

# CHAPTER 7

# Causes of War:
# A Constructivist Account

People were fighting wars in their heads, on the ground, in the air, in their homes. It was impossible not to get involved.[1]

The war was initiated on a political level, but at the end of the day it was finished with the local population killing each other.

—D.C., Zagreb, 1997

At the international or systemic level, structural explanations for the war in Yugoslavia point to the power transition as the Cold War ended, and at the state level to the breakdown of the Yugoslav economy (partly attributable to shifts in systemic power relations) along with the failure to resolve the political crisis exacerbated, if not brought on, by Tito's death in 1980. But Yugoslavia was not the only central or east European state to be affected by the combination of a systemic power shift and an internal political and economic crisis at the end of the Cold War. So while a systemic power transition does help explain uncoordinated policy responses by the Western allies (Germany in the EU), and may even make alliance defections on the question of new state recognition during the early stage of the crisis in 1990 and 1991 more comprehensible,[2] a failure of international leadership coupled with an international power transition is not a sufficient explanation if our question is not simply "why war" but "why *here*," and "why *now*."

From a constructivist perspective, the end of the Cold War signaled not only a restructuring of power, but the collapse of a *socially constructed social arrangement*, to use Onuf's terminology,[3] an arrangement to which the term "Cold War" referred. Using the concepts suggested by Onuf, the rules mediating between social arrangements and agents may be (1) *instructive*—rules that indicate declarations about social reality, how things "are"; (2) *directive* rules that produce hierarchy and organization; or (3) *rules of commitment*—rules that produce associations, patterns, and expectations of agents' behavior in roles and in relation to one another.

As a social arrangement, the Cold War instructed that the United States and Soviet Union constituted a bipolar power structure, that this was the dominant international power structure, and that it was defined in the first instance by the antagonistic relationship between these two powers whose interests were articulated as fundamentally incompatible. Directive rules designated them as "superpowers" and European allies and China as "major powers," thus creating an international order structured by hierarchy. In addition to an arms control regime, an intersection between commitment and directive rules was reflected not only in the association of the superpowers and major powers within the UN system, but in the hierarchy of the relationship between major powers, including the superpowers, and the rest.

The United States–Soviet relationship was characterized by competition for influence in the global system (which alone may have been sufficient for a kind of zero-sum and antagonistic conception of their interests). That competition led to the use of coercive measures to establish Soviet-friendly governments in central and eastern Europe, "hot wars" fought on the turf of formerly colonized non-Western peoples, and the formation of a number of superpower-client relationships exacerbating the volatility of the conflicts in the Middle East and elsewhere. It also produced an initiative among non-Western leaders to carve out a "nonaligned" position, which often found superpower policies resembling divorced parents promising favors as they vied for alliances with their estranged offspring, or a mafia protection racket profiting from arms production and sales to client states living in a world made increasingly insecure by the policies and positions of their patrons.

According to a constructivist account, social arrangements provide a context in which agents and structures co-constitute one another through actions mediated by rules. As Onuf says, "rules tell us who the active participants [agents] in a society are," and they "give agents choices."[4] Yugoslavia, like any state society, was itself constituted by agents as a "stable pattern of rules, institutions, and unintended consequences,"[5] and it was located in the context of the international social arrangement called the Cold War. As argued earlier, Yugoslavia was understood by its citizens (as well as some outside observers) in the Cold War context of nonalignment, a "good" socialist state (as contrasted with the "bad" socialist state of the Soviet Union), a socialist state not entirely isolated from the nonsocialist world, a socialist state indeed, to which many tourists from the nonsocialist world regularly traveled and from which many Yugoslav citizens traveled and even temporarily worked in the nonsocialist world. Yugoslavia was a porous, if not entirely open, socialist society.

As a social arrangement, "Yugoslavia" was also constituted by agents acting within the context of an ongoing and historical international normative discourse about human society and its political forms, about the basis for human societal relations, about the relationship between identity and society formation, the relationship between "ethnic" identity and control over political destiny, and the legitimacy of governments constituted by their citizen-agents rather than by the assertion of authority by agents of the Church or other institutions. It is not my purpose here to recount the entire history of discourses constituting the modern state, but rather to point to the claim, which grew in importance from the mid-eighteenth to the mid-twentieth century, that nationalism is or was an ideology of liberation, of *shifting the agency for legitimating governance from the institutions of the Church, monarchy, and empire to "the people."* Giddens, Jabri notes, rejects psychological explanations of nationalism in favor of a more ideological view linking it with sovereignty and citizenship, while Kedourie "situates the emergence of the relationship between nationalism, sovereignty, and citizenship in the French Revolution": "This event established the relationship between legitimate authority and citizenship in identification with the state."[6]

Jabri's own analysis of the myth of the state as a natural category for political association and polity formation concludes that: "The nation is, therefore, constructed as a totality, built upon an imagined distinctive history and culture, containing a symbolic order that is utilised in times of adversity to mobilize entire collectivities against other bounded communities."[7]

The failure of major powers to intervene against Hitler during the early years of German expansionism under the guise of irredentist discourse is more comprehensible when understood within the context of a nationalism-as-liberatory discourse that had been ongoing in Western societies for nearly two centuries. By framing the problem of war within the realist paradigm in which representation of the state as a naturalized expression of national self-determination is uncontested, the international community has failed as of yet to develop a policy (rule) providing an nonviolent alternative to solving the tensions between identity and statehood.[8]

To a constructivist, growing concerns about conflict rooted in liberatory ethnic discourses (or discourses of ethnic oppression vis-à-vis the state) coupled with efforts to redefine the state in civic rather than national terms might be symptomatic of a breakdown in the rules that mediate agents' choices when acting on behalf of and in relation to the state as a social arrangement rooted, particularly the rules regarding the relationship with ethnicity or nationality and the state.[9] Language that refers to "minorities" in the state, for example, *presumes the existence of an ethnic majority as the norm.* This seems more true for many European states, even for state societies where the agents whose actions constituted the boundaries of the state were mostly "insiders" (China, Thailand, and India come to mind), where they were constructed in connection with national unity movements, or in the dissolution of the Soviet Union making independent states out of formerly constituent republics. But where the construction of territorial and jurisdictional boundaries (within which societies were supposed to form) was heavily influenced by outside (colonial) agents, as in the case of Africa and to a lesser extent in Central and South America, there is quite often a discontinuity between ethnic identity, ethnic majorities, and societal boundaries. Finally, evidence of the "ethnic (majority) rule" can be seen insofar as agents acting against ethnic hegemony within the state or attempting to decenter the state so as to eliminate ethnic preference must act *against the rule* that posits the state as the social arrangement through which ethnic or national identity can reach its fullest expression. In fact, that these agents often identify themselves in terms of ethnic solidarity and then make claims for autonomy, self-determination, or independence further supports the claim that *the ethnic rule* mediates the actions of agents in relation to the formation of polities, keeping in mind that the rule itself is socially constructed, regardless of whether many people have come to regard it as "natural."

The breakdown of the political and economic structures (social arrangements) within Yugoslavia, coupled with the collapse of the international structure (social arrangement) called the Cold War, created what I call a set of *antecedent variables*, not sufficient in themselves to *cause* a brutal and personal war in which officially sanctioned "ethnic cleansing" reminded some people of exactly the kind of horror that the promise of "never again" was intended to prevent. But they did make it possible, or at least more likely. And since these conditions made it less likely that a global hegemonic leader or hegemonic alliance would effectively intervene to arrest the momentum of violence that so quickly gathered in the wake of the Slovenian and Croatian secessions, they made the violence more likely to escalate and spread.

An alternative explanation that takes into account both structure and agency, both institutional and cognitive variables, is this. *The war was a result of a dynamic* interaction *between international and domestic (Yugoslav)* social arrangements *(structures) and the* agency *of specific domestic and international actors in relation to rules instructing them that ethnicity or ethnonational identity is an appropriate basis for the formation of polities.*

In the former category are the political, intellectual, and religious elites, media, individuals with a history of violent behavior such as criminals, and individuals more easily aroused to participate in violence when rationalized by intergroup prejudices. In the category of international agents are those policy-makers, institutions (such as the UN and EU), and observers (journalists and academics) whose discourse about war, power, and the structure of international relations was decentered by the end of the Cold War and who understood themselves to live within a historical narrative about civilization that precluded the possibility of a brutal ethnic war in Europe.

In the case of ex-Yugoslavia and many other postconflict environments, it should be added that *the agency of particular domestic or internal actors was exercised within a sociopolitical environment characterized by narratives of unreconciled grievances and historical narratives of victimization and collective guilt that were conflated with the politicization of ethnic identities.*

A constructivist reading turns our attention to that which connects structures and agency—the social rules in relation to which agents act. Constructivism tells us that agents and structures co-constitute one another in a dynamic and ongoing process. Conflict is to be expected as a regular feature of such a dynamic relationship. An important question is how rule instabilities (the breakdown of a rule or system of rules) and rule conflicts turn violent, or alternatively, how rules structure conflicts. For instance, the "ethnic rule" for polities is appropriated by majorities to proclaim (explicitly or tacitly) their states as "the state of the (Croatian, Serbian, German, Ukrainian, Albanian, Macedonian, and so on) people or nation," as well as by minorities engaged in "national liberation" struggles against states. It seems to me that agency—the actions the follow from agents' choices—is the critical variable in transforming conflict into violence. Even Goldhagen argues that anti-Semitism had a long history in Europe, not only in Germany. But Hitler's rise to power and the Holocaust that followed occurred in the context of the social arrangement called "Germany." Structural instability, which was occurring elsewhere in Europe in the 1930s, was exploited by the agency of a leadership willing and able to do so, and was probably abetted by social beliefs that were particularly pronounced in Germany and not elsewhere. In Germany, as in Yugoslavia, internal as well as systemic structural instability and uncertainty preceded the mobilization of ordinary people to carry out the aggressions of war and crimes against humanity. But as in Yugoslavia, those conditions preceded the war by years, but were not exploited to mobilize violence. The critical variable was *Hitler's willingness to appropriate anti-Semitism* and to interpret structural instability in terms of the scapegoating those prejudices made possible. The emotional vulnerabilities of ordinary people were manipulated through the political rhetoric of German victimization and the scapegoat of collective Jewish guilt. The narrative of anti-Semitism was already a central component of European identity, and the narrative of German victimization was easily fueled by the lived experience of the punishing consequences associated with losing World War I. Both the case of the rise of Nazism and the breakdown and violence in Yugoslavia involved social arrangements called states in the throes of political and economic instability within an international context of power transition (read: breakdown of existing international social arrangements pertaining to the agents and structure of power). The transformation of ordinary people into perpetrators of atrocities in both Germany and Yugoslavia was ultimately, however, made possible by a willing and effective leadership that asserted a high level of control over media, and that was able to exploit structural instabilities by arousing an emotionally vulnerable populace to create a pathology of violence rationalized by ethnic prejudices. The evil of inhumanity is thus truly banal.

In this chapter I will take closer look at the role of agents in the construction of the war in former Yugoslavia, as well as how individuals reflected on and understood the forces that led to violence. In the comments of many respondents and in source documents we will see evidence of the prevalence of a belief that there is a relationship between ethnicity and the state. Many references suggest a belief that ethnic hegemony is the norm, while others insist that we are moving away (or we need to) from the rule that ethnicity legitimates governance or that ethnicity requires control of a state for its fullest expression toward a rule of civic association.

## Elite Mobilization

V. P. Gagnon argues persuasively that the application of realism to "ethnic" conflict fails both because it relies on a concept of the state as a naturalized expression of national identity and because its assumption of rationality is flawed insofar as it focuses exclusively on externally motivated conflict, conflict the nation-state experiences in relation to the outside, international arena.[10] His formulation of rationality in relation to the war in ex-Yugoslavia instead emphasizes in-group competition among elites "seeking to gain or maintain power in the face of challenges from other elites,"[11] defining rationality as "intentional and goal-oriented" behavior "taking into account preferences, costs, and benefits," and noting the heterogeneous environments in which "ethnic groups" are actually located.[12]

From this perspective, it *was* rational for Mr. Milosević to go to war even four times. Perhaps it was also rational for Mr. Tudjman to respond, not only defensively but provocatively. And perhaps it was rational if we presume their objective was to maximize the scope of their respective spheres of influence and thus, for both of them, whether overtly or covertly as an impending secession crisis loomed ahead of them, to savor the prospect of altering the boundaries of their republics to include areas of Bosnia divided between them. The resulting enlarged secessionist states (and the elimination of Bosnia as a consequence) would assert control over a larger territorial, population, and resource base. Both the Croatian and Serbian leaders behaved rationally, if by that we mean that they deployed discourses of ethnonationalism and a promise of territorial expansion as means of securing their own dominance within a field of contenders for elite leadership in the successor states, but why did people follow Milosević and Tudjman? If rational self-interest were sufficient to mobilize support among the ordinary people on whom they had to rely to carry out such plans, then they would not have needed to resort to such emotionally charged rabble-rousing, control of the media and propaganda, appeals to xenophobia, and the deployment of paramilitary terrorism.

Every society has elites. Every modern state is legitimated by an ideology, religion, historical narrative, or some other basis for collective identification with the normative purposes of the state. Realism and other structural accounts, by viewing the state as a naturalized unit of political order and by presuming solidarity (organic or otherwise) among all individuals contained within it, fail to account for either the structure of relations among agents within the state (elites versus the masses or ordinary people) or the relationship between differently situated agents (elites) and the structure of the state itself. This is an especially serious shortcoming when the violence (war) we wish to understand is undertaken in relation to institutions, ideologies, and structures that have become contestable.

Constitutions may and often do contain elements of legitimating narratives, but legitimating narratives are more than that. They are visions of the state, its purpose, and thus its 'identity.' Benedict Anderson describes it as an ideology in the broadest sense—a justification for the state's existence.[13] In spite of the multicultural reality of the majority of states today, we are still inclined to think of the political boundaries of the state as containing people who share something cultural, or, if multicultural, arranged in terms of a dominant culture and one or more "minorities." Gramsci implicates the hegemonic tendencies of dominant or majority cultures to assimilate, marginalize, and suppress minority cultures in the process of modern state-building. Ethnicized culture is more easily appropriated as the basis for political legitimation in more homogeneous settings, such as France, and more antagonistic where multicultural, multinational, social structures have given rise to contentious discourses over the politics of ethnic identity, as in Canada. The construction of a legitimating narrative in Canada, for example, draws more heavily on its historical narrative as a settler state, but to distinguish it from other settler states, a narrative of "Canadian identity" has also emerged, emphasizing its social progressiveness vis-à-vis its powerful neighbor to the south. Canadians may be Anglo, or French, or hyphenated immigrants, but, with the exception of indigenous First Nations, what binds most other nonnative Canadians together is that they are not Americans.

What is the relationship between elites and legitimating narratives? Elites are leaders whose social action takes place in relation to legitimating narratives. Whether to uphold, contest, or transform narratives, elite leadership is exercised in reference to them, much as Onuf describes an actor's relationship to the rules that mediate structure and agency. When a legitimating narrative becomes highly contestable, the narrative itself becomes the central subject of political discourse, and a legitimacy crisis may ensue. Legitimacy crises are often characterized by increasingly nonnormal political action: strikes, protests, and other kinds of direct action, for instance. Extraordinary political action either contests the dominant legitimating narrative or questions the ability of a particular regime to act in accord with it. In the extreme, it can ultimately take the form of antiregime violence.

Yugoslav society floundered on the verge of a legitimacy crisis even before Tito's death, as constitutional and party reforms undertaken in an effort to resolve the crisis failed. The second Yugoslav state was grounded in a legit-imating narrative of antifascist partisan heroism. After the war, Partisan elites, led by Tito, attempted to transform the antifascist Partisan military movement into a more broadly based, pan-Yugoslav, communist, political party by articulating a distinctively Yugoslav socialist ideology as the norma-tive basis for building the new Yugoslav state. These efforts were always in tension with what Banac and others call "the national question."[14] Conse-quently, two competing visions of Yugoslavia emerged, one relying on the transformation of the anti-Nazi Partisan movement into a pro-Yugoslav Communist Party, an integrated socialist state with a uniquely pan-Yugo-slav identity; the other a decentered confederacy of, with the exception of Bosnia, ethnically based republics. Thus, at a rhetorical level the "Yugoslav" vision prevailed in a society where political life was controlled by the Communist Party, while at the local level of most ordinary people's experi-ence, they lived within the political boundaries of republics comprised of ethnonational majorities, and containing symbolic spaces or legitimating symbols, such as Kosovo Polje (site of the Battle of Kosovo) or the squares named after Partisan heroes, to which the historical narratives of national identities referred. In this sense, multiethnic, multinational Bosnia was truly a microcosm of the Yugoslav state: at its center, but surrounded on all sides by republics that, when things fell apart and political action and discourse were "ethnicized," would come to represent ethnic "homelands" to Bosnia's Croats and Serbs.[15]

Attempts to reconcile these visions led to the confederalization of the Yugoslav state in the 1974 Constitution, the creation and strengthening of republican-based communist parties and thus local-level party bureaucracies and "ethnicized" or nationalized Communist Party branches, the creation of two autonomous provinces in Kosovo and Vojvodina and a general trend toward the decentralization of power, the experiment with self-management, the designation of "Muslim" as a national category in Bosnia, and, on the darker side, purges and persecution of accused nationalists and the suppres-sion of national cultures.[16]

By the mid-1980s there were two camps: conservative communists, and integrationist reformers. Political and economic instability exacerbated the struggle. In Serbia the reformers were ousted from the Serbian Socialist Party as Milosević and other nationalists took over (though they identified Serb national interests with the continued existence of Yugoslavia, which was, as they said, the one state in which all Serbs lived). In Croatia the reformers took over the party, which had been made up of both Croatian Croats and Croatian Serbs. The conservatives thus left the party, and in the wake and under the guise of the post–Cold War freedom to form new political parties, Croats went to the nationalist Croatian Democratic Union (HDZ) and Serbs joined the Belgrade controlled Serbian Democratic Party.

The nationalisms that came to dominate Croat–Serb politics individually and in relation to one another were mobilized around grievances articulated as narratives of injustice. As Gagnon argues, to rise and secure their positions of leadership and power, elites often resort to the creation of a credible threat. In the literature on war, this is often called the rally-round-the-flag phenomenon. But there is no reason such a phenomenon should be limited to the relationship between citizens and the political leaders of states. It is a primarily emotional response to the perception of a threat directed toward one's group and against which one seeks defense through collective solidarity. In other words, it is a response by individuals to a threat they perceive is directed *toward* them by virtue of their membership or identification with a group, and *against* which they seek security by strengthening their identification and association with the group.

Prior to the outbreak of violent conflict, grievances in Croatia centered on the alleged draining of "Croatian" revenues to support the "Serb-dominated" communist bureaucracy and to subsidize the poorer regions of Kosovo and Bosnia.[17] Because, as it happened, the newly configured party alignments also actually left communists in power in Serbia, the "Serb" and "Communist" identities were easily conflated by those indulging in stereotypes, and those stereotypes were in turn easily exploited by Croatian nationalists coming into power. Some Croats also complained that under Tito they were as a group more frequently and vigorously persecuted for expressions of national and cultural pride and more frequently arrested and punished for political crimes. They further complained that they were singled out for collective guilt as collaborators during World War II even though the majority of Croats were not Ustaše and many Croats served among the Partisans, and even though there was a Serbian nationalist group, the Četniks, that had also committed atrocities during the occupation and 1941-to-1944 civil war. A corollary to these complaints was the failure of Tito, of the Serbs, of the Communist Party, and of Yugoslav society as a whole to acknowledge the massacre of Bleiburg. The old juxtaposition of nationalism and anticommunist resistance also played into the hands of Croatian elites. The fact that communists *as communists* remained in power in Serbia even after the collapse of the Soviet Union was cited by their opponents as further proof of their backwardness.

Whereas Milosević's rabble-rousing was aimed at exploiting Serbian prejudices toward and fear of Albanians living inside Serbia, Tudjman incited fear among the 12 percent of the Serb population living inside Croatia, though less overtly than his Serbian counterpart. A critical difference between the situation of Albanians in Serbia and that of Serbs in Croatia, however, was the fact that provocation of Albanians and anti-Albanian prejudices were not really a matter of interest to anyone outside Serbia. Both leaders had an interest in provoking conflict between the Croatian Serbs and the Croatian government—Tudjman to secure his position as defender of the (not yet new) state, and Milosević in order to justify the deployment of the Yugoslav National Army (JNA) to "prevent secession" and restore the peace of the Yugoslav state. Thus it was within the republican boundaries of Croatia that the violence began, first in Knin as, in the face of a growing secessionist movement, local Serb leaders railed against any move to change the status of Croatian Serbs from a Yugoslav constituent nation to a minority within a Croatian state, and then in Slavonia, on the border with Serbia and Bosnia. When, in the midst of growing intercommunal tensions, provocateurs, local as well as from Belgrade, fueled fears of persecution, and the JNA under the command of Belgrade was deployed to prevent an escalation of violence, it was not too difficult to convince the Croatian public that the resulting violence was simply an act of aggression against Croatia by the Serb-controlled army under Belgrade's command.

The problem with this scenario is that from the perspective of international norms, aggression can occur only between two internationally recognized states across internationally recognized boundaries, which was not the case among the republics of Yugoslavia at the time. Such subtleties of international law were neither apparent nor important to those Croats who identified themselves with the idea of a Croatian nation attached to a Croatian homeland within the boundaries of the Croatian republic. From their point of view, Croatia, the "national state of the Croatian people," as the 1990 Constitution said, was a victim of Serbian aggression.

Investigations continue into the intentions of the Croatian president and his relationship to the provocation of violence in Croatia and material and logistical support for violence in Bosnia and Herzegovina. His public record suggests an early reluctance to engage in direct and violent confrontation but a reliance on a somewhat inflammatory and certainly exclusivist nationalist rhetoric as the basis for mobilizing and securing support among the Croats both within and beyond the boundaries of the Croatian republic. People also suggested a link between his aspirations in Bosnia and his relationship with Croatian émigré communities (from whom he solicited financial and political support), who are frequently characterized as somewhat more nationalistic than the majority of in-country Croatians. The comments of the following Croatian respondent, who considered himself a loyal though not a "big" Croat (his terminology), are revealing. In his view, emigrant Ustaše supporters may also have played a role in the violence.

*D.C., Croatia, 1997*
One day we may discover the true role of the nationalists in Croatia in starting the war, and whether there was really any provocation from the Croatian side and whether there was there any secret policy among the Croatian politicians in the ruling party to start a war in Croatia. You have to know that a large number of Croats living abroad had long been

involved in an underground movement for the liberation of Croatia from Yugoslavia, and as Croatia became an independent country they came back to Croatia and of course they had that idea of "clean" Croatia. They had that idea in their minds for a very long time—an "ethnically clean" Croatia. This was in their hearts after the Second World War, and they left the country but they kept that dream and then in 1990 they saw their chance.

There was always that question in many people's minds you know— how come Tudjman was allowed to travel out of Croatia in 1970s and 1980s, and when he traveled he was always meeting with Croats outside of Croatia. Maybe he was already plotting a certain political change by meeting with Croatian clubs in Canada, and the United States, and Australia.

Knowing how the Yugoslav government was working at that time, we were always wondering, since Tudjman did not have a passport, why was he allowed to do this traveling? Who gave him the permission to travel and who funded those trips? There were many suspicions like that when it [the war] started.

While these comments reflect how ordinary people may have perceived the link between Tudjman, his party, the HDZ, and the émigré community, Croatian human rights/antiwar activist Vesna Pušić, speaking to the International Forum for Democratic Studies at the National Endowment for Democracy in Washington, D.C., on March 24, 1997, offered a more nuanced and fair interpretation of the role of Croatian émigrés during the early stages of Croatian–Serbian hostility:

An additional force, present in 1990 and growing in influence thereafter, was the Croatian émigré community. Although generally fairly moderate, the émigrés always included in their ranks small but passionate and well-organized groups of extreme nationalists, some of whom were terrorists. These extremist circles, already leaning toward Tudjman and the HDZ, were reinforced in this tendency by Tudjman's first televised speech on behalf of his party, in which he implicitly called for territorial acquisitions in western Herzegovina, a region that was the homeland of key Croat-émigré figures. Extreme nationalists among the émigrés became instrumental in raising funds for Tudjman and the HDZ, although the actual donors were, in many cases, unsuspecting Croats who simply wanted to aid the noncommunist opposition generally or help Croatia fend off Milosević and achieve independence.[18]

Although there have long been suspicions that Tudjman collaborated from the start, even if only tacitly, with his Serbian counterpart to incite localized violence which quickly spread from more ethnically mixed areas of Croatia to virtually all of Bosnia, there is no clear record that in the first few years he did anything more than indulge himself in ethnically inflammatory rhetoric, deploying symbols intended to agitate and stir fear among the Serbian population in Croatia and engaging in rather irresponsible use of the media to create an environment permissive of official (police) and unofficial local verbal and physical assaults stemming from ethnic prejudices. Recent evidence, however, substantiates claims that however unwilling he may have been initially, by 1993 he not only had clear designs on an ethnic partition and likely eventual annexation of Croat Bosnia, but actively advocated the same "cleansing" tactics notoriously used by Bosnian Serbs.[19]

Upon his death from cancer in December 1999, the Bosnia Action Coalition published the following summary of his role in Croatian history:

> Tudjman led Croatia to independence, but governed the country with a heavy hand and virulent nationalism. He backed ethnic Croatian extremists in neighboring Bosnia-Hercegovina and was long accused of seeking to carve up Bosnia between Croatia and Serbia. Western leaders and human-rights activists considered Tudjman a major stumbling block to democracy and stabilization in the region.
>
> He was known to dislike both Muslims and Serbs, and also angered Western leaders by comments such as "Thank God my wife is not a Serb or a Jew" (which he declared while campaigning nine years ago). He also stirred up outrage by questioning the number of Jews exterminated in the Holocaust and claimed the Nazi-allied Croatian Ustaše regime during World War II killed less than 60,000 Serbs, Jews and Gypsies (independent historians believe at least half a million were murdered).
>
> In a 1989 publication called *Impasses*, the *N.Y. Times* notes, he wrote: "A Jew is still a Jew. Even in the camps they retained their bad characteristics: selfishness, perfidy, meanness, slyness and treachery."
>
> "Tudjman confided to friends that he did not really hate Serbs, but that he detested Bosnian Muslims," according to the *Times*. "In May 1995 in London, he told Paddy Ashdown, a Liberal Democratic member of Parliament, that he preferred Milosević to Izetbegović, the Bosnian leader, whom he described as 'an Algerian and a fundamentalist.'"[20]

Though anti-Muslim prejudices were shared by Croats and Serbs alike, it was the more overtly chauvinistic nationalist movements among Serbs (albeit under the guise of the Socialist Party and for the "preservation of the Yugoslav state") and Croats that gave voice to grievances that directly or indirectly incriminated one another. The complaint that Croatian identity and culture had been submerged by Serbian political, cultural, and linguistic hegemony within Yugoslavia after 1990 gave way increasingly to the image of Croats as direct victims of Serb aggression.

In Serbia, claims of injustice centered on the alleged persecution of Serbs living outside Serbia proper—mainly in Kosovo and Croatia at first, and later in a Bosnia that, they claimed, Muslims planned on turning into an Islamic state. Grievances underlying Serb nationalism were articulated in the lengthy Academy of Sciences' Memorandum, which bemoaned the marginalization of the Serbian nation by alleging that the partitioning of Yugoslavia to split the Serb population among four of the six republics, along with the weakening of the Serbian republic by conferring *de facto* republican status on two "autonomous regions" within Serbia, deliberately subverted aspirations to Serb unity within a single republic comparable to the unity enjoyed by Slovenes in Slovenia, Croats in Croatia, and Macedonians in Macedonia.

> On top of its failure to provide for a state for the Serbian nation, the Constitution of the SFRY [Socialist Federative Republic of Yugoslavia] also put insurmountable difficulties in the way of constituting such a state. It is imperative that this constitution be amended so as to satisfy Serbia's legitimate interests. The autonomous provinces should become genuinely integral parts of the Republic of Serbia. . . .[21]

This constitutional injustice, it said, was combined with a growing discontent among Serbs as a result of the failure to assigned greater weight to the Croats for the atrocities of World War II, described below in an excerpt from the lengthy document:

> After the dramatic intercommunal strife in the course of the Second World War, it seemed as though nationalism had run its course and was well on the way to disappearing completely. Such an impression has proven deceptive. Not much time passed before nationalism began to rear its ugly head again, and each successive constitutional change has created more of the institutional prerequisites for it to become full-blown. Nationalism has been generated from the top, its prime initiators being the politicians. The basic cause of the manifold crisis is the ideological defeat which nationalism has inflicted on socialism. The disintegrative processes of all descriptions which have brought the Yugoslav state to the verge of ruin are the consequences of this defeat.[22]

Yugoslavia was being destroyed by nationalism, the Memorandum claimed, which could in turn be traced to the misguided policies of the interwar regime, which were based on the misperception that Serbia had been unfairly privileged following World War I. This misperception subsequently guided the formation of the post–World War II Yugoslav state:

This policy incorporated elements of retribution against the Serbian people as an "oppressor" nation, and it had far-reaching repercussions on inter-communal relations, the social order, the economic system, and the fate of moral and cultural values after the war. The Serbian people were made to feel historical guilt, and they alone did not resolve their national question or gain a state of their own, as did the other national groups. Consequently, it is above all necessary to remove the stigma of historical guilt from the Serbian nation; the charge that the Serbs had a privileged economic status between the two world wars must officially be retracted, and their history of liberation wars and contribution to the formation of Yugoslavia must no longer be denied.[23]

The complicated politics surrounding publication of and responses to the Memorandum, not only in Croatia and Slovenia, but in Serbia itself, are analyzed at length by Olivera Milošavljević.[24] Cautioning all analysts to "resist the temptation to identify the whole [of SANU—Serbian Academy of Arts and Sciences] with its parts," Milošavljević nevertheless argues persuasively that the Memorandum begins as an explanation of the larger crisis in Yugoslav society and ends "as a blueprint for a Serbian national programme. . . ."[25]

[T]he Memorandum met with contradictory interpretations because it attempted to reconcile two irreconcilable motives: it endeavoured to explain the ineffectiveness and the inadequacy of the existing political system which threatened every one of the Yugoslav peoples (this is explicitly stated at one point), and at the same time, it tried to prove the danger inherent in such a system for the Serbian people and Serbia. Because it examined the entire social and economic crisis exclusively through the Serbian national lens, it did not recognize the perspective of the other Yugoslav peoples. As a result, it identified the ineffectiveness of the political system as the basic cause of the crisis, which it then reinterpreted as national, economic, political, and cultural discrimination against Serbia and the Serbian people exclusively.[26]

Although the Memorandum will continue to be, in its own right, a subject for discussion and analysis about its role in creating an ideological justification for the mobilization of Serbian society along nationalistic lines—both within and beyond the borders of the Serbian republic—here there are three key points I wish to make with respect to its role in the complex social processes which culminated in the 1990 to 1995 war. First, the legitimating narrative of the Yugoslav state attempted to transform ethnonational identities into a cohesive Yugoslav socialist identity, and the intelligentsia in all the republics were crucial achieving that transformation. The academy, therefore, held extraordinary influence over the legitimacy of the state. It must be remembered that communist ideology was constructed as a scientific account of social evolution. Second, that the academy conflated Yugoslav communism with the interests of the Serbian people only served to confirm Croatian (and others') fears of Serbian hegemony within the Yugoslav state. Finally, Milosević was able not only to prevail in a struggle among elites for control of the Serbian Socialist Party but to identify his victory with the claim that under his leadership the crisis outlined in the Memorandum would be remedied.[27] It is doubtful that Milosević would have come to power, or at least doubtful that he would have remained in power, without successfully identifying his regime with the Memorandum. It is less clear what the impact of the Memorandum would have been had he not at least initially identified his regime with it.

## The Media, Hate Speech, and Propaganda

Both the Croatian and Serbian leadership inherited control over the media from the old party system. Early war resisters in both republics noted the increasingly inflammatory and propagandistic use of the media to incite intercommunal fear and anger. While antiregime media managed to continue functioning throughout the war in both Serbia and Croatia, both regimes also took extraordinary measures to suppress and harass independent media. A significant number, perhaps a majority of people were willing to believe propaganda. It may be unfair to say that the media caused the violence, but it is also doubtful whether, without the collaboration of the media, elites could have mobilized sufficient support for violence. In both Croatia and Serbia respondents spoke frequently about the role of the media in arousing fear and, in some cases, fabricating for an audience drawn primarily from one ethnic group the threat of violence to them at the hands of another. The political elite used its control of the media to mobilize negative emotions — fears, stereotypes and prejudices — to structure people's thinking, and to provoke, affirm, and inflate fear in a climate in which violence was both spreading and becoming normalized. This theme was repeated in interviews in both Serbia and Croatia, as the following interview excerpts illustrate.

M.Z., Belgrade, 1995
*There is no historic reason for this war. It was created by criminal politicians, by hate speech, by speech alone, and then after that they want to involve us in this stupidity, to find some historical reasons for this war.*[28]
    ["Why did people respond to the hate speech?" I asked.]
    Put yourself in their position. You have only the opportunity to hear our own official state TV program, day in and day out. You see horrible things and you are told these things are being done by your enemies, the

Croats and the radical Muslims. No one knows what these pictures really are. You cannot tell when you see people mutilated whether they are Serbs or Croats or Muslims! You cannot tell when you see housing burning whose houses they are or who set them on fire. After several months you would be completely mad, I am sure. I would be completely mad. I am sure. If I were in a position to have some possibility to influence public opinion, I must say, I would be trying to change it, but I am not in this position.

A Croatian Serb respondent reflected on the relationship between ideology, elites, the use of media for propaganda, and the emotional mobilization of ordinary people who had lived in a relatively closed society. It is also a revealing passage because it refers to the effects of suppressing discussions of history and historical grievances as well as the shift in the international structure of power and its consequences.

*M.P., Zagreb, 1997*

I was just thinking about the relationship between the political elites and the people. There is no doubt that the crucial and substantial and major responsibility for the war is on the side of the political elites. They governed over the heads of the people. With all the means available, particularly their control over the major media, they misused the people's emotions. It started with the question of the westernization of this space, of how to westernize, and the question of whether the people could become a part of Europe as soon as possible. This was the question from one side, I mean the Croatian and Slovenian elite, as they saw it, as the Cold War ended, how could they integrate with the West. From the other side, the Serbian side, they told the people that they have a historical dream to fight against Western hegemony, Western rule over the Balkans, especially Austrians and Germans, and Catholics as representatives of Western imperial domination. This was a misuse of history, of the memories and also the hopes of the people.

So naturally the ideology of communism and ideology of nationalism were always here. Nationalism was used by the communists in a controlled way, but the ideology was already here, and it was not so difficult to transform and step forward from the socialist ideology to nationalistic ideology, from the socialist communist discourse to the nationalistic heuristic type of discourse. Because of the lack of democratic tradition, because one type of ideological discourse was replaced by another type of collectivistic discourse, people just came to have more or less the same type of public opinion, just with a different content, a different type of emotion, and different authorities, different colors, so to speak, different symbols (which is the case more or less in all of eastern Europe).

But here the people awakened as if from hibernation, and they were not able to recognize each other after that. They awakened in a new ideology which was controlled by the old elites but which had been forbidden under the old regime, and it was if they were awakened in the past, which they didn't know because we had not talked openly about the past, only in a controlled way, controlled by Tito and the party. In this new awakened reality they were not able to communicate with each other, the ordinary and common people by themselves were not able to communicate as members of the different church communities, as members of different ethnic communities, as people with different interests. They simply did not know how to understand themselves and interpret their reality in a pluralistic environment.

A Croat respondent from Zadar talks about his impression of the early stages of violence, the "Knin rebellion" of Serbs in Croatia, how the war spread to Bosnia, and the influence of the media.

*D.C., Zadar, 1997*
I always have to think about the pattern of events leading up to the war. First there were some kind of negotiations among the presidents of the republics, maybe even secret agreements, who knows. Then there were secessions. Then came a statement given by the leaders of the Serbian municipalities in Croatia, like Knin, saying that they refuse to be subject to the Zagreb government as a minority and they proclaim the autonomous regions for the Serbs in Serb municipalities [in Croatia] and they refuse to accept the Croatian police, and they put up blockades, and supposedly these are a response to Croatian attacks on Serbian municipalities—that was in Croatia in Krajina or in Slavonia. This is all most people hear on the national news. They do not know whether the police intimidated the Serbs, or what their grievances were about. They are just the rebellious Serbs, and of course the JNA, supposedly to keep Yugoslavia together, comes to their defense. Meanwhile the Croats are already thinking that the republic is their state and if the JNA attacks people it is an attack of Serbia on the Croatian state.

But the media rhetoric was very interesting. The Belgrade station usually referred to these "harmless and unarmed poor Serbian people in that region." They were presented as victims of the Croatian police, but in reality they were armed with AK-47s, rocket-launchers, and so on, yet they were supposed to be a very poorly defended nation, huh?

It was the same in Bosnia-Herzegovina, you know. The majority of the people voted for independence for Bosnia-Herzegovina, but the Serbs would not accept that outcome, and so they declared the autonomous region of Serbian provinces, and again the media portrayed them as innocent victims, this time of so-called radical Muslims, *mujahadeen*. Then the Belgrade media said that some people in Bjelina attacked Serbs, so Arkan's paramilitary was forced to react for the protection of Serbian minorities. It said that Serbian minorities were being slaughtered and there was a big danger for the Serbian people. That was an image easily promoted through the media because there was a lack of information in these areas, people were simply not well informed. And that is very important because the media was very much used to put the pressure in these people specifically living in remote areas, to put the fear in their bones. It is like when you hear that an enemy monster is raping women in the village next to you, and they will come to your village next, I guarantee you that the women will be running away because it will seem to them true, you know if they said it on television it must be true. Then on television they will find or produce some people who saw it, who claim to be eyewitnesses, saying "Yes, I saw it and it is very ugly" and someone will say they saw things that were not true but people start to believe it.

In a 1994 report on hate speech the Center for Anti-War Action described the use of "turbo" folk music to arouse stereotypes and ethnic hostility.[29] Though diverse and sometimes critical currents survived in the arena of contemporary (and dissident rock) music during the war, music, like other dimensions of social and cultural life, became progressively nationalized and "ethnicized."[30] Nationalistic popular music and state controlled media worked in concert to permeate the climate of everyday life with lyrics of victimization, vengeance, heroic nationalism, prejudice, and hate, punctuated with "news" reporting scenes of horror and tragedy in which perhaps only the reporters knew for certain the ethnicity of the victims and perpetrators. Verses analyzed in the hate speech report are said to mirror the propaganda line of the ruling Serbian Socialist Party, including that published in the 1986 Memorandum of the Serbian Academy of Sciences, a document frequently cited as a comprehensive statement on the official rationale for the war. Some verses, the report claims, asserted a particularly strong "mobilizing power" as they were chanted by the masses in political demonstrations. They include, Milinković says, almost direct quotes from speeches by President Milošević, and foreshadowed the coming confrontation with NATO over Kosovo some five years later:

> Jerry wants to come to the Drina, no way Jerry,
> this is where you die!
> Yankee wants to come to Kosovo, no way Yankee,
> It's Serb soil forever!
> Serbia has said her mind. . . .
> Shepherd drives his sheep,
> Serbs drive out the Ustaši,
> far away one-two, Franjo, fuck you![31]

Many of the lyrics analyzed in the report illustrate what the authors tell us that "such powerful, almost mythical images from the collective unconscious, which is the result of frequent wars, are easily transformed into threats."[32]

> Your faith keeps you, my Serbia, with a heroic heart,
> For the same foes are looming,
> your graves are not holy to them!
> When I was small I knew my way,
> they were Catholic and I was Orthodox!
> When I was small I was very lively,
> they cursed my father, I cursed their friar!
> They've always driven me from these lands,
> They sang the Croatian and I sang the Serb hymn!
> I hate you Alija because you're a traitor.
> You've destroyed my dream,
> May the Drina every day carry a hundred mujahedin!

Another song celebrates Serbs' heroic past and the independence of the Serb-majority areas of Croatia, defames Bosnian Muslims, and praises the paramilitary leader Željko Ražnatović, known as Arkan, who was indicted by the Hague Tribunal but was assassinated in Belgrade in 1999:[33]

> Oh Serbia my mother, do not fear the war,
> You'll always have two sisters
> when your brother is no more,
> these two sisters the world has not yet seen,
> the Bosnian Serb Republic and the Serb Krajina!
> The Serb nation is defended,
> Serb lands are protected,
> by Arkan's heroes, warriors without fear,
> These are valiant boys, Serb volunteers![34]

On February 19, 1995, the much-publicized and garish marriage ceremony between the forty-two-year-old paramilitary leader, war profiteer, and—before the war, underground criminal figure Arkan to the twenty-one-year-old "queen of turbo-folk," Svetlana Veličković, known popularly as Ceca, mirrored the gnarled complicity between popular culture and war crimes. As *New York Times* Belgrade correspondent Roger Cohen put it, the "union of a rich thug with a particularly nasty war record and a glamorous young star with a hold on the hearts of Serbia . . . turned into a kitsch pageant of Serbia's disarray."[35] Perhaps this, more than any other single event, illustrates the extent to which both hate speech and normalized violence had penetrated popular culture in Serbia.

Finally, a respondent from Zagreb provides this firsthand account of media propaganda and an opinion of how responsibility for the incitement of war ought to be distributed:

*M.P., Zagreb, 1997*
The war was designed by the political elite and very carefully orchestrated in the media. But some responsibility also rests with the people. I will give you one example. At the beginning, in 1990 in western Slavonia, an area about seventy kilometers away from Zagreb, to the south, an area with no history of Četniks—Serb nationalists known for committing atrocities in World War II—thousands and thousands of people were gathered in a place called Petrinja. Petrinja was a symbol of resistance in World War II. The people from that area came on a certain day to commemorate the Partisans who fought in the war. It was like a veterans' celebration. And they came all dressed in Partisan uniforms which they had kept, preserved, from their husbands and fathers who served during the war. Now on that day also from Belgrade came ten or fifteen, no more than twenty of these paramilitary types, and they came dressed looking like Četniks, and carrying Četnik symbols and flags, and they were playing trumpets, and singing those songs, and drinking. They were drunk! And they went to this veterans' celebration and stood in the front of the microphones, where the speakers would be. Then came the media from Zagreb, and because of them being in front of the crowd, it was just shown on TV cameras these ten or fifteen guys dressed like Četniks in the front of thousands of people in uniforms and it was shown all over Croatia on Croatian TV.

So in addition to elites, the specific people in the media are responsible, and also the people at large because they didn't try hard enough, didn't work hard enough to demand the democratization of institutions, like demanding that the state ownership of the media be ended, and once again the masses of people, the public, accepted the authoritarian ways of governing and representing of their interests. That's the responsibility of the people. Of course other than elites there are also the people, some of them, who are really strongly responsible for the war crimes, for the looting and war profiteering and those kinds of things. So I don't think the responsibility of the people should be dismissed, because they accepted quite easily these kind of messages and these kind of programs.

## Paramilitaries

"It was really a civil war," said one respondent from Belgrade, "and civil war is the worst kind of war. There are no rules, there are many volunteers, and irregulars. Many criminals were engaged by taking on the symbol of patriotism and it gave them the opportunity to engage in crimes, but in the name of patriotism and war."[36]

Paramilitary involvement in the war included not only Arkan and his paramiltary force, Tigers, but an array of irregulars on all sides, though evidence thus far revealed suggests that such groups were far more active among Serbs and Croats.[37] A UN report on the use of paramilitary special forces during the war found such forces active in seventy counties throughout the territory of former Yugoslavia. The report, which gathered information on ethnicity, troop numbers, places of origin, areas of operation, political affiliation, leaders, and alleged activities of paramilitary groups, notes that:

> FRY, Croatia, and BiH [Bosnia and Herzegovina] used paramilitary forces. However, the disproportionate number of paramilitary and special forces of Serbian ethnicity indicates that the Serbs more heavily relied on the use of special forces to accomplish their military and strategic goals. Of 39 counties where Serb paramilitary activity was reported, Serb paramilitary units were operating in conjunction with the JNA in 24 of them. In comparison there were reports for five counties of joint operations between forces operating in support of Croatia, the Croatian Army (HV), and the Croatian Defence Council (HVO), and reports for only two counties of joint operations between the Army of BiH and forces operating in support of the Government of BiH. . . .
>
> Notwithstanding the strong links between these units and the respective armies, the regular armies failed to restrain them from the commission of grave breaches of the Geneva Conventions and other violations of international humanitarian law. Among the most notorious of the special forces are Arkan's "Tigers" and Šešelj's "White Eagles" (also referred to as "Četniks"). Many of these units operate throughout the territory of the former Yugoslavia. Thus, the Serbian units operate in BiH and Croatia, and the Croatian units in BiH. These special forces have committed some of the worst violations of international humanitarian law.[38]

It must be noted that while Serbian and Croatian paramilitaries were the most active, there were Muslim irregulars as well. Again, the UN report discusses the role of paramilitaries operating on behalf of the Bosnian government, including some not from Bosnia:[39]

> Most paramilitary organizations working in support of the government of BiH are referred to by others as "Green Berets" or "MOS." . . . Several reports allege that the Green Berets have committed grave breaches of the Geneva Conventions and other violations of international humanitarian law. The Green Berets have been implicated in the killing of civilians, rapes, the operation of prison camps (in which civilians were unlawfully detained and sometimes tortured or killed), the destruction of property, and interference with humanitarian aid. . . . Mujahedin, or "holy warriors," is a generic term for Muslim volunteers fighting in the former Yugoslavia.

Many Mujahedin originate from Muslim countries outside the former Yugoslavia. It was reported that the Mujahedin began arriving in BiH as early as June 1992. Reports on the number of Mujahedin forces operating in BiH vary, but it is unlikely that the Mujahedin forces have made a significant military contribution to the BiH Government's war effort. The Mujahedin forces came from several Muslim states and many of them were veterans of the Afghan war.[40]

These activities were well known to people from or living in the region at the time of the conflict. Jasminka Udovički and Ejub Štitkovac, for example, counted the total number of paramilitary groups fighting on all sides by 1994 at around forty-five.[41] By employing paramilitaries and mercenaries, the problem of war resistance and emigration to avoid mobilization could be overcome. "All were under the command of an individual," they say, "or were integrated into the action plans of regular armies. Serbian and Croatian paramilitary groups recruited, trained, and armed many criminal elements. Training centers for paramilitaries were located in Erdut, Petrovaradin, and Knin."[42]

With the breakdown of the state and the perception that the military forces under the command of the state were increasingly deployed on behalf of Serbian rather than Yugoslav interests, all military forces became potentially and essentially "irregular," if by that we mean forces not under the command and in the service of the state as a whole. However, the use of paramilitary forces during the wars in ex-Yugoslavia went well beyond the mobilization of soldiers to fight a civil war in the face of a disintegrating state. The greatest concern, of course, was and still is with the role of paramilitary forces in the commission of war crimes. The opening paragraph of the UN report puts both the formation and the misuse of paramilitary forces into the perspective of a civil war in which propaganda confused real with fabricated atrocities:[43]

The conflict in the former Yugoslavia has seen the widespread use of paramilitary organizations within the territories of the Republic of Bosnia and Herzegovina (BiH), the Republic of Croatia, and to a lesser extent, the Federal Republic of Yugoslavia (FRY). The use of paramilitary organizations by all warring factions must be viewed in the context of the breakup of Yugoslavia and the structure of the military before the breakup. . . . In the period of 1989–1991, political ferment indicated that a breakup of Yugoslavia was likely. However, there were no indications as to how the country would be divided. The rise of nationalism and ethnic tension caused Yugoslavs to become concerned for their own safety. This concern over their own self-defence, combined with the rhetoric of nationalist politicians, led many Yugoslavs to arm themselves. Furthermore, uncertainty about the Yugoslav National Army's (JNA) role in post-Communist Yugoslavia led many to conclude that paramilitary organizations were a necessity.

The creation of paramilitary groups was further fueled by the wide circulation of stories of atrocities committed by all sides. Serbs, for example, were shown pictures allegedly depicting the Mujahedin forces holding the severed heads of Serb soldiers. All sides viewed themselves as victims, not as perpetrators, thereby creating a desire for revenge and providing justification for their own deeds.

The paramilitary units were formed under a variety of circumstances at the behest of political parties for the mobilization of territorial defenses or of village or community leadership. The UN found that: "According to some reports, the paramilitary organizations also include criminals released from prison solely for the purpose of forming these units."[44] The UN report found 83 identifiable paramilitary groups: 56 groups, accounting for between 20,000 and 40,000 people, were found to be working in support of the Serbia-dominated "rump" Yugoslavia and the self-declared Serbian republics; 13 groups, including between 12,000 and 20,000 people, in support of the Republic of Croatia; and 14 groups, of between 4,000 and 6,000 individuals, supporting Bosnia-Herzegovina.[45] Furthermore, the report found that:

> In addition to the 83 paramilitary groups, there are groups which consist of persons who have been drawn essentially from outside the former Yugoslavia. Three groups specifically mentioned are the Mujahedin (operating with the BiH Army), the Garibaldi Unit (an Italian unit operating alongside the Croats), and Russian mercenaries (operating in conjunction with the Serbs). There are also general reports of the presence of mercenaries from Denmark, Finland, Sweden, the United Kingdom, and the United States.

How important were paramilitary operations in causing the war? The link between the move from political to violent conflict coincided not only with the infamous secret meeting between Milosević and Tudjman at Karadjordjevo in March 1991, but also with the first known paramilitary activity. Consider the sequence of events, according to Laura Silber's and Allan Little's highly regarded documentary of the war, *Yugoslavia: Death of a Nation*.[46] The Karadjordjevo meeting takes place in March 1991, during which the two leaders are widely alleged to have discussed the partition of Bosnia and Herzegovina and after which Tudjman is said to have "bragged how he doubled the size of Croatia."[47] Tudjman claimed that such a partition was simply the fulfillment of a 1939 Serb-Croat agreement known as the *Sporazum*.[48] One day after the meeting, the Serb Rebellion in Croatia begins, and within two months the eastern Slavonia city of Vukovar is under seige. Notably, among the 1,800 fighters defending Vukovar against the combined Serb paramilitary and JNA forces, *one third are Serbs*, along with other non-Croats from the city. Says the UN report:[49]

> The first report of paramilitary activity occurred in April of 1991. However, Arkan and Vojislav Šešelj began forming paramilitary organizations as early as 1990. The first reported paramilitary operation involved Šešelj's troops in Vukovar County, Croatia. The most active period for Serb paramilitary activity in Croatia was in October of 1991. Those areas reporting the greatest amount of paramilitary activity in Croatia were Knin, Podravska Slatina, and Vukovar.

Among the most active of Croatian irregulars was the Croatian Defense League (HOS), the military arm of the Croatian Party of Rights, the ultra-right wing party reborn in 1990 under the name of the extreme Croatian nationalist party originally founded in 1850 and on which the Ustaše was based nearly a century later. The party, which remains active in Croatian politics today, is frequently referred to as "xenophobic" and "unabashed" regarding its link to the Ustaše. As of the elections in 2000, it claimed four seats in Parliament, though it had split itself into two wings. The party-supported paramilitary wore black shirts, the uniform worn by the Ustaše, and used the Ustaše salute "For the Homeland." Ed Vulliamy quotes its founder, Dobraslav Paraga, as saying in 1993 at the height of the war in Croatia, that the Ustaše was "too liberal in the eyes of the Croatian people," and that "if it had achieved what it set out to do, we would not be in this position now."[50] The first journalist to enter the death camps created by the ethnic cleansing policy in Bosnia, Vulliamy, who traveled extensively in the region during the war, describes the HOS in these terms:

> The black-shirted HOS championed the "Death or Glory" cult imported from American videos and blended it with Ustasha legend. Their recruiting posters showed chisel-jawed young men and girls wearing trendy Ray-Ban sunshades and black leather jackets, and clutching guns with fingers protruding from leather fingerless gloves.[51]

According to the UN report, however, while most paramilitary forces were operating within local arenas, those commanded by Serbian leaders Arkan and Šešelj were the most active throughout the wider area of conflict in both Croatia and Bosnia and Herzegovina. And both of these men also served in the Serbian Parliament in Belgrade during the war. Arkan, whose criminal as well as paramilitary reputation was well known, represented Kosovo, where in a campaign speech he declared himself "an enemy to Albanian infants," in a region that was 90 percent Albanian.[52]

On January 15, 2000, just weeks after a rumor surfaced that he would turn himself into the Hague and attempt to trade information incriminating Milosević for leniency, Željko Ražnatović—a.k.a. Arkan—was assassinated in the Intercontinental Hotel in Belgrade. Patrick Moore, writing for Radio Free Europe, writes of his life of criminality, his paramilitary activity, political career, and association with Milosević:

> Arkan embodied a dark area of Serbian public life where politics, crime, intelligence and police work, paramilitary groups, business, sport, and entertainment come together. The son of a Serbian military officer, he was born in Slovenia on 17 April 1952. His life involved a history of criminal activity together with work for Belgrade's undercover services; in short, a double life. In communist times, for example, he combined bank robbery in Sweden with activities against Croatian émigrés there.
>
> His years in the West earned him a place on Interpol's wanted list, but it is for his activities of the past ten years—that is, during the Milosević era—that he is best known. He led a paramilitary formation called the Tigers in the conflicts in Croatia and Bosnia, and played a role in organizing the paramilitary "police" of the Serbian Interior Ministry in Kosovo as well. Arkan and his men were known for brutality even by the standards of the Serbian paramilitaries, and were instrumental in the ethnic cleansing of eastern Bosnia in early 1992. In 1997, the Hague-based war crimes tribunal indicted him for crimes against humanity.
>
> But Arkan had other interests as well. Wartime Serbia and its sanctions provided abundant opportunities for smuggling and other illicit business activities, at which Arkan excelled. As the cosmopolitan and intellectual class that had long given Belgrade a distinctive image emigrated or struggled to make ends meet, the city increasingly acquired the imprint of the new mafia class.
>
> Arkan was but one of the more famous of these men. He also owned the Obilić soccer club and was married to the flamboyant pop star Svetlana Veličković, "Ceca." Her genre is known as "turbo folk" and is particularly associated with the popular culture of Milosević's wars in the early 1990s. She was his third wife and bore him the last two of his nine children.
>
> A man of pronounced Serbian nationalist views, he headed the small pro-Milosević Party of Serbian Unity. Arkan claimed to have no ties to Milosević, who in turn kept his distance in public from the man whom many regarded as his lieutenant and chief executioner. U.S. Ambassador Richard Holbrooke noted in his memoirs that Milosević dismissed any question of Arkan's activities as a "peanut issue." But Holbrooke also recalled that Milosević was nonetheless "annoyed" over the American's criticism of Arkan in a way that Milosević was not bothered by remarks about Radovan Karadžić or General Ratko Mladič.[53]

I will close this section with the words of a respondent interviewed in Belgrade in early summer, 1995. Because he was a much admired and tireless advocate for human rights and democracy who has since passed away, I would like to reveal his identity as the eminent Professor Miladin Životić of the Philosophy Department, University of Belgrade, and member of the Advisory Committee of the Belgrade Circle. On the day we spoke, he had just received word of the ongoing atrocities of what was later revealed as the massacre in Srebenica. He gestured angrily at the several shelves of dissertations written by his former students who had since left the country: "A whole generation!" he exclaimed. "Exactly those we most need to build a democracy here, and they had to leave Belgrade because of this insanity!" he said. He indicated that he might have left as well, except that his face was so well known that he did not think he would live to leave the country.

His comments are very clear about how he believed the war began and the way paramilitaries were used to terrorize people into a state of violence. I will quote him at some length not only because he links many of the themes I've tried to tie together in this chapter, but also because he is sharply critical of the broader context in which Serbian public opinion was mobilized around the idea of "all Serbs in one state," uniting Serbs in Bosnia and Croatia with those in Serbia, and how illogical and irrational it seemed to him. He is, in a sense, also trying to account for—and take issue with—the large number of Serbs who supported Milosević and the nationalists in general. He finds the nationalist ideology completely irrational and impractical. His remarks also illustrate the link between the ideology of nationalism, the atmosphere of hostility, and the provocation by paramilitary terrorism at a very local level:

*M.Ž., Belgrade, June 1995*
It is an absolute mystification that this conflict, this violence is a product historical inevitability. It is mystification because ordinary people of these nationalities here are not involved in this war. This war was completely planned by the political leadership of this country. Just before this war began I was in Sarajevo and I asked people: "Is it possible to have civil war in this country?" And they all said "that it is impossible! How could we imagine that people from another flat can come to mine to cut my throat just because they are Muslims, and I am Serb? This is impossible." And this is the absolutely right answer. Ordinary people did not start the war. Some groups of criminals came to these small towns, paramilitaries, and they made massacres, and then after that people started to leave, or to defend themselves with weapons. But they know that what they are hearing, that civil war among the people of Yugoslavia in which hatred is the main characteristic, which is said to be historical, those "ancient hatreds," is completely nonsense.

I think that this ideology of a Greater Serbia which is based on the so-called right of self-determination of the Serbian people to have their own state in which all Serbs would be included, is the main source of this war. This is what opportunistic politicians wanted to carry out. I think that it was formulated in the memorandum of the Serbian Academy of Sciences, which I consider to be the main manifesto of Serbian nationalism. And the people who only have the chance to hear this propaganda day in and day out, they don't know what else to think. But it was not their idea. The idea of an all-Serbia, ethnically clean Serbian state is absolutely impossible because in Serbia thirty percent of the people are not even Serbs! In Serbia, thirty percent are Albanians, and Hungarians, and Croats who live in Vojvodina and Kosovo! So I think that even if this end of the Serbian nationalists is fulfilled, then we will still have to confront the problem of Albanian minority in our country because in Kosovo there are only 150,000 Serbs and the majority is Albanian. How can we make a war with Croatia on the basis of the right to self-determination of the Serbs in Croatia and Bosnia, but then deny the right of self-determination to the Albanians right here in Serbia?

You know that ethnic cleansing in this war was supposedly done for Greater Serbia, but this Greater Serbia exists on the premise that inter-communal life is impossible within Bosnia, and within Croatia, especially. But people of different and mixed nationalities lived there and here for so many years. For thousands of years, people live an intercommunal life. If intercommunal life is not possible, then life itself is not possible in Yugoslavia! Yugoslavia is, from the perspective of these national identities which are so mixed, it is like a tiger's skin, you know. Without crimes of ethnic cleansing it is impossible to create new states based on national identity, a new Serbian state, a new Croatian state, and so on.

The problem now is how to stop this tragic ideology which moves us only toward separation, which aims to break apart the whole country. Bosnia was a country in which people lived together for so many centuries. Go, for example, to Subotica, which is multinational part of Vojvodina, and you will understand how these criminals have made civil war, how the paramilitaries went there to kill some citizens. You will have the reality of so-called nationalistic, civil war in Subotica. But it is not a war among the people of Subotica, because if you try to understand how it was possible to make war among the inhabitants, how they came to kill each other in this part, it is impossible! It could *only* happen because outsiders propagandized the people there, and then outsiders began the killing themselves in order to create a civil war.

Hundreds of thousands of young people emigrated from all the republics in order to avoid mobilization. Antiwar resistance in the earliest stages of the political conflict was evident in all of the republics. Ethnic Serbs living in Vukovar, Croatia, even fought along side their Croat neighbors against Serb paramilitaries and the JNA. In order to create an environment of violence, leaders had to resort to the recruitment not only of paramilitary forces, but of foreign mercenaries and domestic criminals to "fight the war." These conditions make any claim of ethnic conflict as a "natural" phenomenon of political violence seem, at least in the former Yugoslavia, absurd.

## Religion and War

Religion and religious institutions played many roles in the social life and articulation of identity in the former Yugoslavia. But people were not fighting over Scripture in the Balkans, any more than in Northern Ireland or the Middle East. "My mother was a Catholic," said a young man from Belgrade despairingly, "my father was Orthodox, my grandmother was Jewish, and they gave me a Muslim first name," he said. "I am going to L.A. and there, I don't want to meet anyone from Yugoslavia," he said despairingly. Then he went on to explain that by "Catholic" he meant "Croat," and by "Orthodox" he meant "Serb." By that time, however, what he meant was perfectly clear to me. These were not designations of religious affiliation, but rather of culture and identity. And he was, after all, a Yugoslav.

There are political dimensions to the historical intermingling of religion and identity. Ramet wrote in 1989 that in all three communities religion was not only "a defining factor in ethnic differentiation," but "perhaps even the single most important factor."[54] The Orthodox tradition evolved specifically in relation to national churches. Not only is the Catholic Church a powerful international nongovernmental institution, but it has also played a central role in European political history from the Holy Roman Empire to the Crusades and in European anti-Semitism.[55] As significant as it was in distinguishing among Croats, Serbs, and Bosniaks or Bosnian Muslims, religious identity was formed within the historical context of imperial "clashes of civilization," to use Huntington's phrase—Byzantine, Roman, Ottoman, Austro-Hungarian, and even Napoleonic—layered over feudalism, peasant cultures, village-centered life, and folkways. Religious practice was therefore often a pastiche of cultural and religious rituals among people whose historical consciousness contained multiple, sometimes contradictory references to conversion. Fouad Ajami describes the unique development of Bosnian Islam within this context:

> There was high religion and low religion. The world of the Balkans was a peasant world of superstition and folk belief. There was little, if any, literacy in the scripture. There was no priestly class of any status. Conversion was easy, and believers were often chameleons. Onto their new faith

the converts grafted their old ways. What emerged, according to the historian Peter Sugar, was a "variety of European or rather Balkan folk-Islam, which tended to include baptism, icons to prevent mental illness and many other basically nonMuslim features." There were mountaineers who called themselves Constantin in front of Christians and Sulayman in front of Muslims. The dead would be given a service by the Orthodox Church and a subsequent burial in a Muslim cemetery.[56]

Islam in Bosnia was both Europeanized and secularized, serving as a focus of cultural as well as religious practice and identity, perhaps on the whole leaning more toward the cultural direction in urban settings and more toward the religious in small villages and rural areas.[57] I was as likely, it seemed, to find myself having a beer (or *slivovica*) with a Bosnian Muslim in downtown Sarajevo as talking about the metaphysics of Sathya Sai Baba with a Bosnian Muslim from Mostar at a café in Croatia. Still, there were more observant Muslims, particularly, though not exclusively in the rural areas, and Alija Izetbegović and other Bosnian Muslim religious intellectuals wrote, spoke, and thought about the relationship between Islam and politics in the modern world. Numerous people from all religious backgrounds commented that people seemed to feel more obliged to behave in a more observant way, to talk about their religious beliefs, attend religious services, and display or wear attire or rosaries and so forth in order to affirm their religious identity during and after the war. Bosnian Muslims I spoke with in Sarajevo said that as the climate of ethnic hostility thickened just before the Serbian attack on Sarajevo, they began to notice an increasing number of women wearing head scarves and other traditional Muslim clothing in the city. They believed this was because smaller cities and villages were under attack or subjected to ethnic cleansing, and the people were fleeing to the Sarajevo for safety. Some also believed that there was an actual increase in the presence of non-Bosnian "outsiders" or "foreigners."[58]

There is little doubt that those non-Muslims, both Croats and Serbs, who were hostile toward Muslims attempted to exploit Western stereotypes about oriental Otherness and Muslims as irrational *mujahadeen* terrorists committed to the creation of an Islamic society and state in Bosnia. "Muslim" had become a constituent nationality in Yugoslavia *only* in relation to Bosnian Muslims. Neither Muslims living in the Sandžak region of Serbia, for instance, nor Albanian Muslims were included in the national category "Muslim."[59] This is one aspect of the politicization of Bosnian Muslim identity. But the delineation of national ethnic identity by the boundaries of religious affiliation was already the norm for Yugoslavia. Additionally, unlike Croats, Serbs, Slovenians, Macedonians, and even Montenegrins, Bosnian Muslims did not have a "homeland republic" within Yugoslavia.

This does not mean that some Bosnian Muslim intellectuals and political leaders, including Izetbegović, did not consider the possibility of Bosnia fitting into a larger scheme of a modern transnational Islamic political alliance. They did. Nor does it mean that the idea of Bosnia being structured as an Islamic state with a Muslim majority was not discussed. It was. Nor does it mean that Bosnian Muslim leaders did not turn to the leaders of Islamic states for support and assistance, particularly as their appeals for help or at least to have arms sanctions lifted so that they could defend themselves were rebuffed by the West.[60] But it must be remembered that both Bosnian Croats and Bosnian Serbs were supported by governments and mercenaries from beyond Bosnia's borders, and that both Croatian and Serbian leadership also engaged in rhetoric and policies aimed at creating a Catholic Croat and an Orthodox Serb state. Ironically, perhaps, the nationalization or politicization of religion seemed less prevalent among ordinary Bosnian Muslims than among their Croat and Serb counterparts, although Islamic practices such as the call to prayer and adherence to traditional dress codes do tend to have a much more public presence than Catholic or Orthodox practices.

There were also observant Catholics, and indeed, religious education returned to public schools after Croatia declared independence from Yugoslavia. Controversy arose, however, over the extent to which non-Catholic, Orthodox children were subject to formal and informal pressure to take part in catechisms conducted in school.[61] In an effort to evoke fears and imagery associated with the Ustaše in World War II, inflammatory rhetoric of "forced conversions" was revived. In spite of the propagandistic nature of this inflated rhetoric, the underlying complaints appear to be supported by evidence reported by the Helsinki Committee of Croatia, which, after the successful return of the formerly Serb-majority areas of Croatia during the controversial Operation Storm, said that:

> We are also worried about the fact that some teachers of religion classes abuse the religion subject for the purpose of molding the Croatian society according to the Catholic mode. There were many cases where children were humiliated and abused for refusing to attend Catholic religion classes; teachers threw away their Holy Bibles merely because they were not printed by Catholic publishers, ridiculed different denominations by calling them sects and conjuring up lies about them. This has contributed to the current social climate, in which all Croatian citizens of Serb nationality, especially those of the Orthodox faith are collectively blamed for the crimes committed by the Serbian aggressors and Četnik paramilitary troops during the war.[62]

Some religious leaders from all three communities became politically active and therefore complicitous in legitimating nationalistic politics as the pluralistic Yugoslav state and society fell apart. Both Croatian Catholic and Serbian

Orthodox religious leaders are said to have traveled to the front lines, where they blessed soldiers and weapons.[63] The Vatican actively supported the secession of Slovenia and Croatia. Serb Orthodox Patriarch Pavle believed there to be a "Vatican-Teheran-fundamentalist plot against the Serbian people."[64] A statement by the Helsinki Committee in Croatia on "Freedom of Religion in Croatia," published in February 1996, reported that:

> The Committee finds it necessary to draw attention to the abuses by religious institutions, religious assemblies and religious media in the promotion of political propaganda, openly disseminating hatred and intolerance, provoking political agitation as well as persecution of intellectualism and the limitation of freedom. Some religious officials have used the media, pulpits, and religious meetings to promote the aggressive and systematic persecution of those who do not share their opinions (opposition, independent intellectuals, labor union activists and national minorities), while not refraining from openly using propaganda to promote totalitarianism . . . and even distorting history.[65]

Acknowledging the complicity of Church leaders and the nationalization of religion in creating a justification for interethnic violence during the first few years of the war, the Interchurch Peace Council, the Helsinki Citizens Assembly, and the European Movement in Serbia jointly organized a "Summer School of Interconfessional Dialogue and Understanding" in August 1993, inviting academic and professional participants from Holland, Italy, Britain, Bosnia and Herzegovina, Denmark, Sweden, Montenegro, Serbia, and the United States. The effort was intended to "contribute to the creation of an atmosphere of peace, mutual confidence, and understanding among people who live in former Yugoslavia as well as those who live in all parts of Europe."[66] The collection of papers published as a result, *Religion and War*, offer significant insight into the complex relationship between politics, religion, and the histories of the region.[67] Mirror images of victimization and persecution are woven into narratives of religious identity and seem to have figured into the rhetoric of the more radical among both the Catholic and the Orthodox clergy. The conference generated a frank and open discussion of the politicization of religious leaders and identities and the role of Church leaders in promoting an atmosphere in which war became increasingly likely. At the least, they lent legitimacy to the historical narratives of interlocking victimization and retribution. At worst, along with political leaders, they deliberately provoked the violence. "Leading Serbian Orthodox theologians focused on the sufferings of the Serbian people, especially at the hands of Croats, Bosnians, and Albanians in Kosovo," says David Steele of the Mennonite Central Committee, who attended the 1993 conference:[68]

Serbian Orthodox newspapers have published such accounts of Serbian victimization since the late 1970s, chasing their claims of the uniqueness of Serbian genocide. In 1991, this perspective was authorized by the Holy Synod of the Serbian Orthodox Church when they referred to the suffering of the Serbian nation, during World War II at the Croatian concentration camp of Jasenovac, as the sins of all sins and equated it with the suffering of Christ.[69]

The theme of equating Serb identity with Jesus' persecution and then appropriating that theme to mobilize support for the subsequent "interethnic" violence is elaborated by Michael Sells in his 1996 book *The Bridge Betrayed: Religion and Genocide in Bosnia*, emphasizing the particular influence of persecutionist ideology among Bosnian Serbs:

On Orthodox Easter 1993, Metropolitan Nikolaj, the highest ranking Serb Orthodox official in Bosnia, stood between Radovan Karadžić and General Ratko Mladić and spoke of the Bosnian Serbs under their leadership as "following the hard road of Christ." Karadžić suggested the problem in Bosnia could be solved if Muslims would just convert to Serb Orthodoxy.[70]

Among Croats, religious persecution was tied to the oppression of communism, which, as argued earlier, implicated the Serbs as the main supporters of communism. Steele quotes from an article in the Catholic publication *Veritas*:

God has by way of his Church, by way of the Holy Father, looked at his faithful people, spoken out on their behalf, directly intervened in history, in the struggle, warring together with his people for their liberation. . . . With this war God has also returned to his people, in its heart and home. [God] returned to the entire mass media, political, social, and state life of Croatia, from where he was driven out 45 years earlier. The cross of Christ stands next to the Croatian flag. . . . The Church is glad for the return of its people from the twofold slavery—Serbian and communist. This is a great kairos of God's grace for the entire Croatian people. . . . Here was not a battle for a piece of Croatian or Serbian land but a war between good and evil, of Christianity and communism, culture and barbarity, civilization and primitivism, democracy and dictatorship, love and hatred. . . . Thank God, it all ended well, due to the Pope and Croatian politics.[71]

Because religion was understood as the most significant marker of identity, churches, mosques, synagogues, and other sites of tremendous cultural significance, such as the library in Sarajevo and the bridge at Mostar, were specifically targeted for destruction. By the end of 1994, one researcher estimated, some 800 mosques, 128 Catholic churches, ten Orthodox churches, and three synagogues had been destroyed.[72]

## War as Pathology: The Normalization of Violence

In his film *Faces of the Enemy*, Sam Keen interviews David Rice, confessed murderer of an unarmed family of four in Seattle in 1984. When explaining his motives, Rice claimed that the family were actually communists. "It is a war," says Rice. "It has always been a war. We have not been fighting the Koreans, Vietnam, South Americans, we have been fighting the Soviets." It is clear, the listener wants to think, that Rice was delusional and that we know that there was no war in which he was a soldier. But how do we know that? And how do we know that the violence which occurred in ex-Yugoslavia was a war? It was certainly not so clear to people there, to people in Sarajevo or Subotica, who, even after hearing about violence in a nearby town, could not believe it would happen to them. It was not clear to people who traveled from Belgrade to Sarajevo in 1992 for an antiwar protest. They did not believe that it could happen, or that it was happening, or that they could not stop it with an antiwar rock concert in Sarajevo.[73]

"In war there is a difference between murder and killing," says Vietnam veteran William Broyles, author of *Brothers in Arms*, in Keen's film. "It is very difficult to put your finger on it but every soldier knows what it is," he says. Perhaps the difference is more elusive when individual responsibility is defused across members of a group. Where violence is collectivized, whether in street gangs, "ethnic groups," or states, it is no longer a matter of "I" killed someone, but "we" killed "them," the enemy. Agency, and any responsibility that we might attach to it, is, like the blame we assign our victims, collectivized. One need not be "following orders" but, rather, simply carrying out an act that has become normalized in the sense that the commission of such acts is widespread. Similar observations were made by Don Foster regarding the violence committed during the era of apartheid in South Africa during a seminar entitled "Truth and Reconciliation Commission Sixth Seminar: Perpetrators."[74] When discussing the social factors that create conditions more likely to foster the psychological process of dehumanization that rationalizes brutality and violence, Foster concluded: "Often you do not need to give the direct orders to do it. The climate is sufficiently there."[75]

In his analysis of the sociopolitical context in which both white and black South Africans carried out acts of violence under apartheid, Foster calls on us to take into account the global and regional as well as local context in which the ideology underlying apartheid and the violence rationalized by it were constructed. His insights are instructive for the case of ex-Yugoslavia, though the international circumstances bearing on the two situations may be different. The perpetrators in South Africa, Foster points out, were acting in a social and political climate in which, first of all, racism was normalized by the ideology of apartheid. Admitting the psychological complexity of the issue, Foster still argues that in general, in the environment of apartheid politics, the dehumanization of black South Africans was normal. And, he adds, that climate was located within the global environment of the Cold War, the rhetoric of communist enemies, and consequently of conspiracy and paranoia. At least some white South Africans, particularly political leaders, were genuinely convinced that a real threat was posed by a global conspiracy by communists to destabilize noncommunist governments by infiltrating and fomenting conflict within the sphere of domestic politics. Finally, he says, human rights violations generally occur in social environments that are militarized.

Joseph Campbell, drawing on the work of Arthur Schopenhauer, believed that acknowledgment of our common humanity was the normal psychological condition (perhaps a defense against the terror of isolation), and that in order to commit aggression, it is necessary to weaken moral constraints against violence.[76] Kelman's work on dehumanization as a rationalization for violence, furthermore, identifies three factors that make the weakening of moral inhibitions against violence possible: authorization, routinization, and dehumanization.[77] Viewed as a social practice, war always involves mobilizing these three factors. In the case of civil war and in the particular case of ex-Yugoslavia, the question of authorization is especially revealing, because we are forced to ask how authority is constructed. Who authorized the Yugoslav war? The state of Yugoslavia? The state of Croatia? Bosnia? Slovenia? The states recognizing the states? The normative order underlying the state system? None of these answers will quite do because what we are looking for is *how authority was constructed in the minds of the perpetrators.* How does an individual know whether he is a soldier or a perpetrator? A killer, or a murderer? Again, examining a case of violence in South Africa under apartheid, social psychologist Lloyd Vogelman observes that:

> Insofar as the individuals see themselves as part of a large group and as having little choice in the authorisation process, they hold themselves less responsible for their conduct. To maintain individual responsibility in mass group aggressive situations is not impossible but is extremely difficult. The tendency to follow the group is even stronger when there is an absence of even a small grouping of leaders adopting a contradictory view.[78]

In a social environment in which political legitimacy was understood by ordinary people to flow from two contradictory sources—intellectuals as trustees of how Marxist ideology applied to the particular vision of the Yugoslav state, and nationalities as the repository of culture and identity (the combination of which was reflected in the republican communist parties, the

Croatian Communist Party, Serbian Communist/Socialist Party, and so on) —
then the willingness of ordinary people to follow the communist intellectuals
Tudjman and Milosević as they turned into nationalist leaders, becomes much
more understandable. To this we can add the general failure after World War
II to reconcile identities constructed on the basis of both lived experiences and
historical narratives in which otherness and victimization were conflated, and
finally, the willingness of elites to manipulate associated emotional vulnerabilities, enabled and magnified by their control of the media. So in the absence
of a willingness by international actors to assert any authority contesting the
descent into civil war in Yugoslavia, domestic political, intellectual, media,
and religious elites aligned to create a structure that authorized violence. In
Serbia, paramilitary leaders served in Parliament. In Croatia, nationalist
parties from Herzegovina supportive of paramilitary activities served in
Tudjman's cabinet as well as in the parliament. What could make them and
their atrocities seem more normal, particularly since Western leaders recognized and conducted diplomatic relations with these governments?

Finally, a confessional account of a Serb soldier offers exceptional insight
into one individual's struggle with the mental and moral tension created by
carrying out the duties of a soldier while trying to resist a digression into the
cognitive process of dehumanizing one's victims. Miroslav Filipović, the independent journalist who reported the story, was subsequently arrested for
publishing this and other exposés on the role of Serbian soldiers in the war
and in committing atrocities in Bosnia and Kosovo. This excerpt was one of
several published just a month before Filipović's arrest:

One retired veteran of the wars in Bosnia and Croatia says the Yugoslav
Army has been responsible for the deaths of countless children over the
past decade.

"I was trained at the country's top military academies and commanded
a crack infantry unit," he said. "Kosovo was the third occasion the army
was responsible for the deaths of children. I didn't see so much of it in
Kosovo because I was more senior by that time — but I fought on the front
line in Croatia and saw some terrible things then."

One officer, Dražen, who took part in the Kosovo campaign, said, "I
watched with my own eyes as a reservist lined up around 30 Albanian
women and children against a wall. I thought he just wanted to frighten
them, but then he crouched down behind an antiaircraft machine-gun and
pulled the trigger. The half-inch bullets just tore their bodies apart. It looked
like a scene from a cheap movie, but it really happened."

Dražen concludes, "I don't know how I will live with these memories,
how I'll be able to raise my own children. I'm not willing to accept the
collective guilt. I want to see those who committed these atrocities stand
trial for their crimes."

For many of the officers, Belgrade's propaganda is wearing thin. The commander of one tank unit was quick to dismiss Serbian claims that the Kosovo campaign was aimed at crushing Albanian separatists. "For the entire time I was in Kosovo, I never saw a single enemy soldier and my unit was never once involved in firing at military targets."

He said state-of-the-art tanks were sent out against defenceless Albanian villages. "The tanks, which cost $2.5 million each, were used to slaughter Albanian children," said the officer. "I am ashamed."

A reconnaissance officer for an engineering brigade said Yugoslav Army reservists in Kosovo ran amok while their commanders did little to intervene. "During one ethnic cleansing operation in a village in south-eastern Kosovo, we gave the villagers half an hour to leave their homes.

"They were standing in a long line along the road leading out of the settlement. A reservist nicknamed Crni (Black) went up to an old man who was holding a child aged around three or four. He grabbed the toddler from the man's arms and demanded a ransom of 20,000 German marks. The Albanian only had 5,000. Crni took the child by the hair, pulled out a knife and hacked off its head.

"'5,000 is only enough for the body,' he said, and walked off past the other villagers, carrying the child's head by its hair."

Vladimir went on, "All of this took place in front of dozens of people. We were all in a state of shock: some soldiers vomited, while our young second lieutenant fainted at the terrible sight of the headless body writhing in the dust.

"Crni was later declared insane, discharged and sent home. But he is still free to walk the streets, even though he committed this terrible crime."[79]

## Constructivism and Causes of War

If the layers, intersections, and dynamic processes of rule making, rule sustaining, rule changing, and rule breaking actions by individual agents and agents acting on behalf of collectivities "add up to a society of staggering complexity and constant change,"[80] can constructivism offer a useful framework for analyzing the problem of political violence? I think it can, but it also seems clear that to do so we must address the interplay between levels of analysis, social arrangements, and social actions, and I will attempt in a preliminary way to do so in the final chapter. In evaluating agents' actions and consequences of actions examined in this chapter, it seems that we are dealing with a variety of rules and agents' actions in relation to them as well as contradictions among rules. For instance, the rule that states ought to be grounded in a shared identity which has historically been articulated in relation to ethnic identity clearly contradicts the rule that citizens in modern societies ought to be tolerant of multiethnic differences. Similarly, the idea that ethnicity is a self-evident and self-defining category delineated by the existence of a shared history (ignoring the social processes that produce histories and privilege some interpretations of events over others) and even distinguishing characteristics and that people prefer "their own kind" suggests and supports a rule of exclusionary identities.

Perhaps one way of understanding the genesis of social conflict is that when social acts that contest commitment rules reach a critical mass sufficient to undermine their legitimacy, or when other events (such as the death of Tito) create a condition of social stress or even a crisis in relation to commitment rules, the potential for other kinds of rules to increase in influence arises, at least among some proportion of the society's members. Leaders may emerge willing to exploit these circumstances in order to advance their own ability to win or to move into leadership roles and, depending on their ability to "get the message out," may mobilize people around rules that had been subordinated to the now-weakened commitment rules. This begins to tell us "why *here*" and even "why *now*," but not yet "why so *brutal.*" For that, I still think we need some understanding of the human psyche and its relationship to rules, and here I think psychoanalytic and cognitive perspectives still have something to offer.

# CHAPTER 8

# The Other Yugoslav Wars: The War against Women and the War against War

The women's organizations are the most active now and during the war. They work mainly in their own home areas. The women from Srebenica right now are here, wanting to find out what happened to their men. Probably the intellectual women are not as organized as the ordinary women were. The intellectuals could have influenced the direct political situation.

—S.R., Sarajevo, 1997

Most structural approaches to the causes-of-war question fail to take into account differences in how the states under study came into existence in the first place: Were they postcolonial, do the boundaries of the modern state coincide roughly with pre-state societal boundaries, were they formed as a result of national unity movements, are they European settler states, and so on? And since the modern state itself is a product of social forces operating in the context of European history, can wars within and among European states really be compared meaningfully with wars in non-European settings, and what are the limitations of doing so? Still, some generalizations emerge from research undertaken from a structural perspective: new states are more prone to violence than older, more settled and stable states (Wright 1942; Singer 1991; Vasquez 1993); states are more violence-prone following a rapid improvement in economic circumstances (Chouchri and North 1975; Cashman 1993); leaders sometimes use war or belligerent rhetoric as a means of mobilizing internal cohesiveness and domestic political support (Ostrom and Job 1986; Russett 1989); violence is associated with state-creation (Holsti 1991; Brogan 1990; Cohen, Organski, and Brown 1981); and ethnonationalism is frequently the justification used for localized and anti-state violence (Carment 1993; Ryan 1990; Gurr 1994). Taken together and viewed from a constructivist perspective, this body of research suggests the existence of a rule instructing and directing the acts of agents in relation to the state: *Violence is an acceptable strategic choice as a means for establishing, mobilizing, or altering the structures of states, especially when framed within the language of ethnonationalist discourses.*

A constructivist account, I think, provides a good answer to the question: Why *here* and why *now?* Here and now because structural crises were exploited by willing political leaders. But even constructivist accounts do not answer the question: *how* and *why* were people mobilized for such *brutal* violence? Structural instabilities and a rule instructing agents to use violence for political purposes are features of social life in many states or settings. The analytical account I began with in Chapter 3 places particular emphasis on how the psyche develops in relation to dichotomous logics in general and how the social construction of gender difference underlies them, especially in relation to Other-directed violence; I return now to a set of theoretically linked issues: exclusionary identities, the masculinization of war and the political, and the feminization of peace and tolerance of difference.

This chapter will examine the Other war, the Unwar, the feminized void, in Lacanian terms, which by its opposition has as much to reveal about the structure of violence as do the overt actions of those who act it out. First, the "woman question" — "where are the women?" — which is really a set of related questions about both the experiences of women as well as epistemological questions pertaining to the structure of gender and gendered relations; and second, where were the sites of resistance, of protest, antiwar activism, particularly through nonviolent means? Finally, I will revisit the question of dichotomies and evaluate their role in structuring our psychic, social, and political life.

## Women: Agents and Symbols

"In the beginning the only strong and serious resistance to the Serbo-Croatian conflict came from the women in both countries," says filmmaker Helke Sander,[1] "But the propaganda machinery in both lands has now succeeded in tying women to the camps of their nationalist leaders." Questions about women and gender in relation to the conflict and violence in ex-Yugoslavia could, and indeed have, filled more than one book and have also been the subject of an internationally acclaimed and award-winning film documenting the experiences of two women, one Muslim and one Croat, in the Omarska camp in Bosnia and their subsequent campaign to bring the issue of rape before the International Criminal Tribunal for Former Yugoslavia.[2] Indeed, rape, for the first time in the history of Western international law, was pronounced a crime against humanity by the International Tribunal. Article 5 of the Tribunal's Statute (adopted May 25, 1993, as amended May 13, 1998), entitled "Crimes Against Humanity," states that:

> The International Tribunal shall have the power to prosecute persons responsible for the following crimes when committed in armed conflict,

whether international or internal in character, and directed against any civilian population: (a) murder; (b) extermination; (c) enslavement; (d) deportation; (e) imprisonment; (f) torture; (g) rape; (h) persecutions on political, racial and religious grounds; (i) other inhumane acts.

Seventeen of the cases for which the court had issued indictments by end of the year 2000 include the charge of rape as a crime against humanity.[3] This was not, of course, the first time rape was employed as a weapon of war, but it is the first time it would be considered a war crime, and it is hard to imagine that it was ever more widely publicized and condemned as it was during the war in ex-Yugoslavia.[4] It is exceedingly difficult to arrive at verifiable figures for rapes, not only for the usual reason that victims have great difficulty in discussing and reporting their ordeals, but also because a huge number of victims were likely to have been subsequently murdered, often in mass executions.[5] Estimates of such murders range from 20,000 to 50,000, according to the Bosnian Ministry of Interior.[6] The majority of cases, probably around 70 percent to 80 percent, were Muslim, with Croatian women likely to be the second largest group.[7] Neither were Serb women immune from rape and other brutalities. Some writers and reporters have emphasized the role of rape as a systematic policy among the Serbs or have attempted on this and other grounds to differentiate either qualitatively or quantitatively between rapes by Serbian perpetrators and rapes by Croatian and Muslim perpetrators, an issue which has also undermined the maintenance of solidarity among feminists from the different republics.[8] Rapes were committed in makeshift brothels in occupied towns and villages, as well as in camps where as many as 7,000 were held prisoner in a single camp.[9] Girls as young as twelve and women over sixty were victims of the terror, which was aimed at so traumatizing them that they would flee their homes and hometowns, never to be able to look at the once-familiar and comforting landscape again without reliving their nightmares. Rape was a tool of ethnic cleansing.

But it was more than that, too. Whether as an act of war or private rage, the motivations for rape are always complex, and all the more so when we try to understand them within the pathological climate of the "normalized violence" we call war. Rape was a means of demoralizing the families and communities of the victims. It was a mechanism for destroying the nexus of relationships—family and community—that located women as mothers, daughters, sisters, and wives at their center. Rape was, for some men in war as in peace, an expression of misogynistic emotions. It was a means by which leaders of paramilitary irregular forces could initiate younger, perhaps less-than-willing recruits into a brotherhood of violence. Rape was a hate crime. It was for some a means of impregnating the enemy, an act of miscegenation.

Serb rapes of Muslim women were also rationalized on the basis of the historical mythologizing of Serbo-Slavic "race miscegenation" by the Ottoman "Turks." Other Serbs were encouraged to view the rape of Croatian women as an act of revenge for the sins of the Ustaše in World War II.[10] And like other acts of dehumanizing violence that those in positions of authority clearly knew to be violations of international laws of warfare, commanding officers probably believed it would more difficult to hold anyone accountable if everyone was guilty.[11] Discussing the application of Susan Brownmiller's *Against Our Will: Men, Women, and Rape* to the case of Bosnia, Obrad Kešić notes that:

> In war, intimidation through rape is done to spread fear through an enemy population in order to either force them to surrender or to flee. Rape in war is also a ritual act of male bonding in the most primitive sense, a ritual of marking territory and desecrating the enemy man's "property." The man who is not able to defend his "property" is humiliated and his masculinity is questioned.[12]

The notion that war as a social practice is grounded in an ideology of masculinity is a common and, I believe, persuasive theme among feminist theorists.[13] The problem, from an empirical perspective, is that while the development of that ideology in conjunction with the development of both the state and the practice of war as an act of state within the historical and social context of Western culture has been persuasively argued, it is difficult to approach the issue comparatively in light of the globalization of Western political and legal normative order. Still, we would benefit from more anthropological research on the proposition that there is a correlation between the extent to which patriarchal and/or misogynistic practices structure the social order and epistemology of a culture, on the one hand, and that culture's proneness to violence, intolerance, and exclusionary identities, on the other, particularly insofar as such studies might provide insight into variations among modern polities.[14]

Men were also victims of sexual violence, though reports and the extent of the sexual violence against men remain exceptional. It does remind us, however, of the important point that sexual violence is about *power*, about the masculinization of power as dominance and the *construction and maintenance* of masculine power as the ability to dominate. To be capable of ordering one man to commit sexual violence against another both dehumanizes both victims and reinforces the assertion of power on the part of the perpetrator.

Sexual violence against women as a *policy* served the practical objective of ethnic cleansing through terror and trauma, but also functioned as an expression of group domination—men carried out the act in their role as members of a particular ethnic group, and they raped particular women because they represented ethnic Otherness. Said differently and without regard for the more complex motives and circumstances, men were recruited to carry out sexual violence *because* they were Serb, Croat, or Muslim men and against women *because* they were Serb, Croat, or Muslim women. The identities of both the perpetrators and victims were reduced to their "ethnicity," which contributed to the creation of a perception inside and outside the war zone, both inside ex-Yugoslavia and outside ex-Yugoslavia, that of all qualities that identify people in former Yugoslavia, *ethnicity mattered most.* Women were raped not only for all the reasons they are raped in peacetime as well as all the reasons they are raped during wars, and in this war as a means of making "ethnic cleansing" more efficient, but also as signs, as symbols of a socially constructed ethnic Otherness.

We must remember, however, that "women" as a category included many individuals in ex-Yugoslavia who were, as they are everywhere else, a complex and multifaceted group acting in a variety of roles and capacities as agents as well as symbols. They were voters in the republics who supported nationalist leaders. They were soldiers, for better and worse. Obrad Kešić reports, for example, that "there were women in all of the militias and national armies throughout the former Yugoslavia."[15] Some were, no doubt, perpetrators. They were also journalists serving the propaganda interests of the nationalistic regimes. They were pop stars who married war criminals. They were the supportive wives of nationalist leaders. Tudjman was glad, he said, that his wife was neither a Serb nor a Jew. Milosević's wife, Mirjana, was the head of a socialist party in Serbia that was purportedly independent but clearly supportive of her husband's party and leadership. In 1987, as her husband heated up the anti-Albanian rhetoric of Serb oppression in Kosovo, for example, Mirjana (Mira) Marković, writing for the regime-controlled *Politika*, took the lead in a media offensive against an early enemy, Dragiša Pavlović.[16] Women were academics, and professional elites, and politicians who contributed to the creation of an environment increasingly dominated by hostile, inflammatory, and exclusionary rhetoric.

I asked everyone I interviewed what they thought about the role of women in war resistance and about the role of women in relation to the conflict in general. Jean Bethke Elshtain would not be surprised that without exception everyone I spoke with in all of the republics said that while women had indeed played a critical role in mobilizing and sustaining war resistance and peace movements, many more observed that women were just as nationalist as their male counterparts, that they supported the nationalistic regimes, voted for nationalistic leaders, and in these and other ways encouraged their husbands, brothers, fathers, and sons to participate in the war.[17]

Having said that, the violence in ex-Yugoslavia highlights the need not only to take gender seriously both in our theorizing and analyses of political violence, but to think in much more complex terms about the relationship between gender, politics, and violence. There is an American joke that "99 percent of lawyers give the rest a bad name." Perhaps we should think about gender in similar terms. Most people, men or women, do not go far toward escaping the limitations of their socialization. How we understand the gendered dimension of our identity begins with how we are socialized about gender. That is the baseline. From this starting point we can ask to what extent and under what circumstances individuals defect or engage in activity that subverts or contradicts gender socialization. I cannot say precisely what percentage of men participated in the war, but many men also defected as war resisters and peace activists. Laura Silber's and Allan Little's book, *Yugoslavia: Death of Nation*, lists a large "cast of characters" at the outset, key figures within the former republics and in the international community, who played some notable role in destruction of the Yugoslav state and the descent into violence.[18] Of the 208 listed who are from the various republics, 204 are men and four are women. Only a handful of those listed were war or antinationalist dissidents. Of the four women, two were notable for having spoken out against the nationalists who were edging closer to violence. One is Ljubinka Trgovčević, a member of Serbia's presidency who spoke out against Milosević at the Eighth Session of the Central Committee in 1987.[19] The other is a Slovenian, Sonja Lokar, who took part in the final and fatal Fourteenth Extraordinary Party Congress on January 23, 1990, where Milosević spearheaded a showdown with the Slovenians that foreshadowed his intentions to force republican tensions to the brink. Lokar is reported to have "wept as her delegation filed silently out of the hall."[20] Before leaving the assembly, the Slovenian delegation warned Milosević that his hard line position would destroy the country.[21]

The remaining two are Mirjana Marković, Milosević's wife who has already been mentioned, and Biljana Plavšić, who served as the vice-president of the self-proclaimed independent state of Republika Srpska under Radovan Karadžić during the war, and who became the president of the Serbian "entity" after the Dayton Accord as Karadžić, now an indicted war criminal, became too controversial. In spite of her association with Karadžić, she won American support by proclaiming two things: that she would defect from her patron's hard line and negotiate an end to the violence, and that, at least after 1995, she no longer supported the creation of a separate Serb state.[22] That is not, however, the whole story on Biljana Plavšić.

During communist rule, she had been dean of the Faculty of Natural Science and Mathematics in Sarajevo, and a member of the B-H Academy of Arts and Sciences, though she was not apparently a member of the Communist Party. As the country broke apart and she cast her political fate with the radical Bosnian Serb nationalists, she seemed to make much more of her nationalist past, claiming always to have been a rabid anticommunist.[23] A geneticist, she became best known, however, for her openly racist views of Muslims, who, she claimed, were descended from "genetically deformed" Serbs who converted to Islam and whose deformity was progressively worsened as it passed through subsequent generations: "And now, of course, with each successive generation this gene simply becomes concentrated. It gets worse and worse, it simply expresses itself and dictates their style of thinking and behaving, which is rooted in their genes. . . ." (Svet Novi Sad, September 6, 1993).[24]

In a statement given to *Borba* in July 1993, she is reported to have claimed that Bosnian Serbs are ethnically-racially superior to Bosnian Muslims, and claimed that:

> Serbs in Bosnia, particularly in border areas, have developed a keen ability to sense danger to the whole nation and have developed a defense mechanism. In my family they used to say that Serbs in Bosnia were much better than Serbs in Serbia . . . and remember, this defense mechanism was not created through a short period of time; it takes decades, centuries. . . . I'm a biologist and I know: most capable of adapting and surviving are those species that live close to other species from whom they are endangered.[25]

The peacemaker at Dayton had, just one year earlier, told the Belgrade media that "One good battle would settle this war."[26] Her most notorious public display of support for the worst elements of the Serbian nationalist cause, however, was her televised kiss of war criminal Arkan in the town of Bijeljina, the very scene of some of the worst atrocities attributed to him during the war in Bosnia. In an article published in 1996, Slobodan Inić, a sociologist at Belgrade University, criticizes her public record, referring to "her monstrous celebration of Arkan as the symbol of Serbdom and heroism."[27] The display was no temporary lapse of judgment, as subsequent statements such as that she "exchanges kisses only with heroes" reveal, but rather intended to project an image of alignment between her political objectives with the folk hero image of Arkan among Bosnian Serbs, however brutal and inhumane he may have been judged in any other court of public opinion or jurisprudence:

> Her conception of heroism is personified by Željko Ražatović—Arkan, the perpetrator of horrific ethnic cleansing in B-H. "When I saw what he'd done in Bijeljina, I at once imagined all his actions being like that. I said: here we have a Serb hero. He's a real Serb, that's the kind of men we need." What is particularly tragicomic is how the Serb Empress saw her dream hero: "Arkan is wonderful . . . he impressed me as a humane person forced by necessity to take up arms." (Bosnian Serb News Agency, 1992)[28]

218 The Social Construction of Man, the State, and War

Leader of the Serb National Alliance (SNS) Party, Biljana Plavšić remained president of the Bosnian Serb "entity" (in the language of the Dayton Accord) until defeated in 1998. Under indictment by the Hague Tribunal, Plavšić surrendered herself at the Hague in January, 2001.

Aside from the exceptional cases of women in positions of high-level political leadership,[29] there was a growing feminist movement in Yugoslavia before the war which during the war provided the organizational basis for the mobilization of antiwar movements. It must be kept in mind that women did not have the right to vote in Yugoslavia until the creation of socialist Yugoslavia in 1945, but not because they did not struggle long before that to gain suffrage.[30] By the mid-1980s, women made up between 13.5 percent (in Kosovo) and 32.1 percent (in Slovenia) of the Communist Party membership, and between 13.2 percent (in Montenegro) and 23.5 percent (in Vojvodina) of the central or provincial committees.[31] Generally speaking, with some exceptions, women's activity both in the party and in its leadership correlated positively with the level of economic development in the various republics and provinces.

Women in the mid-1980s were engaged in antinuclear, ecology, human rights, and peace activism. As increasingly hostile nationalist rhetoric produced escalating fears and tensions throughout the republics, antiwar movements sprang up in most of the major cities. Some women attempted to maintain unity across republican and ethnic lines but were eventually engulfed and disciplined by discourses of patriotism, aggression, victimization, and blame constructed along ethnic lines and conflated with the emergence of state-building nationalisms.[32] Some right-wing women's organizations were in fact instrumental in creating and maintaining an environment in which women's roles were defined exclusively in patriotic and nationalistic terms.[33] But consistent with the notion of the feminization of peace and the masculinization of war, just as we find a predominance of men engaged in war-making, so in the case of ex-Yugoslavia we find a predominance of women in both leadership positions and among the rank and file of the antiwar movements.

## War Resistance

While there were women who supported the war, women who fought in the war, and women who committed atrocities, men were unquestionably the dominant actors, both in leading people into violence and as the majority of those carrying it out. This is not surprising, as war serves to affirm the masculinity of male subjects. It is notable that many men resisted the war, both by leaving the country and by engaging in direct antiwar and resistance action. Still, we must note that many of the dominant actors in the antiwar movements were women, certainly among the antiwar leadership and probably in its rank and file as well. The masculinization of war and the feminization of peace are in this way generally supported in the case of the former Yugoslavia. For example, the antiwar campaigns in both Belgrade and Zagreb were founded by women — Vesna Pešić and Vesna Terselić respectively. Nataša Kandić, who founded the Humanitarian Law Center in 1992 in order to document and monitor human rights violations in former Yugoslavia, remained a persistent thorn in the regime's side during the NATO intervention in Kosovo as she traveled from Belgrade to Kosovo investigating and reporting firsthand on the state of Serb-Albanian relations and the conduct of the military and paramilitary forces in the region. Vesna Pusić was director of another important Croatian antiwar organization, the Erasmus Guild, an Institute for the Culture of Democracy in Croatia.

I am not going to provide here the lengthy and critical analysis the war resistance efforts in ex-Yugoslavia deserve. To my knowledge, no such comprehensive effort has yet been undertaken, though there are two excellent chapters in Udovički and Ridgeway's edited book — "The Resistance in Serbia" by Ivan Torov, and "The Opposition in Croatia" by Sven Balas.[34] The particular peace-building activities of physician Katarina Kruhonja in Osijek along with Vesna Teršelić earned them "The Right Livelihood Award" (also known as the Alternative Nobel Prize) in 1998.[35] With the support of the Centre for Antiwar Action, twenty-one scholars and activists from Serbia published a collection of essays in 1997 in which they critically investigated the "Serb side of the war,"[36] hoping that "all sides" would soon do the same. These scholar-activists examined the emergence and spread of an ideology of bellicose nationalism, the historical narrative, the unresolved psychological "roots of the trauma" that enabled politicians to mobilize support, the role of the media, and the potential for catharsis in postwar Serbian society.

Where political elites used their public speeches and control of the media to spread hate speech and propaganda, an independent media attempted to keep the flow of information open and the voice of criticism alive. Belgrade TV–Studio B and Radio B-92, Zagreb Radio 101, the *Feral Tribune* published in Split, Croatia, the Belgrade weekly *Vreme*, and others became synonymous with the battle to retain a free and open media during the violence from 1990 to 1998.[37]

As the Torov and Balas essays indicate, the independent media was an enormously important source of resistance and opposition, and while the regimes of both Tudjman and Milosević inherited the subsidized, state-controlled media and acted to suppress independent newspapers, television, and radio stations, they never entirely succeeded, though many journalists were harassed, physically threatened, and in some cases killed.[38] Following what some called the "government's final crackdown" in a "wave of bans on independent broadcasters Studio B Radio and Television and Radio B-92 and police brutality against demonstrators who protested against these bans"[39] in May 2000, Belgrade journalist Miroslav Filipović, whose most damning and shocking reportage involved interviews with Serbian soldiers regarding their activities in Kosovo and earlier during the war in Bosnia, was arrested.[40] He was convicted of espionage and disseminating false information in July and sentenced to seven years in prison. After his sentencing, he was awarded the European Internet Journalist of the year award by the NetMedia Foundation "for what it described as a brave article about Yugoslav Army atrocities in Kosovo which could be published only on the Internet."[41] Protests from independent journalists and others in Serbia as well as from the international community continued throughout his imprisonment. In October, following the ouster of Milosević, the new Serbian president Vojislav Kostunica released him from prison. A recent report on his experiences shows high regard for his dissident heroism:

> Crucially, Filipović himself signals the divisions within Serbia. Colleagues who worked with him say his determination to continue his courageous reporting—even after being warned—was based on his own disquiet over the actions of the government carried out in the name of its citizens. Filipović saw his ground-breaking journalism as his expression of patriotism—on behalf of his own country gone wrong.[42]

Serbian journalists in the rump Yugoslavia were not the only ones to pay a heavy price for their courage. In October 1999, Bosnian Serb journalist and publisher Željko Kopanja had both legs amputated after a car bomb went off in front of the Republika Srpska government complex in the Republika Srpska "capital" of Banja Luka. The attack followed Kopanja's publication of a series of articles on Serbian war criminals in which he suggested cooperation with the Hague. Independent journalists and media were constantly harassed, arrested, fined, imprisoned, threatened publically, their facilities vandalized, and their licenses revoked or denied; sometimes they were physically removed and replaced with regime-friendly staff. In Serbia, government attacks on the free media seemed to escalate in proportion to the weakening of support for the Milosević regime, peaking during 2000, and leading up to the electoral defeat of Milosević by Vojislav Koštunica in October.

Just as the independent media constituted an antidote to government propaganda, antiwar action offered resistance to mobilization. In Zagreb some of the wind was taken out of the sails of antiwar protests following the direct involvement of the JNA in attacks inside the republican boundaries of Croatia, particularly after the brutal destruction of Vukovar in November 1991. Some protests and public outcries followed from charges that Tudjman had deliberately sacrificed Vukovar in order to "internationalize" the war.[43] Regardless of the legal status of the territory and the Croatian government's claims to sovereignty, many people simply already regarded or quickly came to regard Croatia as a state—the state of the

Croatian people—and an attack on its territory as an attack on their collective existence. Antiwar activity consisted mainly of attempting to maintain a critical voice in Croatian political discourse, particularly on the treatment of Serbs in Croatia and Zagreb's support of and involvement in Croatian military activities in Bosnia, and after 1995, on the conduct of the Croatian military during Operation Storm, in which Serb occupying forces were driven out of one third of the Croatian republic's territory and hundreds of thousands of Serb civilians fled or were murdered outright. The Croatian antiwar movement also sustained criticism against the conflation of religious identity and citizenship, the revival of conspicuously Ustaše symbols aimed at provoking and intimidating Serbian citizens of Croatia, the polarization of political discourse into attacks on a stereotyped collective "Serb enemy," and general condemnation of the antidemocratic proclivity of exclusionary nationalistic rhetoric, whether originating from government or popular sources. Independent media and activists mutually reinforced one another.

Several parallels and paradoxes were highlighted by antiwar activism in Croatia: between the Serbian government's treatment of Albanians in Kosovo and the Croatian government's treatment of Serbs living in Croatia; between the violence against the territorial integrity of Croatia at the hands of a coalition of Serbs inside and outside Croatia on the one hand, and the violence in Bosnia at least in part at the hands of a coalition of Croats inside and outside Bosnia; between the involvement of paramilitaries supported by both Zagreb and Belgrade; between the hate speech and propaganda of Tudjman and Milosević, and the mutual aspirations of the two leaders in dividing Bosnia.

This is not to say that antiwar activists ever espoused the much despised Tito-era recipe of assigning guilt equally to both sides. If responsibility for aggression falls more heavily and squarely on the shoulders of the party engaging in directly belligerent behavior first, then Milosević is unquestionably responsible for "starting it." At the same time, as the war progressed from what had been essentially a JNA-backed and Belgrade orchestrated Serbian aggression against the Croatian territorial forces and civilians in Slavonia and the Krajina to an all-out war for the partition and "cleansing" of Bosnia, the two leaders seemed to be locked in a dance of war and death, with one doing everything the other did, only backwards (though Milosević may have been clumsier and Tudjman more graceful). Neither did anything to contradict the propaganda emanating from the other side and indeed, both often seemed to behave in ways that reinforced it.

The antiwar movement in Belgrade from very early on focused on opposition to the increasing militarization of Serbian society and the spread and fomentation of intolerance among Serbs by a small circle of increasingly overt and belligerent nationalists whose propaganda and hate speech were rationalized by a rhetoric of persecution. The movement was therefore also closely

linked and identified with various groups whose main aim was the democratization of Yugoslav/Serbian society at both the national and republican
levels, including the Belgrade Circle, the Praxis Group, the Civil Alliance
Party, Women in Black, the Humanitarian Law Center, the Helsinki Committee for Human Rights in Serbia (of which there was a counterpart in
Croatia), and the European Movement in Serbia. The Belgrade Circle, originally known as the "Belgrade Circle—Association of Independent Intellectuals," was founded in 1992 in opposition to the "nationalistic euphoria,
brutal war and the complete criminalisation of Yugoslav society."[44] The
Belgrade Circle was particularly well supported by prominent antiwar,
prodemocracy intellectuals—philosophers, playwrights, writers, literary
critics—with participants from Slovenia and Croatia in addition to those
from Belgrade, and international intellectual and financial support from all
across Europe and the United States. Among the prominent international
guests hosted for visits to the region by the Belgrade Circle were Jacques
Derrida, Christopher Norris, and Richard Rorty. Its founding document
states that it is the primary concern of the organization to "promote the
values of a democratic, civil, open, plural society through various public
forums, open circulation of ideas and defense of independent creative activities."[45] The Circle took a consistently critical position toward:

> totalitarian ideologies on both the left and the right, as well as towards
> intolerance of rights of the Other (cultural, ethnic, political . . . ), hate
> propaganda, aggression and the war, nationalism and ethnocentrism, ethnic
> cleansing, encouraging of war crimes, barbaric destruction of towns and
> forced migrations in the territory of former Yugoslavia.[46]

The Circle also sponsored the creation of a Center for Cultural Deconta-
mination, claiming that: "All forms of cultural life have been contaminated,
they have been infected by a pseudo-religion, a collective national trance,
wherein an individual is lost in relation to the myth of the state and the
populist culture."[47] The Circle sponsored public debates and the creation of
local groups to foster civic dialogue and political pluralism, criticized the
militarization of Serbian society, and held regular public discussions facili-
tated by members of the Circle. In an essay entitled "Why the Belgrade Circle
Journal?" Obrad Savić and Mirko Gaspari offer a scathing description of the
pathological climate that had become normalized between 1990 and 1994:

> The journal has been born in the midst of a terrifying eruption of negative
> signs and events; all those national and religious fanaticisms which we knew
> too well, but never gave enough thought to—the worst kinds of violence,
> crime, xenophobia and racism—have so quickly multiplied throughout—
> now former—Yugoslavia, that they have been mixed beyond recognition.

And it is these primary signs—violence, passion, hate, anger, intolerance, revenge, primitivism, insanity—which have been thoroughly impressed into all types of public discourse.[48]

## War, the State, and Psychoanalytic Theories of Otherness

"During war," as Steven Kull says, "things become very simple, very clear. There are no ambiguities. In times of war suicide rates go down by half, mental health is better, even physical health gets better. It is simpler. All the ambiguities evaporate and we know what we are supposed to do."[49] Antiwar activism resisted the simplicity of hate.

Let me be clear about my position on gender roles and socialization. There is a series of characteristics or qualities coded within Western cultural practice by their association with the socially constructed notions of "masculine" and "feminine" and accordingly, as oppositional and hierarchal—what Peterson calls "asymmetrical dichotomies."[50] These include aggressive/ passive, violent/peaceful, assertive/conciliatory, rational/ emotional, and so on. I do not believe that we can say that men are violent and women peaceful, but rather that within Western culture at least,[51] males are socialized to be masculine, to act consistently with a certain understanding of violence in relation to masculinity,[52] to believe that violence is a "fact of [masculine] life." We come to believe in a gendered social order in which we make distinctions and judgments about violence—good violence and bad violence, violence to be controlled, violence as a necessary evil, violence as noble, violence as sport, violence as inevitable, violence as aggression, violence as defense, and so on.

But what does psychoanalytic theory have to say about the characteristics linked with the socialization of masculinity and how they, in turn, might bear on Kull's observation regarding ambiguity, mental health, and war? First, let's revisit Klein's insights into object relations (1964). Our emotional and cognitive development moves from simplicity toward complexity, from a relatively undefined sense of self, lacking self-consciousness, to a bounded and self-conscious self. The self, we might say, develops as an increasingly bounded locus of agency from the precategorical and undifferentiated world into which it is born. Perhaps we cannot say with certainty precisely when differentiation begins—perhaps with the birth experience itself. Lacan (1975), for example, distinguishes between this precategorical stage, and the emergence of linguistic categories, the first of which is self/Other, or self/not-self, or self-world. But we do move from a psychic position lacking self-identification and boundaries to a progressively complex psychic life in which we come to know the self as the locus of our emotional experience and of our agency. And with that self-consciousness is simultaneously born a consciousness of that which is not self, that which is Other. From a Lacanian perspective, the self is spoken, the Other is silent; the self appears as a thing, while the Other is a void. Exactly why the self as subject appears as masculine and the Other as void appears feminine is the subject of much theorizing and debate, which, though fascinating, is beyond the scope of my analysis.[53]

The process of individuation, the development of self-consciousness, is mediated by the sociocultural system of symbolic discourse, linguistic and nonlinguistic, in which meanings are encoded. The process is progressive, dynamic, and, at least potentially, regressive. There can be some confusion along the way, and categories appear less fixed, less impenetrable, less inviolable and become more fixed, impenetrable, inviolable, a process I will call social discipline. We learn the rules in relation to which we think about and communicate our emotions and experiences, the rules by which speech becomes act. In accepting a distinction between self and Other we must abandon the illusion that the Other is completely located within the self, that our commands can produce acts originating from the Other, that we can command the Other to fulfill our desires. I am not even certain that we ever entirely give up this illusion, which may go far toward explaining the preoccupation of some humans with efforts aimed at controlling Others, particularly Others whom they believe are responsible for their happiness and well-being. Rather, the infantile remains ever with us, an experience leaving emotional imprints and to which we may regress when stressed or in response to trauma. The self/Other relationship, and therefore the emotions aroused by it, is rife with paradox and contradiction as well as frustration and pleasure. And our relationship with the Other is not always or only volatile and ambivalent, since we also seek reunion with or some way of experiencing unity (however impermanent) with the Other or an/Other, which is therefore also the subject of romantic, compassionate, and ennobling behavior.

Klein's account and its political implications as worked out by Alford[54] point us to an understanding of the self/Other relationship as dynamic, and consisting of various "positions" from which we can encounter Otherness. These positions are delineated along two axes, with "paranoid-schizoid" and "depressive" positions marking one axis and "love" and "hate" the other. The paranoid-schizoid position represents a more infantile, undeveloped position from which we love and hate narcissistically. We attach to loved objects out of need, gratification, and fear of loss. From the paranoid-schizoid position we also evacuate that within ourselves that causes discomfort and frustration by projecting it onto Others who are then cast in the role of persecutors. In the infant's world, as in Kull's account of war, "things become very simple, very clear. There are no ambiguities." Is war an infant's world?

Clearly the infantile, paranoid-schizoid position is not something we "grow out of," but rather one to which we are always capable of returning, or "regressing" in psychoanalytic terms. Indeed, in Alford's account, guilt alone (what he calls "true guilt") can resolve the contradiction revealed as we discover ourselves loving and hating (in the infantile, paranoid-schizoid way) the same object (the mother or primary caretaker, our original "object"). The narcissist loves the object when it is perceived to be a source of pleasure, and blames the object for the frustration of needs and for pain. Discovering these contradictory emotions and realizing that our hate can destroy that which we also love, the narcissist feels guilt. Guilt, in turn, also enables us to transform infantile love and hate into *caritas*, love for the Other as a subject rather than an object, on the one hand, and on the other hand, make appropriate judgments regarding Others, hating "what is truly worthy of hate," and also hating "the hating self."[55] It does so by opening up a "depressive position" from which we can repair the damage done by hating the loved object, and thus we can begin to love and hate as mature adults, though Alford's argument suggests that few of us achieve such maturity.

Returning to the parallel between a self interpreting experiences and acting from a paranoid-schizoid position and war, Kull's observation that in war things are simple and clear and mental health is better is a bit disturbing. It suggests that the improvement in a population's mental health derives from the absence of ambiguities about who is worthy of love and who is worthy of hate, but this is precisely the problem. Resolving ambiguities and making appropriate judgments is hard work, it is time-consuming and psychically expensive. How do we decide who is worthy of hate and therefore harm? And what of the problem of "hating the hating self?" Is "hating the hating self" discomforting? Is this what some religions at least attempt to resolve or enable us to live with through concepts such salvation, forgiveness, or learning to live with guilt? Doesn't mental health improve precisely because in war we no longer need to confront our own dark side, our hating self, and we are thus relieved of the psychic costs of laboring over appropriate judgments about "hating what is truly worthy of hate"? Is war seductive precisely because in war *we are given permission to hate without the psychic burden of guilt?* In war (and similarly, as participants of hate groups or subcultures of hate) we no longer need to be vigilant or self-critical about our own capacity for hate and harm-doing, because in times of war we *know* who is deserving of our hate and harm-doing. It is not that humans are "evil," but rather that war and other social practices in which harm-doing and hate are legitimated toward specific Others relieve us of the psychic burden of living with our own capacity for harm-doing and hate, and relieve us of the burden of resolving the paradox, contradiction, and tension that inevitably exist between the need or desire to maintain esteem for ourselves (and thus an ability to love others as subjects) and having to confront that within ourselves which we are doomed to find unworthy of esteem. This, I submit, is what war and hate crimes have in common. They relieve us of these burdens with which we otherwise continuously struggle (or attempt to escape through psychic numbing).

But does this have anything to do with masculinity? The form of masculine identity commonly found in Western culture is constructed in a way that is less tolerant of ambiguity and more reliant on clear and even inviolable boundaries. Evidence can be found in the way social discipline is applied to create and sustain masculinity as distinct from femininity. Language is used to enforce exclusive gender roles and identities when we use derogatory language to designate a homosexual or transsexual violation. So labels like "sissy" or "fairy" are used to connote (and discipline) males engaging in "inappropriate," "feminine" behavior. And there are many more such terms used to punish feminine male behavior than there are to punish masculine behavior by girls and women. In fact, at least one term used to describe masculine behavior by girls is often viewed as complimentary: "tom boy." Will Roscoe, in his study of gender identity among the Zuni Pueblo, suggests a correlation between how gender is socially constructed within a culture and that culture's tolerance for difference and ambiguity.[56]

While I remain open to explanations as to why this is so, I think Chodorow and some of her critics in the psychoanalytic feminist school provide the basis for a plausible account: that because boys are primarily cared for during their first few years by women (on whom they depend for survival and security), and that since gender identification also begins during the same period, males are inclined to perceive "difference" in more threatening terms.[57] Girls, alternatively, perceive the Other (on whom they also depend for survival and security) in terms of sameness rather than difference, and only later, during adolescence, do they begin to focus much more attention on the problem of differentiating themselves from their mothers.

> Masculine development dynamics culminate in the construction of rigid boundaries; in women, very different dynamics result in the creation of more elastic boundaries. Adult women and men construct the self-other, subject-object, distinction in incommensurable ways.[58]

Girls, we might say, are more likely to develop a relationship with Otherness that goes something like "the Other who is not me is also like me," and boys more likely to perceive "the Other who is not me is not like me." Could it be that the first position is more tolerant of ambiguity and paradox or has a less troublesome relationship with ambiguity and paradox? Or perhaps because girls can move from the infantile toward the adult position under conditions of a less problematic relationship with the Other—the problems of individuation being delayed at least until adolescence—they can develop a more fluid notion of the self/Other relationship and the boundaries that delineate it.

Again, it seems plausible that the tendency to associate masculinity with a more acute concern for boundaries and their defense and with self-interested behavior may derive from the way in which these early relation-ships with Otherness are constructed.[59] Two cautions must be issued here. First, I am not arguing that the structure of gender in infant-caretaker rela-tions produces rage, frustration, and the "disagreeable emotions," especially in so far as they produce violence and aggression, in men alone. Women rage and are frustrated, violent, and aggressive. The puzzle to be solved here is, first of all: Why are rage, frustration, violence, and aggression so often socially constructed as *overtly* masculine traits and problems, why are we so much more concerned with men's rage than women's? And then, why, in relation to the social construction of masculinity, do they seem to occur in relation to greater anxiety over difference? The second cautionary note is that these tendencies can be attenuated by the nature of the relationship with same-gender adults, by the configuration of the family and the structure of child-rearing, and this, I think, could be a very fruitful area for more cross-cultural research.[60] For instance, though male infants are largely cared for by women, at least during the first two years, the relationship between male infants and male adults varies significantly across cultures, with some cultures involving men in child-rearing and caregiving at the earliest stages. Indeed, Chodorow (1978) attributes the high degree of male anxiety over difference to the restructuring of family relations under conditions of moder-nity, in particular, taking the father out of the home to work and the general tendency of modernity to alienate the father from the family.

Does a relationship with the Other constructed in terms of "the Other who is not me, but like me" but in which the Other is an object of love and hate, coupled with the fact that female differentiation is stretched out over the longer period from infancy to adolescence, incline girls and women toward less anxiety over difference and a tendency toward more empathetic relations with Others? This is not to suggest in any way that girls and women do not rage, and that they do not rage against women,[61] nor that the capacity for empathy is exclusively female, nor that empathy leads only to caring behavior. The same circumstances that incline women to develop an empa-thetic capability can also lead to more negotiable self-boundaries and even the failure to recognize the individual agency of others in a rather infantile way, failing to make a clear distinction between self and Other. It is not diffi-cult to imagine how insufficiently developed boundaries can also lead to controlling behavior, albeit more likely to manifest as passive (or caretaking) rather than active aggression.

Just as aggression and violence have been masculinized, so have empathy and compassion (and tolerance?) been feminized. To be empathetic and compassionate is to be soft and weak, to be rendered vulnerable rather than secure, to need protection. Where do politics and emotions intersect on the question of sameness, difference, and identity? The following table extends the list of some of the ways gender-coded differences are associated with a dichotomous set of characteristics and traits reflecting rules about how the relationship between gender identity, the state, and civic identity is constructed.

| Masculine/Masculinity is (constructed as) | Feminine/Feminity is (constructed as) |
|---|---|
| war | peace |
| security | vulnerabiity |
| decisive | negotiable |
| absolute | relative |
| logical | contradictory |
| certainty | ambiguity |
| rational | emotional |
| discriminating | tolerant |
| rigorous | permissive |
| objectivity | subjectivity |
| equality | empathy |

The idea of the modern state is based on an idea of a "community of sameness" or like individuals, expressed linguistically as "nationality." The concept of nationality, in turn, derives from presumed organic, ethnic roots of kinship. The family becomes a metaphor for the naturalization of the state. I say metaphoric because (aside from all the obvious rhetorical references to founding fathers, fathers of nations, motherland and fatherland, and so on) even though no one believes that all citizens within the state today are literally blood relatives, they are presumed to be alike in ways that make reference to familial and/or ethnic relationships. They are assumed to have one or more of the following shared characteristics: language, culture, religion, beliefs/ideology/worldview, ethnic identity, and/or narrative history. While we try theoretically to explain the modern state as a product of social transition from ethnic to civic forms of obligation and identity, in reality the imagery of kinship, or "the ethnic rule," as I called it in the previous chapter, remains a powerful theme in the political rhetoric of state leaders. Zimbabwe's President Robert Mugabe, for instance, who enjoys widespread support among blacks in his formerly colonized and white-dominated country, announced in a June 2000 speech that "The whites can be citizens in our country, or residents, but not our cousins."[62] The story's headline, "Mugabe: Whites Must Recognize Nation's for Blacks," in fact underscored Mugabe's claim as well as convoluting the ideas of nation and state. Defending the illegal occupation of over 1,400 white-owned farms (not to say that white settlement was a legal act in the first place), Mugabe explained that: "The British are saying that they are squatting on white man's land. Where is black man's land in Europe? Zimbabwe is a black man's land and a black man will determine who gets it."[63]

Now there is nothing peculiarly African or black about Mugabe's statements, and I should note that he is increasingly being criticized among his own people for these and other positions. But they could just as well have been made with respect to foreigners or nonwhites by Europeans or Americans, though one would hope that in the present time such ideas represent fringe elements. Historically, however, there has been plenty of ethnic nationalism in both Europe and its settler states in the Americas and elsewhere. My point is that even though most of us realize that states have more often been created by force, structural or direct, rather than by "nature," the "ethnic origins of states," in Anthony Smith's (1991) terminology, underlies much of the rhetoric used to mobilize support for state-building, whether in eighteenth and nineteenth century Europe and the United States, or twentieth-century postcolonial Africa, or in the Balkans. The Croat Constitution, after all, opens its preamble with: "The millennial national identity of the Croatian nation and the continuity of its statehood, confirmed by the course of its entire historical experience in various political forms and by the perpetuation and growth of state-building ideas based on the historical right to full sovereignty of the Croatian nation . . ." and then proceeds with a historical recitation beginning in the seventh century. And in Article 10 entitled "Citizens Abroad," it again affirms the "natural" relationship between Croatian ethnonational identity and citizenship in the Croatian state by declaring that: "Parts of the Croatian nation in other states are guaranteed special concern and protection by the Republic of Croatia."[64]

Now, returning to the qualities associated with masculinity and femininity, what is the purpose of the state in relation to its ethnonational family? Its primary purpose, at least until the late twentieth century, was to protect its "family" inside from "outside" threats, from Others. Yet the problem for the modern state is precisely its (presumed) transition from an identity based on ethnic sameness to an association of mutually obligated but diverse citizens. This is sometimes referred to as the shift from ethnic to civic identity. But I would like to call into question the extent to which this transition has occurred in the so-called older, more mature states, or whether it has been entirely left behind as laws are reformed to accommodate pluralism and dismantle a history of legal discrimination. Mugabe's statements suggest that even as European and settler states struggle to reform themselves, state-building in formerly colonized parts of the world is still patterned on the nation-state model historically rooted in European experience.

## The Psychic Life of States and Citizens

As argued earlier, sameness can simply be constructed along the lines of same/not same, or in an infantile way, as consciousness of a bounded self develops, by making the distinction between "me/like me" in contrast with "not me/not like me," for example, in the early development of consciousness about self/Other gender identity. A more complex formulation, however, might be "not me, and not like me, but *similarly situated* to me," which supposes the ability to understand one's position abstractly and to perceive others who occupy the same position, or to empathize. Citizens can be different but similarly situated in legal terms when they share the same set of rights and obligations by virtue of their being situated as citizens within the same polity rather than because they share organic traits such as common ancestry. "Equality before the law," for example, is a principle that situates citizens similarly.

When we construct social systems in which we are obligated to refrain from doing harm to others and in which we are obligated to afford others the same respect we expect for ourselves, we are forming what I and others have called a "moral community," a community structured by relationships of obligation grounded in a rule of reciprocity.[65] Similarly situated citizens share moral equality deriving from their legal status. Fairness requires that punishment for violating one's obligations is applied to all individuals more or less equally (as a legal ideal), including the ultimate sanction: exclusion from the moral community, or moral exclusion. But more exclusion need not always be a sanction for abrogating one's obligations. An innocuous example of moral exclusion is the prohibition against children holding sole ownership of material property until they reach an age of majority. Until then, they are subjected to adult supervision in legal and material matters. The assumption underlying this rule is that their ability to make judgments regarding their own interests and the interests of others is not sufficiently developed or mature. Children grow up, however, so they will reach maturity and with it will obtain the entitlements and responsibilities having legal consequence. Debates about holding minors accountable to the same laws and punishments as adults center on the presumption that a child lacks the moral maturity to make appropriate ethical judgments for which he or she should be help accountable on the same basis as an adult. The child and the adult occupy different positions as a result of differences in their moral maturity.

For the purposes of my argument, the manifestation of moral community relevant here is that which forms the basis for citizenship, equality before the law, or reciprocity. Efforts to reform the modern state in the direction of civic-based rather than ethnic-based identity, and in the direction of pluralism and equality rather than assimilation and discrimination, are deeply rooted in the idea of reciprocity, equality of legal rights, and equality of political and economic opportunities.

What is the relationship between moral communities of inclusion and exclusion, and the exclusionary practices implicated in the cognitive process of dehumanization, a process that rationalizes denying the humanity of others? Moral communities are formalized as legal and political rules of inclusion/exclusion, but they can also be constituted through social rules and practices, for example, as in-group/out-group prejudices and preferences, and the two can be in contradiction, even in opposition. Individuals may learn rules regarding the exclusion and even dehumanization of others within their families, neighborhoods, and churches, on the one hand, but be subject to legal rules restraining them from acting on such informal and learned exclusionary rules, on the other. If reciprocity is the foundation of civility, then dehumanization, denying others' humanity, destroys civility by relieving us of any responsibility for reciprocity. Dehumanization characterizes acts of racism, hate crimes, and some kinds of war.

So is reciprocity enough to create and sustain a civil society? Are legal fairness in relations among citizens, equality before the law, and rules that bind citizens by mutual obligation sufficient to mitigate the prejudices we learn to associate with difference? Prejudices, I have argued, are also rules that mediate between agents and structures. Reciprocity imposes a legal rule that trumps other kinds of social rules, such as prejudice, but it does not foster the development of any relationship or connection in a positive way, it does not entail an acknowledgment of shared humanity among individuals whose identities are different but who share the same civic space.

What does this have to do with the construction of dichotomous gender hierarchies? The public sphere, with rules that structure it, is a masculinized space to the extent that masculinized individuals have largely shaped it and created the rules. A masculinized formulation of fairness emphasizes objectivity, which is satisfied by a rule of reciprocity. But it does not create a rule of empathy, a characteristic associated with both the feminine and the subjective. The moral implications of empathy and subjectivity, the feminized counterparts to equality and objectivity, are that we must not only treat one another on the basis of rule-derived equality, but we must be able to see ourselves as *interchangeable* with one another's circumstances. We must be able to ask: How would I feel walking in the Other's shoes? If I am interchangeable with all other citizens, then the quality of my citizenship is only as good as the quality of citizenship enjoyed by every other citizen. Said differently, inequalities in citizenship represent a kind of shared fate, a shared burden, because citizens are interchangeable. South Africa's system of apartheid is only an extreme example. Segregation in the United States is another, albeit less extreme example.

In a multicultural society, if more than one language is spoken as the first language among citizens, then those who must learn a second language in order to engage in civic discourse are marginalized just as those for whom the official language of civic discourse is a first language are privileged. The same can be applied to religious, cultural, and traditional practices to the extent that they enter into the public sphere as symbols and practices constituting the collective identity of citizens.

A moral community based only on reciprocity rationalized on the basis of sameness is really a community of narcissists. But this is exactly the way claims about the nation-state or polities (and aspirations to polities) based on ethnic sameness are constructed. The ideal of a pluralistic society is not fully achieved through a rule of reciprocity, but requires that citizens learn to see themselves as interchangeable with one another. Interchangeability provides a measure of the fairness in the way in which power structures relationships—by our willingness to occupy the Other's circumstances, the fairness with which power is used across citizens whose identities are different.

Perhaps an illustration will help. The moral exclusion of blacks in American history was legally remedied by civil rights and voting rights legislation that eliminated barriers to reciprocity. This move achieved legal fairness. But interchangeability and political fairness are only achieved when whites are able to empathize, to understand the fate of black citizens as their own fate. Political and social fairness is achieved when whites are willing to change places with blacks because there is no difference in the way power operates in relation to variations in racial identity. Similarly, men should fight alongside women for equal rights, and so on.

Comedian Chris Rock made this point in a routine in which he asks his audience: "How many white guys out there would like to be me? None!" he says, "Even though I am a well-off black guy, I am rich, and good looking, I am privileged. But none of y'all would want to trade places with me, no matter how bad off you are and no matter how well off I am, you still know it's better to be white than black in this country."[66] Civil society, I want to argue, requires embracing the Other who is different and seeing his or her fate as our own. The quality of my citizenship is diminished by the degradation of the citizenship of any other member of my community.

In the case of former Yugoslavia, the majority of Serbs in Serbia, including the rhetoric of the political leadership, empathized only with the fate of other Serbs in Croatia and Bosnia, while within Serbia they treated the Albanians just as badly or worse than their Croatian neighbors treated their Serb "brothers." Theirs was a moral community founded on narratives of sameness, not interchangeability. Similarly, Croats in Croatia (probably a majority and certainly the leadership) bemoaned the discrimination against their "brothers" in Herzegovina while themselves discriminating against Serbs in Croatia in exactly the same way. They claimed that they had a right to intervene in Bosnia-Herzegovina and to unite their fellow Croats in Bosnia with the "motherland" of Croatia while at the same time declaring as unlawfully rebellious the Croatian Serbs who wished to do the same with Serbia. But why shouldn't they? Western political discourses are rife with nationalistic rhetoric of self-determination and ethnonational bases for liberation. Indeed, when I interviewed a high-ranking member of the Serbian Socialist Party on the issue of ethnic cleansing, he said: "Why shouldn't we do this? Isn't this what you Americans did to Native Americans? And in France they established a French state and then said, well everyone who lives here will be French citizens and will now speak French. Why shouldn't we require that the Albanians speak Serbian?"[67]

What distinguishes people who resisted the war is their insistence on maintaining ambiguities, on seeing the common humanity across categories of identity, of seeing their fate as interchangeable with Others. As the respondent cited in Chapter 4 said, "I was Croat when Serbs bombed Dubrovnik, I was Muslim when Croats bombed the old bridge in Mostar. It is all part of my culture, part of who I am."[68] Or in the words of the title of Slavenka Drakulić's article in *The Nation*, "We Are all Albanians." "The young women on TV used the expression 'Serbian citizens,' but her use of this phrase suggested that those Serbian citizens are people struggling to maintain the normality of their daily lives. By 'Serbian citizens' she evidently meant only Serbs." Drakulić says:

> Others—that is, Albanians—are simply never mentioned in that context. Their problems are not addressed, by her or other Serbs. In the perception of ordinary Serbs, Albanians are not included in the category of Serbian citizen and therefore are absent from the language as well.
>
> Why? The problem is that Serbs—or anyone else for that matter—cannot identify with the suffering of others if they are not able to see them as equals. In Yugoslav society Albanians were never visible. There was no need to construct their "otherness"—as, for example, with Jews in prewar Germany or recently with Serbs in Croatia. . . .
>
> It was clear that they belonged to a different category from Serbs, Croats, Macedonians, Montenegrins, or Slovenes. Serbs could even fight a war against Croats, but they never perceived each other in the same way they both perceived Albanians. The prejudice against Albanians can be compared to that against Jews or blacks or Gypsies in other cultures. Today every Serb will tell you that Albanians multiply like rabbits—that this is their secret weapon in the war they are waging against Serbs in Kosovo.[69]

## Living with and beyond Dichotomies

The world of the self and Other is messy, whether at the individual or group level. Some Others are outsiders against whom we need protection, and some are insiders whom we regard as parasites and inferiors. Others are our intimates, our neighbors, our loved ones, our enemies. Others are repositories for our own dark side, returning to us as perpetrators, enabling us to see ourselves as innocent victims, providing a relief for the discomfort of guilt. Others are the evil that we struggle to expel. We need them, it seems, to define ourselves, to establish and stabilize our own identity. Others are what we are not. Or are they? Try as we may to keep ourselves and Others contained within their respective categories of identity, we remain intimately linked, twin-born, inescapably interdependent, and, paradoxically, mutually constituted. The self needs the Other, indeed, cannot exist without the Other.

A number of critical perspectives—postmodern, feminist, postcolonial, and other postpositivist/poststructuralist modes of analysis—contest the usefulness of dichotomies, particularly hierarchical dichotomies, sometimes going so far as to characterize dichotomous thinking as itself a source of oppression. I think those who focus on a critique of hierarchical dichotomies (or binary oppositions) are closer to the mark in that it is not *dichotomies per se* that are problematic, but rather the way we relate to them, the way they are used to structure thinking. My own position is that we need to learn how to live with them by relating to them in ways that are emancipatory rather than oppressive.

While too extensive a topic to take up here, one can readily think of alternatives to dichotomous thinking: unity is one—the unity and interdependence of opposites, rather than opposition as separation. That can also lead us to a triangular cognitive structure, where a thing is both the opposite of and unified with another thing. Paradox and contradiction may also be triangular cognitive structures. Contextualizing things adds yet another dimension, the thing, its opposite, and the context in which we find them. Alford's use of Kleinian analysis is based on a four-way construction of our psychic life, four possible positions from which we can interpret our emotional experiences. Game theory offers another quadrangular structure for cognitive analysis. And so on.

Perhaps the self is not entirely reducible to opposition. As the Buddhist nun Pema Chödrön observes, "Form is that which simply *is* before we project our beliefs onto it."[70] Everything is what it is, or, in the Old Testament, "I am that I am." But we cannot say much about anything without words to express and describe and thus project our beliefs, project meanings onto things. Contrast and opposition are one but not the only way of doing so, and I find the insights suggested by psychoanalytic theory persuasive. Self-consciousness is achieved through a cognitive move from a state in which the self is not perceived to be separate from its environment to one in which it is, though I also believe that our cognitive life must become more complex lest we move about the world interpreting our emotions and experiences purely from the dichotomous perspective of an infant.

But the claim I have made here—and one that I find supported both by evidence regarding the collapse of cognitive complexity indicated by the rhetoric of ethnonational ideology as well as by resistance to such cognitive reductionism so among those who opposed the war and its psychopathic mentality—is that under conditions of psychic stress and trauma, as Steven Kull claims, ambiguities disappear, and things become very simple. When economic and political systems fail, people become psychically vulnerable to cognitive regression. Only by educating and socializing a citizenry to resist that move can we ultimately reduce the probability that they will respond to the toxic rhetoric that preys on their prejudices in times of crisis. The question I wish to take up here is really whether opposition must always and only be antagonistic, whether psychoanalytic inquiry into the self/Other relationship can help us understand the way identity operates in political life. I think it can. The breakdown of civility and the onset of violence in former Yugoslavia can be instructive.

The mature narcissist, as Alford argues, must be able to "hate the hating self" and "hate that which is worthy of hate" in others. The mature narcissist must therefore resist and even avoid two things which we might think of as psychic laziness. First, she must resist the idea that she is completely virtuous and without a capacity for evil or harm-doing. We cannot "hate the hating self" unless we first acknowledge its existence. Perhaps we would not act the Hitler, but we have the capacity to do so. We must therefore be vigilant and attentive to the perpetual potential to disown our own dark side, to project it onto others, even (or especially) in times of extreme stress and trauma.

To be good citizens, we must be mature narcissists. We must resist stereotypes and the temptation to attribute destructive motives or evil nature to Others categorically. This means we must do the hard work of judging others by their actions, in contexts, and restrict our judgment to their actions without condemning the person or providing justification for the denial of the Other's humanity. And we must do so by doing the hard work of reason, of judging a particular act by a particular person in a particular context. We must hate or condemn only that which is truly worthy of condemnation. Actions may be worthy of condemnation, but are people? Certainly not whole groups of people on the basis of their identification (or our identification of them) with a particular category—whites, blacks, Serbs, Croats, Germans, Jews, men, women, and so on. We cannot take the shortcuts prejudices offer and remain civil. *Vigilance over our own capacity to do harm, our own dark side, our capacity to split and project, and resistance to prejudices and stereotypes necessitates self-criticism.*

Is there a role or even a need to bring empathy into our civic life? I believe there is. Rules requiring reciprocity break down when political systems disintegrate or undergo crisis, but learning to see through the eyes of the Other is not easily unlearned. Respondent after respondent agonized over not only the destructiveness of violence, but the destruction of their relationships with friends and neighbors with whom, in spite of cultural and religious differences, they had shared holidays, and family birthdays and had even attended one another's churches.

Empathy respects the boundaries of the Other without consuming the

Other. It does not presume to know the Other as oneself. Rather, it makes the effort to perceive from the Other's vantage point, to make the effort to feel what the Other is feeling. It is not so difficult, as Chris Rock's dry political humor suggests; people do it, albeit unconsciously, all the time. That's why his comments evoke knowing laughter. And they remind those of us who are Americans that as long as whites in general would not want to change places with blacks in general, then there we must continue to struggle for fairness in the way power structures relationships. But I do not think we can truly engage in empathy as long as we are indulging ourselves in a world of Others on whom we have simply projected parts of ourselves — whether romanticized or demonized parts of the self. Empathy requires acknowledgment of and respect for the agency of the Other.

And what about tolerance? Isn't tolerance the antidote for prejudice? I suggested earlier that we are inclined to view tolerance as a feminized trait and discrimination or discernment as masculinized, particularly since the latter is concerned with constructing and maintaining boundaries, I do not mean to suggest that women are tolerant and men intolerant. Rather, when tolerance and discrimination are thought of in terms of asymmetrical dichotomies, patriarchal societies will tend to privilege discrimination as a desirable or "necessary" trait and view tolerance as weakness. But it is not that simple. J. J. Ray revisits Adorno's work on the authoritarian personality, reviewing recent efforts further to understand what is being measured by F scale tests for authoritarianism.[71] Though once thought to correlate with racism and intolerance, more recent studies indicate that what is really being measured is what researchers have begun to call the "old fashioned personality," one with a fondness for tradition, that the F scale "correlated with assent to popular myths and superstitions of the past,"[72] particularly the 1920s or what Ray calls "Victorian values." But the authoritarianism of the F scale correlation is not entirely out of the picture, because, as Ray says, "the pro-authority content of the F scale is an important part of its "old-fashionedness.'" He also cites research that documents "the authoritarian nature of child-rearing practices in the 1920s and 1930s" in both the United States and Germany.[73] This is not, however, evidence either "that all old-fashioned people are Nazis," nor that "the Nazis were old-fashioned."[74]

Perhaps we cannot think a "tolerant" personality can be accepting of others, of their differences, and can be nonjudgmental. From the perspective of much of my argument, we might think this is a good thing. But an "overly tolerant" personality may also be unable to make ethical judgments and take authorial responsibility for them. An overly tolerant person would not be able to "hate that which is worthy of hating." An overly authoritative personality, on the other hand, is intolerant of ambiguities and differences and might be inclined to ground ethical claims in external authorities, such as nature, God, truth, science, tradition, or a stereotyped, categorical truth.

Now, in former Yugoslavia we had a situation where political leaders deliberately exploited infantile emotions, arousing people to fear and scapegoating of Others, and urging them to find themselves in narratives of victimization and thereby blame and rationalize the destruction of the Other. But we also had a significant number of people who resisted these moves, who understood the pathological nature of this process and the climate it created, a climate that seemed inevitable.

Finally, though Milgram's studies remain controversial for a number of reasons, I believe that his work still offers some insight into the configuration of support for and opposition to the war within the populations of the republics. A majority, or at least a critically large plurality of people, seemed to support the nationalisms of exclusion, warmongering, and images of victimization and vindication, while a small proportion of people maintained a critical position. In Milgram's studies (eventually involving more than a thousand participants at several universities), he found only a small percentage of people willing to make an independent ethical judgment about their participation in the experiments.[75] Most people were "obedient." Says Milgram:

> It is the extreme willingness of adults to go to almost any lengths on the command of an authority that constitutes the chief finding of the study and the fact most urgently demanding explanation.
>
> A commonly offered explanation is that those who shocked the victim at the most severe level were monsters, the sadistic fringe of society. But if one considers that almost two-thirds fall into the category of "obedient" subjects, and that they represented ordinary people drawn from working, managerial, and professional classes, the argument becomes very shaky.[76]

Milgram then went on to explore a variety of explanations, including cognitive adjustments such as dehumanization. But by his own admission, "the most adjustment of thought in the obedient subject is for him to see himself as not responsible for his own actions. He divests himself of responsibility by attributing all initiative to the experimenter, a legitimate authority."[77]

The subject is thus embedded within a system of social meaning through which authority is legitimized to act in certain ways, and he or she becomes an agent of that system. The state is such a system, and itself is embedded within a state system of international norms, particularly those pertaining to the social practice of war. Milgram's subjects did not even require arousal provoked by narratives of victimization and vindication. And as earlier chapters have shown, nationalistic leaders, particularly in Serbia, deliberately involved those on the "sadistic fringe of society" as mercenaries and even as military leaders. But as Milgram might also have predicted, a minority of people *were* able to retain a sense of responsibility, to answer only to their own authority, to make morally independent judgments about "hating what is truly worthy of hate," and to maintain vigilance over their own vulnerability to regress into the infantile narcissism of the splitting and projecting personality. They hated hate, and they hated the nationalists who depended on it.

# CHAPTER 9

# Identity, Conflict, and Violence

I know I should have asked myself at this point whether the murdered people were Croats or Serbs and who killed them; perhaps I should have felt rage or a desire for revenge. But as I gazed at the dark, gaping hole, at the blood-caked pulp, I only felt an unspeakable revulsion towards humankind. The naked brain is stronger than such questions, it is evidence that we are all potential criminals.

——Slavenka Drakulić, *Balkan Express*, 1993: 47

Love, compassion, and tolerance are needs, not luxuries. Without them humanity cannot survive.

——His Holiness the Dalai Lama, *Buddha Heart, Buddha Mind*, 2000: cover

Many, maybe even all cultures have a concept of humanity, or "personhood." The African concept of *Ubuntu*, Michael Battle explains, derives from the Xhosa expression, *umuntu ngumuntu ngabanye bantu*, which translates roughly into "a person depends on other persons to be a person."[1] It is on the principle of *Ubuntu* that Desmond Tutu bases his efforts to lead South African citizens, black, white, and all people of color, toward reconciliation. Writes Tutu:

In the African *Weltanschauung*, a person is not basically an independent solitary entity. A person is human precisely in being enveloped in the community of other human beings, in being caught up in the bundle of life. To be is to participate. The summum bonum here is not independence, but interdependence. And what is true of the human person is surely true of human aggregations.[2]

"[F]or Tutu," says Battle, "*Ubuntu* is the environment of vulnerability, i.e. a set of relationships in which people are able to recognize that their humanity is bound up in the other's humanity."[3]

The problem I've set out to, if not explain, at least obtain more insight into is the perennial issue of human beings" inhumanity toward one another, specifically focusing on the question of what politics has to do with it. I have tried to stop thinking about "war" as an entirely discreet category of violence but rather as a kind of politicized violence, and then to think about politicized violence itself on a continuum of more or less politicized violence. Perhaps, for instance, a higher crime rate among those whose identities are linked with the historical experience of direct and structural violence, and for whom that history has consequences that negatively impact their economic, social, and political experiences today also has antisocial political underpinnings, even if some or even most of those engaged in such violence do not consciously regard their motives as political.[4] After all, the reverse seems to be true: people engaging in politically rationalized violence who were the subject of this study frequently dissociated from the intensely personal quality of their behavior. That dissociation, however, does not make such violence less personal.

I have tried to follow the advice of feminists and abandon the distinction between public and private,[5] and then see what insights are possible by doing so. If, as Tutu and the African concept of *Ubuntu* suggest, our humanity is bound up with the humanity of others, then so is our inhumanity: our own humanity is also diminished by acts of inhumanity toward others. Does justifying such acts within the rhetorical or ideological framework of political language and political necessity alter that fact?

Contemporary debates over the issue of "man's inhumanity to man" frequently begin with an explicit or implicit assumption that the convergence of politics, violence, and identity produced unprecedented and self-evidently unacceptable acts of inhumanity in the Holocaust. Hitler's "willing executioners" should have known that what they were doing was so wrong that, should they be defeated, they would face certain and severe consequences. But is the Holocaust, like Freud's psychopath, really an exaggeration of other acts of inhumanity undertaken in the name of political objectives, particularly state-building or reconfiguring? The Holocaust, we all seem willing to say, was unquestionably a genocide, even while we debate whether or not the term "genocide" can be applied to other acts involving the widespread and brutal decimation of people, whether it takes place within months, years, or decades, on the basis of their identity. Even as we fail to prevent or intervene in other tragedies, we might still reassure ourselves that surely we would not fail to act decisively were the circumstances as clear to us in foresight as they are in hindsight when looking back on the Holocaust. Holocaust survivor and director of the American Jewish Congress in 1997, Henry Seigman makes the comparison this way:

> To compare Bosnia and the Holocaust is to invite angry disagreement from some Jewish critics who correctly see the Holocaust as a unique evil, an

unprecedented descent into hell. But the uniqueness of the Holocaust does not diminish the force of powerful parallels that do exist between the two tragedies, and no one should better understand these commonalities than the Jews.[6]

What can we really say of the human capacity for brutality and its political implications? That the Holocaust was the worst historical case in modern times, but that the capacity for inhumanity is ubiquitous? Or do we really believe that it was uniquely produced by the convergence of a willing leadership with an authoritarian and anti-Semitic political culture in Germany? During the Holocaust, compared to other genocides, more people were murdered in cold blood, during a shorter period of time, and more people were brutally and icily tortured, and both mass killings and torture were carried out as acts of state, encouraged and sanctioned by political institutions and the rule of law and tolerated by the community of civilized nations. But perhaps the Holocaust is most offensive to us now because the ideology which rationalized it was in part a product of the Western cultural myth of human reason and progress, a myth that seems central to the social construction of a European concept of "civilization." Hitler, in this view, was a product of, rather than a deviant from, Western social practices.[7] The very social engineering we believed would follow from scientific enlightenment was turned toward the destruction of humanity, not the enhancement of it. Though it had happened before and it has happened since, albeit on a smaller scale, over a longer period of time, or absent the sterility of scientific rationalism, the Holocaust brought the word *genocide* into the vocabulary of ordinary people as well as their political leaders throughout the Western world.

If the Holocaust was the genocide of high technology, Rwanda was the genocide of low technology. Within the period of several months in the summer of 1994, during the third year of violence in Bosnia, more than 500,000 of Rwanda's 657,000 Tutsis were killed—about 77 percent of the entire Tutsi population there—mostly with machetes.[8] And what of the genocides against indigenous peoples, or the Armenians, if by genocide we mean, more or less, violence carried out against people for the purpose of destroying the ability of the group to survive as a group?[9] Where and how do we classify the Khmer Rouge killing of several million intellectual and commercial elites in Cambodia? And what of the "ordinary" violence carried out by ordinary people against others whom they hate and target simply because they are different?

As humans, we have a capacity to become self-conscious of our humanity—at least in Western cultures we believe this to be so. Through the humanities—history, literature, the art of narrative, philosophy—we are moved to reflect on our humanity, on that which is common to the human experience. Sadness, grief, joy, happiness, endurance, conflict, tragedy, enlightenment, catharsis, and struggles over ethical questions, however differently these are understood within various cultural and linguistic systems, are common human experiences. But we also have the capacity to deny, perhaps even destroy, our own humanity through the dehumanization of others, no less so when we do it "unconsciously." That, at least, is what I believe we do when we engage in acts of dehumanization, because our humanity remains intact only as a presence linking us one to the other. Denying another's humanity breaks that link with our own. In a search to understand dehumanization, we will also come to a better understanding of our humanity.

We have failed, I think, to examine critically the relationship between exclusionary ideologies and the political rationalization of doing harm to others, particularly because it may implicate the nationalistic foundations of the modern state itself. Perhaps we can lay responsibility for the Holocaust at the feet of a historical anti-Semitic ideology fertilized within a relatively authoritarian political culture (particularly acute in but not exclusive to Germany) and appropriated by German leaders to mobilize ordinary people to do extraordinary and inhuman things. But isn't this also a way of reassuring ourselves that "we," the speakers making such an assessment, would never do such a thing ourselves? Isn't this a way of locating the human capacity for evil in Others? Of denying our own capacity for inhumanity by depositing it in the Nazis? Is that "hating the hating self" or hating the hating Other as a means of denying our own capacity to hate? Doesn't an indictment resting on the particulars of German political culture and leadership distract us from an equally, if not more important question: Why did "we" not intervene to stop it sooner? Why were "we" (some of us) collaborators? Why do we (some of us) also dehumanize and act cruelly toward others, as a matter both of public policy and private miscreance? Where is our own dark side?

The notion that ethnic identity must inevitably drive us toward the cognitive processes of exclusion and dehumanization, of denying the humanity that renders us equal to others who are different, equally human in spite of our differences, is not, in my opinion, well supported by the evidence presented in the previous four chapters, though it certainly can be deployed by political leaders in order to arouse those emotions in individuals that will make many of them more inclined to dehumanize others. Some people did seem more readily mobilized to adopt such a position and to act on it violently, but others struggled over the loss of connection and civility with their friends, neighbors, fellow citizens, relatives, and even strangers who were "different." Still others who were victims of such violence, sadly but more understandably, responded in kind. And some resisted ceaselessly. Some simply left the country, if they had the means to do so. As the political environment became increasingly polarized and intolerant, those in the "grey area," could no longer find themselves in the political rhetoric of toxic nationalism, victimization, and hate. Like the young man quoted in Chapter 7 said, "My mother was Catholic, my father was Orthodox, my grandmother was Jewish, and they gave me a Muslim first name. I am going to Los Angeles and when I get there I don't want to meet any Yugoslavs."

Perhaps the question we should be asking is: "What makes resistance to the cognitive process of exclusion and the emotions of hate more likely, and what can be done from the level of "outside" forces to make such resistance more likely to prevail in a climate of escalating violence? But can we approach this question in honesty and with scientific integrity without being able to look in the mirror, to move beyond explanations that implicate the uniquely heinous character of the "others" who would commit such atrocities? It seems plausible, for instance, that the way the practice of politics in an arena of social life we call "international relations" is currently constructed relies on an understanding of power in general, and legitimate or authoritative power in particular, that rests on an assumed link between exclusionary identities and political claims. We must interrogate the relationship between violence and rationalizations that reference exclusionary identities wherever they are found.

Constructivists ask: How do language practices reveal rules that mediate between agents' actions and the structures created, maintained, destroyed, and transformed by them? One kind of language practice is found in the historical narrative and the production of political identities. It is within historical narratives that individuals locate themselves in relation to social practice and social relations. Historical narratives also serve to affirm the legitimacy of political institutions and the legitimacy of the state as it is understood (constructed) within the European experience, and thus they become the narratives of the state, narratives of civilizations, to use Huntington's terminology (1993). The contemporary state, the Westphalia state, is European in origin and is intimately tied to and at least historically reliant on narratives of nationalism. Somewhat ironically, nationalism in the nineteenth century was a narrative of liberation, of shifting the locus of authority and control over political life from institutions of monarchical rule, with its roots in the legitimating narrative of "divine right," toward the creation of populist-controlled political institutions (even though the societies remained highly stratified along the lines of race, class, and gender). Nineteenth-century nationalism was, in other words, a narrative of resistance to domination. As the historical narrative on which the legitimacy of the populist-controlled state rests, however, nationalism has itself become a narrative of domination over those who, given the nationalist origins of the state, become "minorities." Ethnic cleansing, genocide, and the various means by which minorities are put at risk within the state and as a consequence of state-building practices provide more than ample evidence of nationalism as a narrative of domination and exclusion.

### Words Matter: Cognition, Narrative Practice, and International Relations Theory

In the social world, speaking is acting. Because the language we use and the meanings contained in it and altered by it frame our thinking, and because thought precedes speech, then thinking is a social act as well. How we talk about things contributes to making them what they are or at least how actors in social settings will perceive them, and thus how actors will devise strategies (including speech acts) intended to influence the social world in light of how they perceive it to be. If we talk about the state as if its claim to legitimacy rests on a naturalized relationship between organic identities and political authority, then "nationalists" will continue to appropriate the language of inclusion and exclusion, of ethnic nations and minorities within them, and they will rouse willing combatants along with willing perpetrators of cruelty who require few or no rationalizations in order to expel their own evil through acts of brutality against others.

The title of this book invokes Kenneth Waltz and his first excursion into the intersections between political and international relations theory: *Man, the State, and War: A Theoretical Analysis*. Although his later work, *Theory of International Politics*, is widely regarded as a more rigorous development of the theory International Relations (IR) students would come to know as neorealism, my invocation is intentionally directed toward a contestation of his earlier argument regarding levels of analysis: that theories based neither on human psychology nor on the ideological content of the social contract on which the political order within states rests are sufficient to account for the central problematic of IR: war. It is from this reasoning that Waltz proceeds to build his theory of international politics on a structural foundation, namely, the structure of the relations between states, or the state "system." But I should say straight out that I am not simply arguing in opposition to Waltz. Rather, I believe that any attempt to understand contemporary political violence must bring both the cognitive and the constitutive back into the picture, along with the structural. It is a messier business, and it fails to meet Waltz's criteria for scientific elegance—it does not explain a lot with a little, it explains a little with a lot. But it does, I think, provide insights that can lead us toward more effective intellectual, moral, and policy-oriented engagement with the problem of contemporary political violence.

What caused the war in ex-Yugoslavia? Let's begin by reviewing the reasons various investigators and participants have identified:

- *The state of Yugoslavia was not universally regarded by people living in it as a legitimate state and so was doomed from the start.* (If this is a cause of war, then there are many states at risk.) It was not legitimate for one of two reasons (which can be understood also as variations on the same claim): it had no common ethnocultural basis (or the ethnocultural basis was perceived to be artificial, which speaks to the presumption of international normative order that such a link *ought* to exist); or it was an artificial state because it was created by dominant Western European powers and their allies, forces outside the boundaries of anything which could be regarded as the "natural" community or communities in the Balkans;[10]

- *Economic and political instability precipitated a crisis that led leaders to revert to their nationalistic rather than multinational pan-Yugoslav basis for political support,* eventually leading to increasingly belligerent nationalist rhetorics culminating in an aggressive use of force by Serbian President Milosević;[11]

- *Faced with the immanent breakdown of the Yugoslav state, political leaders at the republican level sought to maximize their gains under a reconfigured system of successor states,* with Bosnia-Herzegovina being the republic with the most contestable boundaries in light of its lack of a dominant ethnic majority population;[12]

- *The end of the Cold War created a level of uncertainty in the international system, a power transition from bipolar to unipolar/hegemonic.* In this climate, political leaders were more likely to take risks in the form of contesting state boundaries, given the uncertainty of interventions against their aggressions;[13]

- *Historical memories of the Yugoslav civil war during World War II left unresolved and unreconciled grievances that were at the least unaddressed under the Tito regime and, at worst, exacerbated by Tito's policies,* such as splitting Serbs among several republics in order to diminish their potential for domination, discriminating against Croats' expressions of nationalism, which tacitly implied punishment for their collective guilt as Nazi collaborators, and the contradictory claim of applying a recipe of equally distributed punishments and denunciations across all ethnic groups;[14]

- *The notorious and widely discredited and criticized "ancient hatreds" thesis that patterns of conflict among the Balkans peoples were the rule rather than the exception and that they had never been able to devise a political system capable of mitigating them;*[15] (What are "ancient hatreds"? Did ancient hatred drive the centuries-long war between the English and French? Is anti-Semitism an ancient hatred? It seems that the writers of Western history regard only people in non-Western spaces as having "ancient hatreds," while providing much more elaborate explanations for wars in the Western world.)

- *Samuel Huntington's related "clash of civilizations" theory*, which argues that the inability of people to form political communities across civilizational divides, such as Catholicism, Orthodox Christianity, and Islam, is at the root of contemporary "ethnic" conflicts;[16]

- *Variations on some of the above themes, but within the framework of "ethnic conflict" theories*, such as the instrumentalization of ethnic identity because of its perceived claim to political stakes, including the rhetoric of "self-determination," or a primordial approach that holds ethnic identity as a powerful mobilizer (without explaining why), or elite mobilization which seems to integrate the two by claiming that elites specifically employ a strategy of appropriating ethnic identity as a means of constructing political discourse and action on the basis of grievances and injustices coterminous with ethnic boundaries;[17]

- *Individual psychological inclinations toward scapegoating, projection, and reliance on exclusionary identities* render us vulnerable to the manipulations of elites under circumstances of collective psychological stress.[18]

Is it possible or useful to think systematically about these diverse and sometimes overlapping claims, all (with the exception of the "ancient hatreds" thesis) based on case studies and plenty of empirical evidence? First, I would note that they all provide some understanding of the sociopolitical dynamics that culminated in the war in ex-Yugoslavia, though none gives us very much help in understanding why it was so personal and so particularly brutal. Even the widely criticized and often dismissed "ancient hatreds" thesis contains some insight in the sense that people can be mobilized to act violently on the basis of socially learned prejudices. It is also, after all, in a way the basis for arguments about the role of historical narratives in the construction of identity. And there is a mostly unspoken, politically incorrect corollary to the "ancient hatreds" thesis, which holds that as one moves culturally or "civilizationally" eastward through Europe and toward the Orient in general, the peoples and cultures encountered are increasingly primitive and uncivilized.[19] The point is not that such perspectives are in any way accurate, but that at least some western Europeans and their allies, including policy-makers, often make assumptions about the backwardness of Eastern/Oriental peoples or cultures, and that assumption, in turn, informs their policy positions.

We begin by revisiting the question at the heart of contructivists' thinking, the relationship between agency and structure, particularly as it reflects critically on the deficiencies of structuralists' thinking. The main problem with the structuralist approach, critics argue, is not so much that structures don't matter, but that prevailing accounts rely on a kind of structural determinism by failing to identify any agency through which structures assert influence on international actors. They also provide no account of how structures change. At the other extreme, we have the problem of disembodied agency, an agent without a structure, without even any way of talking about agency or structure, or IR theory, for that matter, because language itself is a structure. Agency without structure is thus equally problematic, though contructivists do not necessarily go this far but instead place agency within "context." But if structures do *cause* things, if language rules among Westerners "cause" most Westerners to develop a view of non-Western people as not only different, but backward, then we should ask *how*?

First, structures do matter, but only in relation to social consequences— that things are as they are in the social world in part because of the way the social world is structured. Both agents and structures are products of social interaction, which also limits the usefulness of exclusively adapting either the epistemology or methodology of the physical/natural sciences to the task of acquiring knowledge about social reality. Most writers from Giddens to Onuf seem to agree that agents and structures are mutually constituted.[20] Language itself is also a structure. Precategorical, prelinguistic agency is meaningless from the perspective of social analysis. Whatever emotions and experiences we have prior to the acquisition of language, their social consequence is limited by our inability to act on them in a socially meaningful way. Said differently, agency without structure is meaningless and unintelligible, for language itself is a structure. What we need, then, is a way of thinking about the relationship between the two, to which Onuf's work has contributed much insight.[21] The dynamic nature of the agent-structure relationship is mediated by *rules*, and it is through discovery of the rules that we understand how agents' actions affect structures, and vice-versa.

There is no such thing as presocial order, for the existence of language itself structures social relations, and language is socially produced. But of course, structures do change. While structural theorizing may be concerned with explaining how the international system moves from hegemonic to bipolar, to multipolar, modified bipolar power configurations, and the like, it fails to interrogate the structure of the state itself as a product of social action and therefore to anticipate how changes in the structure of the state might impact changes in the structure of the state system. Thus if we do indeed find ourselves in an historical context in which the structure of the state is changing, what does that do to the usefulness of structural theorizing? What we need in order to evaluate the proposition that the state is changing is to understand the rules mediating between states and agents, particularly if agents' actions seem increasingly to be against states. In Onuf's terminology, they are not acting against states as much as *acting against the rules by which the social arrangement we call the state is maintained.*

A constructivist approach is one that places an event (or process) such as the war in ex-Yugoslavia within the context of social interactions, including the interactions between structures and agents, speech acts, and the construction and adaptations of identities and interests, when interests are understood as having the potential to vary according to self-perception. I am by no means a theorist at the level of intellectual sophistication at which the agent-structure and constructivism debate is currently taking place,[22] but rather I am here concerned with whether taking a constructivist approach seriously will lead to better thinking about the problem of political violence when applied to the case of the war in ex-Yugoslavia and the way the conflict and the forces leading up to it were understood by the people on the ground there. I think it can. As Harry Gould has argued,[23] many of the exchanges in the agent-structure debate have raised the issue of whether, and if so how, constructivism alters our thinking about levels of analysis. The three dimensions, or levels of analysis, employed by conventional IR theorists, however, are not very useful as we presently understand them, however much it seems to make common sense to order theorizing around the idea of individual, state, and state system "levels." The idea of "levels" of analysis seems implicitly to refer to the kind of ordering and cataloging that takes place within the physical sciences. The problem with adapting them to the social sciences is precisely the constructivists' point, I think. That deploying these terms uncritically, without attending to the social construction of the things they are meant to represent, is misleading. What do we mean by "individual"? How did the "state" come into existence and what, exactly, is it? What are the historical and social processes that created the state, and the "state system," and might the two even be mutually constituted? What rules mediate agents and structures at each level? What rules make the individual a part of the state, and the state a part of the state system?

While I realize that a full discussion of these issues could generate a book or two in itself, here I wish only to use a constructivist perspective as a means of both critiquing and reconstituting a slightly more complicated schema that will allow us to take into account some of a constructivist perspective and suggest a relationship between structure and agency.

### The Psychological and Cognitive Level or Dimension[24]

At one level of social interaction, we find the individual, but rather than appearing "fully formed," as Hobbes's mushroom man does, our individual is somewhat more ephemeral, less fixed, and constituted by boundaries of identity that wax and wane; in love perhaps, they even seem to disappear, at least at times. Our individual is emotional, mental and social. Our individual is located within a network of social interactions, narratives of identity and history, within relationships of family and community, born to a community of speakers whose thinking is framed in terms of a certain language, a world of enemies and allies and of gendered beings (the meaning of which varies across cultures and languages) with whom she or he may or may not strongly and clearly identify. Our individual is constantly struggling with contradictions and inner conflicts, and struggling to define perpetually elusive states of mind, such as peace, happiness, contentment. Our individual's sense of self is sometimes felt to be threatened and at other times secured. Instead of the perennial structuralist question "What is human nature?"[25] we take psychologists seriously. Human beings are capable of both caring and destructive behavior, of rage and adoration, dissociation and attachment, and a full range of emotions. Our emotional life is characterized not by a move from one stage of development to another (infant to adult, immature to mature) but by a layering on of increasingly complex options for perception and behavior. Adult is layered onto infant, mature onto immature. And we may peel those layers back and choose to act from a number of psychological positions or options that have been layered on as a result of agents' choices in relation to rules and structures.

Human beings are emotional, but they are also *cognitive*. Their emotions interact with their thinking processes. How we think about things determines, to some extent, how we feel about them. We may also disguise our feelings by dressing them up in thinking outfits. Our agency is enacted in relation to the system of social rules governing our emotional-mental or psychological-cognitive existence. These rules enables us to ascribe meaning to experiences and choose actions relative to those meanings. We learn them in stories, in poetry, in a parent's rage, in historical narratives, in all of our social interactions. Agents may develop a variety of interpretations of events and choose to behave differently in relation to them. Behavioral psychology and social psychology aim to understand the probabilities that behaviors will be similar, but there is always that variance, the exception. In an essay on "The Meaning of Meaning" Aaron T. Beck describes it this way:

> Although we seem to respond almost instantaneously to assaults, whether physical or physiological, we do not always experience anger. Whether we do so or not depends on the context of the injury and the explanation for it. A young child subjected to an injection by the family doctor will fight and scream to protect herself from an inexplicable infliction of pain. An adult receiving such an injection, and experience the same kind of pain, may have some anxiety, but will not typically respond with anger.[26]

We even know something about the conditions under which individuals are more likely to behave one way or another. The crucial difference between the child's reaction and the adult's reaction to pain, Beck says, is *meaning*. Beck's approach to psychological theorizing about hostility and aggression first draws on a school that focuses on the interaction between external, environmental circumstances and the innate, internal human capacity for violence. The roots of our "fight–flight" behaviors, Beck argues, can be

traced to "primordial encounters with group rejection, which led to deprivation of good resources and loss of protection by other members of the
group."[27] Under these circumstances, "Encounters with others had to be
rapidly categorized as either threat or non-threat, with a distinct boundary
between them. There was no latitude for ambiguity. This crude either–or
categorization is the prototype of the dichotomous thinking that we see in
chronically angry, hypercritical, or hyperirritable individuals."[28]

But, he says, our social circumstances have changed, and such fight–flight
behavior is not only no longer necessary to our survival or to prolonging
our lives, but in fact works against us:

> [I]t is the hyperactivity of these defensive strategies that poses problems in
> contemporary society, where the perceived threats are for the most part
> psychological rather than physical. Disparagement, domination, and decep-
> tion, which represent threats to our status in a group and diminish our self-
> esteem, do not in themselves constitute dangers to physical well-being or
> survival. Yet we often react as strong to a verbal attack as we would to a
> physical one, and become just as intent on retaliating.[29]

It is not simply that we have the capacity to become angry and to act
destructively against others as a response to anger, but that, like the child
receiving an injection, a cognitive process intervenes between the experience
of hurt and an angry response, and again between an angry response and
behavior. That cognitive process is the process of interpretation, of assigning
meaning to our experiences. Again, Beck explains hostility in terms familiar
to any psychologist:

> Hostility—whether experienced by a group or an individual—stems from
> the same principles: seeing the adversary as wrong or bad, and the self as
> right and good. In either case, the aggressor shows the same "thinking
> disorder": construing the facts in his favor, exaggerating the supposed
> transgression, and attributing malice to the opposition.[30]

Our adult dental patient, however, certainly would not see the dentist as an
adversary, so the where does the idea that someone should be responsible for
our distress come from?

## The Sociocultural Level or Dimension

Perhaps psychoanalytic accounts of the individual and its feminist variations
are not yet well theorized, but they do provide a starting point for posing
the question of whether we can find a way of talking about psychological
constructs, such as self/Other boundaries, that transcend cultural, and

perhaps even historical, differences. Beck's account, for example, suggests that the constant feature of human psychic life is the inclination toward dichotomous thinking. Perhaps this is a good place to begin. How do different cultures handle the problem of dichotomous thinking differently? And have specific cultures over time altered the meaning of dichotomies, or has dichotomous thinking played a different role at different points in the historical experience of a culture? Similarly, the question of self/Other boundaries may provide a starting point for cross-cultural research (and these are not mutually exclusive starting points, but may be different ways of viewing the same phenomenon). Do all cultures have a concept of self? How is that concept related to the Other? Are the boundaries more or less negotiable within different cultures? Are they negotiated and constructed differently in different cultures? Some of the cross-cultural research on gender, for example, points in this direction. Other than history and culture, in what other ways can context vary?

Cultural processes and social life, including language and narrative practices, contain the rules that mediate not only agents' actions, but cognition. They provide the meaning indicated by Beck's perspective on emotional and cognitive processes. Linguistic order, other symbolic forms of representation, socialization practices, and education, for instance, mediate between the individual's emotional experience of self/Other boundaries and the individual's choice to act on them by framing the experience and choice within a culturally structured dichotomous thinking.

While the agency of the individual to choose different responses to the pain inflicted by the dentist, as opposed to the mugger, is mediated by the sociocultural processes by which we understand (and tolerate) one as beneficial to us and the other as harmful seems rather straightforward, how is it that we come to believe that a government or political leader or people whom we identify as members of a different group are potentially harmful to us even when we do not experience them as the direct agents of pain? Let's talk about distress and uncertainty rather than direct physical pain. I have argued in Chapter 3 that the structure of the psyche is such that we share a human capacity for splitting, projecting, and scapegoating, but that we differ in our capacity to manage the stresses that make us prone to such behavior. Furthermore, we should understand these processes and our capacity to engage in them as more or less ordinary and a constant feature in our lives. When we are having a "bad day," we may simply mean that the state of our emotional life on that particular day is more vulnerable to irritations and anxieties.

But our capacity for distress, anxiety, and Other-directed stress is also mediated by social and cultural variables. Cultural and social processes create a context of meaning in which we interpret those things that we experience as distressful, whether an agent attaches to them, and what the agent's intentions are. They tell us how to think about distressful experiences. Cultural and social processes include the historical and cultural narratives in which we locate ourselves. Answering the question "Who am I?" locates us within these narratives. Is the historical narrative in which we find ourselves primarily one of oppression and victimization, a struggle for liberation, or a narrative of enlightenment and progress, manifest destiny and triumph? Is it mixed, that is, does it refer to a broad range of possibilities and experiences? Does it take into account our ability as individuals and in our collective life to commit acts of brutality, to be reprehensible as well as noble?

Cultural and social processes also create the rules and norms to which contructivists refer. To what extent do our cultural narrative and the rules and norms contained within it tend to structure social relations along more authoritarian, patriarchal, tolerant, or self-critical lines? How does our collective self-definition as reflected in those narratives refer to or regard Others? To what extent is our own collective self-definition and collective self-understanding structured by reference to others? For example, are postcolonial Africans, as Fanon argues, more susceptible to a self-image that lacks confidence, that internalizes the colonizers' claim of Western superiority and African inferiority, of Western progress and non-Western backwardness?

Now, clearly we must make room for variations in the capacity of different individuals even within the same culture to handle distress, as well as the degree to which they are likely to respond to distress with anxiety, and to act on anxiety in Other-destructive ways. But we can also probably agree that there are some collective experiences, some traumas, that are very likely to evoke widespread and deep feelings of distress and anxiety in a broader spectrum of the population within a society. When most people feel that their individual needs are met more often than frustrated, when their sense of relative deprivation is low to negligible, then we would expect the level of distress and anxiety and related processes of scapegoating, splitting, projecting, harmdoing, and violence also to be relatively low. But when traumatic events unfold, then two things matter very much: the historical and identity narratives in which we locate ourselves and our relationship to others; and the willingness of leaders to mobilize collective distress and anxiety as a mechanism for strengthening their own claims to legitimate leadership. At least that's what I make of the experience of the peoples of former Yugoslavia.

## The Structural Level or Dimension

First, let me explain what I mean by structural, particularly since I have already said that language structures thought (and I still think it is possible to think outside the lines of language, which is the magic of poetry, art, and other expressions of imagination). Here I mean, more or less, institutions and relationships among institutions, including patterned or "structured" relationships, such as regimes or systems. I am specifically concerned here with two kinds of structures across two levels of social interaction: economic structures and political structures, at local and international levels. Perhaps the number of levels should be increased, because in terms of political structures there are possibilities beyond the limits of the state and interstate system, such as local, communal,[31] religious, and tribal structures on the one hand, and transnational, nongovernmental, and regional communities of states, on the other. Economic structures are a little more straightforward, because states manage economies, including the value of currencies as well as fiscal and other aspects of monetary policy; as well as states and the arrangements and regimes formed among states at the international and regional levels, we might want to think about the European Union, or at least the "Euro-11" in a category of its own—something more than a regional regime, but less than a state itself.[32]

I have placed norms in the previous analytical category, though I should say here that I think norms do create structures, and agency, in turn, creates norms. Specifically, norms are created as a result not of the behavior or agency of a single individual, but because of the way an individual's behavior is situated within a network of relationships, a network of other individuals acting. A norm is a norm precisely because more than one individual engages in behavior consistent with it. So perhaps there is room here to contribute to contructivists' thinking about the agent-structure problem.

It may, however, disquiet some contructivists to hear that I also find some of the theorizing and research undertaken by our structuralist colleagues useful. I do not go so far as to believe that the structure itself causes something to occur, but rather that it makes some things more likely and others less likely. Structures change precisely because some agents "think outside the lines," or act beyond the limits of prevailing norms—they act in ways that alter norms. Furthermore, it is not so much the structure, but the way it is interpreted, the meaning agents assign to it, that matters. The state, for example, is perceived to be the structure through which identity groups can best secure their control over their own sociocultural practices (language, religion, and so on). Perhaps it is. But perhaps the reason for this being so is precisely what needs to be changed within the state structure in order to adapt it to the need for peaceful coexistence among diverse identity groups. The prevailing international norms at this time are often interpreted and acted on by identity groups—and their leaders—as if the state were the highest expression of nationhood. More specifically, political leaders are able to mobilize people on the basis of such identities because of the normative structure of the contemporary state. The very concept of national minorities refers to the position of nondominant identities within the state, implying a "normal" relationship between an identity group constituting a majority within the state and the ability of that group and its leaders to appropriate state authority in ways that provide greater security for the practices associated with hegemonic identity. Zimbabwe's President Mugabe's statement (in Chapter 8) that "the nation's for blacks" reflects his interpretation of the state as a nation, and the nation as constituted by ethnic identity.

In an attempt to understand the war in former Yugoslavia, both the interviews and other documented materials presented here as well as the long and much-discussed "national question" in Yugoslav politics point to the assumption of a privileged relationship between national identity and control over the institutions that constitute a state. Similarly, the prospect of being or becoming a "minority" within a state evokes fear (often well-founded) among members of such groups. That fear, in turn, becomes an important variable in relation to how ordinary people interpret specific events and respond to ethnonationalist rhetoric and propaganda. This was true, for example, of Serbs in Croatia, Croatians in Bosnia, and Albanians and Serbs in Kosovo.

My argument, then, is something like this: violent conflict along ethnic cleavages is provoked by elites in order to create a domestic political context where ethnicity becomes the only politically relevant identity. Identity, in turn, constructs the individual interest of the broader population in terms of the threat to the community defined in ethnic terms. Such a strategy is a response by ruling elites to shifts in the structure of domestic political and economic power—by constructing individual interest in terms of the threat to the group, endangered elites can fend off domestic challengers who seek to mobilize the population against the status quo, and can better position themselves to deal with future challenges to their authority.

It is possible for elites to play this "identity card" both because it taps deeply into the psychological and cognitive life of the individual, and because (or to the extent that) it is socially constructed by narratives of shared history, particularly those elements of historical narrative that refer to victimization of the group. These dynamics are not limited to environments of "ethnic conflict," as evidenced by the 1999 rise of Austria's Haider, with his political rhetoric of xenophobia and thinly veiled racism,[33] or the increase in neo-Nazi violence in Germany,[34] or indeed the persistence of racial hate groups in the United States. All three are environments of economic and political stability and relative affluence, though demographic changes may result in the loss of privilege by groups previously unaware, for the most part, of having had them, which in turn may make some individuals in those groups more vulnerable to scapegoating. In each case, the emotional appeal is articulated not only in terms of hate for the Other, but of the *justification of exclusion, hate, and harm on the grounds that the Other threatens the group to whom such appeals are made.* Even the dehumanizing violence of America's settlers toward indigenous peoples was "justified" in terms of political (and later historical) narratives making reference to the "hostile" Indians attacking "innocent" settlers, often, it was claimed, including women and children.[35]

How effective appeals aimed at arousing toxic emotions toward and the justification for dehumanizing others will be depends, to some extent, on the degree to which those they are intended to mobilize perceive themselves as and interpret their experiences from the perspective of actual or potential victims. For reasons I will discuss later, some individuals may not be very susceptible at all to such appeals because of the way they interpret their own injurious experiences. The political culture, I believe, can also make a difference, as I have suggested earlier in this chapter and in the previous one. Because identities are constructed in part in relation to historical narratives, the failure to reconcile historical harm may also therefore make future violence more likely. But even when combined with sociocultural variables that rely heavily on narratives of victimization and with historical narratives in which past harms remain unreconciled, appealing to the fears associated with exclusive identities will not necessarily provoke widespread violence without the convergence of structural variables, namely, political and economic insecurity and/or instability. Structural insecurity generates uncertainty, which is a source of stress and, as such, can weaken our psychic defenses against the cognitive processes that evoke fear and Other-directed violence.

## Violence, Cruelty, and Politics: The Modern Problematic

We stand at an extraordinary moment in human history. Human cruelty is certainly not a new phenomenon. But there are two relatively recent developments that focus our attention on it in a new way. One is the fact that during the second half of the twentieth century there seems to be a growing consensus that we, as human beings, want to do something to reduce or eliminate the incidence of human cruelty and political violence. We seem, in other words, to want to do something about it. The other development, and it has been at the center of political struggles over the period of the past three to four centuries, is the emergence of the state as the inimitable arbiter of authoritative power. These two developments share a paradoxical, and in some ways antithetical relationship, for it is precisely the emergence of the state in the image of an absolute sovereign that has enabled humans to engage in cruelty toward one another on an unprecedented scale.

Neither the state nor the sovereignty we attribute to it is natural or immutable, yet the degree to which ordinary people, people who have little reason to question either, take the notion of the sovereign state as both natural and even desirable is striking. Yet it is precisely that belief which enables those in positions of power, and those who aspire to positions of power, to make what are fundamentally emotional appeals to those who would follow or support them to engage in cruelty and violence against those who would not, or against those designated as enemies of the group. Cruelty and violence are emotional, not rational acts. They may be wanton acts, they may be acts of revenge, and they may be perpetrated by individuals who are emotionally dissociated.

Self-defense would be, intuitively as well as legally, the exception. In a twisted, pathological way, however, if our sense of self is completely identified with the group, the boundaries of the self obliterated,[36] and we are convinced that our group is the target of violence, then we may be deluded by the belief that violence *en masse* is a kind of appropriate act of self-defense. Nazi propaganda, for instance, preyed on mythologized prejudices and fears that underscored a centuries-old ideology of anti-Semitic intolerance in Europe. But would we find credibility in any claim that supporting and even participating in carrying out the Holocaust was an appropriate act of self-defense on the part of ordinary Germans? Of course not. So the question is how to diminish the occurrence of human cruelty and violence *other than self-defense* by restraining and holding accountable individuals acting in their capacity as agents of institutional authority and as ordinary people supporting and carrying out acts of cruelty and violence that they believe are sanctioned, and therefore protected, by institutional authority.[37]

It is in this respect that a series of related normative questions about violence now confronts us as international citizens. One question is whether or not we will continue to accept the view that war is a legitimate act of state, an instrument of foreign policy (the international dimension of war), and a means of contesting the right of a particular regime to maintain control of the state (the internal or "civil" dimension of war), particularly as in some cases, like Yugoslavia, it may be difficult to distinguish between international and civil war. Keeping in mind that the state as we now know it is a product of historical forces occurring primarily within and among European societies, those same historical forces have been pushing us in the direction of distinguishing between war as an act of aggression and as an act of self-defense, and away from a norm that holds war simply as an act of state, an instrument for achieving state interests in relation to other states, to be implemented arbitrarily and without restraint with respect to international norms. Having said that, it is also true that the origins of international law lie in discourses about war and peace,[38] discourses that occurred in connection with contestations over state versus church sovereignty, and from which the norm of state sovereignty emerged and evolved into a kind of Austinian legal norm,[39] in the process of which the notion of international normative constraints remained a subject of skepticism and debate. Many developments mark the progression toward acceptance of the distinction between illicit and legitimate uses of force by states: the defeat of Napoleon and more importantly, the response to it in the form of the Congress of Vienna, the codification of laws of warfare, the attempt to outlaw aggression in the Kellogg-Briand Pact, the formation of two international organizations through which collective security could be realized (the league and the UN), and efforts within the United Nations to define aggression and delineate acts prohibited by it and by the customary practice of states pertaining to acts of aggression.

What had been lacking until the end of the Cold War was the political will among a critical mass of states powerful enough to undertake enforcement actions successfully with respect to acts of aggression. This lack of political will was reflected both in the inability of the UN Security Council to agree to condemn specific suspect acts as violations of norms prohibiting aggression, and the unwillingness of any coalition of states to engage in collective security, collective enforcement, or collective self-defense in the face of suspect acts outside the framework of the United Nations. The politics of the Cold War, combined with the failure of either the European Union or NATO to articulate any common security policy outside the framework of the Cold War, resulted in the politicization of international norms regulating the use of force in most, but not all cases.[40]

The path leading away from a security policy rationalized entirely in terms of self-interested national security toward the concept of international security, however, is neither smooth nor straight. The question now confronting policy-makers and philosophers alike is whether, and if so, how, we can reconceptualize security and interests within the framework of international norms prohibiting acts of aggression by states. Those who think in terms of rational self-interest must address whether or not order itself is a value that promotes prosperity through globalization and whether aggression is an act of international violence that diminishes prosperity by disrupting the flow of people, goods, and services. Those who think in terms of humanitarian values must address whether the loss of life that is more or less inevitable as a consequence of interventions to stop aggression is justified. And these questions lead us to a second set of concerns raised by efforts to reduce violence and cruelty, concerns raised within the context of norms for the protection of human rights.

Human rights as a legal concept has evolved, not surprisingly, in relation to and in conjunction with the rise and institutionalization of the state in Western society, the notion of due process as a limitation on the state's application of coercive power against its citizens, and efforts to regulate the state's use of force in its relations with other states, or the laws of warfare. The proceedings at Nuremberg identified three categories of violations to be considered by the court: the crime of war-making or aggression (which included deliberately planning a war), war crimes or violations pertaining to the conduct of war once begun, and crimes against humanity. The first two categories regulate the state in its relations with other states, but the last category had no basis in codified, positive, international law, and therefore relied on natural-law arguments regarding acts so patently offensive to one's sense of humanity that any human being would have to conclude that these acts violate our common humanity. This is an interesting argument because it also suggests that acts which are inhuman are acts that reveal the transcendent quality of humanity. Humanity is that which makes us human, is present within every human but cannot be contained by any individual human, binds human beings to one another in a common moral community, and acting in violation of it results in a loss of our own possession of it.

It is from the perspective of an emerging international normative community that I find these prohibitions against certain acts of state most intriguing. Claims pertaining both to acts of aggression and violations of human rights are addressed to states, they regulate states as subjects of international law, and thus they move international normative discourses out of the realm of law, as simply the institutionalization of interests, into the realm of legal order, where power becomes authoritative, and authority, in turn, rests on compliance with a legal normative structure, or what Hans Kelsen called a *Grund norm*. States thus have moved from being free to exercise power arbitrarily to exercising power *authoritatively* according to the rule of law. As long as states may make, interpret, and apply norms as they see fit, without accountability to norms in any way determined by forces beyond their borders, they are not constrained by the rule of law. But when states must act within a normative framework of legal restraint, the rule of law in the interstate system becomes a reality.

Said in a slightly different way, politics and law can never be wholly divorced, as it is through power that law is ultimately sanctioned and enforceable. The rule of law begins to operate when the use of power is limited to the enforcement of the law, when power itself is subjected to legal norms. Progress in the development of the rule of law can be measured by the relative balance in the relationship between law and power or law and politics. Even in what we think of as some of the most highly developed states, as measured by the independence of the rule of law and a balance in which politics is constrained by law, it remains true that the structure of power produces an uneven and therefore somewhat arbitrary application of the law. Examples can be found in the United States and elsewhere of law failing the test of blindness on the basis of race, class, or gender privileges. The question is *to what extent and how frequently politics trumps law*, not whether law is entirely independent of power and politics. In the second half of the twentieth century we have witnessed the emergence of the political will to "do something" at an international level to reduce or even eliminate acts of cruelty and inhumanity carried out as political projects, whether in the form of war, state-making, state-destroying, ethnic conflict, human rights violations, or any degrading and discriminatory treatment of people, whether state-sponsored or state-enabled.

### Implications for Policies of Conflict Prevention and Resolution: Creating Sustainable Peace

South Africa has shed the cruelty of apartheid, civil and otherwise "dirty" wars have ended in Guatemala, El Salvador, Chile, and Argentina, North and South Korea may be on the verge of a reconciliation, if not a reunion. But elsewhere, notably Ireland and the Middle East, permanent and sustainable peace seems as elusive as ever.[41] We settle for "peace processes." We have settled for a peace process in the former Yugoslavia, and the evaluations of that process are beginning to come in. They do not look particularly hopeful, particularly if we are interested in permanent, stable, and sustainable peace.[42]

I agree with Gagnon's criticism of realist thinking[43]—that its failure to explain the war in Yugoslavia is reason enough to warrant a serious examination of other approaches. Burg and Shoup also criticize the limits of applying realist analysis to conflicts where ethnic identity is used to mobilize fear, insecurity, and violence:

> Realist theorists of international conflict suggest that such conflicts can be averted by ensuring a balance of military capabilities among the successor states, ignoring the fact that the emotions aroused by ethnonational conflict may lead each side to use newly acquired capabilities in pursuit of maximalist agendas, rather than considering them instruments of deterrence.[44]

Accordingly, the mere substitution of "ethnic groups" as actors in the role realists normally assign to states is also incapable of providing a satisfactory analysis and explanation. How we think about a problem determines how we think about possible solutions. Put simply, if the violence we call war is not understood by academics and policy makers as it is understood, experienced, and orchestrated by those involved in it, then policies and interventions aimed at solving, managing, or minimizing its occurrence will not be effective.

Perhaps some interstate wars have been as we imagine them: ordinary people, willing to become noble soldiers, defending a polity in which citizens' common identity is defined either in an organic sense of homogeneous nationality or because they are bound together by a social contract of common values, and whose way of life and physical security are under attack by aggressive Others. Most interstate wars were probably not like this. Others may have resembled our imagined wars to some extent, but also deviated in dramatic ways, such as World War II. The war in ex-Yugoslavia (like that in Rwanda), however, was a war created by political elites who used hate speech to arouse and manipulate the emotions and the fears of ordinary people; who employed pathological and criminal elements as soldiers; who exploited prejudices and circumstances of structural instability both internal to Yugoslavia and within the state system; and who created the climate of war and rallied emotions against a clear idea of the enemy, where emotions were manipulated and aroused in their most toxic and virulent form. But doesn't this scenario also in many ways resemble elements in the genesis of Hitler's rise to power and mobilization of violence in Nazi Germany?

Violent conflicts, both societal and interstate, appear to have reached a peak during the 1980s and, since 1992, have been in decline, according to a recent study of armed conflict.[45] "The challenge," say Gurr, Marshall, and Khosla, authors of the study, "is to sustain these positive trends. They result from concerted efforts to build and strengthen democratic institutions in post-Communist states and in the global South, and to negotiate settlements of revolutionary and ethnic conflicts."[46]

But violent conflict does not have to be getting worse, becoming more widespread, or increasing in occurrence for us to believe that we ought to know more about the causes of violent conflict and strategies for preventing them or building a sustainable peace in their aftermath of violence. One would hope, for instance, that we will not see another Holocaust, nor for that matter, another Rwanda or Yugoslavia. The position I have taken here is that by understanding the deeper connections between emotion, cognition, sociocultural process, and economic and political structures as they pertain to one of these cases—Yugoslavia—we can gain useful insights into forces that weaken the bonds of civility and underlie political rhetoric and actions that foster exclusion, scapegoating, and justify violence in a variety of settings. There are lessons for other conflict environments where the potential for violence waxes and wanes with the uneasiness and uncertainty of an inexperienced tightrope artist—in at-risk societies in Africa and central Eurasia, for example. There may be lessons for parties to protracted low-intensity conflicts and interminable peace processes, such as the Middle East and Northern Ireland. There may be lessons for what appear now to be older and more stable societies experiencing an increase in hate crimes and exclusionary violence. There may be lessons for those who, in the aftermath of conflict and violence, attempt reconciliation and a reconstruction of the bonds of civility in hopes of achieving stable, long-term, sustainable peace. And there may be lessons for multicultural societies in which relations among identity groups has been characterized by a history of harm-doing and injury, whether through the direct violence of war or structural violence, such as slavery and forced relocations.

## Lesson 1

*The structure of the human psyche is such that all human beings are capable of both empathy and caring as well as hostility and harm-doing toward others.*

Our capacities for humanity and inhumanity are inseparable. The capacity for human cruelty is ubiquitous. The very structure of identity itself, the ability of the individual to locate agency (and therefore responsibility) within the self and to perceive the boundaries that constitute the self, is intimately connected with our perception of the twin-born Other. The capacity for dichotomous thinking is pervasive. All humans have the potential to understand themselves in relation to others as enemies or allies, to locate the self within a metaphysical world constituted by a struggle between opposing forces. We are capable of seeing ourselves in others, for better or worse.

That ability can lead us toward a consciousness of our common humanity or into a process of projecting unwanted elements of the self onto others. But we are also capable of perceiving ambiguities and contradictions, of transcending or conceiving of alternatives to life in a world of antagonistic dichotomies. We can see ourselves in a complex world of multiple and infinite Otherness; we can also see ourselves living in a world of underlying unity. We need not be restricted by our inclination for dichotomous thinking. Perhaps it is only the first layer in the development of an individuated psyche. Our common humanity unites us with Others, but does not necessarily reduce Others to a reproduction or part of the self. We can experience and respect the agency of the other. How do we do that? By acknowledging our own capacity to do harm, we find the basis for equality with others underlying all of our differences. This does not mean that we cannot make judgments; indeed, I think it means that our judgments will have a stronger moral foundation. We can judge the actions of others as long as we are also willing to have our actions judged. Judgment entails attaching agency to an effect and holding an agent accountable. We are not judging the agent, but the agent's action. By learning to hate or condemn "what is truly worthy of hate" in ourselves and in others, and by hating "the hating self," we exercise a responsibility to judge while remaining vigilant over our own capacity to engage in exactly that behavior which we must condemn.

## Lesson 2

*Culture, social practice, historical, and other kinds of narratives intervene in the cognitive and emotional processes that determine the likelihood that individuals will be able to transcend dichotomous thinking and acknowledge and remain vigilant over their own capacity to do harm.*

Some cultures, I think, encourage the development of critical thinking — the ability to view a situation from diverse perspectives, the ability to "walk in the other's shoes," and to debate ideas without diminishing the person who has them. Some cultures contain a capacity for self-criticism, for acknowledging their own capacity to do harm as a collectivity. Societal reconciliation is therefore a benefit not only to the specific groups and individuals engaged in reconciliation but to the larger process of constructing historical narratives, because reconciliation entails an admission, at the societal, group, and individual level, of the capacity to commit harm. The implications here are for the development of a free, open, independent, and self-critical press; for educational materials that engage students in critical thinking as well as collective self-criticism. In some cases encounter groups may be helpful, as they have been in postwar Europe. In some cases truth commissions will be useful.[47]

There are many efforts and experiments in reconciliation taking place today.[48] One thing is clear, however, and that is that there must be opportunities for encounter in order for reconciliation to take place. In South Africa, for example, Wilhelm Verwoerd and others have advocated active reconciliation by encouraging white South Africans to make a commitment to find ways of acting on feelings of remorse, volunteering their time and talents for projects undertaken in black townships, for instance.[49] One of the problems in Northern Ireland, for example, is the relatively segregated structure of the Catholic and Protestant communities—most students go to schools where their own group predominates, neighborhoods tend to be separated, and, of course, people attend different churches, which are also the center of many community activities. Reconciliation is occurring, but the low level of opportunities for encounter between Catholics and Protestants has somewhat hindered its progress. A similar problem exists in the Palestinian–Israeli relationship.

## Lesson 3

*Under conditions of economic and political instability, psychic stress is more likely to induce cognitive and emotional changes that make scapegoating, projection, and ultimately violent behavior more likely.*

Here it is not so much deprivation or even relative deprivation but rapid changes in the structural conditions and the structure of power in relationships that create an environment of escalating uncertainty in which psychic stress is more likely. Germany prior to the rise of Hitler and the Nazi Party, for instance, was in the midst of wild swings in the economy. It was not only the problems of hyperinflation and depression that contributed to the social instability, but the effect these had on rapid and unpredictable redistributions of income, privilege, status, and the means necessary for daily life. In fact, we know from voting studies that the chronically poor tend to participate in political life at a much lower rate than the middle and upper classes. It was not, therefore, simply the rapid rise and fall of currency values, prices, wages, and interest rates, that created the economic conditions antecedent to war propaganda, but the effect these fluctuations had on the classes with a proportionately greater influence over political processes. It was from the ranks of the middle class that Hitler rose to power.

In the case of former Yugoslavia, the economy struggled throughout the 1980s, and when the Cold War ended and the West was no longer as strategically interested in buttressing the Yugoslav economy, for all intents and purposes it began to collapse. The decline was all the more severe because Yugoslavs were relatively successful socialists, or so they believed, with a standard of living that had been more or less steadily improving for decades but began to level off in 1979 and then rapidly decline between 1989 and 1990.[50] As discussed earlier, the rising nationalist leaders in both Croatia and Serbia traded on the discontent and distress (with the associated ethnically based prejudices and blaming) such changes provoked in order to mobilize and advance their own political interests. At the international level, the collapse of communism and the emergence of a more cohesive EU than ever before further destabilized pan-Yugoslav identity and left uncertainty about who would act should a war break out, and how.

## Lesson 4

*We must transform state polities based on imagined and mythologized kinship into truly civil societies grounded in civic identities capable of accommodating multiple identities without marginalizing any of them.*

Michael Ignatieff describes the move in terms of "ethnic nationalism" and "civic nationalism." Most Westerners think of themselves as living in societies grounded in identities of civic nationalism because they live in democracies. Not so, says Ignatieff, and I agree. Like Freud's psychopath, the former Yugoslavia is an exaggeration of the same forces present within all multicultural, multiethnic societies. The argument that ethnic nationalism is not to be found in democratic societies where much political capital has been devoted to the cultivation of civic identity, and will be found only in societies where the development of civic culture has been repressed, is not supported by reality. "If so," says Ignatieff:

> [I]t ought to be true that ethnic nationalism does not sink deep roots in societies with extensive democratic traditions. Unfortunately, this is not the case. European racism is a form of white ethnic nationalism—indeed, it is a revolt against civic nationalism itself, against the very idea of a nation based in citizenship rather than ethnicity. This revolt is gaining ground in states like Britain, Italy, France, Germany, and Spain with ample, if varying degrees of democratic experience.[51]

Ethnic identity has been endowed with what Burg and Shoup call "state-constituting status," and this claim was at the heart of the ability of republican nationalists in Croatia and Serbia to appropriate the rhetoric of ethnic identity as the basis for claims to the creation of secessionist states.[52] Anthony Smith identifies six attributes that correlate with the notion of ethnic identity:

1. A collective proper name;
2. A myth of common ancestry;
3. Shared historical memories;

4. One or more differentiating elements of common culture;
5. An association with a specific "homeland";
6. A sense of solidarity for significant sectors of the population.[53]

What became clear to me in interviews with both mid-range leaders and ordinary people in the former Yugoslavia is that, as the Croatian constitution affirms, whether international norms explicitly support this version of the nationalists' claim to statehood or not (and I think they do not), the *perception in the minds of most people* is that this relationship exists and that state-constituting claims based on ethnonationalism are legitimate. This is clearly still a basis for the ability of secessionists to maintain support among many ordinary Kosovar Albanians, though to their credit, Western policy-makers have never legitimated that claim.

In itself this is a terribly complex issue, and I cannot do justice here to the theoretical debates surrounding it.[54] There seems to be a growing recognition within both academic and policy circles of the need to take a stronger position on the distinction between protecting minorities from arbitrary and injurious treatment within states and the notion that "minorities at risk," to use Gurr's term,[55] can achieve remedy and protection only through secession, as indicated by the NATO position that while acting to end the violence in Kosovo, it did not intend to support the secession of Kosovo from Serbia.

The nation-state is a product of Western normative order stemming from, first, the incorporation (often by force or coercion) of diverse local communities united by the Roman Catholic Church under the Holy Roman Empire into a system of secular European states under a system of monarchies who rule on the basis of divine right, followed, in the eighteenth and nineteenth centuries, by the liberation of those states from the arbitrary rule of divinely ordained monarchs to populist governments within stratified societies that ruled on the basis of nationalist ideologies. Since Western political hegemony means that the Westphalia/European state is the normative basis for state-building in the rest of the world, non-Western and eastern European peoples can hardly be blamed if it is their impression that nationalist ideology is a proper basis for claims to statehood. But if interstate war was the central problem for IR experts in the twentieth century, figuring out how to foster the development of polities containing civil societies grounded in cultures of civic nationalism, within the framework of an international civil society in which states do not repress or marginalize groups or individuals on the basis of group identity, may be the central problem for the twenty-first.

## Lesson 5

*The problem of identity, politics and violence needs to be approached from an interdisciplinary and multidisciplinary perspective.*

The usefulness of an analytical schema focusing on the relationship between psychological/cognitive, sociocultural, and structural variables can be tested only by studies involving both collaborative efforts across disciplinary boundaries and social scientists and humanists willing to think "outside the lines" of their own disciplinary training and orientation. There is room here for psychologists, philosophers, political scientists, sociologists, economists, and anthropologists, to begin with.

## Lesson 6

*Feminist theorizing should not be viewed exclusively as theorizing by, about, and for women. It is also more broadly about how rules construct gender and, in turn, how gender rules construct social relations.*

Not that being by, about, and for women would not be enough, but the epistemological issues raised by feminist theorizing are pertinent to the development of constructivist analysis, and vice versa, as Elisabeth Prügl has elaborated.[56] This is not a new insight or lesson, but worth repeating here. From psychoanalytic theorizing to Wendy Brown's *Manhood and Politics*,[57] to Peterson's edited volume on *Gendered States* (1992), feminists interrogate the rules by which gender—masculinity and femininity—is constructed and their consequences for social life. Feminist theorizing is rich and diverse and while the debates among feminists as theorists continue, all theorizing, in my opinion, should be subjected to the question: How is this theory/thinking gendered?

## Lesson 7

*Democracy as we currently understand it (majority rule and minority rights, with freedom of expression and association, and due process) is not an antidote to intolerance and political violence mobilized by intolerance.*

If the case of Yugoslavia can be thought of as an exaggeration of the circumstances found elsewhere that can lead to political violence mobilized by the rhetoric of exclusion and intolerance, then what is lesson to be learned here? The breakdown of social, political, and economic structures (signaled by a breakdown in the rules constituting them) can create the antecedent conditions that enable leaders willing to exploit the human capacity for violence-producing intolerance. Democracies may even make it easier for such leaders to arise and assert influence, particularly through the use of mass media. Is there an antidote, then? Only the development of critical thinking and a citizenry willing and able to engage in it, socialization that includes an understanding of the ubiquity of the human capacity for cruelty, that teaches us to be mindful of the existence of our own "dark side" in our lives as individuals and as citizens of the polity, and learning to be vigilant self and social critics.

## Lesson 7

*Social reality is different from material reality, and we need different ways of thinking about and understanding it.*

I would not yet go so far as to say that adapting methodologies and theoretical orientations from those used to study the material world is not useful in studying the social world, only that their usefulness is limited by the fact of the social world's difference. Not only do we imagine communities, but we imagine conflicts. Those who wish to mobilize ordinary people to engage in political violence do so by appealing to our emotional life and cognitive processes. Before there is an enemy, there is the *idea* of the enemy. Before we begin to kill each other, we *think* each other to death. Before the idea of defending one's state or ethnic group is meaningful to an individual, the individual must come to *believe in the existence of the state or ethnic group*. We need models and theories for thinking about and methodologies for studying the social world that encompass its existence both in the external world of social action and in the internal life of the human psyche. Constructivism may offer an alternative, but it does not address the role of emotion. We need to know not only what the "psychological causes" of war are as well as the "structural causes," but how they are *linked*.

### The Ethical and Moral Dimension of Violence in the Former Yugoslavia

Perhaps no other event since the Holocaust has so deeply engaged the moral and ethical concerns of policy-makers, academics, and ordinary citizens than the "ethnic cleansing," rape, and deeply personal nature of violence in former Yugoslavia. It is not that other events should not have so engaged us, particularly the genocide in Rwanda, but Yugoslavia did—perhaps because Westerners could more readily identify with Yugoslavs and because even the most strategically-oriented policy-makers still found themselves puzzling over the ethical questions. So in closing, I should make some mention of the moral issues that inform so much of this study but which have not been explicitly addressed. At the heart of the analysis is the question as to whether we can develop a political framework in which humans are less likely to act injuriously toward one another on the basis of consciously or unconsciously toxic emotions (hate, fear, envy, a desire to escape one's own capacity for evil, and so on). I do not believe this is another of those idealists' calls for a reform of human nature, but rather a call for more deliberately and consciously engaging our social actions, from education to societal reconciliation and foreign policy, with the reality of the human capacity for harm as well as for caring.

One set of moral issues pertains to the question of responsibility and how to sort it out among various parties, including individuals (political leaders, war criminals), institutional actors (media and church leaders), and collective actors (people in organizations who voted for and supported nationalist leaders and their agendas, such as the HVO, HDZ, Serbian Socialist Party, paramilitary organizations, and so on). In this regard, one question confronting all of us is what the role and value are of an international tribunal in relation to the process of holding people accountable, and what kinds of domestic processes are also necessary. President Kostunica has said he supports the creation of a truth commission modeled on the Truth and Reconciliation Commission (TRC) in South Africa.[58] The Hague Tribunal has been more effective and more durable than most believed it would be. On the other hand, some South Africans believe the TRC is not enough to address and reconcile the crimes of the state there, and the appropriate parallel between South Africa and ex-Yugoslavia is not a truth commission in Serbia but a truth commission in, at least, Bosnia and preferably involving all the parties to the former conflict, meaning Serbia, including Kosovo, and Croatia, including Croatian Serbs, as well.

A second kind of moral question pertains to the role and responsibility of the international community, which admittedly is more or less a shorthand for the Western alliance rather than something representative of the larger constituency of 190 states. Though it has not been the subject of this analysis, the intervention in Kosovo, I think, was in many ways an attempt to compensate for the failure to intervene in Bosnia. But both raise the question of intervention in order to stop ongoing human atrocities. The Hague Tribunal was, after all, created before the war was over, even before the NATO intervention in 1995, and some of the worst atrocities occurred after the tribunal had opened for business. During the Kosovo intervention, some argued that the intervention itself may have *caused* Milosević to escalate his campaign against Albanians—that the intervention, in other words, would be responsible for atrocities committed in response to it. I had to wonder at the time, though, whether we could draw a parallel with the experience of World War II and the failure to confront Hitler. Hindsight is perfect, of course, but had we (the Western alliance) intervened, say, after it was clear that atrocities were being committed and a million or more innocent people had been murdered, suppose we were not actually able to stop the atrocities until Hitler had succeeded in killing one million more innocent civilians. *We would have never known that an intervention at that point had saved another four million lives.* A decision to intervene can only be made as the best judgment possible under the circumstances.

A related issue is something I believe peace researchers began to confront during the Kosovo intervention, and that was whether it is possible to distinguish between "good violence" and "bad violence." Ironically, a pamphlet I read while in Belgrade in 1995 provided some provocative ideas on this issue.[59] Nonviolence or pacifism as a philosophy, it said, meant refraining from violence toward others, but defending against violations of one's own rights with the least violent alternative possible. Violence and nonviolence, it argued, were on a continuum, each representing an extreme, and nonviolence an ideal. One should strive toward the ideal, but at the same time not allow a violation of one's rights. "Good violence," then, is violence that meets two criteria. First, it is used only as a necessary defense against the violation of one's rights, and second, the form used must be the least violent alternative capable of doing so. I am not addressing the question exhaustively here, but rather asking the reader concerned with this ethical issue to examine this proposition in relation to the violence in ex-Yugoslavia. It should also be said that once a course of intervention involving force is chosen as the least violent alternative to stop an ongoing harm, the commitment should be wholehearted. I question the integrity of an intervention in Kosovo that placated domestic political concerns among alliance members by attempting to minimize the risk to NATO pilots by flying so far above that they were more likely to inflict unintended harm on innocents.

A third moral issue is one referred to earlier, and that is whether we are witnessing the development of a kind of global civil society. Mathias Albert, Lothar Brock, Klaus Dieter Wolf, and members of the World Society Research Group writing in *Civilizing World Politics*, seem to think so. Building on the earlier work of sociologists including Weber, Simmel, Durkheim, and Tönnies, and the IR theory developed within the English School, as well as world and international society theorists such as John Burton and Hedley Bull, these authors look not only to the decline of the state as an effective manager of economic and political life, but to the emergence of a normative structure approximating a global civic community.[60] Returning to the idea of a moral community in which norms of reciprocity and interchangeability delimit the boundaries of mutual obligation as citizens, I would argue that minimally the boundaries of the community need to extend as far as the consequences of one's actions. In other words, if my actions have consequences for individuals living in Beijing, then Beijing is in my moral community. A broader interpretation, however, would include not only actions, but inactions, failures to act when action is possible. In that sense, knowing of a harm and failing to act also places individuals within the boundaries of a common moral community.

Finally, there is an ethical issue which is something of a corollary to lessons four and five above, and that is that *civil societies require a commitment to reconciliation*. There are 4,000 to 5,000 ethnic or identity groups in the world, living in fewer than 200 states. Virtually all societies are multiethnic, and even those less so are in theory open to immigration and thus potentially more multiethnic in the future. Restructuring the basis of civic obligation within the state from one based on a perception of sameness to one of mutual respect, of reciprocity and interchangeability even in light of difference, is not a moral luxury, it is a necessity. But beyond that is the equally urgent need to reconcile the basis of relationships among existing states in light of the prevalence of norms enabling majority ethnic groups to dominate the political life of the state.

Most minorities have come to live within states as a result of past conflicts with ethnic majorities. Such relationships are structured by historical narratives of injustice and injury, in which the identities of minorities are often entrenched. Transformation of the state from a polity whose ethnic majority enjoys social and cultural privilege, greater access to power, control of the political institutions, and economic advantage, into a civic polity for which the historical narrative in which civic identity is located is multifaceted, is a necessity for sustainable peace and social stability. We take the case of ex-Yugoslavia as an exaggeration of social processes found in many states in which the construction and maintenance of political identities are ongoing and contentious, and which in turn structure relationships among identity groups along lines with a potential for conflict, given the convergence of other structure and sociocultural variables. Reconciliation is a process that is not limited to the case of postconflict societies, where we take conflict to mean "violence," but it is also relevant to those societies characterized by a history of structural violence or of coping with the stress of increasingly diverse demographics, such as the United States, Canada, New Zealand, Australia, and other settler states in the Americas, or Europe, where societies are becoming more diverse as a result of postcolonial immigration, not to mention long-standing, ethnic, cold and warm wars, such as with the Basques.

Both within and among societies we must come to a new understanding of citizenship and its obligations. Only by acknowledging our capacity for inhumanity can we embrace our humanity, the *Ubuntu* on which our personhood depends. South Africa has emerged from a history of cruelty both institutionalized and personal in which up to 80 percent of the population were targets and potential victims, yet it has so far done so with unparalleled grace and relative nonviolence. There is no future, says Desmond Tutu, without forgiveness. Or, in the words of the Dalai Lama quoted at the opening of this chapter, "Love, compassion, and tolerance are needs, not luxuries. Without them humanity cannot survive." Perhaps that is the new definition of what it means to be a realist.

# Appendix I:
# Notes on Methodology

My first trip to former Yugoslavia was in the spring of 1995. I had no idea at the time how soon the war would end, though I am now certain that there were people at the time who did, or at least who knew about, planned, or anticipated the Western-supported offensive called Operation Storm, which by the end of that summer resulted in the recapturing of territory in the Croatian republic that had been held and occupied by Serbs for the previous three years. Operation Storm also resulted in the mass expulsion and exodus of hundreds of thousands of Serbs, many of whom were the original occupants of these war zones and others who had wittingly and unwittingly abetted the military occupation by moving into the area after having been cleansed and/or evicted from other areas in which they had been in the minority. And it was followed by long-overdue NATO use of air strikes, after which all parties agreed to enter into the negotiations that produced the Dayton Accord.

It was also during this period that the "safe areas," declared so by the United Nations—Gorazde, Zepa, and Srebenica—were brutally overtaken in a final Bosnian Serb offensive. Not only was Srebenica the site of what was probably the single worst case of war crimes and crimes against humanity during the war—as many as six thousand people were summarily executed—but the name of the town became synonymous with atrocities that, but for scale, provoked the criticism that the Yugoslav war represented a failure of the Atlantic alliance to make good on the promise of "never again" made at the end of World War II. Some of the people I interviewed in Belgrade in 1995, at the time these events were taking place or being planned made obscure, cryptic, and hypothetical references that I later suspected revealed their knowledge of them. In Belgrade, the war was both omnipresent and subterranean, a condition captured by the talented and acclaimed filmmaker Emir Kusturica in his award-winning 1995 movie *Underground*. Ironically, perhaps, the outdoor cinema just across the street from the apartment where I stayed played the film for nearly three weeks straight. As the city swelled with refugees, a growing number of families were showing the stress of hosting too many traumatized people, of not having enough of anything—food, beds, medicine, fuel, normalcy—and of living in a political house of mirrors. With the war on one side and sanctions on the other, the list of goods available in Belgrade was short: cigarettes, squash, tomatoes, cucumbers, cheese, eggs, and bread. McDonald's was open, and I confess to having resorted to the familiarity and reliability of a meal or two there, though I'd never seen a McDonald's where the manager wore a handgun and holster, at least not openly displayed as they were in Belgrade. Still, I had money to buy what food was available and many people didn't, and I never really got used to that. Exchanging my dollars for local currency was another matter. The banks were open but empty. The official exchange rate offered by the banks was "one for one." For a denomination of one in any currency, you could get one dinar. I was very fortunate to have made friends who showed me how to exchange my money at the local shoe store, in the back, though I had to find my own sources to determine the exchange rate of dollars for deutsch marks and then change them into dinars at the local black-market rate.

I add these personal observations not because they contribute anything to the understanding of those who lived through the war (in contrast to my privileged position of popping in and out of it once, and afterward in and out of postwar ex-Yugoslavia once or twice a year over the next few years), but for the benefit of some of my colleagues and other readers who will better understand the way in which my experience of the situation (my positioning, my context, as it were) informed what I learned from this study and how I learned it. One of my most important learning experiences occurred on my first night in Belgrade, when I got lost walking back to the apartment from the anti-war center and found myself in the midst of a gathering (and madding) crowd, all singing the same songs and moving in the direction of the Parliament grounds. (The first thing I learned was the importance of spending some time each day learning the Cyrillic alphabet used on all the street signs!) Thousands collected around a rise near the Parliament building, where they had set on fire what looked to me like their own flag (which I had seen on the back of my Berlitz pocket guide to Yugoslavia). For a few minutes I couldn't make any sense out of what was happening, and had to rely on purely intuitive instincts in order, minimally, to determine whether or not I was in danger. And I could think of only one thing: this was the emotional power of nationalism, in spite of the apparent contradiction between that perception and the flag being burned. And I also quickly reasoned that this was no place for an American who was not with the press or with local friends. Later I found out that the flag was not a Yugoslav flag, but the Croatian flag, and the demonstration was precipitated by a basketball game won by the Serbian team but which provoked a walkout by the Croatian team in protest.

The hardships endured by the people in Belgrade were experienced in varying degrees by the people elsewhere in former Yugoslavia, with an important exception: to the extent that people expected that the territorial space of the former republics ought to represent "zones of safety" to those whose national identities were celebrated by the names of the republics (Slovenia for Slovenes, Croatia for Croats, Serbia for Serbs, Macedonia for Macedonians and Bosnia for everyone), the territorial spaces in other republics became the central war zones, the places where the killing and cruelty took place. But even here, even to say that Serbia was not in the war zone, we must note an exception, and that is Kosovo. In many ways, the war—the "ethnic cleansing," the blurring of the lines distinguishing the territory of one nation from another, police officer from soldier, and soldier from civilian, the stereotyping that underlies hate speech and war mongering and makes prejudices into an ideology—these things began in Kosovo. And Kosovo is "in" Serbia. But did the cosmopolitan people in Zagreb really live any closer to the war than the cosmopolitan people in Belgrade just because the war zone was inside the boundaries of the Croatian republic? One of the central issues that confronted and confounded the people in former Yugoslavia, as well as their European neighbors and others, was how the violence contested the relationship between socially constructed ethnonational identities and the territorial boundaries of states. This was in many ways a war over incongruous claims to the legitimate location of boundaries delineating inside/outside.

Several psychologists I interviewed spoke of a Yugoslav "Vietnam syndrome." Many of the young men walking the streets and frequenting the bars and cafes in Belgrade were undoubtedly veterans of an unimaginably inhumane war taking place a half-day's drive away. Many were, in fact, AWOL until Milosević carried out a "mobilization" in which the identity cards of every man of military age were checked, and if born in Bosnia, the men were forcibly returned to the killing fields. I heard some of their stories, firsthand and second, though in these conversations I dispensed with the formality of the more structured interviews and interview questions. I listened to every story anyone wanted to tell. Some certainly trusted in me with little or no reason to do so other than that they were possessed of some self-consciousness about the profundity of the events taking place and in which they had a role. Some may have trusted me because of who I associated with, or because they felt misunderstood, or because the others simply told stories as they wished them to be told (particularly by a Western academic). The same mixed motives no doubt informed all of my respondents.

Although I had hoped to go from Belgrade to Zagreb during the 1995 trip, the logistical problems seemed insurmountable and unnecessarily risky. Spending all of the time and money I had by staying in Belgrade, it turned out, offered more than enough opportunities to interview key people whose perspectives and politics were dramatically diverse. My remaining trips to the region, therefore, took place in the aftermath of the war, the Dayton Accord, and efforts to implement it. It would have been ideal both to obtain a "representative sample" of respondents from all republics and to have interviewed them in roughly the same or comparable historical moments. None of this was possible. I talked more to what John Paul Lederach (1997) characterizes as "mid-range" leaders, educated elites whose professional or political roles placed them in a position to mediate between events and policies originating at the national level but with the most significant and tangible consequences at the local level, in the towns and cities (or as the Western press like to call them all, the "villages") that became the front lines of this uncivil war. I also interviewed a very few people who rubbed shoulders with national leaders as advisors, as high-ranking party members, or as fellow politicians.

Although initially most of my respondents in Belgrade were involved in one way or another with an antiwar movement, I was also able to spend considerable time talking with people who occupied a variety of political positions in relation to the dissolution crisis. While no doubt the antiwar folks knew of my sympathies for nonviolence (and democracy and reason), my discussions with those more or less supportive of Mr. Milosević in particular, or who articulated variations on the nationalist project in general, did not seem particularly inhibited by any suspicion regarding my sympathies. They talked with me as much from a philosophical as a political level, something I regarded as rather chilling and deeply disturbing. I couldn't help but think that they regarded themselves as philosopher-kings but, from my perspective, kings who took no responsibility whatsoever for the cruel and brutal ways their visions were carried out by ordinary people under the leadership of criminals. There were many complex lessons here about denial, its role in political life, and about how easily narratives of victimization, even when they originate from the experience of victimization, can be converted into ideologies of violence.

My remaining trips to the region took place as people tried to reconstruct and reconcile. Anti-war activism had turned into reconciliation activism. Perceptions of winning and losing were reshaping histories. Winners were less apologetic for their tactics, losers were beginning to construct their own new victimization narratives. Dissenting opinions on why and how the war started were in some ways both more tolerated and more obscure. Thoughtful and critical minds across time and space found common ground. In Croatia and Bosnia I also interviewed a disproportionate number of mid-range leaders and a few national politicians, but I spent more time with other, ordinary people in informal encounters as well. I found mirror-image nationalisms in Croatia and Serbia, both emanating from unique historical perspectives in which their own marginalization played a central role in rationalizing violence during the 1990 to 1995 wars. I found many Slovenes both sympathetic and aloof, unselfconscious of the degree to which their own fate was shaped favorably by the fact of near-homogeneity among the Slovene people. Others very definitely understood how and why they were spared more violence, and this, in turn, emphasized their sympathy for everyone who was not spared, without assigning responsibility in a simplistic way to one side or the other.

The material facts regarding my methodology are, first of all, that I was not an expert or specialist in the area (regionally, the Balkans, southeast Europe) or in the politics of communist or postcommunist states, or on Yugoslavia. I did not speak the language (or any of its variations) and did not have the resources to learn other than in the field and for the purpose of getting around and showing respect for the people by making the effort to learn their languages. The vast majority of people spoke to me in English, and elsewhere I used interpreters. The disadvantages of my nonspecialization are obvious. The advantages had to do with being able to come to the task of understanding what was happening on its own terms, within an analytical framework of intergroup conflict and of the role of historical injuries and the consequences of failing to reconcile them in constructing intergroup conflict, and with an open and even skeptical view of the relationship between identity and state-building or state-destroying. Second, as I have pointed out, most of the people I interviewed formally were educated and professional. I reason that they were thoughtful, reflective, and critical about the genesis of events culminating in violence, as well as about how to reconstitute civil societies in its aftermath. At the same time they were in touch on a daily basis and as part of the routine of their professional lives with ordinary people at the grassroots level. I also spent some time talking with people in collective (or refugee) centers, and in a variety of social settings as opportunities arose. Third, most of the people I interviewed in depth were from the larger, metropolitan areas of Belgrade, Zagreb, Sarajevo, and Ljubljana. But I did travel around a bit, had many informal encounters and discussions, and many of the people I met in collective centers were from rural areas. Finally, while many of the respondents were opposed to the violence in one way or another, others were complicitous in it. Besides, there was already an extensive public record of the position and perspectives of those who favored or even conjured the violence. I have made extensive use of those sources in addition to the lengthy interviews with individual respondents.

As the time approached for my first trip, I developed a set of questions and an introduction to them in order to structure interview sessions around issues of the war, history, identity, and the future. Any modifications or variations on these questions during actual interviews over the next four years were minor and did not substantively alter the context of the interviews (this would primarily apply to the content of the introduction). When I first traveled to Croatia, I had the questions translated into the language then widely regarded as a distinct Croatian language. I did not, as I have done in tele-phone survey research, read the introductory statement each time. To put respondents at ease, I often ad-libbed, and I often asked follow-up questions.

## Interview Introduction and Questions

Although I am a political scientist, I am interested in learning more about the psychological dimension of the current war: how and why it started, why it continued, what it will take to heal from the war and create the condi-tions necessary for a lasting and stable peace. I know these are complicated questions, and I do not underestimate the difficulty of answering them. I would just like to know your perspective. I hope you will understand that I need to ask everyone the same questions. I realize that these are sensitive and difficult issues. I am also trying to research the issue of identity and its rela-tionship to conflict. From my point of view, these are not problems unique to the Balkans, though they have been more of a problem with very sad and more severe consequences here recently. Are there any questions you would like to ask me before we begin?

### On the War

1. What would you say caused the war? How do you understand the events leading to the war?
2. Do you believe there was an aggressor? Do you believe it was started by one side or another?
3. When thinking about how the war started, what role, if any, do you think was played by the media? The Church? The economy?
4. I know that not everyone wanted a war, not everyone was involved in fighting or supporting the war. There are/were antiwar groups who actually opposed the war, for example. What percentage of the popu-lation would you say is/was actually involved in fighting or supporting the war? What age group, mostly?
5. I realize that political leaders are largely responsible for starting the war, but why do you think people followed them and carried out the violence and the relocations?
6. Is there anything you would like to add on this topic?

### On History

1. From what I have studied so far, it looks like as many as one in five people in World War II were either fighting or were killed. Are you aware of any effects World War II had on your family? If so, would you elaborate?
2. Did you learn about World War II from your family, friends, or neigh-bors? If so, what? In school?

3. What impressions about World War II do you recall during the years when Tito was president of Yugoslavia?
4. Do you recall getting any impressions from your family or neighbors about other ethnic groups? About ethnic relations?
5. What else did you learn in general about the history of Yugoslavia in school or in your family?
6. Is there anything else you would like to add on this topic?

*On Identity*

1. How did you identify yourself before the recent war? What did that mean to you? Did you see yourself as both a Croat/Serb/Muslim/Bosnian and a Yugoslav?
2. How did you think of Yugoslavia as compared to the rest of the world, for instance, the Soviet countries, or Western Europe, or the other countries of central and eastern Europe?
3. Before the recent war, were you aware of ethnic prejudices?
4. Did being Yugoslav have any meaning for you? If so, could you talk about that a little bit?
5. Were you aware of changes in people's identities that took place during the recent war?
6. Is there anything else you would like to add on this topic?

*On the Future*

1. What role do you think the international community—the European Community and the UN—could have played to prevent the war or to end it sooner?
2. What role do you think the international community could play now to prevent further violence?
3. What do you think of the War Crimes Tribunal?
4. Where do you come from? What are the main problems in your community today?
5. Do you think there is hope for rebuilding a civil society in Croatia/Bosnia/Serbia? What are the main obstacles?
6. Were there any problems with civil society in your community before the war? Did people of different ethnic groups get along well before the war? Were there any problems with the local authorities, the police, before the war?
7. What was the ethnic composition of your community before the war? After the war?
8. What do you think will be the future of your country?

# NOTES

## Preface

1. Taken from "Quiet Voices from the Balkans," *New Yorker* March 15, 1993, pp. 4–6.
2 Nicholas Onuf, "Constructivisim: A User's Manual," in Kubálková, Onuf, and Kowert, eds., *International Relations in a Constructed World* (New York: M. E. Sharpe, 1998).

## Chapter 1: International Relations Theory and the Problem of Violence

1. Philip Gourevitch, *We Wish to Inform You that Tomorrow We Will Be Killed with Our Families: Stories from Rwanda* (New York: Farrar Straus and Giroux, 1998), p. 202.
2. Robert F. Heizer and Alan F. Almquist, *The Other Californians* (Berkeley, CA: University of California Press, 1971), p. 13.
3. Ibid., p. 30.
4. Report from the Leadership Conference on Civil Rights, Arnold Aronson, President, Leadership Conference on Education Fund, and Dorothy I. Height, Chair of the Leadership Conference on Civil Rights, found at: http://www.civilrights.org/lcef/hate/toc.html, accessed November 16, 1999.
5. Mary Williams Walsh, "A Tribunal in a Time of Atrocities," *Los Angeles Times*, August 30, 1995.
6. Matt Bai and Vern E. Smith, "Evil to the End: A Racist is Sentenced for a Gruesome Murder. But the Hateful Fringe He Represents Will Certainly Outlive Him." *Newsweek,* March 8, 1999.
7. Crystal Maxwell, News Director, Wyoming Network, Inc., "McKinney Guilty of Felony Murder, Second Degree Murder," updated November, 3, 1999, found on the internet at: http://www.cheyennenetwork.com/news/, accessed November 16, 1999.
8. Crystal Maxwell, News Director, Wyoming Network, Inc., "Prosecution Rests," updated October 29, 1999. Available at: http://www.cheyennenetwork.com/news/, accessed November 16, 1999.
9. Daniel Jonah Goldhagen, *Hitler's Willing Executioners: Ordinary Germans and the Holocaust* (New York: Vintage Press, 1997), p. 190.
10. See V. Spike Peterson, "Introduction," *Gendered States: Feminist (Re)visions of International Relations Theory* (Boulder, CO: Lynne Rienner, 1992). This book also contains an excellent bibliography of feminist work in IR.
11. John Darby and Roger Mac Ginty, ed., *The Management of Peace Processes* (London: Macmillan Press, 2000), p. 2.
12. Hate Crimes Sentencing Enhancement Act of 1994, as quoted in Aronson and Height, "Report from the Leadership Conference on Civil Rights."
13. On the connection between violence and state-making, see Youssef Cohen, Brian R. Brown, and A. F. K. Organski, "The Paradoxical Nature of State Making: A Violent Creation of Order." *American Political Science Review* 75:4 (1981): 901–910.

14. As reported in *The Guardian*, "Huge Rise in Race Crime, Reveals Government." Accessed March 12, 2001 at: http://www.guardianunlimited.co.uk/racism/Story/0,2763,424016,00.html "Special Report: Policing Crime," Thursday January 18, 2001. See also European Monitoring Centre of Racism and Xenophobia (EUMC), Annual Report Part II, 1998, "Looking Reality in the Face: The Situation regarding Racism and Xenophobia in the European Community," and Annual Report 1999.
15. The number of war deaths has become a subject of debate, with political implications attaching to all perspectives. A figure that often appears is 250,000. According to Project Ploughshares staffmember Ken Epps, who participated in the Department of National Defense's Security and Defense Forum field excursion to Bosnia and Croatia in April 2000, the UN estimates that during the war in Bosnia, 156,500 civilians were killed before the Srebenica and Zepa massacres in the summer of 1995, and 81,500 military deaths. To this total of 238,000 might then be added some estimate of the Srebenica and Zepa civilian deaths. The *International War and Peace Reporter*, in its *Tribunal Updates*, estimates that 7,000 men and boys were killed in Srebenica alone. More liberal estimates go as far as 8,000–10,000 (including those of Ken Epps). Finally, somewhere around 10,000 were killed during the six-month war in Croatia, bringing a fair estimate of the total to between 251,000 and 258,000 combined civilian and military deaths, of which approximately 70 percent would be civilians. See *Ploughshares Monitor,* June 2000, "Bosnia-Herzegovina: Attaining Human Security" by Ken Epps. Available at: http://www.ploughshares.ca/content/monitor/monj00e.html.
16. Walker Connor, "Nation-Building or Nation-Destroying?" *World Politics* 24 (1972): 319–355; "A Nation Is a Nation, Is a State, Is an Ethnic Group Is a . . ." *Ethnic and Racial Studies* 1 (1978): 377–400; "When Is a Nation?" *Ethnic and Racial Studies* 13 (1990): 99; "From Tribe to Nation," *History of European Ideas*, vol. 13 (New York: Pergamon, 1991), pp. 5–18; and *Ethnonationalism: The Quest for Understanding* (Princeton, NJ: Princeton University Press, 1994).
17. See Homi K. Bhabha, ed., *Nation and Narration* (New York: Routledge, 1990).
18. Michael Ignatieff, *Blood and Belonging: Journeys into the New Nationalism* (New York: The Noonday Press, Farrar, Straus, and Giroux, 1993).
19. "Mugabe: Whites Must Recognize Nation's for Blacks," *Bozeman Chronicle*, June 18, 2000, p. 42.
20. Cynthia Weber, *Simulating Sovereignty: Intervention, the State, and Symbolic Exchange* (Cambridge, U.K.: Cambridge University Press, 1995), p. 27.
21. We will see how the history of Croatia as a "thousand year old state" is recounted in the new Croatian Constitution. Perhaps the perceived threat to organic identities is also at work in the apparently growing appeal of racist groups in Europe. See European Monitoring Centre of Racism and Xenophobia (EUMC), Annual Report Part II, 1998, "Looking Reality in the Face: The Situation regarding Racism and Xenophobia in the European Community," and Annual Report 1999.
22. Durkheim, however, referred to these alternative forms of solidarity as "mechanical" and "organic." See Emile Durkheim, *The Division of Labor in Society* (New York: Free Press, 1893/1964).
23. An objection to or concern with this argument is sometimes raised in connection with the claims of indigenous peoples, but I would counter that what indigenous peoples seek is the ability to control their own political destiny within the framework of their own society as constituted by cultural affinities and traditions over time. That those cultural affinities often occur in conjunc-

tion with perceived organic or genetically based distinctions is less important than who controls the allocation of values within self-identified indigenous societies.

24. See Fritjof Capra, *The Tao of Physics* (Berkeley, CA: Shambala, 1975).
25. Pierre Bourdieu, *Language and Symbolic Power*, trans. Gino Raymond and Matthew Adamson, ed., intro. by John B. Thompson (Cambridge, MA: Harvard University Press, 1991).
26. William Connolly, "The Liberal Image of the Nation," in D. Ivison, P. Patton, and W. Sanders, eds., *Political Theory and the Rights of Indigenous Peoples.* (Cambridge, U.K.: Cambridge University Press, 2000).
27. "Tutu and Franklin: A Journey towards Peace," *Teachers Guide* (Washington, DC: Wisdom Works, 2001), p. 9.
28. While it may be useful to draw a contrast between these two societal forms, I do not subscribe to the simplistic view that the smaller, more local society is a less evolved antecedent social form in relation to the more complex modern state.
29. See Vamik D. Volkan, *The Need to Have Enemies and Allies: From Clinical Practice to International Relationships* (Northvale, NJ: Jason Aronson, Inc., 1988).
30. Anne Pitsch, "1995–1998 Groups in Open Rebellion with the State." July 3, 1998, Minorities at Risk Project. Available at http://www.bsos.umd.edu/cidcm/mar/autonomy.htm, accessed December 7, 1999.
31. I also realize that there is a case to be made from a structural perspective in explaining the failure at first and then intervention later in both World War II and the former Yugoslavia. I am not rejecting such explanations, only arguing that they are partial and, on questions like genocide, inadequate.
32. Anatol Rappoport, *Peace: An Idea Whose Time Has Come* (Ann Arbor, MI: University of Michigan Press, 1992).
33. See Ole Waever, "Figures of International Thought: Introducing Persons Instead of Paradigms," in Iver B. Neumann and Ole Waever, eds., *The Future of International Relations: Masters in the Making* (New York: Routledge, 1997).
34. Kalevi J. Holsti, *The State, War, and the State of War* (Cambridge, U.K.: Cambridge University Press, 1996), pp. 25–26.
35. See also Christopher R. Browning, *Ordinary Men: Reserve Battalion 101 and the Final Solution in Poland* (New York: Harper Collins, 1992).
36. I would like to point out here that history operates as both an intermediary and an instrumental variable; intermediary in the sense of representing experiences interpreted and passed on from one generation to the next, and instrumental when the interpretation of history is undertaken by calculating elites in service to their objective of mobilizing people to action, or to support elite actions.
37. The psychological dimension has not been entirely overlooked (see Volkan 1996), but has not been applied to an integrated analysis of the interplay between history, identity, culture and intergroup conflict in the case of the Balkans
38. C. F. Alford, *What Evil Means to Us* (Ithaca, NY: Cornell University Press, 1999), p. 7.

## Chapter 2: What Happened in Yugoslavia?

1. Priscilla B. Hayner, *Unspeakable Truths: Confronting State Terror and Atrocity* (New York: Routledge, 2001).
2. This issue will be taken up later, in Chapter 8.

3. This may seem like a harsh view, but I believe the Allied action was ultimately mobilized around the issue of Hitler's aggression rather than his atrocities, and the concentration camp liberations occurred only after his death and defeat. I too remember filmed images of grateful survivors, but I always think at the same time of silent voices of those who did not survive. It is from their point of view that I make the statement regarding the Allies' failure to intervene in the Holocaust.

4. The dissonance created by the destruction of and in the former Yugoslavia was eventually resolved with the "realization" in Europe and the United States that "Yugoslavia" was *not actually in Europe*. It was in the *Balkans*, after all!

5. Mark Almond, *Europe's Backyard War: The War in the Balkans* (London: Heinemann, 1994).

6. Though it is raised in most books on Yugoslav politics and the war, the most comprehensive single source on the role of the "national question" in prewar Yugoslavia in Ivo Banac, *The National Question in Yugoslavia: Origins, History, Politics* (Ithaca, NY: Cornell University Press, 1984).

7. I quote from personal correspondence with Hans-Joachim Lanksch on the term *"shqiptar"* because it was used in a derogatory way by some Serbs, but also as the proper Albanian language word for Albanians. Says Mr. Lanksch: "Nowadays, many Albanians in Kosova try to adopt standard Albanian and, therefore, write and pronounce *shqiptar,* whereas it is mainly older people (mainly in the villages) who maintain *shqyptar.* It is true that in Serbian the term was *"siptar,"* conceived by Albanians in Kosova as derogative as the ethnonym "Albanian" in Serbian is *"albanac."* It was still in the time before Milosevic's regime that Serbians abandoned the term *"siptar."* E-mail correspondence, May 22, 2000.

8. Interview June 1995, Belgrade.

9. Dubravka Ugrešić, *Cultures of Lies* (University Park, PA: Pennsylvania University Press, 1998), p. 272. Published originally in Dutch in 1995, quoted from the English translation.

10. Although it is an edited compilation, my first recommendation would be *Burn This House: The Making and Unmaking of Yugoslavia,* ed., Jasminka Udovički and James Ridgeway (Durham, NC: Duke University Press, 1997). The chapters, written by a variety of authors including scholars, intellectuals, former diplomats, and journalists from both in and out of the area, is a surprisingly coherent read, beginning with a chapter summary of the shifting boundaries, territorial control, and cultural layering under imperial and feudal influences, proceeding to the period of state-building, Yugoslavia under Tito, and then focusing the majority of the book on the recent conflict including important chapters on war resistance movements in the region and international dimensions of the conflict. A by no means exhaustive list (over 150 books have been written on the subject in the past six years!) of more detailed and conventional histories are: Lampe (1996) on the whole of the former Yugoslavia; Donia and Fine (1994) and Malcolm (1994) on Bosnia; and more journalistic (but well researched, comprehensive, and richly analyzed) accounts are Glenny (1992), Silber and Little (1997), Maass (1996), P. Cohen (1998), and Hall (1994). Susan Woodward (1995) and Sabrina Ramet (1996) have written very detailed, political analyses on the breakup of the former Yugoslavia. The Donia and Fine book also contains an excellent bibliography of historical readings by period. Many readers still find that Rebecca West's *Black Lamb and Grey Falcon,* written after a six-week trip through Yugoslavia just before Hitler's takeover of the area, is still a uniquely informative, though very long, read. She is also criticized for being too pro-

Serbian and anti-German, though almost all nonacademic (and some academic) accounts contain such sympathies or affinities for one or the other culture/group/perspective. Editorial and reader reviews are readily available, particularly on the Web, and this should help any reader of any book make an assessment of the completeness, bias, or comparative value of any book available on the subject today.

11. Interview by the author with L. C., September 27, 1998.

12. Some Albanians claim to be descendants of the Illyrians. Other early tribes include the Thracians and Dardanians, though the latter may have belonged in the Illyrian grouping. The relationship is debated among academics. See Malcolm (1998),Vickers (1998), and Wilkes (1992). From the perspective of my argument, particularly in chapters 5 and 6, these are significant assertions and contestations because they reflect the way legitimacy is believed to follow from naturalized claims about the relationship between identity and territory.

13. This is somewhat ironic, because the Croatian nationalism that emerged in conjunction with the most recent secession, independence, and conflict in Bosnia has claimed the Kajkavian or Kajkavski dialect spoken in Zagreb and northwest Croatia as its official language, though this is not without controversy even today.

14. The revived unification movement came to be known as "Yugoslavism" in the late nineteenth century.

15. Southern Serbia, where Kosovo is located, also known as "old Serbia," remained under Ottoman control until the First Balkan War of 1912.

16. See Lampe, op. cit., pp. 39–62.

17. Significantly, the Ottoman army used to try to suppress the Serbian rebellion was "led by the irregular units of Bosnian Muslims that were the closest at hand" (Lampe 1996:48).

18. Sven Balas, "The Opposition in Croatia," in Udovički and Ridgeway, eds. *Burn this House: The Making an Unmaking of Yugoslavia*, pp. 265–278.

19. Tito downplayed this history, which remains controversial. Tudjman, a historian, has offended the Serbs by claiming that no more than 60,000 people were killed at the compound of camps known as Jasenovac, whereas the most exaggerated Serb sources claim over one million. A number of sources who seem to have no interest in biasing the data have always held the number to be closer to 600,000. Additionally, Jasenovac was the worst, but not the only camp run by the Ustaše, and many more deaths occurred directly at the hands of the Nazi occupiers with whom the Croatian government was collaborating. According to Lampe (1996) only about 2,000 of the 36,000 Jews who lived in Croatia and Bosnia-Herzegovina before the war survived.

20. According to Crnobrnja (1994), the "notion of a Muslim 'nation' was introduced by the constitution in 1963" (p. 21), but according to Ramet (1992), this designation did not entail equal status to the other constitutive nations until after 1971 (p. 55). The designation as a nation was reserved for Bosnian Muslims, and was distinct from the designation of an individual as religious Muslim.

21. The rationale, for example, for relegating Albanians to the status of protected minorities or nationality but not including them as a constitutive nation, was that, like Hungarians and others, they were a national minority for whom there was a national state outside the Yugoslav framework.

22. Some of the change may be attributed to the structural change in the status of "Muslim" as a category of ethnic identification to a nationality with participatory rights equal to the other "constituent nations" of Yugoslavia. It is not clear that this is the case, however, for while a sharp decline in those

identifying themselves as "Yugoslavs," some of whom were of "mixed" heritage, occurred just before the constitutional recognition of Muslim nationality, it just as sharply increased afterward.

23. As a result of the conflict, the Serb population in Eastern Slavonia has declined from approximately 600,000 to 200,000.

24. Attempts to reform the economy in a market-oriented direction had begun as early as the mid-1960s but were implemented inconsistently and resulted in high unemployment, and Yugoslav political leaders abandoned them (Kovacevic and Dajic 1994:13).

25. Interview with Sonja Biserko, July 7, 1995, Belgrade.

26. Interview with Alexander Romanovic, June 1998.

27. I found these suspicions of conspiracy and collusion common among mid-level leaders, many but not all of whom were antiwar, in all four republics I visited (Slovenia, Serbia, Croatia, and Bosnia).

28. See note 15 in Chapter 1.

29. Interview in July 1997 with Nina Kadic, who is compiling data for the War Crimes Tribunal.

30. Patrick Moore, "Bosnian Croat Nationalists Declare Federation Null and Void," *Radio Free Europe/Radio Liberty Newsline*, March 1, 2001, no. 42, Part II. Available at: http://www.rferl.org/newsline/search/

31. SFOR Transcript, Joint Press Conference January 11, 1999, 11:30 hours, Coalition Press Information Center, Tito Barracks. Available at: www.nato.int/ifor/trans/trans.htm

32. Mihailo Marković, interview July 15, 1995.

33. Mladin Životić, interview July 18, 1995.

34. IWPR'S Tribunal Update, No. 224, June 4–9, 2001.

35. IWPR'S Balkan Crisis Report, No. 258, June 22, 2001.

36. Op. cit. See "Bosnian Serbs Spurn Reconciliation," by Gordana Katana, and "Croatian Government Falling Apart? By Dragutin Hedl in that issue.

## Chapter 3: The Social Construction of Man

1. See also Ronnie D. Lipschutz and Beverly Crawford, *The Myth of "Ethnic Conflict": Politics, Economics, and Cultural Violence* (Berkeley, CA: University of California, 1999).

2. Roy Gutman notes in his Forward to Alexandra Stiglmayer's book *Mass Rape: The War against Women in Bosnia-Herzegovina* (Lincoln, NE: University of Nebraska Press, 1993) that:

> Women of childbearing age were the primary targets. . . . In this sense the pattern of the rapes of unmarried women of childbearing age fulfills another definition of genocide—the attempt to block procreation of the group. Yet so many cases have come to light of women of sixty and girls under twelve being raped, gang-raped, often in front of their relatives, that genocide seems too dry a description of unreined savagery. Sexual humiliation was not restricted to females; in repeated instances, men held in detention camps report being forced to commit sexual acts on each other and to witness pubic castrations that prisoners had to carry out against each other. (x)

3. Interview in Zagreb, July 1997, with Nina Kadic, who reported these figures from her work at the Hague Tribunal.

4. Stipe Šuvar, *Consequences of Ethnic Cleansing in the Area of the Former Yugoslavia*, paper presented to the International Summer School Conference of the Southeast European Research Unit of University of Glasgow, September 1998, Korčula, Croatia.

5.  J. W. Honig and N. Both *Srebenica: Record of a War Crime* (Penguin Books, 1996), and Roy Gutman, *A Witness to Genocide* (New York: MacMillan Press, 1993). The Omarska camp discovery probably generated the most press coverage and controversy of any event in the war, including accusations of misrepresentation by photojournalists.

6.  Alexandra Stiglmayer, ed., trans. Marion Faber (Lincoln, NE: University of Nebraska Press, 1993).

7.  International Criminal Tribunal for the Former Yugoslavia (ICTY), Case Number IT-95–12-R61, unofficial transcripts, April 2, 1996. During this stage of the testimony, the attorney for the prosecution is entering into the record, as a sworn statement, a summary of the testimony given to him by several "protected" witnesses. This procedure enables the sworn testimony of witnesses who have requested that their identity is not made public to be presented orally as evidence to the tribunal.

8.  The language used here—a report about the testimony by a third party— would in trial proceedings in U.S. courts be considered hearsay evidence. The tribunal proceedings are directed by Rules of Procedure which can be read at www.un.org/icty/basic/rpe/IT32_rev17con.htm This particular hearing was conducted pursuant to Rule 61, "Procedure in Case of Failure to Execute a Warrant," which is a pretrial proceeding and during which the witness's identity remains protected and undisclosed., If this case reaches the trial stage, as I understand the rules, the witnesses' identities will be revealed to the court in a closed session.

9.  "HVO" refers to the Croat Council of Defense, the military arm of the Bosnian Croats supplied by the ruling party in Zagreb (see Silber and Little 1997:293).

10. I will leave out here several lines of questioning pertaining to the whereabouts of her husband.

11. C. Fred Alford, *What Evil Means to Us* (Ithaca, NY: Cornell University Press, 1997). I am paraphrasing Alford's claim that the experience of "evil" in Western culture consists of "Pleasure in hurting and lack of remorse" (which is also the title of his second chapter). I would add that we are assuming here that this definition applies to only to morally mature, that is, adult, individuals, conceding that courts routinely struggle with the issue as to what (age, mental capacity, etc.) constitutes moral maturity.

12. *Faces of the Enemy*, a film by Sam Keen, 1987.

13. This is a paraphrase of the 1948 Genocide Convention.

14. Some have taken up this issue. See Leslie E. Sponsel and Thomas Gregor, eds., *The Anthropology of Peace and Nonviolence* (Boulder, CO: Lynne Rienner, 1994) and Bruce D. Bonta, *Peaceful Peoples: An Annotated Bibliography* (Scarecrow Press, 1993).

15. This rationalization can take the form of an ideological construct, dehumanization, or, as in the case of capital punishment and other forms of retribution, a belief that harm-doing is a justifiable response to the victim's own actions.

16. This is a paraphrase of Nagel, "Constructing Ethnicity: Creating and Recreating Identity and Culture," in *Social Problems*: 41 (1994): 153–176.

17. Dzevad Karahasan, *Sarajevo: Exodus of a City* (New York: Kodansha International, 1993), pp. 69–70.

18. C. Fred Alford, *Group Psychology and Political Theory* (New Haven, CT: Yale University Press, 1994).

19. These references by no means exhaust work on the intersection between psychoanalytic, feminist, and political theory, but among them one will find

threads leading elsewhere. I should also note that I am not engaging these theorists in a critical discourse either with my account or among themselves, but rather as the platform from which my own theoretical thinking on the structure of the self and the problem of difference is launched., Finally, while the theoretical literature in the past decade or so, particularly in the areas of postcolonial and critical theory, has been very much concerned with the "self/Other question," and Iver Neumann (1997) has even critiqued the limits of self/Other analysis, I take its usefulness here as unproblematic.

20. Jacques Lacan, *The Language of the Self: The Function of Language in Psychoanalysis*, trans. Anthony Wilden (New York: Delta Publishers, 1968), p. 163.

21. Iver Neumann, *The Limits of Subject/Other Perspectives*, paper presented to the panel Beyond Self/Other: Security Identities After the Cold War, 38th Annual ISA Convention, Toronto, March 18–22, 1997.

22. Anthropological studies indicate that in some societies the "self" and "other" are constructed in different ways, ways Westerners might say are not "self/Other" at all, but something of a more seamless stream of agency distributed across a contextualized relationship, and sets of relationships constructed as "we" and "they" in ways that do not resemble in-group/out-group identities in Western cultures. I am drawing here very much on the work of Western thinkers—Klein, Lacan, Alford—and am myself a Western thinker, so in this sense, this story is the story of a Western self.

23. Interview with Kull by Sam Keen, in the film *Faces of the Enemy*, 1986.

24. I am not contrasting indigenous and modern cultures as opposites, nor am I suggesting that there are not patriarchal, intolerant non-Western cultures, but rather that in contrast to modernist Western cultures, the incidence of gender ambiguity and tolerance of difference and even pacifist cultures is much higher among indigenous peoples.

25. According to Chodorow (1978), Girls also seem to undergo the process of individuation at a later age, roughly, adolescence.

26. This does not mean that such contact needs to be parental. It may be provided by variety of sources—other relatives, friends, or community members, for example.

27. Nancy Chodorow, *The Reproduction of Mothering* (Berkeley, CA: University of California Press, 1978).

28. Vamik Volkan, *The Need to Have Enemies and Allies: From Clinical Practice to International Relationships* (Northvale, NJ: Jason Aronson, 1988).

29. Rhoda E. Howard, "Human Rights and the Culture Wars: Globalization and the Universality of Human Rights," *International Journal*, 53:1 (Winter 1997–98): 94–112, and Rhoda E. Howard-Hassmann, "Identity, Empathy and International Relations," a paper prepared for the symposium Looking at the World Through Non-Western Eyes, Walker Institute for International Relations, University of South Carolina, April 14–16, 2000.

30. Ziauddin Sardar, *Postmodernism and the Other* (Chicago: Pluto Press, 1998), p. 13.

31. Neumann, op. cit. p. 21. A more recent version of the paper appears as the final chapter in Neumann, *Uses of the Other*, 1999.

32. See the collection of essays in Charles B. Strozier and Michael Flynn, *Trauma and Self* (Landham, MD: Rowman and Littlefield, 1996).

33. Interview with Joseph Campbell by Sam Keen, in the film *Faces of the Enemy*, 1986.

34. Aaron T. Beck, M.D., *Prisoners of Hate: The Cognitive Basis of Anger, Hostility, and Violence* (New York: Harper Collins, 1998).

35. Habermas, of course, was concerned with the political implications of communicative action, and democracy as well as civility would having us employ communicative action in a world of selves regarded as having equal capacity. Onuf has elaborated a theory of social construction, or in his terms, "constructivism," by referring specifically to the rules encoded within communicative mechanisms and practice which mediate between agents (social actors) and structures are patterns of agent relations. See Nicholas Greenwood Onuf, *World of Our Making: Rules and Rule in Social Theory and International Relations* (Columbia, SC: University of South Carolina Press, 1989), and Vendulka Kubálková, Nicholas Onuf, and Paul Klowert, eds., *International Relations in a Constructed World* (New York: M. E. Sharpe, 1998).

36. Their differences along these variables matters from to a comparativist, but this is not a study of the social relations between them so much as a comparison of the social patterns that characterize each in relation to similar others.

37. For an excellent exploration of the contrast between Western/European and Indian/Buddhist constructions of the self, see Mark Epstein's *Thoughts without a Thinker* (New York: Harper Collins, 1995).

38. Franke Wilmer, "Postmodernism and Indigenous World Views," in *Race, Gender, and Class,* 3:2 (1996): 42. See also C. Vescey, *Imagine Ourselves Richly: Mythic Narratives of North American Indians* (New York: Harper Collins), and S. R. Dixon, "The Essential Spirit," *Northeast Indian Quarterly* 7:4 (Winter, 1990): 2–12.

39. Lao-tze, *Tao Te Ching,* trans. with forward and notes by Stephen Mitchell (New York: Harper Collins, 1988), p. 2.

40. The concept of "ethnic" itself is a socially constructed category of meaning, primarily through Western academic discourses.

41. The boundaries of subfields themselves, such as between comparative politics and international relations, are not strictly bounded, as indicated in varying degrees by the work of Walker Connor (1972), and David Horowitz (1985).

42. Perhaps this is one way in which the end of the Cold War reoriented—or disoriented—the discipline. Examples of those examining the IR–Ethnic conflict intersection include Gurr (1993), Carment and James (1997), and Schechterman and Slann (1993). In my own work on indigenous peoples, I originally compared ethnic mobilization theory with prevailing theories of IR as frameworks for analyzing the global political activism of indigenous peoples (1993).

43. See V. P. Gagnon (1994/95).

44. Benedict Anderson, *Imagined Communities* (London: Verso Books, 1991) and Anthony Smith, *National Identity* (Harmondsworth, U.K.: Penguin Books, 1991).

## Chapter 4: Identity and (Ethnic) Conflict in the Former Yugoslavia

1. Youssef Cohen, Brian R. Brown, and A. F. K. Organski, "The Paradoxical Nature of State Making: A Violent Creation of Order," *American Political Science Review* 75:4 (1981): 901–910.

2. Yugoslav Federal Government statistical reports list "Ruthenians" (Belgrade 1953–1989) as a category of ethnic nationality in 1955–1968. The identity originates in Slovakia, speaks a Ukranian dialect, and has its own "Uniate Church of the Little Russians," representing a communion between the Orthodox and Roman Catholic churches. They are sometimes referred to as "Little Russians."

3. The concept of "tribalism," in turn, defines the otherness against which "modern" identities are sustained., See F. Wilmer, *The Indigenous Voice in World Politics* (Newbury Park, CA: Sage, 1993) for a fuller development of this argument.
4. Diane Duffy has done some very interesting research exploring precisely this question in relation to Native American identity and patriotism.
5. Laurence M. Hauptmann, *The Iroquois Struggle for Survival: World War II to Red Power* (Syracuse, NY: Syracuse University Press, 1986).
6. See Appendix I, "Notes on Methodology."
7. As critical writers and as Croatian Yugoslavs, they have been more critical of the climate and leadership of Croatian nationalism. I cannot presume to know how either of them identify themselves at this point.
8. S. B., interview in Belgrade, 1995.
9. Interviews, also see Tone Bringa, *Being Muslim the Bosnian Way: Identity and Community in a Central Bosnian Village* (Princeton, NJ: Princeton University Press, 1995). I use the past tense here to indicate the period prior to the breakup and war beginning in 1990–1991.
10. T. G., Durham NC, in the essay entitled "We Shall Have to Build a Whole New National Identity," in *Children of Atlantis: Voices from the Former Yugoslavia*, Zdenko Lešić ed. (Budapest, Central European University Press), pp. 158–160.
11. Unlike the Soviet model, in Yugoslavia "the influx of Western mass and high culture was taken for granted," says Jasminka Udovički (Udovički and Ridgeway 1997). In the Belgrade University Department of Philosophy, for example, readings by western social theorists and philosophers were studied., Critics argue, however, that within the context of top-down political ideology and action such apparent openness failed to foster a genuinely open public discourse.
12. Ugrešić (1998), pp. 3–4.
13. Zdenko Lešić, ed., from an essay by A. M. in Tubingen, Germany, in *Children of Atlantis*, p. 146.
14. There was a census category which read "Moslems (in ethnic sense)" included in the official tabulation of "Population by Ethnic Group." None of the other ethnic nationalities included such parenthetic qualification, though the category "Yugoslav" was also listed with the parenthetical reference "nationality undeclared." There was clearly a difference between "nationality," which had the connotation of *"narod"* or constituting a "people," and "ethnic" identity, which was construed as a less significant category. In earlier census forms, Muslims had to choose between "Serb-Muslim," "Croat-Muslim," and "ethnically undeclared Muslim," so the inclusion of "Muslim" as an unqualified category in 1971 was viewed as a move toward Muslim equality with other nationalities. "Bosniak" was recognized in 1961, though Muslim leaders did not consider this a satisfactory recognition of Bosnian Muslim nationality. See Ramet (1984), pp. 177–187.
15. *Children of Atlantis*, op. cit., p. 144.
16. Edited by Zdenko Lešić (Budapest: Central European University Press, 1995).
17. Slavenka Drakulić, *Balkan Express: Fragments from the Other Side of the War* (New York: Norton, 1993), p. 50.
18. See also Ramet (1992).
19. Drakulić, op. cit. p. 49.
20. D. J., interview with the author in Belgrade, 1995.
21. See Ramet (1992) chap. 6 and 7.
22. Drakulić, op. cit. p. 52.

23. Drakulić, op. cit. p. 52.
24. Interview with a war crimes investigator, Nina Kadić, Zagreb, 1997.
25. ICTY Transcripts from November19, 1998, in open session, questioning of the witness Miroslav Pejcinović.
26. Interview with the author, Belgrade, July 1995.
27. Drakulić, op. cit., p. 120.
28. By "ordinary" I mean as distinct from highly educated elites.
29. Drakulić, "We Are All Albanians," *The Nation*, June 7, 1999.
30. IWPR Balkan Crisis Report, No. 81, October 5, 1999.
31. See especially Tone Bringa, *Being Muslim the Bosnian Way*.
32. Many of the transcripts from open sessions of the court are accessible to the public on the Internet at www.icty.org.
33. Interview with the author, September 1998.
34. Interview, Korcula, 1998.
35. Interviews with the author, June 1995, Belgrade.
36. Kull, Stephen J., in Sam Keen's film "Faces of the Enemy."
37. Figures given by the United Nations High Commissioner for Refugees. These are "displaced people" who have lost their homes due to the war, whether subsequently located within their home country or elsewhere.
38. The notion that perpetrators often suffer psychological injury is no doubt controversial.
39. Interviews in Belgrade, 1995.
40. I recommend reading all of Drakulić's book of essays mentioned earlier — *Balkan Express: Fragments from the Other Side of the War*, written during the war in Croatia — for a firsthand journal of life in Zagreb at the time.
41. Drakulić, op. cit. p. 64.
42. A. R. London (*Only Because I Was Not One of Them*, pp. 115–116).
43. L. Z., London (*They Became Refugees in Their Own Country*, p. 77).
44. Case No. IT 96–22, heard on appeal in the Hague, January 14, 1998. The transcript is quoted verbatim here without grammatical or other corrrections.
45. See materials produced and archived by Zum Beispeil: Dacahau (or Z. B. Dachau) at http://members.aol.com/zbdachau/history/caceng.htm; also the film *Shoah*, directed by Claude Lanzmann. Studio: New Yorker Films, 1985.
46. Drakulić, op. cit. p. 149.

## Chapter 5: The Social Construction of the State

1. See Ejub Štitkovac, "Croatia: The First War," in Jasminka Udovički and James Ridgeway, eds., *Burn This House: The Making and Unmaking of Yugoslavia* (Durham, NC: Duke University Press, 1997), p. 155.
2. This remained so even in 1997 and 1998 when I finally visited Croatia. There seemed to be no escaping its presence.
3. Štitkovac, op. cit., pp. 154–156.
4. Drakulić, op. cit., p. 53, 1993.
5. See for example Giddens, 1987, 1991; Smith, 1981, 1991; Anderson, 1987; and Hobsbawm and Ranger, 1983.
6. See for example Shapiro and Alker, eds., 1996; Lapid and Kratochwil, eds., 1997; and Campbell, 1998.
7. See for example Bourdieu, 1991; Bhabha, ed., 1990; and Bakhtin, Holquist, and Emerson, 1981.
8. H. Lasswell. *Politics: Who Gets What, When, and How* (New York: Peter Smith, 1950).
9. V. Spike Peterson, "The Gender of Rhetoric, Reason, and Realism," in Francis A. Beer and Robert Hariman, eds., *Post-Realism: The Rhetorical Turn in Inter-*

*national Relations* (East Lansing, MI: Michigan State University Press, 1996), pp. 257–276.

10. Michael Ignatieff, *Blood and Belonging: Journeys into the New Nationalism* (New York: Noonday Press, 1993), esp. pp. 3–18.

11. William E. Connolly, "The Liberal Image of the Nation," in Duncan Ivison, Paul Patton, and Will Sanders, eds., *Political Theory and the Rights of Indigenous Peoples* (Oakleigh, Victoria, Australia: Cambridge University Press, 2000), p. xxx.

12. Interviews by the author with Aboriginal Australians, July 1996.

13. Ernst Cassirer, *The Myth of the State* (New Haven, CT: Yale University Press, 1946), pp. 226–227.

14. See Wilmer (1993) chap. 3 and 4.

15. This equation has by no means disappeared from common usage, even by heads of state. In June 2000, a headline referring to comments made by Zimbabwe's President Mugabe respecting the relationship between blacks and whites, citizenship, and the state, announced that "White Must Recognize Nation's for Blacks." *Bozeman Chronicle*, June 18, 2000, p. 42.

16. Donald L. Horowitz, *Ethnic Groups in Conflict* (Berkeley, CA: University of California Press, 1985) includes a chapter entitled "A Family Resemblance."

17. Kathleen B. Jones, "Citizenship in a Woman-Friendly Polity," *Signs*, 15:4 (Summer 1990): 781–812.

18. See especially Chapter 3 in Franke Wilmer, *The Indigenous Voice in World Politics: Since Time Immemorial* (Newbury Park, CA: Sage, 1993).

19. See Pierre Bourdieu, *Language and Symbolic Power* (Cambridge, MA: Harvard University Press, 1991).

20. J. Ann Tickner, Foreword to *Gendered States: Feminist (Re)Visions of International Relations Theory*, V. S. Peterson, ed. (Boulder, CO: Lynn Rienner, 1992), p. ix. See also Cynthia Weber, *Simulating Sovereignty: Intervention, the State and Symbolic Exchange* (Cambridge, U.K.: Cambridge University Press, 1995).

21. In addition to Peterson, op. cit., on feminist theory see for example, Christine Di Stefano, *Configurations of Masculinity: A Feminist Perspective on Modern Political Theory* (Ithaca, NY: Cornell University Press, 1991) and Wendy Brown, *Manhood and Politics: A Feminist Reading in Political Theory* (Totowa, NJ: Rowman and Littlefield, 1988); in comparative politics and political theory, David Held, ed., *States and Societies* (New York: New York University Press, 1983); William T. Bluhm, *Theories of the Political System* (Englewood Cliffs, NJ: Prentice-Hall, 1978); and for an overview, Murray Knuttila, *State Theories: From Liberalism to the Challenge of Feminism* (Toronto, Canada: Garamond Press, 1987).

22. Ernst Gellner, *Nations and Nationalism* (Ithaca, NY: Cornell University Press, 1983), p. 5.

23. See the discussion of the historical state in Yale H. Ferguson and Richard W. Mansbach, *The Elusive Quest: Theory and International Politics* (Columbia, SC: University of South Carolina Press, 1988), pp. 117–125.

24. Bourdieu, op. cit.

25. Peterson, op. cit.

26. Di Stefano, op. cit.

27. Wendy Brown, op. cit.

28. I follow Steven Vertovec's lead here. He identifies five "normative political philosophies" on which the modern state as a civil society can be grounded: Marxism, welfarism, liberalism, communitarianism, and associationalism. See Steve Vertovec, "Introduction," in *Migration and Social Cohesion*, S. Vertovec, ed. (Aldershot, U.K.: Edward Elgar, 1999), pp. xi–xxxvii.

29. For a good review of the feminist critique of liberalism and a feminist response to it, see Mona Harrington, "What Exactly Is Wrong with the Liberal State as an Agent of Change?" in Peterson, ed., op. cit., pp. 65–82.
30. Anthony Giddens, *The Nation-State and Violence* (Berkeley, CA: University of California Press, 1985), p. 7.
31. David Easton, *A Framework for Political Analysis* (Englewood Cliffs, NJ: Prentice-Hall, 1965), p. 22.
32. I emphasize the "narrative" issue here because "organic" sameness must still be socially constructed., The genome project, for example, indicates a basis for organic sameness among all humans, and the issue of basing "racial" categories on the *perception* of genetic sameness has become highly contestable. Americans are especially oriented toward visual difference, but I wish to emphasize that even this is a *perceptual* (and socially constructed) rather than *organic* difference.
33. V. Cohen, B. R. Brown, and A. F. K. Organski (1981).
34. Sabrina Petra Ramet, *Balkan Babel*, 2nd. ed. (Boulder, CO: Westview Press, 1996), p. 199.
35. Ugrešić, *Culture of Lies* (1998), p. 69.
36. This is the figure given by Mirko Tepavac, Yugoslav minister of foreign affairs in the 1960s and early 1970s, in M. Tepavac, "Tito: 1945–1980" in *Burn This House: The Making and Unmaking of Yugoslavia*, Jasminka Udovički and James Ridgeway, eds. (Durham, NC: Duke University Press, 1997).
37. Drakulić, op. cit., 1998, pp. 74–75.
38. Tepavac, op. cit. p. 65.
39. Ugrešić, *The Culture of Lies*, 1998, p. 80.
40. S. P. Huntington, S. P. (1993). "The Clash of Civilizations?" *Foreign Affairs* 72 (Summer): 22–49.
41. Ibid., p. 81.
42. I doubt if these "white" American speakers were thinking about what "the Alamo" means to either Native or Latino, especially Chicano or Mexican, Americans.
43. Drakulić, op. cit., p. 51.
44. Connolly, op. cit., and James N. Rosenau, "The Complexities and Contradictions of Globalization," *Current History*, November 1997, pp. 360–364.

## Chapter 6: The Social Construction of War

1. This is the conclusion drawn by Fintan O'Toole regarding violence in Northern Ireland in his review of *Lost Lives: The Stories of the Men, Women and Children Who Died as a Result of the Northern Ireland Troubles*, by Brian Feeney and Chris Thornton (Edinburgh: Mainstream Publishing) in the *New York Review of Books*, October 5, 2000, pp. 10–13.
2. I would also note that although the prevailing perception of the Holocaust is that of a highly organized and implemented project, one could view Goldhagen's research as revealing the extent to which it was also carried out in a decentralized, unauthorized manner.
3. Daniel Jonah Goldhagen, *Hitler's Willing Executioners: Ordinary Germans and the Holocaust* (New York: Vintage, 1997).
4. Interview in Zagreb, June 1997.
5. Lešić (1995).
6. Interviews, M.O., Belgrade, 1995.
7. Croatian Helsinki Committee Statement 5, "On Mobilization of the Croatian Citizens for the War in Bosnia and Herzegovina," December 29, 1993, signed by CHC President Ivan Zvonimir Eieak.

8. Independent Belgrade Radio "B92," June 11, 1995.
9. Interviews in Belgrade, 1995; Croatia and Bosnia, 1997; and Croatia, 1998. See also Chuck Sudetić, *Blood and Vengeance: One Family's Story of the War in Bosnia* (New York: Penguin Books, 1998); Sara Sharratt and Ellyn Kaschak, eds., *Assault on the Soul: Women in the Former Yugoslavia* (Binghamton, NY: Haworth Press, 1999); and Alexandra Stiglmayer, ed., *Mass Rape: The War against Women in Bosnia-Herzegovina* (Lincoln, NE: University of Nebraska Press, 1993).
10. David Campbell, ed., Introduction, *The Political Subject of Violence*, D. Campbell and M. Dillon, eds. (Manchester, U.K.: Manchester University Press, 1993), p. 1.
11. These are also known as the *jus ad bellum, jus anti bella*, and *jus in bello*.
12. Vivienne Jabri, *Discourses on Violence: Conflict Analysis Reconsidered* (Manchester, U.K.: Manchester University Press, 1996); Kalevi J. Holsti, *The State, War, and the State of War* (Cambridge, U.K.: Cambridge University Press, 1996); David Campbell, *National Deconstruction: Violence, Identity, and Justice in Bosnia* (Minneapolis, MN: University of Minnesota Press, 1998).
13. Peter Paret, with Gordon A. Craig and Felix Gilbert, *Makers of Modern Strategy: From Machiavelli to the Nuclear Age* (Princeton, NJ: Princeton University Press, 1986); Martin van Creveld, *The Transformation of War: The Most Radical Reinterpretation of Armed Conflict Since Clausewitz* (New York: Simon and Schuster, 1991).
14. See Paret, op. cit., and van Creveld, op. cit.; also Janice Thomson, *Mercenaries, Pirates, and Sovereigns: State-Building and Extraterritorial Violence in Early Modern Europe* (Princeton, NJ: Princeton University Press, 1994). Barbara Ehrenreich offers a feminist critique of the history of war written for an educated, nonexpert audience in *Blood Rites: Origins and History of the Passions of War* (New York: Henry Holt, 1997). Other feminist writings on war include Jean Bethke Elshtain, *Women and War* (New York: Basic Books, 1987); Elshtain and Sheila Tobias, eds., *Women, Militarism, and War* (Savage, MD: Roman and Littlefield, 1990); and among the works by Cynthia Enloe that address the issue of war in IR, *Bananas, Beaches, and Bases: Making Feminist Sense of International Politics* (Berkeley, CA: University of California Press, 1990); For an excellent bibliography, see Peterson (1992).
15. John Keegan, *A History of Warfare* (New York: Knopf, 1993).
16. Kalevi J. Holsti, op. cit.
17. See Jabri, op. cit., pp. 30–32, though this approach is also reflected in the earlier works of John Burton and Johan Galtung, for example.
18. Jabri, op. cit., p. 30.
19. John Keegan, *A History of Warfare* (New York: Knopf, 1993).
20. John Burton, 1979, 1987, 1990; Louis Kriesberg, 1982, 1998; Johan Galtung, 1969; and Ted Robert Gurr, 1970; among others, have been concerned with war-as-conflict throughout their careers. Elise Boulding's work, including her most recent, *Cultures of Peace: The Hidden Side of History* (Syracuse, NY: Syracuse University Press, 2000), and the classic *Building a Global Civic Culture: Education for an Interdependent World* (Syracuse, NY: Syracuse University Press, 1990). Gordon Fellman, *Rambo and the Dalai Lama: The Compulsion to Win and Its Threat to Human Survival* (Albany, NY: State University of New York Press, 1998); and Robin J. Burns and Robert Aspeslagh, eds., *Three Decades of Peace Education Around the World: An Anthology* (Garland Reference Library of Social Science, vol. 600) indicate the range and variety of works in peace education. Peace educator Betty Reardon's

work often addresses the intersection between sexism and war. See Betty A. Reardon, *Women and Peace: Feminist Visions of Global Security* (State University of New York, 1993).

21. Campbell and Dillon, 1993.
22. Vivienne Jabri, op. cit.
23. Jabri, op. cit., p. 132.
24. Jabri, op. cit., pp. 133–134.
25. Nicholas Onuf, "Constructivism: A User's Manual," in Vendulka Kubálková, Nicholas Onuf, and Paul Kowert, ed., *International Relations in a Constructed World* (New York: M. E. Sharpe, 1998), pp. 58–78.
26. CNN, *Our Planetary Police*, September 23, 1994.
27. Mark Almond, *Europe's Backyard War: The War in the Balkans* (London: Hienemann, Ltd., 1994), p. 308.
28. Ivo Banac, *The National Question in Yugoslavia: Origins, History, and Politics* (Ithaca, NY: Cornell University Press, 1984).
29. It is widely asserted that it was as a Milosević-directed JNA war, initially at least, Milosević was willing to let Slovenia secede without much official resistance because there was only a negligible Serb (and non-Slovenian in general) presence in Slovenia. But both because Macedonia is neither as homogeneous as Slovenia with a 25 percent to 30 percent non-Macedonian, mostly Albanian population and because a closer cultural affinity could be asserted between Serbia and Macedonia (both are Orthodox, for example) in purely structural terms there should also have been a high probability of civil war in Macedonia. Alice Ackerman (2000) argues that the peaceful secession of Macedonia was due in large part to the success of UN peacekeeping operations there. Though it has recently become a more violent conflict, it in no way compares to the brutal conflicts in Bosnia.
30. Branko Milinković, ed., *Hate Speech: An Analysis of the Contents of Domestic Media in the First Part of 1993*, published in Belgrade by the Center for Antiwar Action, 1994, p. 5.
31. Yigal Chazan, "Zagreb Cracks Down on Dissent: Reporters, Opposition Leaders Could Face Prosecution," *The Gazette*, September 6, 1992. (Montreal, Quebec, Canada, 1992), p. 12.
32. I. Z. Èièak, President, CHC. "Statement: Concerning the Freedom of the Media," and "The Freedom of Media in Croatia Proposals to the Croatian Prime Minister Mr. Nikica Valentae," July 7, 1993 (Zagreb, Croatia; Croatian Helsinki Committee, 1993).
33. Helsinki Committee for Human Rights in Serbia, "Report on the State of Human Rights in Serbia," Belgrade, October 4, 1994.
34. Lazar Lalić, *Three TV Years in Serbia* (Belgrade: Independent Media Union, 1995).
35. Filip David, "An Essential Handbook," preface to *Three TV Years in Serbia*, Lazar Lalić (Belgrade: Independent Media Union, 1995).
36. Op. cit., p. 6.
37. Helsinki Committee for Human Rights in Serbia, p. 6, citing the report by Varadi Grubać for Women in Black, "Deserters from the War in Yugoslavia," Belgrade, 1994.
38. Independent Belgrade Radio "B92," daily email service, printed English version, June 11, 1995.
39. Tone Bringa, *Being Muslim the Bosnian Way* (Princeton, NJ: Princeton University Press, 1995). See also Julie A. Mertus, *Kosovo: How Myths and Truths Started a War* (Berkeley, CA: University of California Press, 1999).

40. Mark Thompson, *A Paper House: The Ending of Yugoslavia* (London: Vintage Books, 1992), p. 91.
41. I was told rather frequently, for example, how neighbors helped one another with house repairs, or how they shared tractors for cultivating small gardens, or traded skills such as mechanical skills and masonry.
42. Izetbegović was tried with twelve others in Sarajevo, charged with "hostile and counter-revolutionary acts derived from Muslim nationalism. For an excellent discussion of both the rise of Muslim nationalism and debates among Muslims about secular versus religious identity, national versus communist interests, pan-Bosnian versus Bosnian Muslim interests, and the rise of Serb and Croat nationalism in Bosnia, see Noel Malcolm's *Bosnia: A Short History* (New York: New York University Press, 1994), pp. 200–210.
43. Slavenka Drakulić, "We Are All Albanians," *The Nation*, June 7, 1999.
44. See Julie A. Mertus, op. cit.
45. Susan L. Woodward, *Balkan Tragedy: Chaos and Dissolution after the Cold War* (Washington, DC: Brookings Institution, 1995).
46. CNN Headline News, February 23, 1999. Drasković also compared the Albanian leadership to Nazis; see "Drasković Charges Kosovars with 'Nazi' Program," Radio Free Europe/Radio Liberty, *Newsline* vol. 3, no. 30, Part II, February 12, 1999.
47. They were within one to two percent more or less than each of these in the 1971 and 1981 census, although by 1991 there were approximately 40 percent more Albanians than Macedonians in the total Yugoslav population, split between the republics of Serbia and Macedonia, *Statistical Yearbook of the Federal Republic of Yugoslavia, 1952–1992* (Belgrade).
48. *Statistical Yearbook of the Federal Republic of Yugoslavia, 1952–1992.*
49. Mertus, op. cit., p. 108.
50. Misha Glenny, *The Fall of Yugoslavia: The Third Balkan War* (London: Penguin Books, 1992).
51. Misha Glenny, "Yugoslavia: The Revenger's Tragedy," *New York Review of Books*, August 13, 1992, p. 39.
52. Op. cit., p. 39. Glenny, August 13, 1992.
53. Sam Keen, *Faces of the Enemy*, PBS video, 1986.
54. ICTY Monday, April 12, 1999 (open session), testimony of Mr. Nezirević during the trial of Cerkez and Kordić.
55. I have quoted the passage as it appears in the translated text, *Hate Speech*, Branko Milinković, ed. (Belgrade, Center for Antiwar Action, 1994), pp. 16–17.
56. See Dubravko Horvatić, *Croatia* (Zagreb: Pegaz, 1996), p. 79. It is worth noting that Horvatić was (according to the book jacket) "stigmatized because of his literary activities during the 1970s and 1980s" but in the newly independent Croatia became "again fully affirmed." This is a reference to the nationalist cultural pride movement among Croatian artists and intelligentsia in the 1970s known as the Croatian Spring. They were apparently vindicated by the break-up of Yugoslavia and the consequent independence of Croatia.
57. Ibid., p. 79.
58. Ibid., p. 79.
59. Ibid., p. 95–96.
60. Ibid., p. 96
61. Ibid.
62. Constitution of Croatia, Preamble, "Chapter I Historical Foundations."
63. Respondents often pointed out that the alliance with Hitler was not as significant as the historical fact of Croatia's independence during World War II. Thus

renaming streets and squares after collaborationists or exclusionary nationalists was interpreted as an expression of continuity with aspirations for an independent Croatian state, not sympathy with a pro-Nazi regime.
64. Yigal Chazan, "Zagreb Cracks Down in Dissent: Reporters, Opposition
Leaders Could Face Prosecution," *The Gazette*, June 9, 1992, Montreal,
Canada. Available at www.cdsp.neu.edu/info/students, accessed July, 2000.
65. Vesna Pešić, "Bellicose Virtues and Elementary School Readers," in Ružica
Rosandić and Pešić, ed., *Warfare, Patriotism, and Patriarchy* (Belgrade: Centre
for Antiwar Action, 1994).
66. Paul Parin, "Ethnopsychoanalytical Reflections," in Alexandra Stiglmayer, ed.,
*Mass Rape: The War Against Women in Bosnia-Herzegovina* (Lincoln, NE:
University of Nebraska Press, 1994), p. 37.
67. Her story also appears in Franke Wilmer, "Identity, Culture, and Historicity:
the Social Construction of Ethnicity in the Balkans," *World Affairs* 160:1
(Summer 1997): 3–16.

## Chapter 7: Causes of War

1. L. Lešić, *Children of Atlantis* (Budapest: Open Society Institute, 1995),
pp. 115–116.
2. See Raju G. C. Thomas, "Self-Determination and International Recognition
Policy: An Alternative Interpretation of Why Yugoslavia Disintegrated," in
*World Affairs* 160:1 (1997): 17–31, though I do not agree with Thomas that
the failure of the international community was entirely at fault and that
nationalisms within Yugoslavia were insufficient to bring about the war.
3. Nicholas Onuf, "Constructivism: A User's Manual," in Vendulka Kubálková,
Nicholas Onuf, and Paul Kowert, eds., *International Relations in a
Constructed World* (New York: M. E. Sharpe, 1998), pp. 58–78.
4. Ibid., pp. 59–60.
5. Ibid., p. 61.
6. Vivienne Jabri, *Discourses on Violence: Conflict Analysis Reconsidered*
(Manchester, UK: Manchester University Press, 1996), p. 136. Jabri cites E.
Kedourie, *Nationalism* (London: Hutchinson University Library, 1966).
7. Ibid., p. 137.
8. I take this problem also to be a key issue in finding a stable solution to the
Kosovo situation. As it is, many Kosovar nationalists view the NATO intervention as an indication of support for their separatist aspirations on the basis
that ethnic self-determination must ultimately find its expression in statehood.
9. This is not to say that many expressions of ethnic oppression do not arise from
the real experience of oppression. Nor do I mean to imply that what we call
"ethnic conflict" is on the rise or decline but rather that concern with violence
in which collectivities identify their motives with ethnic discourses is increasing
over the past decade or two.
10. V. P. Gagnon, "Ethnic Conflict as an Intra-Group Phenomenon: A Preliminary
Framework," *Revija za sociologiju* (Zagreb), no. 1–2, 1995, copy received via
email from the author.
11. Ibid., p. 3.
12. Ibid., p. 3.
13. Benedict Anderson, *Imagined Communities* (New York: Verso Books, 1991).
14. See Ivo Banac, *The National Question in Yugoslavia: Origins, History, Politics*
(Ithaca, NY: Cornell University Press, 1984) and also V. P. Gagnon, "The
Historical Roots of the Yugoslav Conflict," *International Organizations and
Ethnic Conflict*, Milton J. Esman and Shibley Telhami, eds. (Ithaca, NY:
Cornell University Press, 1995), pp. 179–197.

15. Montenegro is "homeland" to some of the most prominent Serbian political and military leaders in the war, and so in this sense, Montenegro together with Serbia, including Kosovo, represents the Serbian "homeland," and not coincidentally, also constitutes the rump "Yugoslav" state. As Slovenia, with its Slovenian majority, and later Macedonia, with its Macedonian majòrity, seceded to become successor states with ethnic majorities, so, many must have thought, Bosnia could be divided between a new Croatian and new Serbian successor state, leaving only the Bosnian Muslims without a homeland.
16. See Gagnon, op. cit (1995), note 14.
17. Constituting only 40 percent of the population in all of Yugoslavia, Serbs accounted for 50 percent of those employed by the state. Of course the Yugoslav capital was also located in Belgrade. Though not showing exactly a "dominance" of the state bureaucracy, these facts together were enough to reinforce the prejudices of non-Serbs, particularly Croats, as well as the perception that Serbs used the communist bureaucracy to assert greater influence over the state.
18. Vesna Pusić, Untitled essay, *Journal of Democracy* 9:1 (1998): 112.
19. Drago Hedl, "Bosnian Trade Off," Balkan Crisis Report no. 179, September 5, 2000, International War and Peace Reporting. The story reports on the revelations contained in recorded conversations between Tudjman and Bosnian Croat leader Mate Boban, brought to light by Tudjman's successor, Stipe Mešić, in September 2000. For earlier suspicions, see Thomas L. Friedman, "Whose Balkan Menu," September 1995, *New York Times Commentary.* Available at www.bosnet.org/archive/bosnet.w3archive/9509/, accessed October 2, 2000.
20. December 20, 1999, "This Week in Bosnia-Hercegovina," Bosnia Action Coalition. Available at at: http://www.applicom.com/twibih/, accessed December 20, 1999.
21. "Memorandum of the Serbian Academy of Sciences and Arts," translated by Margot and Bosko Miloslavjević, printed by GIP "Kultura" Belgrade, Maršala Birjužova 28, Belgrade 1995, p. 42.
22. Memorandum, p. 40.
23. Memorandum, p. 40.
24. Olivera Milosavljević, "The Abuse of the Authority of Science," in *The Road to War in Serbia: Trauma and Catharsis*, Nebojša Popov, ed. (Budapest: Central European University Press, 1996). English translation published 2000.
25. Ibid., p. 277, English version.
26. Ibid., p. 277.
27. Ibid., p. 286.
28. Interview in Belgrade, June 1995, with italics added to indicate that the respondent was clearly emphasizing, even angrily shouting, this sentence.
29. "Turbo" folk referred to a particular genre of music in the Yugoslav or Serbian youth culture of the 1990s. One of its most popular performers was "Ceca," who married the infamous alleged war criminal Arkan in February 1995.
30. For an excellent discussion of the nationalization of popular culture, see Sabrina Petra Ramet, *Balkan Babel: The Disintegration of Yugoslavia from the Death of Tito to Ethnic War* (Boulder, CO: Westview Press, 1996), especially chap. 5 and 13. Also see *The Road to War in Serbia*, Popov, ed., op. cit., especially Mirko Djordjević, "Populist Wave Literature"; Ivan Čolović, "Football, Hooligans, and War"; Zoran Marković, "The Nation: Victim and Vengeance"; and Snježana Milovojević "The Nationalization of Everyday Life."
31. Milinković, op. cit., p. 83.

32. Branka Milinković, *Hate Speech*, Center for Antiwar Action, Belgrade, 1994, pp. 82–83.

33. He was reported to have indicated his willingness to turn himself into the tribunal just before his assassination.

34. Milinković, op. cit., p. 84.

35. Roger Cohen, "Serbia Dazzles Itself: Terror Suspect Weds Singer," February 20, 1995, *New York Times*, International section, p. 24.

36. Interview with author R.N., Belgrade, June 1995.

37. "Special Forces," Annex III A., "The military structure, strategy and tactics of the warring factions," United Nations—Security Council, Document No. S/1994/674/Add.2 (vol. I) December 28, 1994, Final report of the United Nations Commission of Experts established pursuant to Security Council Resolution 780 (1992), Annex II, prepared by M. Cherif, Bassiouni, Chairman and Rapporteur on the Gathering and Analysis of the Facts, Commission of Experts, with the assistance of Edmund A. McAlister, Assistant to M. Cherif Bassiouni, Richard Janney, IHRLI Staff Attorney, and Peter M. Manikas, IHRLI Staff Attorney.

38. Ibid., p. 6.

39. I should also note, as Robert J. Donia did during testimony at the Hague when asked about the participation of "outside" forces in assisting the Bosnian Muslims, that the Bosnian Croats and Bosnian Serbs were also assisted by outside forces, and there is no reason—aside from anti-Muslim prejudices—to single out Bosnian Muslims for accepting or even recruiting non-Bosnians as allies.

40. Final report of the United Nations Commission of Experts established pursuant to Security Council Resolution 780 (1992) Annex III.A "Special Forces," Section B. "Forces operating in support of BiH—the Green Berets and Mujahedin," and 1(b) "Ties" with the Government and regular military of BiH. Available at http://www.ess.uwe.ac.uk/comexpert/ANX/III-A.htm#II.B, accessed March 27, 2001.

41. Jasminka Udovički and Ejub Štitkovac, "Bosnia and Hercegovina: The Second War," in Jasminka Udovički and James Ridgeway, eds., *Burn This House: The Making and Unmaking of Yugoslavia* (Durham, NC: Duke University Press, 1997), p. 207.

42. Udovički and Štitkovac cite as their sources Aleksandarčirić, "Svi smo mi dobrovoljci," *Vreme*, May 31, 1993, pp. 20–21; and Duska Anastasijević and Denisa Kostović, "Zločini rezultat strategije," *Vreme*, July 11, 1994, pp. 19–23. It is also worth noting that *Vreme* was one of the independent news magazines which continued publication in Belgrade throughout the war.

43. Op. cit. note 38.

44. Op. cit., p. 1.

45. Op. cit., Section C.a. p. 5 of the report. The report also notes that the number of people active in paramilitaries fluctuated with the intensity of the conflict.

46. Both a book and a documentary film (L. Silber and A. Little, *Yugoslavia: Death of a Nation* [New York: Penguin Books, 1995, 1996, 1997]), so well respected is this account of events leading up to and occurring during the war, that, while observing the proceedings at the Hague tribunal in July 1999, I watched both the prosecution and defense as well as the academic expert witness they were questioning, Robert Donia, refer repeatedly to events as reported and recorded in the Silber and Little book. When asked to refer to a passage in the book and whether he was familiar with it, Professor Donia said, jokingly, "Yes, I have it. I never leave home without it."

47. Silber and Little, p. 131.

48. Sporazum is a Serbo-Croatian word for "agreement" or "settlement."
49. Op cit. note 38.
50. Ed Vulliamy, *Seasons in Hell: Understanding Bosnia's War* (New York: Simon and Schuster, 1994), pp. 61–62.
51. Vulliamy, op. cit., p. 62.
52. UN Report on "Special Forces," op. cit., p. 21.
53. Patrick Moore, "Running with Wolves," Radio Free Europe/Radio Liberty, *Newsline*, vol. 4, no. 11, part II, January 17, 2000.
54. Pedro Ramet, subsequently called Sabrina Petra Ramet, "Religion and Nationalism in Yugoslavia," in Pedro Ramet, ed., *Religion and Nationalism in Soviet and East European Politics* (Durham, NC: Duke University Press, 1989), p. 299.
55. See especially Goldhagen, 1997.
56. Fouad Ajami, "In Europe's Shadows," in Nader Mousavizadeh, ed., *The Black Book of Bosnia: The Consequences of Appeasement* (New York: Basic Books, 1995), p. 41.
57. See Tone Bringa, *Being Muslim the Bosnian Way: Identity and Community in a Central Bosnian Village* (Princeton, NJ: Princeton University Press, 1995); Noel Malcolm, *Bosnia: A Short History* (New York: New York University Press, 1994); Robert J. Donia and John V. A. Fine, Jr., *Bosnia and Herzegovina* (New York: Columbia University Press, 1994); and Fouad Ajami, "In Europe's Shadows," in Nader Mousavizadeh, op. cit.
58. The perceived urban–rural difference was believed by many respondents to be more significant than ethnic differences. Tone Bringa also offers insight into this phenomenon in *Being Muslim the Bosnian Way*, op. cit., fn. 42.
59. It should also be noted that not all Albanians, either in Serbia or in Albania, are Muslim, nor are all Albanians religious.
60. The level of support from Islamic states was neither extensive nor consistent. Iran, for example, said Martin Peretz in an editorial in *The New Republic*, "sent mullahs to the Bosnians, but it was caught red handed selling oil to the Serbs." August 7, 1995, reprinted in Mousavizadeh, ed., *The Black Book of Bosnia*, op. cit., p. 148.
61. "Fist as Political Argument: What We Can Learn from the Political Scandal in the Croatian Parliament," A. Radošović, trans. Jelena Marković, *Nas Glas*, Zagreb, December 6, 1994.
62. "Statement 33, On Freedom of Religion in Croatia," Helsinki Committee of Croatia, February 26, 1996, signed by Ivan Zvonimir Èièak, President.
63. See David Steele, "Religion as a Fount of Ethnic Hostility or an Agent of Reconciliation?" in Dušan Janjić, ed., *Religion and War* (Belgrade: European Movement in Serbia, 1994).
64. Steele, op. cit., p. 174.
65. "Ivan Zvonimir Èièak, President, Croatian Helsinki Committee, Statement 33, "On Freedom of Religion in Croatia," February 26, 1996, Zagreb, Croatia.
66. Janjić, op. cit., "Editorial Note."
67. Dusan Janjić, ed., op. cit.
68. David Steele, op. cit., p. 173.
69. Ibid., Steele, p. 174.
70. Michael Sells, *The Bridge Betrayed: Religion and Genocide in Bosnia* (Berkeley, CA: University of California Press, 1996), pp. 81–82.
71. Steele, op. cit, p. 176, quoting Josip Beljan, "Priznata Vjernost," *Veritas*, nos. 9–10, September-October 1992, pp. 22–25 (trans. Paul Mojzes).
72. Nina Kadić, interview in Zagreb, June 1997.

73. From comments made to the author by a former Belgrade resident now living in the United States who attended the antiwar protest and continued to be active in the antiwar movement in Belgrade until leaving in 1995.
74. Conference held in Capetown, South Africa, May 28, 1997. Professor Foster, the first speaker during the seminar, is a professor of Social Psychology at the University of Cape Town.
75. Ibid., Professor Foster.
76. Interview with Joseph Campbell by Sam Keen in the film, *Faces of the Enemy*, and see also Arthur Schopenhauer, *On the Basis of Morality* (Oxford, U.K.: Berghahn Books, 1995); the revised 1995 edition is based on Schopenhauer's original 1839 work "On the Foundation of Morality."
77. Herbert C. Kelman, ed., *International Behavior: A Social Psychogical Analyzes* (New York: Holt, Rinehart, and Winston, 1965) and H. C. Kelman "Violence without Moral Restraint: Reflections on the Dehumanization of Victims and Victimizers, *American Psychologist*, 27: 989–1016.
78. Lloyd Vogelman, "Psychological Factors to Consider in Strikes, Collective Violence and the Killing of Non-Strikers," in Violence in Contemporary South Africa, South African Breweries (SAB) conference proceedings (1991). Lloyd Vogelman is the former Director of the Centre for the Study of Violence and Reconciliation. Available at: www.wits.ac.za/csvr/papbusl2.htm, accessed November 10, 2000.
79. Miroslav Filipović, "Serb Officers Relive Killings," International War and Peace Reporter's *Balkan Crisis Report*, no. 130, April 4, 2000, Anthony Borden, editor-in-chief. The Institute for War & Peace Reporting, London. Miroslav Filipović, a regular contributor to IWPR and independent journalist from Kraljevo, was imprisoned in Serbia for six months in 2000 after publishing a series of exposés on Serbian security forces.
80. Onuf, op. cit., p. 74.

## Chapter 8: The Other Yugoslav Wars

1. Helke Sander, "Prologue," in Alexandra Stiglmayer, ed., *Mass Rape: The War against Women in Bosnia-Herzegovina* (Lincoln, NE: University of Nebraska Press, 1994), xviii.
2. Alexandra Stiglmayer, ed., *Mass Rape: The War against Women in Bosnia-Herzegovina*; Sara Sharratt and Ellyn Kaschak, eds., *Assault on the Soul: Women in the Former Yugoslavia* (New York: Haworth Press, 1999); Sabrina P. Ramet, *Gender Politics in the Western Balkans: Women and Society in Yugoslavia and the Yugoslav Successor States* (University Park, PA: Pennsylvania State University Press, 1999); Vesna Nikolić-Ristanović, ed., *Women, Violence and War: Wartime Victimzation of Refugees in the Balkans* (Budapest: Central European University Press, 2000); and *Calling the Ghosts: A Story about Rape, War, and Women*, Mandy Jacobson and Karmen Jelinčić, Directors (Bowery Productions, US and Croatia, 1996).
3. See International Criminal Tribunal for the former Yugoslavia home page available at www.un.org/ICTY/ for index to documents, cases, judgments, indictments, and proceedings.
4. During the first month of the "Rape of Nanking" during World War II, which referred not only to the actual raping of Chinese women by Japanese invaders but the overall brutality of the Japanese takeover, an estimated 20,000 women were raped in the first month alone, and during the Bengali war for independence from Pakistan, Susan Brownmiller reports that some 200,000 Bengali women were raped., See Rhonda Copelon, "Surfacing Gender: Reconceptualizing Crimes against Women in Time of War," in Stiglmayer, op.cit.,

300 The Social Construction of Man, the State, and War

pp. 197–218, and Susan Brownmiller, *Against Our Will: Men, Women, and Rape* (New York: Simon and Schuster, 1975)

5. Interview with Nina Kadić, June 1997, Zagreb.

6. As reported by Alexandra Stiglmayer in "The Rapes in Bosnia-Herzegovina," in Stiglmayer, op. cit., p. 85.

7. I base this figure on the fact that roughly 80 percent of the 200,000 casualties by the end of 1993 were believed to be Muslim, and the fact that the majority of death and rape camps were in Bosnia and created and run by Serbs, making Croatian women likely to be the second largest group. Nonpartisan observers agree that women of all nationalities were raped during the war.

8. This problem is addressed by Obrad Kešić in "Women and Gender Imagery in Bosnia: Amazons, Sluts, Victims, Witches, and Wombs," in Sarbina P. Ramet, ed., *Gender Politics in the Western Balkans: Women and Society in Yugoslavia and the Yugoslav Successor States* (University Park, PA: Pennsylvania State University Press, 1999), pp. 187–202.

9. Andrea Dworkin, "The Real Pornography of a Brutal War against Women," *Los Angeles Times*, April 5, 1993, p. M2.

10. See *Calling the Ghosts: A Story about Rape, War, and Women,* op. cit.

11. On admitting to crimes against humanity, though not including rape, Drazen Erdemovic described his own experience in Srebenica in these terms. Erdemovic, Case No. IT 96–22, 1 Wednesday, January 14, 1998, ICTY, The Hague.

12. Obrad Kešić, op. cit., p. 193.

13. The literature is now rich and varied., See for example, Christine Di Stefano, *Configurations of Masculinity: A Feminist Perspective on Modern Political Theory* (Ithaca, NY: Cornell University Press, 1991); Christine Di Stefano, "Masculinity as Ideology in Political Thought: Hobbesian Man Considered," in *Women's Studies International Forum* 6 (1983): 633–44; Wendy Brown, *Manhood and Politics: A Feminist Reading in Political Theory* (Totowa, NJ: Rowman and Littlefield, 1988); Eileen Boris and Peter Bardaglio, "The Transformation of Patriarchy: The Historic Role of the State," in *Families, Politics, and Public Policy,* Irene Diamond, ed. (New York, Longman, 1983); Cynthia Enloe, *Bananas, Beaches, and Bases: Making Feminist Sense out of International Politics* (Berkeley, CA: University of California Press, 1990); and the entire collection in V. Spike Peterson, ed., *Gendered States: Feminist (Re)Visions of International Relations Theory* (Boulder, CO: Lynne Rienner, 1992).

14. I realize that this is a complex question for feminist scholars and others, especially within the field of anthropology, and it is additionally difficult to determine whether the rise in misogyny and patriarchy in relation to war may be a function of arousing latent factors that exist in all cultures, but the question remains of why does it seem to be *easier* to arouse Other-directed violence rationalized by exclusionary identities in some cultural and social contexts than others. This is the central question for a group of Yugoslav researchers whose work appears in the edited book *Warfare, Patriotism and Patriarchy*, Ružica Rosandić and Vesna Pešić (Belgrade: Centre for Antiwar Action, 1994), and the theme addressed by the contributors to Sabrina Petra Ramet's edited collection of essays, *Gender Politics in the Western Balkans: Women and Society in Yugoslavia and the Yugoslav Successor States* (University Park, PA: Pennsylvania State University Press, 1999). Though he is dealing with small scale, nonstate, indigenous, non-European cultures, Will Roscoe suggests in his book *Zuni Man-Woman* (Albuquerque: University of New Mexico Press, 1991) that cultures characterized by more ambiguous and complex

conceptions of gender and gender roles might be less prone toward Other-directed violence.

15. Obrad Kešić, op. cit., p. 188.
16. Laura Silber and Allan Little, *Yugoslavia: Death of a Nation* (New York, Penguin Books, 1997), pp. 40–41.
17. Jean Bethke Elshtain, *Women and War* (New York, Basic Books, 1987).
18. Silber and Little, op. cit., pp. 15–23.
19. Silber and Little, op. cit., p. 45.
20. Silber and Little, op. cit., pp. 79–80.
21. The incident was apparently reported in the media, according to an account told to the author by Bojana Šušak, a young Serbian woman who would later become active in the antiwar movement in Belgrade.
22. Richard Holbrooke, *To End a War* (New York: Random House, 1998), pp. 353–354.
23. Slobodan Inić, "Biljana Plavšić: Geneticist in the Service of a Great Crime," *Bosnia Report* translated from *Helsinska povelja* [Helsinki Charter], Belgrade, November 1996. Slobodan Inic teaches sociology at the University of Belgrade. Available on the web at: www.barnsdle.demon.co.uk/bosnia/plavsic.html
24. Inić, op. cit., including the reference to *Svet, Novi* as the source of Plavšić's statement. Sad, September 6, 1993.
25. Branko Milinković, *Hate Speech* (Belgrade, Center for Antiwar Action, 1994), p. 15.
26. Inić, op. cit, reports the quote as appearing in the Belgrade publication *Telegraf,* on July 15, 1994.
27. Inić, op. cit.
28. Inić, op. cit.
29. There were a few women involved in high-profile political and military roles. Dusica Nikolić, for example, was both a volunteer fighter for Serbs in Croatia and the vice-president of the most radical nationalist party in Serbia, the Serbian Radical Party, whose president was the notorious paramilitary leader Vojislav Seselj. Both Seselj and Nikolić served in the Serbian party. Since the political and social structure of Yugoslav society was, I believe, highly patriarchal before becoming militarized, the women who remained "fully immersed in patriarchal ideology," in the words of Obrad Kešić (rather than resistant to it) were more often engaged in activities supportive of the war rather than directly engaged in conflict either as combatants or politicians.
30. Vlasta Jalušić, "Women in Post-Socialist Slovenia," in Sabrina P. Ramet, ed., op. cit., p. 111. Many of the essays in this volume discuss the history of the suffrage and other women's movements in Yugoslavia.
31. Sabrina P. Ramet, "In Tito's Time," in Ramet, ed., op. cit., p. 102.
32. See Kešić, op. cit.
33. See the essays in Ramet, op. cit.
34. Ivan Torov, "The Resistance in Serbia," and Sven Balas "The Opposition in Croatia," in Jasminka Udovićki and James Ridgeway, eds., *Burn this House: The Making and Unmaking of Yugoslavia* (Durham, NC: Duke University Press, 1997), pp. 245–264; and Sr. Mary Evelyn Jegen, *Sign of Hope: The Center for Peace, Nonviolence and Human Rights in Osijek* (Uppsala, Sweden: Life and Peace Institute, 1996) which is also summarized in a brief essay, "The Center for Peace, Nonviolence and Human Rights in Osijek, Croatia: Working to Establish Civil Society," in *People Building Peace: 35 Inspiring Stories from Around the World* (Utrecht, Netherlands: European Center for Conflict Prevention, 1999), pp. 186–191.

35. For more information, write The Right Livelihood Award Foundation, PO Box 15072, S-10465 Stockholm, Sweden, or see http://oneworld.org/chronicle98/awards.htm.

36. Nebojša Popov, ed., *The Road to War in Serbia: Trauma and Catharsis* (Budapest: Central European University Press, 2000). Popov is the former president of the Yugoslav Association of Sociology and is a research fellow at the Institute of Philosophy and Social Theory of Belgrade University.

37. In addition to the Torov and Balas chapters, see also another piece in the Udovicki and Ridgeway book, "The Media Wars: 1987–1997," by Milan Milošević, as well as many of the chapters (four specifically in a section on "Media Wars") in Popov, op. cit.

38. The most recent and well-known case was the murder of Slavko Ćuruvija, who was gunned down—shot 15 times in the back—in front of his home a few days after NATO initiated the bombing campaign. He was the founder and owner of the daily *Dnevni Telegraf* and weekly *Evropljanin*, and according to the International War and Peace Report's Balkan Crisis Report no. 34, May 18, 1999, he "had been an influential member of Serbian society, an insider critical of the regime and the course Milosević had set for Serbia."

39. Media Watch, ANEM press release, "Journalist Sentenced to Seven Years' Imprisonment," July 27, 2000.

40. The previous chapter concludes with an excerpt from one of Filipović's reports.

41. Anem's Weekly Report on Media Repression in Serbia, July 8–July 14, 2000, received from "mediawatch@freeb92.net," which is a moderated list for distribution of information on the media situation in Yugoslavia.

42. International War and Peace Reporter, internet version, Balkan Crisis Report, no. 139, May 12, 2000. Available http://www.iwpr.net

43. See Silber and Little 1997, especially chap. 13, pp. 169–189.

44. Mladin Životić and Branka Baletić, "Spreading of Circles," in "Brief History of the Belgrade Circle," *Beogradski Krug/Belgrade Circle* no. 0/1994, p. 267.

45. Ibid., p. 267.

46. Ibid., p. 267.

47. Ibid., p. 267.

48. Obrad Savić and Mirko Gaspari, "Why the Belgrade Circle," in *Beogradski Krug/Belgrade Circle*, no. 0/1994, p. 5.

49. Interview with Kull by Sam Keen, in the film *Faces of the Enemy*, 1986, also see Chapter 3.

50. V. Spike Peterson, "Introduction," in V. Spike Peterson, ed., *Gendered States: Feminist (Re)Visions of International Relations Theory* (Boulder, CO: Lynne Rienner, 1992), p. 7. See also Susan Bordo, "Feminism, Postmodernism, and Gender-Scepticism," in Linda Nicholson, ed., *Feminism/Postmodernism* (New York and London: Routledge, 1990).

51. Rather than repeating myself, the reader should know that I am limiting this discussion to the construction of masculinity in Western cultures. My work on indigenous peoples has proven to me that gender can be constructed in a variety of ways and I will refer to that in some of this discussion. The apparent pervasiveness of, for instance, masculine gender hierarchy within modern societies, Western and non-Western, may be as much a result of either the influence of modernity as a cultural force, or Western hegemony, or both, rather than because masculine hierarchy is either a cultural universal or a function of societal complexity, though I know some anthropologists make that argument. The same applies to arguments about the development of the psyche and the concept of the self, which I admit may vary across cultures but about which we

can speak in similar terms across Western cultures. See Ashis Nandy, *The Savage Freud and Other Essays on Possible and Retrievable Selves* (Princeton, NJ: Princeton University Press, 1995).

52. I do not deny that physiological variables may be contributing factors, but this is an enormously complex and highly contestable issue, whether viewed from the social or material sciences. The fact remains that there are significant cultural variations, and that many men are peaceful and many women violent, so my concern here is how socially constructed beliefs about masculinity and femininity intervene or mediate between physiological factors and behavior.

53. See, for example, Slavoj Žižek, *Tarrying with the Negative* (Durham, NC: Duke University Press, 1993), Linda M. G. Zerilli, *Signifying Woman: Culture and Chaos in Rousseau, Burke, and Mill (Contestations)* (Ithaca, NY: Cornell University Press, 1994), and the words of Julia Kristeva in general, for instance, *The Kristeva Reader* by Julia Kristeva, Toril Moi, ed. (New York: Columbia University Press, 1986).

54. C. Fred Alford, *Melanie Klein and Critical Social Theory* (New Haven, CT: Yale University Press, 1989), see esp. Chapter 2, "Psychoanalyst of the Passions."

55. Ibid., p. 39.

56. Will Roscoe, op. cit.

57. There is a rich and complex theoretical debate among feminist social theorists such as Chodorow (1978) regarding the issue of how infantile gender development is affected by relations with caregivers, and I cannot do justice to the debate here, though I draw from it rather freely. See Cynthia Burack, *The Problem of the Passions: Feminism, Psychoanalysis and Social Theory* (New York: New York University Press, 1994) for a good and thorough discussion of these questions and their implications for political and social theory.

58. Ibid., p. 83.

59. Christine Di Stefano, *Configurations of Masculinity: A Feminist Perspective on Modern Political Theory* (Ithaca, NY: Cornell University Press, 1991), offers an elaborate version of this argument and applies it to the discourse of Western political theory.

60. See Isaac Balbus, "Mother-Monopolized Child Rearing and the Instrumental Mode of Symbolization," in Issac Balbus, *Marxism and Domination: A Neo-Hegelian, Feminist, Psychoanalysic Theory of Sexual, Political and Technological Liberation* (Princeton, NJ: Princeton University Press, 1982); and also Franke Wilmer, "Taking Indigenous Critiques Seriously: The Enemy 'R' Us," in Karen T. Litfin, ed., *The Greening of Sovereignty in World Politics* (Cambridge, MA: MIT Press, 1998).

61. See Burack's discussion of this question in feminist social theory, op. cit., pp. 82–87.

62. "Mugabe: Whites Must Recognize Nation's for Blacks," *Bozeman Chronicle*, June 18, 2000, p. 42.

63. Ibid., p. 42.

64. Comparable references to nationality and statehood are not found in the constitutions of the other former republics, though Serbian is declared the official language of Yugoslavia, consisting of the voluntary association of Montenegro and Serbia, and the rights of "other national minorities" are discussed, which presumes a national majority of Serbs or at least, a majority of Serbian-language speakers.

65. See Chapter 4 in F. Wilmer, *The Indigenous Voice in World Politics: Since Time Immemorial* (Newbury Park, CA: Sage, 1993), and Susan Opotow, "Moral

Exclusion and Injustice: An Introduction," *Journal of Social Issues* 46(1), 1990, as well as the work of Herbert Kelman in general.

66. Chris Rock Show, HBO, January 31, 2001. I have paraphrased his comments.
67. Interview with Mihailo Marković, July 6, 1995, Belgrade.
68. Interviews with the author, June 1995, Belgrade.
69. June 7, 1999.
70. Pema Chödrön, "The Awakened Heart," *Shambala Sun*, September 2001, p 36.
71. In Ray, J. J. "The Old Fashioned Personality," *Human Relations* 43 (1990): 997–1015.
72. Ibid., p. 997.
73. Ibid., p. 1014.
74. Ibid., p. 1015.
75. Stanley Milgram, *Obedience to Authority: An Experimental View* (New York: Harper and Row, 1974). For those not familiar with his work, Milgram recruited subjects to role play "teacher" and "learner" in which the "teacher" was eventually instructed to administer legal levels of electrical shock to the learner. Most did, though Milgram actually substituted actors for the learners and, unbeknownst to the teacher subjects, no electrical shocks were actually transmitted., Among the controversies surrounding his work is the ethical issue of his having led people to believe they were actually hurting another person.
76. Milgram, op. cit., p. 5.
77. Ibid., pp. 7–8.

## Chapter 9: Identity, Conflict, and Violence

1. Michael Battle, "The Ubuntu Theology of Desmond Tutu," in *Archbishop Tutu: Prophetic Witness in South Africa*, Leonard Hulley, Louise Kretzschmar and Luke Lungile Pato, eds. (Cape Town, South Africa: Human and Rousseau, 1996), pp. 99–100.
2. Ibid., p. 100. This is a quote for Tutu, who here uses the German word for worldview, *Weltanschauung.*
3. Ibid., p. 103.
4. See *The Management of Peace Processes*, John Darby and Roger Mac Ginty, ed. (New York: St. Martin's Press, 2000), where the authors look at the increase or decrease in crime rates as an indicator of political stability in post-conflict environments.
5. See V. Spike Peterson, ed., *Gendered States: (Re)Visions of International Relations Theory* (Boulder, CO: Lynne Rienner, 1992), especially Peterson, "Introduction" and "Security and Sovereign States: What Is at Stake in Taking Feminism Seriously."
6. Henry Siegman, "The Holocaust Analogy Is Too True," *Los Angeles Times*, July 11, 1997, p. 24.
7. This point is also raised by Michael Shapiro, quoting anticolonialist Black Martinique poet Aimé Césaire in his "Introduction," in Michael J. Shapiro and Hayward R. Alker, eds., *Challenging Boundaries: Global Flows, Territorial Identities* (Minneapolis, MN: University of Minnesota Press, 1996), p. xix.
8. Human Rights Watch, Report 171–1, March 1999, "Leave None to Tell the Story: Genocide in Rwanda." Available at: www.hrw.org/reports/1999/rwanda/Geno1–3-04.htm#P95_39230, accessed November 10, 2000.
9. The Convention on the Prevention and Punishment of the Crime of Genocide (1948) defines the act more or less in this way.

10. See David Campbell's excellent application of deconstructionist analysis to the destruction of Yugoslav identity in *National Deconstruction: Violence, Identity, and Justice in Bosnia* (Minneapolis, MN: University of Minnesota Press, 1998). This perspective as well as criticisms of it are also reflected in the opinions of some the local participants, for instance, in some of the interview material used in this book. The claim of 'artificiality' was often voiced by nationalist/republican political leaders, but who knows whether this reflects an actual belief or a rhetoric of propaganda.

11. See Woodward, 1995.

12. See, for example, Sabrina Petra Ramet, *Balkan Babel: The Disintegration of Yugoslavia from the Death of Tito to Ethnic War*, 2nd ed. (Boulder, CO: Westview Press, 1996). A critical perspective on the relationship between the 'ethnic card' and the war for new state boundaries is outlined in Vesna Pešić, "The War for Ethnic States," in Nebojša Popov, ed., *The Road to War in Serbia: Trauma and Catharsis* (Budapest: Central European Press, 1996).

13. Barry Posen, "The Security Dilemma and Ethnic Conflict," *Survival*, 35(1) (Spring 1993): 27–47. This essentially realist perspective is also reflected in analyses which simply substitute ethnic groups for states as the relevant collective actors in the anarchic environment of international relations. For a critique of this perspective, see V. P. Gagnon, Jr., "Ethnic Nationalism and International Conflict: The Case of Serbia," *International Security* 19(3) (Winter 1994/95): 130–166.

14. This was, as argued in earlier chapters, the subject of controversy raised, for example, by the Serbian Academy of Sciences Memorandum and responses to it, mostly from Croats, but also Slovene writers.

15. This argument was espoused more by journalists than academics, the most extended version of which was Robert D. Kaplan's *Balkan Ghosts* (New York: Vintage Books, 1993). Kaplan also wrote articles reflecting this perspective for *New Republic* and *The Atlantic*.

16. Samuel P. Huntington, "The Clash of Civilizations?" *Foreign Affairs* 72 (Summer) 1993: 22–49. For a critique of Huntington specifically as applied to the case of ex-Yugoslavia, see Michael Ignatieff, *The Warrior's Honor: Ethnic War and the Modern Conscience* (New York: Henry Holt, 1998).

17. For an excellent critique of this literature, see V. P. Gagnon, "Ethnic Conflict as Demobilizer: The Case of Serbia," published as an *Institute for European Studies Working Paper* (Cornell University), no. 96.1 (May 1996). Donald Horowitz's *Ethnic Groups in Conflict* (Berkeley, CA: University of California Press, 1985) is still probably the classic statement on the claim that ethnicity provides some kind of natural or inevitable basis for intergroup conflict mobilization.

18. This is really the crux of my argument here, but is hardly new or original. See the work of Vamik D. Volkan and his collaborators in general, and particularly *The Need to Have Enemies and Allies: From Clinical Practice to International Relationships* (Northvale, NJ: Jason Aronson, 1988), and Vamik D. Volkan, "Bosnia-Herzegovina: Ancient Fuel of a Modern Inferno," *Journal of Mind and Conflict* (Fall 1996): 110–127. I will argue that such conflicts and the resulting violence, however, are neither inevitable nor unpreventable.

19. See the critical perspective in Todorova, 1997. This point is also made specifically in relation to complex claims and configurations of Western/civilized/European identities as they bear on the war in *Why Bosnia? Writings on the Balkan War,* Rabia Ali and Lawrence Lifschultz, ed. (Stoney Creek, CT: Pamphleteer's Press, 1994).

20. See Kubálková, Onuf, and Kowert, eds., *International Relations in a Constructed World* (Armonk, NY: M. E. Sharpe, 1998), especially Harry D. Gould, "What *Is* at Stake in the Agent-Structure Debate?" pp. 79–100, A. Giddens, *The Constitution of Society* (Oxford, U.K.: Polity, 1984).
21. Onuf, 1989, op. cit.
22. See Onuf, and Kowert, op. cit., and Wendt 1999, for instance. I just mean that I am not primarily a theorist, and am more a user than a developer of IR theory.
23. Harry D. Gould (1998), op. cit.
24. I prefer the term "dimension" because while these three categories of variables are never found in isolation from one another, each one adds contextual complexity and depth to the others. They can also be seen as a kind of reformulation of levels-of-analysis thinking, with the psychological and cognitive replacing the idea of "the individual," the sociocultural replacing the idea of "the state" or "society," and the structural replacing the idea of "the state system" or "global" level of analysis.
25. Here I am suggesting that both classical realists and classical liberals can be viewed as structuralists because they begin with an assumption about human nature and then prescribe different structural arrangements relative to those assumptions.
26. Aaron T. Beck, M.D. *Prisoners of Hate: The Cognitive Basis of Anger, Hostility, and Violence* (New York: Harper Collins, 1998), p. 42.
27. Ibid., p. 39.
28. Ibid., p. 38.
29. Ibid., p. 38.
30. Ibid., p. 26.
31. By "communal" I mean both community in a literal sense and other kinds of group associations normally referred to by their religious, ethnic, or cultural identities but which I will include as "communal groups."
32. "Euro-11" refers to the eleven members of the EU that converted to the "Euro" currency.
33. See "Joerg Haider: The Rise of an Austrian Extreme Rightist." Available: http://www.adl.org/ backgrounders/joerg_haider.html, Anti-Defamation League Backgrounder home page, accessed March 9, 2001. Haider has apparently managed to evade implications that he is anti-Semitic, though many of his supporters are and he openly defends Nazi policies.
34. "Neo-Nazi Crimes Move Upward in Germany," (AP) *Bozeman Daily Chronicle*, March 3, 2001, p. 24.
35. See Wilmer, 1993, especially chap. 3.
36. I will address the issue of self/group boundaries and identification later, for it is much more complicated, I think, and has implications for the pathology of intergroup violence we think of as "ethnic" conflict.
37. This is also the present status of international legal norms pertaining to violence, though self-defense can be undertaken collectively, which blurs a distinction between collective self-defense and an "enforcement" action. One could argue, however, that self-defense merely represents the most primitive, least refined, least well defined, and developed, and most decentralized act of enforcement in the absence of centrally coordinated, well-defined, and developed norms regarding the use of violence as a mechanism of enforcement.
38. I am referring mainly to Hugo Grotius, *On the Law of War and Peace*, written in 1625, but these issues were also the subject of many early writings on international law.

39. By Austinian I mean law as "the command of the sovereign," as John Austin defined it. See Michael Curtis, ed., *Great Political Theories, Volume 2*. (New York: Avon Books, 1962), p. 103.

40. Clearly it was not a straightforward matter of there being no effort to conform to or take into account and act on such international norms, but that a very high degree of inconsistency existed as a consequence of the way the Cold War framed all other security questions among the Western states, in whose hands the power to enforce international norms mostly rests. Efforts by the United States to conduct a security policy consistent with international legal norms during the Cuban missile crisis, for example, are contradicted by an interventionist U.S. foreign policy in Vietnam and elsewhere, in which the idea of aggression was completely politicized in favor of a Cold War interpretation of security interests. The United States was caught in at least one contradiction resulting in a case brought by Nicaragua before the International Court of Justice in the 1980s.

41. As this book goes to press, sustainable peace in the Middle East and Northern Ireland remain elusive, but that could change. The peace process in Ireland, for example, produced two failed initiatives in 1973 and 1985, a new initiative in 1993 followed by a 1994 ceasefire and then in 1996, the ceasefire was broken. Between 1990 and 1994, 400 people were killed in N. Ireland, compared with 363 in the previous four years. See S. Smith, ed., *The State of War and Peace Atlas* (London: Penguin Books, 1997).

42. Ivana Drazenovic (AIM, Sarajevo) "Four Years after Dayton: Three Big Delusions in B&H," AIM Sarajevo, November 14, 1999. Available: http://www.aimpress.org/dyn/trae/archive/data/199911/91120–001-trae-sar.htm, accessed March 9, 2001; International Crisis Group, "Is Dayton Failing? Bosnia Four Years After the Peace Agreement," October 28, 1999. Available: 212.212.165.2/ICGold/projects/bosnia/reports/bh51main.htm, accessed accessed March 9, 2001. David Chandler, *Bosnia: Faking Democracy After Dayton* (London: Pluto Press, 1999); Radha Kumar, *Divide and Fall? Bosnia in the Annals of Partition* (London: Verso Books, 1997).

43. V. P. Gagnon, "Ethnic Nationalism and International Conflict: The Case of Serbia," *International Security*, 19(3) (Winter 1994/95): 130–166.

44. Steven L. Burg and Paul S. Shoup, *The War in Bosnia Herzegovina: Ethnic Conflict and International Intervention* (New York: M.E. Sharpe, 1999), p. 8; Burg and Shoup also refer to Barry R. Posen's article "The Security Dilemma and Ethnic Conflict," *Ethnic Conflict and International Security*, Michael E. Brown, ed. (Princeton, NJ: Princeton University Press, 1993) for an outline of this realist position.

45. Ted Robert Gurr, Monty G. Marshall, and Deepa Khosla, *Peace and Violent Conflict: A Global Survey of Armed Conflicts, Self-Determination Movements, and Democracy* (College Park, MD: Center for International Development and Conflict Management, 2000).

46. Ibid. "Highlights," p. i.

47. See Priscilla B. Hayner, *Unspeakable Truths: Confronting State Terror and Atrocity* (New York: Routledge, 2001).

48. See not only Hayner, op. cit., but also Antije Krog, *Country of My Skull: Guilt, Sorrow, and the Limits of Forgiveness* (South Africa: Random House South Africa, 1998); and also the video *Tutu and Franklin: A Journey Towards Peace* (Washington, DC: Wisdom Works, 2001).

49. Interview with the author, December 23, 2000. Verwoerd, an Afrikaans member of the ANC is one of the originators of a movement in South Africa to move beyond verbal apologies and toward reconciliation as action.

50. Susan Woodward, *Balkan Tragedy*, chap. 3, "The Politics of Economic Reform and Global Integration" (Washington DC: Brookings Institution, 1995).
51. Michael Ignatieff, *Blood and Belonging: Journeys into the New Nationalism* (New York: Noonday, 1993).
52. Steven L. Burg and Paul S. Shoup. *The War in Nosnia-Herzegovina: Ethnic Conflict and Internatioanl Intervention* (New York: M. E. Sharp, 1999).
53. Anthony D. Smith, *National Identity* (Las Vegas, NV: University of Nevada Press, 1991), p. 21.
54. See, for example, Timothy D. Sisk, *Power Sharing and International Mediation in Ethnic Conflicts* (Washington, DC: U.S. Institute of Peace Press, 1996); Burg and Shoup, op. cit., chap. 1; and Ignatieff, op. cit.
55. Ted Robert Gurr, *Peoples Versus States: Minorities at Risk in the New Century* (Washington, DC: U.S. Institute of Peace Press, 2000), and Ted Robert Gurr, *Minorities at Risk: A Global View of Ethnopolitical Conflicts* (Washington, DC: U.S. Institute of Peace Press, 1993).
56. Elisabeth Prügl, "Feminist Struggle as Social Construction," in Kubálková, Onuf, and Kowert, eds., *International Relations in a Constructed World* (London: M. E. Sharpe, 1998), pp. 123–146.
57. Wendy Brown, *Manhood and Politics: A Feminist Reading in Political Theory* (Totowa, NJ: Rowman and Littlefield, 1988).
58. Aryeh Neier, "The Quest for Justice," *New York Review of Books*, March 8, 2001. Neier reviews six recent books addressing the question of reconciliation and responsibility for political crimes within the framework of truth commissions and international tribunals.
59. I have not been able to locate the pamphlet since, but it was written by Dutch peace activist Pat Patfort.
60. Mathias Albert, Lothar Brock, and Klaus Dieter Wolf, eds., *Civilizing World Politics: Society and Community Beyond the State* (Lanham, MD: Rowman and Littlefield, 2000).

# REFERENCES

## Books

Ackerman, A. (2000). *Making Peace Prevail: Preventing Violent Conflict in Macedonia (Peace and Conflict Resolution.* Syracuse: Syracuse University Press.

Adamic, L. (1943). *My Native Land.* New York: London, Harper.

Akhavan, P., ed. (1995). *Yugoslavia, the Former and Future: Reflections by Scholars from the Region.* Washington, DC: Brookings Institution and Geneva, Switzerland: United Nations Research for Social Development.

Albert, M., Brock, L. and Wolf, K. D., ed. (2000). *Civilizing World Politics: Society and Community Beyond the State.* New York: Rowman and Littlefield.

Alford, C. F. (1994). *Group Psychology and Political Theory.* New Haven, CT: Yale University Press.

Alford, C. F. (1989). *Melanie Klein and Critical Social Theory.* New Haven: Yale University Press.

Alford, C. F. (1997). *What Evil Means to Us.* Ithaca: Cornell University Press.

Ali, R. and Lifschultz, L., eds., (1994). *Why Bosnia? Writings on the Balkan War.* Stoney Creek, CT: Pamphleteer's Press.

Almond, M. (1994). *Europe's Backyard War: The War in the Balkans.* London: William Heinemann.

Almond, G., and Verba, S. (1963). *The Civic Culture; Political Attitudes and Democracy in Five Nations.* Princeton, NJ: Princeton University Press.

Anderson, B. (1991). *Imagined Communities.* London: Verso Books.

Arcel, L. T, ed. (1998). *War, Violence, Trauma, and the Coping Process: Armed Conflict in Europe and Survivor Responses.* Copenhagen, Denmark: Rehabilitation Center for Torture Victims.

Aronson, E. (1984). *The Social Animal.* New York: Freeman

Babad, E. Y, Birnbaum, M., and Benne, K. D. (1983). *The Social Self: Group Influences on Personal Identity.* Beverly Hills: Sage Publications.

Bakhtin, M., Holquist, M., and Emerson, C., eds. (1981). *The Dialogic Imagination.* Austin, TX: University of Texas Press.

Banac, I. (1984). *The National Question in Yugoslavia: Origins, History, Politics.* Ithaca, NY: Cornell University Press, 1984.

Basta-Posavec, L., Nakarada, R., Samardžić, S., Teokarević, J., and Kovačević, D. (1992). *Inter-Ethnic Conflicts and War in Former Yugoslavia.* Belgrade, Yugoslavia: Institute for European Studies.

Baumeister, R. F. (1999). *Evil: Inside Human Violence and Cruelty.* New York: Freeman.

Beck, A. T. (1999). *Prisoners of Hate: The Cognitive Basis of Anger, Hostility, and Violence.* New York: HarperCollins.

Belgrade Circle Journal (1994). No.0/1994. Obrad Savić, Editor-in-Chief. Belgrade: Belgrade Circle.

Bhabha, H., ed. (1990). *Nation and Narration.* New York: Routledge.

Bluhm, W. T. (1978). *Theories of the Political System: Classics of Political Thought and Modern Political Analysis.* Englewood Cliffs, NJ: Prentice-Hall.

Bonta B. D. (1993). *Peaceful Peoples.* Lanham, MD: Scarecrow Press.

Boulding, E. (1990). *Building a Global Civic Culture: Education for an Interdependent World*. Syracuse, NY: Syracuse University Press.

Boulding, E. (2000). *Cultures of Peace: The Hidden Side of History*. Syracuse, NY: Syracuse University Press.

Bourdieu, P. (1991). *Language and Symbolic Power*. Cambridge, MA: Harvard University Press.

Bringa, T. (1995). *Being Muslim the Bosnian Way: Identity and Community in a Central Bosnian Village*. Princeton, NJ: Princeton University Press.

Brogan, P. (1990). *The Fighting Never Stopped: A Comprehensive Guide to Conflict since 1945*. New York: Vintage.

Brown, M. E. ed. (1993). *Ethnic Conflict and International Security*. Princeton, NJ: Princeton University Press.

Brown, W. (1988). *Manhood and Politics: A Feminist Reading in Political Theory*. Totowa, NJ: Rowman & Littlefield.

Browning, C. R. (1992). *Ordinary Men: Reserve Battalion 101 and the Final Solution in Poland*. New York: HarperCollins.

Brownmiller, S. (1975). *Against Our Will: Men, Women, and Rape*. New York: Simon and Schuster.

Burack, C. (1994). *The Problem of the Passions: Feminism, Psychoanalysis, and Social Theory*. New York: New York University Press.

Burg, S., and Shoup, P. (1999). *The War in Bosnia-Herzegovina: Ethnic Conflict and International Intervention*. New York: M. E. Sharpe.

Burns, R. J., and Aspeslagh, R., eds. (1996). *Three Decades of Peace Education around the World: An Anthology*. New York: Garland Publishing.

Burton, J. W. (1990). *Conflict: Resolution and Prevention*. London: Macmillan.

Burton, J. W. (1979). *Deviance, Terrorism, and War*. Oxford, U.K.: Martin Robertson.

Burton, J. W. (1987). *Resolving Deep-Rooted Conflict: A Handbook*. Lanham, MD: University Press of America.

Campbell, D. (1998). *National Deconstruction: Violence, Identity, and Justice in Bosnia*. Minneapolis, MN: University of Minnesota Press.

Campbell, D., and Dillon, M., eds. (1993). *The Political Subject of Violence*. Manchester, U.K.: Manchester University Press.

Capra, F. (1975). *The Tao of Physics*. Berkeley, CA: Shambala.

Carment, D., and James, P. (1997). *Wars in the Midst of Peace: The International Politics of Ethnic Conflict*. Pittsburgh, PA: University of Pittsburgh Press.

Cashman, G. (1993). *What Causes War? An Introduction to Theories of International Conflict*. New York: Lexington Books.

Cassirer, E. (1946). *The Myth of the State*. New Haven, CT: Yale University Press and London: G. Cumberlege, Oxford University Press.

Chandler, D. (1999). *Bosnia: Faking Democracy after Dayton*. London: Pluto Press.

Chodorow, N. (1978). *The Reproduction of Mothering*. Berkeley, CA: University of California Press.

Choucri, N. and North, R. C. (1975). *Nations in Conflict*. San Francisco: Freeman.

Cohen R. (1998). *Hearts Grown Brutal: Sagas of Sarajevo*. New York: Random House.

Cohen, P. (1996). *Serbia's Secret War: Propaganda and the Deceit of History*. College Station, TX: Texas A & M University Press.

Connor, W. (1994). *Ethnonationalism: The Quest for Understanding*, Princeton, NJ: Princeton University Press.

Crnobrnja, M. (1994). *The Yugoslav Drama*. McGill-Queen's University Press.

Danforth, L. M. (1995). *The Macedonian Conflict: Ethnic Nationalism in a Transnational World.* Princeton, NJ: Princeton University Press.

Davis, G. S. (1996). *Religion and Justice in the War over Bosnia.* New York: Routledge.

Darby, J., and R. MacGinty, ed. (2000). *The Management of Peace Processes.* New York: St. Martin's and London: Macmillan.

Di Stefano, C. (1991). *Configurations of Masculinity: A Feminist Perspective on Modern Political Theory.* Ithaca, NY: Cornell University Press.

Dimitrijević, N. (2000). *Managing Multiethnic Local Communities in the Countries of the Former Yugoslavia.* Budapest, Hungary: Open Society Institute.

Donia, R. J., and Fine, J. (1994). *Bosnia and Hercegovina: A Tradition Betrayed.* New York: Columbia University Press.

Doubt, K. (2000). *Sociology after Bosnia and Kosovo: Recovering Justice.* Lanham, MD: Rowman & Littlefield.

Drakulić, S. (1996). *Café Europea: Life After Communism.* New York: Penguin Books.

Drakulić, S. (1993). *The Balkan Express: Fragments from the Other Side of the War.* New York: Norton.

Durkheim, E. (1893/1964). *The Division of Labor in Society.* New York: Free Press.

Easton, D. (1965). *A Framework for Political Analysis.* Englewood Cliffs, NJ: Prentice-Hall.

Ehrenreich, B. (1997). *Blood Rites: Origins and History of the Passions of War.* New York: Henry Holt and Company.

Eller, J. D. (1999). *From Culture to Ethnicity to Conflict.* Ann Arbor: University of Michigan Press.

Elshtain, J. B. (1987). *Women and War.* New York: Basic Books.

Elshtain, J. B., and Tobias, S., eds. (1990). *Women, Militarism, and War.* Savage, MD: Rowman and Littlefield.

Enloe, C. (1990). *Bananas, Beaches and Bases: Making Feminist Sense of International Politics.* Berkeley, CA: University of California Press.

Epstein, M. (1995). *Thoughts without a Thinker.* New York: HarperCollins.

European Centre for Conflict Prevention. (1999). *People Building Peace: 35 Inspiring Stories from Around the World.* Published in cooperation with the International Fellowship of Reconciliation (IFOR) and the Coexistence Initiative of State of the World Forum. Utrecht, Netherlands: Author.

Fellman, G. (1998). *Rambo and the Dalai Lama: The Compulsion to Win and Its Threat to Human Survival.* New York: State University of New York.

Fenton, S. (1999). *Ethnicity, Racism, Class and Culture.* Lanham, MD: Rowman and Littlefield.

Ferguson, Y., and Mansbach, R. W. (1988). *The Elusive Quest: Theory and International Politics* Columbia, SC: University of South Carolina Press.

Ferguson, R. B., and Farragher, L. E., eds. (1988). *The Anthropology of War: A Bibliogaphy.* New York: Harry Guggenheim Foundation.

Ferguson, R. B., ed. (1984). *Warfare, Culture and Environment.* New York: Academic Press.

Filipović, Z. (1993). *Zlata's Diary: A Child's Life in Sarajevo.* New York: Viking Press.

Gellner, E. (1983). *Nations and Nationalism.* Ithaca, NY: Cornell University Press.

Giddens, A. (1991). *Modernity and Self Identity: Self and Society in the Late Modern Age.* Stanford, CA: Stanford University Press.

Giddens, A. (1987). *The Nation-State and Violence: Volume Two of A Contemporary Critique of Historical Materialism.* Berkeley, CA: University of California Press.

Glenny, M. (1992). *The Fall of Yugoslavia: The Third Balkan War.* New York: Penguin Books.

Goldhagen, D. J. (1997). *Hitler's Willing Executioners: Ordinary Germans and the Holocaust.* New York: Vintage Press.

Goswami, A. (1993). *The Self-Aware Universe: How Consciousness Creates the Material World.* New York: Penguin Putnam.

Gourevitch, P. (1998). *We Wish to Inform You That Tomorrow We Will Be Killed with Our Families: Stories from Rwanda,* New York: Farrar Straus and Giroux.

Grotius, H. (1925). *De Jure Belli Ac Pacis* [The Law of War and Peace], translated by E. Kelsey. Washington, D.C.: Carnegie Endowment for International Peace.

Gurr, T. R., Marshall, M. G., and Khosla, D. (2000). *Peace and Violent Conflict 2001: A Global Survey of Armed Conflicts, Self-Determination Movements, and Democracy.* College Park, MD: Center for International Development and Conflict Management.

Gurr, T. R. (2000). *Peoples versus States: Minorities at Risk in the New Century.* Washington, DC: U.S. Institute of Peace Press.

Gurr, T. (1993). *Minorities at Risk: A Global View of Ethnopolitical Conflict.* Washington, DC: U.S. Institute of Peace.

Gurr, T. R. (1970). *Why Men Rebel.* Princeton, NJ: Princeton University Press.

Gutman, R. (1993). *A Witness to Genocide.* New York: Macmillan.

Hall, B. (1994). *The Impossible Country: A Journey Through the Last Days of Yugoslavia.* Penguin USA.

Hauptmann, L. (1986). *The Iroquois Struggle for Survival: World War II to Red Power.* Syracuse, NY: Syracuse University Press.

Hayner, P. B. (2001). *Unspeakable Truths: Confronting State Terror and Atrocity.* New York: Routledge.

Heizer, R. F., and Almquist, A. F. (1971). *The Other Californians,* Berkeley, CA: University of California Press.

Held, D., ed. (1983). *States and Societies.* New York: New York University Press.

Hobsbawm, E., and Ranger, T., eds. (1983). *The Invention of Tradition.* New York: Cambridge University Press.

Hodge, C., and Grbin, M. (1996). *A Test for Europe, Report: Confidence Building in Former Yugoslavia.* Glasgow: Institute of Russian and East European Studies.

Holbrooke, R. (1998). *To End a War.* New York: Random House.

Holsti, K. (1991). *Peace and War: Armed Conflicts and International Order, 1648–1989.* Cambridge, U.K.: Cambridge University Press.

Holsti, K. (1996). *The State, War, and the State of War.* Cambridge, U.K.: Cambridge University Press.

Honig, J. W., and N. Both. (1997). *Srebrenica: Record of a War Crime.* London: Penguin Books.

Horowitz, D. L. (1985). *Ethnic Groups in Conflict.* Berkeley, CA: University of California Press.

Horvatić, D. (1996). *Croatia.* Zagreb, Croatia: Pegaz.

Hukanović, R. (1993). *The Tenth Circle of Hell: A Memoir of Life in the Death Camps of Bosnia.* Translated from the Bosnian by Colleen London and Midhat Ridjanović. New York: A New Republic Book, Basic Books,

Human Rights Watch/Helsinki. (1993). *Open Wounds: Human Rights Abuses in Kosovo.* New York: Human Rights Watch.

Hutchinson, J., and Smith, A. D., eds. (1996). *Ethnicity*. Oxford, U.K. and New York: Oxford University Press.

Ignatieff, M. (1993). *Blood and Belonging: Journeys into the New Nationalism*. New York: Noonday Press.

Ignatieff, M. (1998). *The Warrior's Honor: Ethnic War and the Modern Conscience*, New York: Henry Holt.

Ingram, D. (2000). *Group Rights: Reconciling Equality and Difference*. Lawrence, KS: University Press of Kansas.

Ivison. D., Patton, P., and Sanders, W., eds. (2000). *Political Theory and the Rights of Indigenous Peoples*. Oakleigh, Victoria, Australia: Cambridge University Press.

Jabri, V. (1996). *Discourses on Violence: Conflict Analysis Reconsidered*. Manchester, U.K.: Manchester University Press.

Jakšić, B., ed. (1995). *Interkulturalnost/Interculturality (Interculturality in Multiethnic Societies)*. Belgrade, Yugoslavia: IP "Hobisport" Yu.

Janjić, D., ed. (1995). *Serbia Between the Past and the Future*. Belgrade, Yugoslavia: Institute of Social Sciences Forum for Ethnic Relations.

Janjić, D., ed. (1994). *Religion and War*. Belgrade: European Movement in Serbia.

Janjić, D., and Maliqi, S., eds. (1994). *Conflict or Dialogue: Serbian-Albanian Relations and integration of the Balkans, Studies and Essays*. Subotica, Yugoslavia: Open University European Civic Centre for Conflict Resolution.

Jegen, M. E., Sr. (1996). *Sign of Hope: The Center for Peace, Nonviolence and Human Rights in Osijek*. Uppsala, Sweden: Life and Peace Institute.

Kandić, N. (1995). *Spotlight on Human Rights in Times of Armed Conflict*. Belgrade, Yugoslavia: Humanitarian Law Center.

Kaplan, R. (1993). *Balkan Ghosts: A Journey through History*. New York: Vintage Books.

Karahasan, D. (1993). *Sarajevo: Exodus of a City*. New York: Kodansha International.

Katzenstein, P. J. (1996). *The Culture of National Security: Norms and Identity in World Politics*. New York: Columbia University Press.

Kedourie, E. (1966). *Nationalism*. London: Hutchinson University Library.

Keen, S. (1986). *Faces of the Enemy: Reflections of the Hostile Imagination*. San Francisco: Harper & Row.

Kelly, R. (2000). *Warless Societies and the Origin of War*. Ann Arbor, MI: University of Michigan Press.

Kelman, H. C. (ed.). (1965). International Behavior: A Social-Psychological Analysis. New York: Holt, Rinehart and Winston.

Klein, M., and Riviere, J. (1964). *Love, Hate, and Reparation*. New York: Norton.

Knuttila, M. (1987). *State Theories: From Liberalism to the Challenge of Feminism*. Toronto, Canada: Garamond Press.

Kovačević, S., and Dajić, P. (1994). *Chronology of the Yugoslav Crisis 1942–1993*. Belgrade, Yugoslavia: Institute for European Studies.

Kratochwil, F. (1989). *Rules, Norms, and Decisions: On the Conditions of Practical and Legal Reasoning in International Relations and Domestic Affairs*. Cambridge, U.K.: Cambridge University Press.

Kriesberg, L. (1982). *Social Conflicts*. Englewood Cliffs, NJ: Prentice-Hall.

Kriesberg, L. (1998). *Constructive Conflicts: From Escalation to Resolution*. New York: Rowman and Littlefield.

Kristeva, J. (1993). *Nations without Nationalism*. New York: Columbia University Press.

Krog, A. (1998). *Country of My Skull: Guilt, Sorrow, and the Limits of Forgiveness*. South Africa: Random House South Africa.

Kubálková, V., Onuf, N., and Kowert, P., eds. (1998). *International Relations in a Constructed World*. Armonk, NY: M. E. Sharpe.

Kumar, R. (1997). *Divide and Fall? Bosnia in the Annals of Partition*. London: Verso Books.

Kymlicka, W. (1995). *Multicultural Citizenship*. Oxford, U.K.: Oxford University Press.

Lacan, J. (1975). *The Language of the Self: The Function of Language in Psychoanalysis*. Translated with notes and commentary by Anthony Wilden. New York: Dell.

Lalić, L. (1995). *Three Years in TV Serbia*. Belgrade, Yugoslavia: Independent Media Union.

Lampe, J. R. (1996). *Yugoslavia as History: Twice There Was a Country*. New York: Cambridge University Press.

Lao-tze. *Tao Te Ching*. (1988). Translated with forward and notes by Stephen Mitchell. New York: HarperCollins

Lapid, Y., and Kratochwil, F. (1997). *The Return of Culture and Identity in International Relations Theory*. Boulder, CO: Rienner.

Layder, D. (1997). *Modern Social Theory: Key Debates and New Directions*. London: University College Press.

Lederach, J. P. (1997). *Building Peace: Sustainable Reconciliation in Divided Societies*, Washington, DC: U.S. Institute of Peace Press.

Lešić, Z., ed. (1995). *Children of Atlantis: Voices from the Former Yugoslavia*. Budapest, Hungary: Central European University.

Levinsohn, F. H. (1994). *Belgrade Among the Serbs*. Chicago: Ivan R. Dee.

Levinson, D. (1998). *Ethnic Groups Worldwide: A Ready Reference Handbook*. Phoenix, AZ: Oryx Press.

Lipschutz, R., and Crawford, B. (1999). *The Myth of "Ethnic Conflict": Politics, Economics, and Cultural Violence*. Berkeley, CA: University of California.

Maass, P. (1996). *Love Thy Neighbor: A Story of War*. New York: Knopf.

Malcolm, N. (1994). *Bosnia: A Short History*. New York: New York University Press.

Marković, M. (1994). *Selected Writings*. Belgrade, Yugoslavia: Bigz Genes-s Prosveta Skz.

McKinnon, C. (1993). *Only Words*. Cambridge, MA: Harvard University Press.

Mehmedinović, S. (1998). *Sarajevo Blues*. Translated from Bosnian by Ammiel Alcalay. San Francisco: City Light Books.

Mertus, J. Tesanovic, J., Metikos, H., and Boric, R., eds. (1997). *The Suitcase: Refugee Voices from Bosnia and Croatia*. Berkeley, CA: University of California Press.

Mertus, J. A. (1999). *Kosovo: How Myths and Truths Started A War*. Berkeley, CA: University of California Press.

Milgram, S. (1974). *Obedience to Authority: An Experimental View*. New York: Harper and Rowe.

Milinković, B., ed. (1994). *Hate Speech: An Analysis of the Contents of Domestic Media in the First Par of 1993*. Belgrade, Yugoslavia: Center for Antiwar Action.

Miller, A. (1983). *Hidden Cruelty in Child-Rearing and the Roots of Violence*. Translated by Hildegaarde and Hunter Hannum. New York: Farrar, Strauss, and Giroux.

Moore, J., ed. (1998). *Hard Choices: Moral Dilemmas in Humanitarian Intervention*. Lanham, MD: Rowman and Littlefield.

Mousavizadeh, N., ed. (1995). *The Black Book of Bosnia: The Consequences of Appeasement*. New York: Basic Books.

Nakarada, R., ed. (1994). *Europe and the Disintegration of Yugoslavia*. Belgrade, Yugoslavia: Institute for European Studies.

Nandy, A. (1995). *The Savage Freud and Other Essays on Possible and Retrievable Selves*. Princeton, NJ: Princeton University Press.

Neuman, I. (1999). *Uses of the Other: "The East" in European Identity Formation*. Minneapolis, MN: University of Minneapolis Press.

Neumann, I. B., and Wĺver, O. (1997). *The Future of International Relations: Masters in the Making*, London: Routledge.

Nikolić-Ristanović, V. (2000). *Women, Violence, and War: Wartime Victimization of Refugees in the Balkans*. Budapest, Hungary: Central European University Press.

Obradović, M. (1995). *Narodna Demokratija u Jugoslaviji 1945–52*. Belgrade, Yugoslavia: INIS.

Onuf, N. (1989). *World of Our Making: Rules and Rule in Social Theory and International Relations*. Columbia, SC: University of South Carolina Press.

Paret, P., with Craig, G. A., and Gilbert, F. (1986). *Makers of Modern Strategy: From Machiavelli to the Nuclear Age*. Princeton, NJ: Princeton University Press, 1986.

Peterson, V. S., ed. (1992). *Gendered States: Feminist (Re)Visions of International Relations Theory*. Boulder, CO: Lynne Rienner.

Popov, N., ed. (1996). *The Road to War in Serbia: Trauma and Catharsis*. Budapest, Hungary: Central European University Press.

Pribichevich, S. (1982). *Macedonia, Its People and History*. University Park, PA: Pennsylvania State University Press.

Prstojević, M. (1993). *Greetings from Sunny Sarajevo!* Sarajevo: FAMA.

Pusić, V. (1998). *Journal of Democracy* 9(1), (1998): 112.

Ramet, S. P. (1996). *Balkan Babel: The Disintegration of Yugoslavia from the Death of Tito to Ethnic War*. Boulder, CO: Westview Press.

Ramet, S. P. (1992). *Nationalism and Federalism in Yuoslavia, 1962–1991*, 2nd ed. Bloomington, IN: Indiana University Press.

Ramet, S., ed. (1999). *Gender Politics in the Western Balkans: Women and Society in Yugoslavia and the Yugoslav Successor States*. University Park, PA: Pennsylvania State University Press.

Rappaport, A. (1992). *Peace: An Idea Whose Time Has Come*. Ann Arbor, MI: University of Michigan Press

Reardon, B. A. (1993). *Women and Peace: Feminist Visions of Global Security*. New York: State University of New York.

Rieff, D. (1995). *Slaughterhouse: Bosnia and the Failure of the West*. New York: Simon and Schuster.

Rosandić, R., and Pesić, V., eds. (1994). *Warfare, Patriotism and Patriarchy: An Analysis of Elementary School Textbooks*. Belgrade, Yugoslavia: Centre for Antiwar Action, Association MOST.

Roscoe, W. (1991). *The Zuni Man-Woman*. Albuquerque, NM: University of New Mexico Press.

Ruggie, J. (1998). *Constructing the World Polity: Essays on International Institutionalization*. New York: Routledge.

Ryan, S. (1990). *Ethnic Conflict and International Relations*. Brookfield, VT: Gower.

Said, E. (1979). *Orientalism*. New York: Random House

Sardar, S. (1998). *Postmodernism and the Other: The New Imperialism of Western Culture*. Chicago: Pluto Press.

Schechterman, B., and Slann, M., eds. (1993). *The Ethnic Dimension in International Relations*, Westport, CN: Praeger Publishers.

Schopenhauer, A. (1995). *On the Basis of Morality*. Translated by David E. Cartwright. Oxford, U.K.: Berghahn Books.

Sells, M. (1996). *The Bridge Betrayed: Religion and Genocide in Bosnia*. Berkeley, CA: University of California Press.

Shapiro, M. and Alker, H, eds. (1996). *Challenging Boundaries: Global Flows, Territorial Identities*. Minneapolis, MN: University of Minnesota Press.

Sharratt, S., and Kaschak, E., eds. (1999). *Assault on the Soul: Women in the Former Yugoslavia*. New York: Haworth Press.

Silber, L., and Little, A. (1997). *Yugoslavia: Death of a Nation*. New York: Penguin Books.

Sisk, T. D. (1996). *Power Sharing and International Mediation in Ethnic Conflicts*. Washington, DC: U.S. Institute of Peace Press.

Smith, A. D. (1981). *The Ethnic Revival*. Cambridge, U.K., and New York: Cambridge University Press.

Smith, A. D. (1991). *National Identity*. Harmondsworth, U.K.: Penguin Books.

Smith, E., ed., (1997). *The State of War and Peace Atlast*. London: Penguin Books.

Sponsel, L. E., and Thomas, G. (1994). *The Anthropology of Peace and Nonviolence*. Boulder, CO: Lynne Reinner.

Stiglmayer, A. (1994). *Mass Rape: The War against Women in Bosnia-Herzegovina*. Lincoln, NE: University of Nebraska Press.

Stover, E., and Claude, R. (1996). *War Crimes in the Balkans: Medicine under Siege in the Former Yugoslavia 1991–95*. Boston: Physicians for Human Rights.

Strozier, C. B., and Flynn, M. (1996). *Trauma and Self*. Lanham, MD: Rowman and Littlefield.

Sudetić, C. (1998). *Blood and Vengeance: One Family's Story of the War in Bosnia*. New York: Penguin Books.

Tanner, M. (1997). *Croatia: A Nation Forged in War*. New Haven, CT: Yale University Press.

Thomas, R. (1999). *The Politics of Serbia in the 1990s*. New York: Columbia University Press.

Thompson, M. (1992). *A Paper House: The Ending of Yugoslavia*. New York: Pantheon Books.

Thomson, J. (1994). *Mercenaries, Pirates, and Sovereigns: State-Building and Extraterritorial Violence in Early Modern Europe*. Princeton, NJ: University Press.

Todorova M. (1997). *Imagining the Balkans*. New York: Oxford University Press.

Turner, P. R., and Pitt, D. (1988). *The Anthropology of War and Peace*. Westport, CT: Greenwood Publishing Group.

Udovički, J., and Ridgeway, J., eds. (1997). *Burn This House: The Making and Unmaking of Yugoslavia*. Durham, NC: Duke University Press.

Ugresić, D. (1998). *The Culture of Lies*. University Park, PA: Pennsylvania University Press.

Ugresić, D. (1996). *The Museum of Unconditional Surrender*. Translated by Celia Hawkesworth. New York: New Directions Books.

van Creveld, M. (1991). *The Transformation of War: The Most Radical Reinterpretation of Armed Conflict Since Clausewitz*. New York: Simon and Schuster.

Vasquez, J. (1993). *The War Puzzle*. Cambridge: Cambridge University Press.

Vertovec, S., ed. (1999). "Introduction," in *Migration and Social Cohesion*. Aldershot: Edward Elgar.

Vickers, M. (1998). *Between Serb and Albanian: A History of Kosovo*, New York: Columbia University Press.

Volkan, V. D. (1988). *The Need to Have Enemies and Allies: From Clinical Practice to International Relationships*, Northvale, NJ: Jason Aronson.

Volkan, V., Julius, D., and Montville, J., eds. (1990). *The Psychodynamics of International Relationships, Volumes 1 and 2.* Lexington, MA: Lexington Books.

Vulliamy, E. (1994). *Seasons in Hell: Understanding Bosnia's War.* London: Simon and Schuster.

Wachtel, A. (1998). *Making a Nation, Breaking a Nation: Literature and Cultural Politics in Yugoslavia.* Stanford, CA: Stanford University Press.

Waltz, K. (1954). *Man, the State, and War: A Theoretical Analysis.* New York: Columbia University Press.

Waltz, K. (1979). *Theory of International Politics.* Reading, MA: Addison-Wesley.

Weber, C. (1995). *Simulating Sovereignty: Intervention, the State, and Symbolic Exchange*, Cambridge, U.K.: Cambridge University Press.

Weber, S. (1991). *Return to Freud: Jacques Lacan's Dislocation of Psychoanalysis.* Translated by Michael Levine. New York: Cambridge University Press.

Weiner, A. (1998). *European Citizenship Practice—Building Institutions of a Non-State.* Boulder, CO: Westview Press.

Wendt, A. (1999). *Social Theory in International Relations*, Cambridge, U.K.: Cambridge University Press.

West, R. (1943). *Black Lamb and Grey Falcon: A Journey through Yugoslavia.* New York: Viking Press.

Wilkes, J. (1992). *The Illyrians.* Oxford, U.K.: Blackwell.

Wilmer, F. (1993). *The Indigenous Voice in World Politics: Since Time Immemorial.* Newbury Park, CA: Sage.

Wilson, E. O. (2000). *Sociobiology: The New Synthesis.* Cambridge, MA: Belknap Press of Harvard University Press.

Wilson, E. O. (1998). *Consilience: The Unity of Knowledge.* New York: Knopf.

Woodward, S. (1995). *Balkan Tragedy: Chaos and Dissolution after the Cold War.* Washington, DC: Brookings Institution.

Wright, Q. (1942). *A Study of War.* Chicago: University of Chicago Press.

Young, I. M. (1990). *Justice and the Politics of Difference.* Princeton, NJ: Princeton University Press.

## Articles and Book Chapters

Ajami, F. (1996). "Shadows," in N. Mousavizadeh, ed. *The Black Book of Bosnia: The Consequences of Appeasement.* New York: Basic Books.

Balas, S. (1997). "The Opposition in Croatia," in Jasminka Udovićki and James Ridgeway, eds., *Burn this House: The Making an Unmaking of Yugoslavia.* Durham, NC: Duke University Press.

Balbus, I. (1982). "Mother-Monopolized Child Rearing and the Instrumental Mode of Symbolization," in Issac Balbus, *Marxism and Domination: A Neo-Hegelian, Feminist, Psychoanalytic Theory of Sexual, Political and Technological Liberation.* Princeton, NJ: Princeton University Press.

Battle, M. (1996). "The Ubuntu Theology of Desmond Tutu," in *Archibishop Tutu: Prophetic Witness in South Africa*, Leonard Hulley, Louise Kretzschmar and Luke Lungile Pato, eds. Cape Town, South Africa: Human and Rousseau.

Bauman, Z. (1996). "From Pilgrim to Tourist–or A Short History of Identity," in Stuart Hall and Paul du Gay, ed., *Questions of Cultural Identity.* London: Sage.

Bordo, S. (1990). "Feminism, Postmodernism, and Gender-Scepticism," in Linda Nicholson, ed., *Feminism/Postmodernism.* New York: Routledge.

Boris, E., and P. Bardaglio. (1983). "The Transformation of Patriarchy: The Historic Role of the State," in I. Diamond, ed., *Families, Politics, and Public Policy*. New York: Longman.

*Bozeman Chronicle*. (2000). "Mugabe: Whites Must Recognize Nation's for Blacks." June 18, p. 42.

*Bozeman Chronicle*. (2001). "Neo-Nazi Crimes Move Upward in Germany." March 3, p. 24.

Carment, D. (1993). "The International Dimensions of Ethnic Conflict," *Journal of Peace Research* 30 (May) 137–150.

Chazan, Y. (1992). "Zagreb Cracks Down on Dissent: Reporters, Opposition Leaders Could Face Prosecution," *The Gazette*, September 6. Montreal, Quebec, Canada: CanWest Global Communications Corporation.

Chodorow, N. (1978). "The Reproduction of Mothering: A Methodological Debate," *Signs* 6(3): 500–514.

Chödrön, P. (2001). "The Awakened Heart," *Shambala Sun*, September 2001.

Cohen, Y., Brown, B. R., and Organski, A. F. K. (1981). "The Paradoxical Nature of State Making: A Violent Creation of Order." *American Political Science Review* 75(4), 901–910.

Cohen, R. (1995). "Serbia Dazzles Itself: Terror Suspect Weds Singer," *New York Times*, February 20, p. 24.

Čolović, I. (2000). "Football, Hooligans, and War," in N. Popov, ed., *The Road to War in Serbia: Trauma and Catharsis*. Budapest, Hungary: Central European University.

Connolly, W. (2000). "The Liberal Image of the Nation," in D. Ivison, P. Patton, and W. Sanders, eds., *Political Theory and the Rights of Indigenous Peoples*. Cambridge, U.K.: Cambridge University Press.

Connor, W. (1978). "A Nation Is a Nation, Is a State, Is an Ethnic Group Is a . . ." *Ethnic and Racial Studies* 1 (1978): 377–400

Connor, W. (1972). "Nation-Building or Nation-Destroying?" *World Politics* 24 (1972): 319–55.

Connor, W. (1990). "When Is a Nation?" *Ethnic and Racial Studies* 13:99.

Connor, W. (1991). "From Tribe to Nation." *History Of European Ideas* 13:5–18.

Copelon, R. (1994). "Surfacing Gender: Reconceptualizing Crimes against Women in Times of War," in A. Stiglmayer, ed., *Mass Rape: The War against Women in Bosnia-Herzegovina*. Lincoln, NE: University of Nebraska Press.

David, F. (1995). "An Essential Handbook," in L. Lalić, ed., *Three Years in TV Serbia*. Belgrade, Yugoslavia: Independent Media Union.

Di Stefano, C. (1983). "Masculinity as Ideology in Political Thought: Hobbesian Man Considered." *Women's Studies International Forum* 6: 633–44.

Dixon, S. R. (1990). "The Esssential Spirit," *Northeast Indian Quarterly* 7(4) (Winter): 2–12.

Djordjević, M. (2000). "Populist Wave Literature," in N. Popov, ed., *The Road to War in Serbia: Trauma and Catharsis*. Budapest, Hungary: Central European University.

Drakulić, S. (1999). "We Are All Albanians." *The Nation*, June 7.

Drazenovic, I. (1999). "Four Years after Dayton: Three Big Delusions in B&H," AIM Sarajevo, November14, 1999. Available: http://www.aimpress.org/dyn/trae/archive/data/199911/91120–001-trae-sar.htm, accessed March 9, 2001.

Dworkin, A. (1993). "The Real Pornography of a Brutal War against Women," *Los Angeles Times, April 5, 1993, p. M2.*

European Centre for Conflict Prevention. (1999). "The Center for Peace, Nonviolence and Human Rights in Osajek, Croatia: Working to Establish a Civil Society," in *People Building Peace: 35 Inspiring Stories from Around the*

*World*, European Platform for Conflict Prevention and Transformation, pp. 186–191. Utrecht, Netherlands: Author.

European Monitoring Centre on Racism and Xenophobia (EUMC). (1999). *Annual Report 1999—Diversity and Equality for Europe*. Vienna: Author.

Feeney, B., and Thornton C. (2000). Book Review, "Lost Lives: The Stories of the Men, Women, and Children Who Died as Result of the Northern Ireland Troubles," in *New York Review of Books,* October 5, pp. 10–13.

Filipović, M. (2000). "Serb Officers Relive Killings." International War and Peace Reporter's *Balkan Crisis Report*, no. 130, April 4. London: The Institute for War & Peace Reporting.

Gagnon, V. P. (1995a). "Ethnic Conflict as an Intra-Group Phenomenon: A Preliminary Framework. *Revija za sociologiju*, no. 1–2, Zagreb.

Gagnon, V. P. (1995b). "The Historical Roots of the Yugoslav Conflict," in Milton J. Esman and Shibley Telhami, eds., *International Organizations and Ethnic Conflict* (pp. 179–197). Ithaca, NY: Cornell University Press.

Gagnon, V. P. (1996). "Ethnic Conflict as Demobilizer: The Case of Serbia," published as an *Institute for European Studies Working Paper*, no. 96.1. Ithaca, NY: Cornell University.

Gagnon, V. P. (1994/95). "Ethnic Nationalism and International Conflict: The Case of Serbia," in *International Security* 19(3) (Winter 1994/95): 130–166.

Galtung, J. (1969). "Violence, Peace, and Peace Research." *Journal of Peace Research* 6:3, 167–91.

Glenny, M. (1992). "Yugoslavia: The Revenger's Tragedy," *New York Review of Books*, August 13, 1992.

Gould, H. D. (1998). "What *Is* at Stake in the Agent-Structure Debate?" in V. Kubláková, N. Onuf, and P. Kowert, eds., *International Relations in a Constructed World*. New York: M. E. Sharpe.

Gurr, T. R. (1994). "Peoples Against States: Ethnopolitical Conflict and the Changing World System," *International Studies Quarterly* 38 (September): 347–377.

Harrington, M. (1992). "What Exactly is Wrong with the Liberal State as an Agent of Change" in V. S. Peterson, ed., *Gendered States: Feminsit (Re)Visions of International Relations Theory*. Boulder, CO: Lynne Reinner.

Hedl, D. (2000). "Bosnian Trade Off," in *Balkan Crisis Report 179*. September 5. London: Institute for War and Peace Reporting.

Howard, R. E. (1997). "Human Rights and the Culture Wars: Globalization and the Universality of Human Rights," *International Journal* 53(1) (Winter 1997–98): 94–112.

Howard-Hassmann, R. E. (2000). "Identity, Empathy and International Relations," a paper prepared for the symposium Looking at the World Through Non-Western Eyes, Walker Institute for International Relations, University of South Carolina, April 14–16.

Huntington, S. P. (1993). "The Clash of Civilizations?" *Foreign Affairs* 72 (Summer): 22–49.

Inić, S. (1996). "Biljana Plavšić: geneticist in the service of a great crime," *Bosnia Report*, translated from *Helsinska povelja* [Helsinki Charter], Belgrade, Yugoslavia. Available: www.barnsdle.demon.co.uk/bosnia/plavsic.html.

International Crisis Group. (1999). "Is Dayton Failing? Bosnia Four Years After the Peace Agreement," October 28, 1999. Available: 212.212.165.2/ICGold/projects/bosnia/reports/ bh51main.htm, accessed March 9, 2001.

Jalušić, V. (1999). "Women in Post-Socialist Slovenia," in Sabrina Ramet, ed., *Gender politics in the Western Balkans: Women and Society in Yugoslavia and the Yugoslav Successor States.* University Park, PA: Pennsylvania State University Press.

Kelman, H. C. (1972). "The Rights of the Subject in Social Research: An Analysis in Terms of Relative Power and Legitimacy." *American Psychologist,* 27: 989–1016.

Kešić, O. (1999). "Women and Gender Imagery in Bosnia: Amazons, Sluts, Victims, Witches, and Wombs," in Sabrina P. Ramet, ed., *Gender Politics in the Western Balkans: Women and Society in Yugoslavia and the Yugoslav Successor States.* University Park, PA: Pennsylvania State University Press.

Kruhonja, K. (1999). "The Center for Peace, Nonviolence and Human Rights in Osijek, Croatia," in *People Building Peace: 35 Inspiring Stories from Around the World,* a publication of the European Centre for Conflict Prevention, in cooperation with the International Fellowship of Reconciliation (IFOR) and the Coexistence Initiative of State of the World Forum, pp. 186–191.

Jones, K. B. (1990). "Citizenship in a Woman-Friendly Polity," *Signs* 15(4) (Summer): 781–812.

Marković, Z. (2000). "The Nation: Victim and Vengeance," in N. Popov, ed., *The Road to War in Serbia: Trauma and Catharsis.* Budapest, Hungary: Central European University.

Milovojević, S. (2000). "The Nationalization of Everyday Life," in N. Popov, ed., *The Road to War in Serbia: Trauma and Catharsis.* Budapest, Hungary: Central European University.

Mirosavljević, O. (2000). "The Abuse of the Authority of Science," in N. Popov, ed., *The Road to War in Serbia: Trauma and Catharsis.* Budapest, Hungary: Central European University.

Nagel, J. (1994). "Constructing Ethnicity: Creating and Recreating Identity and Culture," in *Social Problems* 41: 153–176.

Neuman, I. B. (1997). "The Limits of Subject/Other Perspectives," unpublished paper presented to the panel Beyond Self/Other: Security Identities after the Cold War," 38th ISA Convention, Toronto, March 18–22, 1997.

Onuf, N. (1998). "Constructivism: A User's Manual," in V. Kublaková, N. Onuf, and P. Kowert, ed., *International Relations in a Constructed World.* New York: M. E. Sharpe.

Opotow, S. (1990). "Moral Exclusion and Injustice: An Introduction," *Journal of Social Issues* 46(1) 120.

Ostrom, C. W. and Job, B. L. (1986). "The President and the Use of Force," *American Political Science Review* 80 (June): 554–566.

O'Toole, F. (2000). Book Review of *Lost Lives: The Stories of the Men, Women and Children Who Died as a Result of the Northern Ireland Troubles* by Brian Feeney and Chris Thornton. Edinburgh: Mainstream Publishing, in the *New York Review of Books,* October 5, 2000, pp. 10–13.

Parin, P. (1994). "Ethnopsychoanalytical Reflections," in A. Stiglmayer, ed., *Mass Rape: The War Against Women in Bosnia-Herzegovina.* Lincoln, NE: University of Nebraska Press.

Pešić, V. (1994). "Bellicose Virtues and Elementary School Readers," in V. Pešić and R. Rosandić. *Warfare, Patriotism, and Patriarchy.* Belgrade, Yugoslavia: Center for Antiwar Action.

Peterson, V. S. (1992a). "Introduction," in V. S. Peterson, ed., *Gendered States: (Re)Visions of International Relations Theory.* Boulder, CO: Lynne Reinner.

Peterson, V. S. (1992b). "Security and Sovereign States: What Is at Stake in Taking Feminism Seriously," in V. S. Peterson, ed., *Gendered States: (Re)Visions of International Relations Theory.* Boulder, CO: Lynne Reinner.

Posen, B. (1993). "The Security Dilemma and Ethnic Conflict," in Brown, ed. *Ethnic Growth and International Security*. Princeton, NJ: Princeton University Press.

Prpa-Jovanōvic, B. (1997). "The Making of Yugoslavia: 1830–1945, in J. Udovički and J. Ridgeway, ed., *Burn this House: The Making and Unmaking of Yugoslavia*. Durham, NC: Duke University Press.

Pusić, V. (1998). Essay based on talk to the International Forum for Democratic Studies of the National Endowment for Democracy in Washington, DC, on March 24, 1997. *Journal of Democracy* 9(1): 111–124.

Radošević, A. (1994). "Fist as Political Argument: What we can learn from the political scandal in the Croatian Parliament," translated by Jelena Marković, *Nas Glas* 6 December 1994. Zagreb, Croatia.

Ramet, P. (1989). "Religion and Nationalism in Yugoslavia," in P. Ramet, ed., *Religion and Nationalism in Soviet and East European Politics*. Durham, NC: Duke University Press.

Ramet, S. P. (1999). "In Tito's Time," in Sabrina P. Ramet, ed., *Gender Politics in the Western Balkans: Women and Society in Yugoslavia and the Yugoslav Successor States*. University Park, PA: Pennsylvania State University Press.

Ray, J. J. (1990). "The Old Fashioned Personality," *Human Relations*. 43(4): 997–1015.

Russett, B. (1989). "Economic Decline, Electoral Pressure, and the Initiation of Interstate Conflict," in C. Gochman and A. N. Sabrosky, eds., *Prisoners of War? Nation-States in the Modern Era*. Lexington, MA: D. C. Heath.

Savić, O., and Gaspari, M. (1994). "Why the Belgrade Circle," in *Belgrade Circle Journal* No. 0/1994: 5–6.

Singer, D. (1991). "Peace in the Global System: Displacement, Interregnum, or Transformation?" in C. W. Kegley, ed., *The Long Postwar Peace*. New York: HarperCollins.

Steele, D. (1994). "Religion as a Fount of Ethnic Hostility or an Agent of Reconciliation?" in Dušan Janjić, editor, *Religion and War*. Belgrade, European Movement in Serbia.

Tepavac, M. (1997). "Tito: 1945–1980," in J. Udovički and J. Ridgeway, ed., *Burn This House: The Making and Unmaking of Yugoslavia*. Durham, NC: Duke University Press.

Torov, I. (1997). "The Resistance in Serbia," in Jasminka Udovicki and James Ridgeway, eds., *Burn This House: The Making and Unmaking of Yugoslavia*, pp. 186–191. Durham, NC: Duke University Press.

Štitkovac, E. (1997). "Croatia: the First Way," in J. Udovički and J. Ridgeway, eds., *Burn This House: The Making and Unmaking of Yugoslavia*. Durham, NC: Duke University Press.

Šuvar, S. (1998). "Consequences of Ethnic Cleansing in the Area of the Former Yugoslavia," paper presented to the International Summer School Conference of the Southeast European Research Unit of University of Glasgow, September, Korcula, Croatia.

Thomas, R. G. C. (1997). "Self-Determination and International Recognition Policy: An Alternative Interpretation of Why Yugoslavia Disintegrated." *World Affairs* 160(1): 17–31.

Vogelman, L. (1991). "Psychological Factors to Consider in Strikes, Collective Violence and the Killing of Non-Strikers," in *Violence in Contemporary South Africa*, South African Breweries (SAB) conference proceedings.

Volkan, V. D. (1996). "Bosnia-Herzegovina: Ancient Fuel of a Modern Inferno," *Journal of Mind and Conflict* (Fall): 110–127.

Wendt, A. (1987). "The Agent-Structure Problem in International Relations Theory." *International Organization* 41(3): 335–350.

Wilmer, F. (1998). "Taking Indigenous Critiques Seriously: The Enemy 'R' Us," in Karen T. Litfin, ed., *The Greening of Sovereignty in World Politics*. Cambridge, MA: MIT Press.

Wilmer, F. (1997). "Identity, Culture, and Historicity: The Social Construction of Ethnicity in the Balkans." *World Affairs*, 160(1): 3–16.

Wilmer, F. (1997). "Postmodernism and Indigenous World Views," in *Race, Gender, and Class* 3(2): 35–58.

Wisdom Works Inc. (2001). "Tutu and Franklin: A Journey towards Peace." *Teachers Guide* Washington, DC: Author.

Youniss. J., McLellan, J., and Yates, M. (1998). "What We Know about Engendering Civic Identity," *American Behavioral Scientist* vol. 40, no. 5 March/April.

## Films

Cohen, P., director, and van Breugel, R., producer. (1999). *Ethnic Identity, Regional Conflict, and Peacekeeping Initiatives*. Amsterdam: Netherlands Ministry of Foreign Affairs, RNTV. Director, Palm Plus Productions.

CNN, Frontline September 23, 1994, with Bernard Shaw. (1994). *Our Planetary Police*. Atlanta, GA: Cable News Network.

Jacobson, M., and Jelinčić, K. (1996). *Calling the Ghosts: A Story about Rape, War, and Women*. Directors, US and Croatia: Bowery Productions.

Maly, S. Producer. (1999). *On Tour with the Blue Berets*. Documentary film. Helena, Montana: Light Brigade and Helena Television Coalition.

Keen, S. (1987). *Faces of the Enemy*. Videorecording. Berkeley, CA: Quest Productions

Poussaint, R., Producer. (2001). *Tutu and Franklin: A Journey Towards Peace*. Videorecording. Washington, DC: Wisdom Works.

## Documents and Other Sources

Beogradski Krug/Belgrade Circle. (1994). *Kritika Centrizma/Critique of Centrism*. No. 0, 1994. Obrad Savić, Editor.

Biserko, S. (1997). "Reporting from the Writing Fields, or How to Prepare Genocide in Five Years," for the Helsinki Committee for Human Rights in Serbia, April 11, 1997, speech given to Human Rights Center University of California at Berkeley.

Croatian Helsinki Committee. (1993). "Statement 1 of July 7, 1993." Zagreb, Croatia: Croatian Helsinki Committee.

Èièak, I. Z., President, CHC. (1996). "Statement 33: On Freedom of Religion in Croatia," February 26. Zagreb, Croatia: Helsinki Committee in Croatia.

Èièak, I. Z., President, CHC. (1993). "Statement 1: Concerning the Freedom of the Media," and "The Freedom of Media in Croatia Proposals to the Croatian Prime Minister Mr. Nikica Valentl." July 7. Zagreb, Croatia: Helsinki Committee in Croatia.

Èièak, I. Z., President, CHC (1993). "Statement 2: The Stance of the International Helsinki Federation for Human Rights Related to the Events Taking Place in Bosnia and Hercegovina." Zagreb, Croatia: Helsinki Committee in Croatia.

Èièak, I. Z., President, CHC (1993). "Statement 5: On Mobilization of the Croatian Citizens for the War in Bosnia and Herzegovina." December 29. Zagreb, Croatia: Helsinki Committee in Croatia.

Èièak, I. Z., President, CHC (1994). "Statement 6: On Turning the Croatian State into a Purely Catholic State." January 4. Zagreb, Croatia: Helsinki Committee in Croatia.

Èièak, I. Z., President, CHC (1994). "Statement 15: Forcible Evictions from Apartments." July 18. Zagreb, Croatia: Helsinki Committee in Croatia.

Helsinki Committee for Human Rights in Serbia. (1994). "Report on the State of Human Rights in Serbia, no. 1." October 4. Belgrade: Helsinki Committee for Human Rights in Serbia.

Helsinki Committee for Human Rights in Serbia. (1995). "Report on Media No. 2," January 27. Belgrade: Helsinki Committee for Human Rights in Serbia.

Helsinki Committee for Human Rights in Serbia. (1994). "Situation in Media— 'Soft Repression.'" September. Belgrade: Helsinki Committee for Human Rights in Serbia.

Helsinki Committee for Human Rights in Serbia. (1994). "Kosovo Report: Forced Repression in Function of Possible Dialogue." December 15. Belgrade: Helsinki Committee for Human Rights in Serbia.

Helsinki Committee for Human Rights in Serbia. (1994). "Deserters from the War in Yugoslavia." December 21. Belgrade: Helsinki Committee for Human Rights in Serbia.

Helsinki Committee for Human Rights in Serbia. (1995). *International Convention on the Elimination of All Forms of Racial Discrimination—A Review of Legislation and Practice in FR Yugoslavia.* January. Belgrade: Helsinki Committee for Human Rights in Serbia.

International Criminal Tribunal for the Former Yugoslavia (ICTY), Case Number IT-95-12-R61, unofficial transcripts, April 2, 1996.

International Criminal Tribunal for the Former Yugoslavia. (ICTY ) Monday, April 12th, 1999 (Open session), testimony of Mr. Nezirevic during the trial of Cerkez and Kordić.

Socialist Federal Republic of Yugoslavia. (1972–92). *Statistical Yearbook of the Federal Republic of Yugoslavia, 1972–1992.* Belgrade, Yugoslavia: Government of SFRY.

United Nations Security Council, Final Report of the United Nations Commission of Experts established pursuant to Security Council Resolution 780 (1992). Annex III.A "Special forces," Section B. "Forces operating in support of BiH— the Green Berets and Mujahedin," and 1 (b) Ties with the Government and regular military of BiH. Available: www.ess. uwe.ac.uk/comexpert/ANX/III-A.htm#II.B, accessed March 27, 2001.

United Nations Security Council, Document No. S/1994/674/Add.2 (Vol. I) December 28, 1994. "Special Forces," Annex III A., "The military structure, strategy and tactics of the warring factions," Final report of the United Nations Commission of Experts established pursuant to Security Council Resolution 780 (1992)., Annex II, prepared by M. Cherif Bassiouni, Chairman and Rapporteur on the Gathering and Analysis of the Facts, Commission of Experts, with the assistance of Edmund A. McAlister, Assistant to M. Cherif Bassiouni, Richard Janney, IHRLI Staff Attorney, and Peter M. Manikas, IHRLI Staff Attorney.

Serbian Academy of Science and Arts (SANU). (1987). "Memorandum of the Serbian Academy of Sciences and Arts." translated by Margot and Bosko Miloslavjević, printed by GIP "Kultura" Belgrade, Maršala Birjužova 28, Belgrade 1995.

## Media and Internet Sources

ARKZIN, Zagreb, Croatia, http://www.arkzin.com ad http://mediafilter.org/MFF/
    ARKzin.html
B92 Radio, Belgrade, http://www.b92.net
Balkan Media Policy Monitor, http://mediafilter.org/MFF/MonIdx.html
Bosnia Action Coalition, *This Week in Bosnia*, http://www.applicom.com/twibih/
Feral Tribune, Croatia, at http://www.feral-tribune.com/ and English version:
    www.feral-tribune.com/english
Institute for War & Peace Reporting, *Tribunal Update*, http://www.iwpr.net/index.
    pl?tribunal_index.html
Institute for War & Peace Reporting, *Balkan Crisis Report*, http://www.iwpr.net/
    index.pl? Balkans index.html
NATO Press Releases, from NATO Integrated Data Service, distributed via email
    by: natodoc@HQ.NATO.IN
Radio 101, Zagreb, http://public.srce.hr/r101/, Audio version: http://radio101.
    purger.com
Radio Free Europe/RadioLiberty, RFE/RL Newsline, via email from newsline@
    list.rferl.org, online at: http://www.rferl.org/newsline/search
Vreme News Digest, translated into English, Vreme International, distributed via
    email by: vremeint@ping.at

# INDEX

de Tocqueville, Alexis, ix
dehumanization
  rationalization and, 285n15
democracy, x
  conflict, violence and, 86
  ethnic identities and, 86
  inclusionary history and, 129
  intolerance, political violence and,
    265
Derrida, Jacques, 222
difference
  development of bounded self and,
    79–80
  urban vs. rural, 298n58
  Western vs. non-Western tolerance
    of, 286n24
*Discourses on Violence,* 150
discrimination
  masculinity and, 236
DiStefano, Christine, 75, 148
Dole, Bob, 50
"domestic jurisdiction"
  doctrine of, xi
dominance, ethnic
  ethnic minorities vs., 12
Drakulić, Slavenka, 87, 91–92, 94,
    96, 100, 101, 108, 130, 160, 233
  betrayal of "Others" and, 114
  loss of cosmopolitan identity in
    Yugoslavia and, 141
Drašković, Vuk, 160
Durkheim, E., 10, 268

Eastern Europe
  power shift, internal political,
    economic crises in, 173
Easton, David, 126
Eichmann, Adolf, 63
elites
  legitimizing narratives and, 179
Elshtain, Jean Bethke, 215
empathy, 231
Erasmus Guild, Institute for the
  Culture of Democracy in Croatia,
  219
Erdemović, Drazen, 110–113
Erdut Agreement, 52

ethnic cleansing, 184
  in Belgrade, 96
  in Kosovo, 273
  Manifest Destiny and, 84–85
  sexual violence and, 213, 215
  in Yugoslavia, 39, 40, 41, 60,
    111–113, 176, 266
ethnic groups
  definition of, 31
  "national" identities within, 8
  political destiny of, 12
*Ethnic Identity, Regional Conflict,
  and Peacekeeping Initiatives,* 84
ethnic prejudices
  Albanians and, 159–160
ethnic purification
  Yugoslav Civil War and, 39, 40, 41
ethnicity
  civic association and, 178
  intergroup conflict mobilization
    and, 305n17
  political difference and, 11–12
  political significance of, 81
  state and, 178
  as "stock," 119
ethnonationalism, 9, 264
European Free Trade Association, 44
European Movement in Serbia, 203,
  222
European Union (EU), 54
*Europe's Backyard War,* 28
evil
  experience of, 285n11
  understanding of self and, 64
exclusion
  cognitive processes of, 242–243
existence, collective
  paradox of interdependent
    individual and, xiii

*Faces of the Enemy,* 205
fairness
  masculinized formulation of,
    231
Fanon, 252
Federal Republic of Yugoslavia (FRY).
  *See* Yugoslavia